KW-299-407

Nuclear Waste
Law, Policy and Pragmatism

PETER RILEY
De Montfort University, Leicester, UK

ASHGATE

© Peter Riley 2004

All rights reserved. No part of this publication may be reproduced, stored in a retrieval system or transmitted in any form or by any means, electronic, mechanical, photocopying, recording or otherwise without the prior permission of the publisher.

The author hereby asserts his moral right to be identified as the author of the work in accordance with the Copyright, Designs and Patents Act, 1988.

Published by
Ashgate Publishing Limited
Gower House
Croft Road
Aldershot
Hants GU11 3HR
England

Ashgate Publishing Company
Suite 420
101 Cherry Street
Burlington, VT 05401-4405
USA

Ashgate website: http://www.ashgate.com

British Library Cataloguing in Publication Data
Riley, Peter
  Nuclear waste : law, policy and pragmatism
  1. Radioactive waste disposal - Law and legislation
  2. Radioactive waste disposal - Law and legislation - Great
  Britain 3. Radioactive waste disposal - Government policy
  4. Radioactive waste disposal - Government policy - Great
  Britain
  I. Title
  344'.04622

UNIVERSITY OF PLYMOUTH
900639025X

Library of Congress Cataloging-in-Publication Data
Riley, Peter, 1936-
  Nuclear waste : law, policy and pragmatism / Peter Riley.
      p. cm.
Includes bibliographical references and index.
  ISBN 0-7546-2318-1
  1. Radioactive waste disposal--Law and legislation. I. Title.

  K3671.R55 2004
  344.04'622--dc22
                                                                2003024253

ISBN 0 7546 2318 1

Printed and bound by Athenaeum Press, Ltd.,
Gateshead, Tyne & Wear.

NUCLEAR WASTE

Contents

Preface

In the optimistic days of the 1950s when nuclear energy was being developed to provide an alternative to coal and oil for the energy to produce electricity, the management of final disposal of radioactive waste was low on the list of priorities. Today it is an obstacle to the continued use of a form of energy that provides near to one fifth of the electrical energy produced in the United Kingdom and much larger proportions in France and the Republic of Korea.

Through employment in the nuclear construction industry I have indirectly contributed to the production of a significant part of that waste and also to solutions for its immobilisation and storage. Over the past fifteen years I have helped to teach environmental law at postgraduate level and in particular the laws associated with nuclear pollution. I can claim, therefore, to have a broad understanding of the question of radioactive waste.

This work sets the context of radioactive waste and energy in the United Kingdom; the nature and classification of radioactive waste is described and for comparison the way it is treated in four other states, the USA, France, Finland and Korea is also described. Those states were selected as they all have active nuclear programmes and are pursuing to different degrees a solution to the long-term disposal of radioactive waste. National policies, the laws, regulations and the experience of the practice of the legal control of radioactive waste are described. Having identified the experience in the United Kingdom the main obstacles to a satisfactory strategy for the management of radioactive waste are identified. As far as I am able to tell the work takes into account published material to 1 August 2004.

I owe the completion of this work to my wife Myra for her patience and assistance with typing, to Dr W J Leigh, Senior Legal Adviser, British Nuclear Fuels plc for his advice and Professor Neil Hawke of De Montfort Law School for his encouragement and for his comments on drafts.

Peter Riley
Hinckley, August 2004.

Table of Cases

United Kingdom Cases

United States Cases

Cases from other Jurisdictions

Table of International Instruments

Table of European Instruments

Table of United Kingdom Legislation

Legislation Before Parliament

Table of Legislation from Other Jurisdictions

Finnish Legislation

Korean Legislation

Glossary

Actinides – the group of 15 elements with atomic numbers from that of actinium (89) to lawrencium (103) inclusive. All are radioactive. The group includes thorium, protactinium, uranium, neptunium, plutonium, americium and curium.

Activation Products – radionuclides produced in materials as a result of neutron capture by atoms that constitute either the materials or impurities in those materials.

AGR – Advanced Gas-cooled Reactor.

ALARA – As Low As Reasonably Achievable.

ALARP – As Low As Reasonably Practicable.

Alpha Activity – radioactivity associated with the emission of alpha particles.

Alpha Particle – a particle emitted during the radioactive decay of some atoms (predominantly actinides and their daughter radionuclides). It is composed of two protons and two neutrons. It loses its energy over a very short range in air and has little penetrating power.

ANDRA – Agence nationale pour la gestion des déchets radioactifs (France).

AWE – the Atomic Weapons Establishment.

BE – British Energy Generation Ltd; an operator of several UK nuclear power stations.

Becquerel (Bq) – the SI unit of radioactivity, equivalent to one disintegration per second. The activity of a source is the number of disintegrations it undergoes per unit time.

kBq – kilobecquerel, 1,000 Bq.

GBq – gigabecquerel, 1,000 million Bq.

Beta/Gamma Activity – radioactivity associated with the emission of beta particles and/or gamma radiation.

Beta Particle – electron (beta-minus) or positron (beta-plus), emitted during the decay of some atoms.

Beta Radiation – fast moving electrons emitted from the nucleus of a decaying atom, smaller than alpha particles and with more, although limited, penetrating power.

Bioshield – biological shield. A mass of material that reduces ionising radiation in a given region to acceptable levels. In particular, the term is applied to the shield placed round the core of a nuclear reactor for the purpose of absorbing neutrons and gamma radiation.

BNFL – British Nuclear Fuels plc; a Government-owned company with interests in electricity generation, nuclear fuel manufacture and spent fuel management, and nuclear decommissioning and clean up of nuclear power plants.

BPEO – Best Practicable Environmental Option. In its Twelfth Report (1988 Cmnd 310) the Royal Commission on Environmental Protection defined BPEO as '... the outcome of a systematic consultative and decision making procedure which emphasises the protection and conservation of the environment across land, air and water. The BPEO procedure establishes, for a given set of objectives, the option that provides the most benefit or at least damage to the environment as a whole, at acceptable cost, in the long term as well as in the short term'.

BPM – Best Practicable Means; within a particular waste management option, the level of management and engineering control that minimises, as far as practicable, the release of radioactivity to the environment whilst taking account of a wide range of factors, including cost effectiveness, technological status, operational safety, and social and environmental factors.

BWR – Boiling Water Reactor.

Carbon-14 – a radionuclide that emits soft beta particles, with a half-life of about 5,700 years.

Catalyst – a substance that aids or speeds up a chemical reaction while remaining chemically unchanged itself.

CEA – the Commissariat à l'energie atomique (France).

CEED – the Centre for Economic and Environmental Development (UK).

Cladding – the sheath within which the reactor fuel is sealed.

Clean-up – the decontamination and decommissioning of a nuclear licensed site.

COGEMA – Compagnie générale des matières nucléaires (France).

Conditioning – a general term for operations that transform waste into a form suitable for transport, storage and/or disposal. The operations may include converting the waste to another form (e.g. incineration), immobilising the waste in some suitable matrix (e.g. cementation, vitrification) and enclosing the waste in containers (packaging).

Containment – a leak tight steel or steel and concrete building surrounding a reactor and its primary circuit; or any arrangement for the physical retention of radioactive material.

Control Rod – a rod or blade of neutron-absorbing material inserted into the reactor in order to assist in changing the reactivity balance and hence the neutron population.

Coolant – the fluid (liquid or gas) used to carry heat away from the reactor core.

Core – the region of the reactor containing the fuel (and the moderator if present) within which fission reactions take place.

Daughter – a nuclide produced by the radioactive decay of a given radionuclide (*parent*).

Decay – reduction with time in the rate of emission of particles and/or energy. This rate is dependent upon the number of radioactive atoms present; as the number of atoms is reduced by disintegration the activity or rate of particle/energy emission reduces and is said to decay.

Decommissioning – the dismantling of a reactor, process plant or other facility following the end of its operational life.

Decontamination – removal or reduction of radioactive contamination.

DEFRA – the Department for Environment, Food and Rural Affairs, the Government department responsible for environmental protection policy in England.

Depleted Uranium (DU) – Uranium that contains less than the natural proportion of 0.7 percent uranium–235.

Disposal – in the context of solid waste, disposal is the emplacement of waste in a suitable facility without intent to retrieve it at a later date; retrieval may be possible but, if intended, the appropriate term is storage. Disposal may also refer to the release of airborne or liquid wastes to the environment (i.e. emissions and discharges).

DOD – the Department of Defence (United States).

DOE – the Department of Energy (United States).

Dounreay – a site licensed under the *Nuclear Installations Act (NIA65)*, managed by UKAEA, formerly the UK centre for research into experimental fast reactor technology, now being decommissioned.

Dounreay Pits – a facility at Dounreay consisting of seven trenches, used for the disposal of low activity wastes above VLRM levels, which are now full.

DPRK – the Democratic Peoples Republic of Korea.

Drigg – the facility for the near-surface disposal of most of the UK's solid LLW operated by BNFL, near the company's Sellafield site, in Cumbria.

DSRP – the Dounreay Site Restoration Plan; UKAEA's strategy for decommissioning Dounreay's nuclear facilities, decontaminating the site, and managing the resulting wastes.

DTI – the Department of Trade and Industry.

Dustbin Disposal – the process of collection of VLLW from small user sites by local authority refuse collectors and its disposal with ordinary waste to landfill.

EA – the Environment Agency; one of the regulators for radioactive waste management in England and Wales. EA's powers are provided under *RSA93;* the Agency's role is the enforcement of specified laws and regulations aimed at protecting the environment, in the context of sustainable development, predominantly by authorising and controlling radioactive discharges and waste disposals to air, water (surface water, groundwater) and land. In addition to authorisations issued under the *RSA93*, the EA also regulates nuclear sites under the *Pollution Prevention and Control Regulations* and issues consents for non–radioactive discharges. The equivalent body in Scotland is the Scottish Environment Protection Agency (SEPA).

EARP – the Enhanced Actinide Removal Plant (at Sellafield site).

EIA – Environmental Impact Assessment.

Electron – one of the particles composing the atom, carrying a single negative charge and orbiting the atomic nucleus. It is identical to the beta–minus particle.

Elements – atoms classified according to the number of protons in their nuclei, which determines their chemical identity (see also *Fuel Element*).

EM – Environmental Management (United States).

Enrichment – the process of increasing the proportion of one isotope relative to another of the same element.

EOs – Exemption Orders; regulations made under *RSA93* which remove the need for individual regulatory approval of some activities and some classes of materials/wastes where provisions included in the orders themselves are sufficient to assure protection of the public.

EPA – the Environmental Protection Agency (United States).

EURATOM – the European Atomic Energy Community – within the European Union, nuclear matters are the subject of a separate Treaty dating from 1957. This established the European Atomic Energy Community (EAEC) or EURATOM, which was set up to encourage progress in the field of nuclear energy.

Fast Neutrons – neutrons that have a large amount of energy (in excess of 0.1 MeV).

Fast Reactor – a reactor in which there is no moderator. The chain reaction is sustained using fast neutrons.

FDA – the Food and Drug Administration (United States).

FED – fuel element debris.

Fission – the splitting of heavy atomic nuclei with a corresponding energy release. Fission can be spontaneous or caused by the impact of a neutron, high-energy charged particle or high-energy gamma rays. In nuclear power reactors, the core is normally designed for neutron fission.

Fission Products – the two (or very rarely more) lighter nuclei produced when a heavy nucleus is split (i.e. undergoes fission).

Flask – a thick-walled sealed metal container, designed for the safe storage and transport of radioactive material.

Floc – sludge-like residue produced during flocculation.

Fuel Element – an assembly consisting of a grouping of fuel pins. In Magnox reactors the element is a single fuel pin of large diameter.

Fuel Pin – a sealed tube containing nuclear fuel.

Fusion – the building of more complex nuclei by the combination of simpler ones, usually accompanied by the release of energy.

Gamma Particles – energy emitted from the nucleus of atoms but without the movement of material (i.e., similar to X-rays). Gamma radiation has great penetrating power and substantial shielding is needed.

Half-life – the time required for the rate of radioactive emission from a particular radionuclide to fall to half its original value; a characteristic of that radionuclide.

HLW – High Level Waste. Radioactive wastes are commonly classified in terms of the nature and quantity of radioactivity they contain and their heat generating capacity. HLW has the greatest concentration of radioactivity, and generates substantial quantities of heat. It is produced in relatively small volumes from the reprocessing of irradiated nuclear fuel, but contains about 95 percent of the radioactivity in all wastes arising from the nuclear power generation programme. It is produced as a concentrated aqueous residue during the primary stages in the separation of uranium and plutonium from irradiated nuclear fuel. This concentrated residue is conditioned by vitrification. Spent fuel would be included in this category if it were to be disposed of without reprocessing.

HSE – the Health and Safety Executive; a statutory body whose role is the enforcement of work related health and safety law under the general direction of the Health and Safety Commission established by the *Health and Safety at Work Act 1974*. HSE is the licensing authority for nuclear installations. The Nuclear Safety Directorate of HSE exercises this delegated authority through the Nuclear

Installations Inspectorate (NII) who are responsible for regulating the nuclear, radiological and industrial safety of nuclear installations UK wide.

IAEA – the International Atomic Energy Agency.

ICRP – the International Committee for Radiological Protection (see appendix 2).

ILW – Intermediate Level Waste - Wastes with radioactivity exceeding the upper limits for LLW but of a lower radioactivity and heat output than HLW. Intermediate level waste consists principally of materials that have been irradiated in a nuclear reactor (e.g. fuel cladding and reactor components), and equipment and materials that have been used in the processing of radioactive materials (e.g. ion exchange resins and filters).

In-situ Burial – the concept of the authorised burial of solid waste at the site at which it arises, including leaving contaminated soil in place.

Ion-exchange Resin – an insoluble material that exchanges ions with a solution. Resins are used widely to soften water, purify certain industrial chemicals and for the removal of radioactive contaminants from liquid effluent and coolant.

Irradiated Material – material that has been exposed to radiation. In the nuclear industry this commonly refers to material that has been exposed to and has captured neutrons, and thus contains activation products.

Isotopes – atoms of a given element with different numbers of neutrons within their nuclei.

KAERI – the Korea Atomic Energy Research Institute (ROK).

KEDO – the Korean Peninsula Energy Development Organisation (ROK).

KEPCO – the Korea Electric Power Company (ROK).

KINS – the Korean Institute of Nuclear Safety (ROK).

KIST – the Korean Institute of Science and Technology (ROK).

KSNP – Korean Standard Nuclear Power Plant (ROK).

Landfill Disposal – the burial of waste, including some radioactive waste, in near surface excavations, or landfills, operated by local authorities and the private sector.

L/ILW – Low and Intermediate Level Waste.

LLW – Low Level Waste - Wastes containing radioactive materials not exceeding 4 GBq/t alpha or 12 GBq/t beta/gamma, but more radioactive than VLLW. LLW consists of general rubbish (such as used paper towels and discarded laboratory clothing) and other lightly contaminated plant items and equipment, as well as some materials that have been irradiated, arising predominately from the operation of nuclear facilities. Building materials and larger items of plant and equipment are also produced from the decommissioning of facilities. Since 1959 most of the UK arisings of solid LLW have been disposed of at Drigg in Cumbria. There is also a LLW disposal facility at Dounreay for wastes from this site.

LSA – Low Specific Activity; a term mainly used for LLW produced by the oil and gas industry (predominantly radioactively contaminated pipe work scale). LSA scale has relatively high radium content and, consequently, the majority of LSA waste streams do not meet the Drigg waste acceptance criteria.

LWMO – Licensed Waste Management Operator (Finland).

MAC – Miscellaneous Activated Components.

Magnox – an alloy of magnesium used for fuel element cladding in natural uranium fuelled gas-cooled power reactors, and hence a generic name for this type of reactor.

Moderator – a substance used in thermal reactors to reduce the energy of neutrons produced in the fission process in order that they may cause further fissions more readily.

MOST – the Ministry of Science and Technology (Korea).

MOX – Mixed Oxide; a term used for nuclear fuel containing plutonium.

MRWS – a commonly used abbreviation for 'Managing Radioactive Waste Safely', a UK Government consultation paper on the future management of long-lived solid radioactive waste, published in September 2001.

MTR – Materials Testing Reactor; a specialised type of reactor designed for the irradiation of material samples.

MTU – Metric Tons of Uranium.

NAW – the National Assembly for Wales; the elected assembly for Wales, and the body responsible for most aspects of environmental protection policy in Wales under devolution arrangements.

NEA – the Nuclear Energy Agency of the OECD.

NETEC – the Nuclear Environment Technology Institute (Korea).

Neutron – a particle of zero net charge, having mass approximately equal to that of the proton. It is a basic component of the atomic nucleus.

NII – the Nuclear Installations Inspectorate – (part of HSE).

Nimonic – an alloy of the elements nickel, chromium and other minor constituents.

Nimonic Spring – a component of a Magnox fuel element, which because of its material composition becomes highly activated. The high concentration of Co-60 is significant for waste management.

Nirex – United Kingdom Nirex Ltd; a company owned by the Government and the civil nuclear industry, the work of which mainly relates to advice on the management of intermediate level radioactive waste and some LLW, and production of the RWI.

NIST – the National Institute of Standards and Technology (United States).

NLIP– the Nuclear Liabilities Investment Portfolio. Investment assets in BNFL's balance sheet earmarked for the discharge of future nuclear liabilities.

NORM – Naturally Occurring Radioactive Materials.

NPP – Nuclear Power Plant.

NRC – the Nuclear Regulatory Commission (United States).

NRPB – the National Radiological Protection Board.

Nuclear Fuel Cycle – processes connected with nuclear power production, including obtaining, using, storing, reprocessing, recycling and disposing of nuclear materials used in the operation of nuclear reactors.

Nucleus – the part of an atom containing most of its mass.

Nuclide – species of a given element characterised by the number of neutrons within the atomic nucleus.

OCRWM – Office of Civilian Radioactive Waste Management (United States).

OECD – Organisation for Economic Co-operation and Development.

ONDRAF/NIRAS – Organisme national des déchets radioactifs et des matières fissiles (France).

Parent – that radionuclide from which a *daughter* nuclide is produced by radioactive decay.

Partitioning – the separation of certain radionuclides from other wastes so they can be subjected to transmutation.

PCM – Plutonium Contaminated Material.

PCSC – Post Closure Safety Case; a means of appraising a radioactive waste disposal site, in terms of compliance with radiological protection standards, focusing on assurance that the site can eventually be closed and on its post closure performance.

PFR – Prototype Fast Reactor (at Dounreay site; shut down in 1994).

Pressure Vessel – a large steel or pre-stressed concrete container housing the whole of the reactor core and primary coolant in those reactor systems where the primary coolant is pressurised.

Proton – a particle that is a basic component of the atomic nucleus, and carries a single positive charge. It has a mass approximately equal to that of the neutron.

PWR – Pressurised Water Reactor.

Radiation – the emission of energetic particles or electromagnetic waves.

Radioactivity – the spontaneous disintegration of atomic nuclei.

Radioisotope – an older term for radionuclide.

Radionuclide – a general term for an unstable atom or nucleus that emits ionising radiation.

Radium-226 – a radionuclide that emits alpha particles, with a half-life of 1,600 years, often used in the manufacture of luminising materials R&D Research and Development.

Recycling – the re-use of uranium and plutonium recovered from irradiated nuclear fuel by reprocessing.

Reprocessing – the chemical treatment of spent fuel from a reactor in order to separate unused uranium and plutonium from the fission products.

ROK – the Republic of Korea.

RWI – the United Kingdom Radioactive Waste Inventory; a published record of information on the origins, quantities and properties of radioactive wastes in the UK, both currently managed and predicted to arise.

RWMAC – the Radioactive Waste Management Committee.

Safeguards – under the Non-proliferation Treaty (NPT), states are required to enter into a Safeguards Agreement with the IAEA that allows the IAEA inspectorate to carry out periodic, systematic inspections of nuclear installations.

Safestore – a strategy for decommissioning gas-cooled power stations that involves the construction of containments around all buildings containing active plant. The purpose is to protect the buildings and their contents from deterioration due to weathering so that complete dismantling can be deferred. The more active buildings would be prepared for a long (around 100 years) period during which no routine maintenance would be required, the intention being to facilitate radioactive decay prior to final dismantling.

SE – the Scottish Executive; the Cabinet of the Scottish Parliament, which, in turn, is the body responsible for most aspects of environmental protection policy in Scotland under devolution arrangements.

SEPA – the Scottish Environment Protection Agency; the regulators for radioactive materials and radioactive wastes in Scotland. SEPA's powers are provided under *RSA93*.

Sievert – a measure of radiation that takes into account the type of radiation involved, the energy deposited in the tissues irradiated, and the sensitivity of the different body tissues to radiation. Typically, doses are expressed in milli Sieverts (mSv); 1 Sievert = 1,000 mSv. The annual average dose to an individual in the UK is 2.2 mSv from natural radiation and 0.4 mSv from man-made radiation, of which 0.37 mSv is from medical uses of radiation and radioactive materials.

SIXEP – the Site Ion-exchange Effluent Plant (at Sellafield site).

Small Users – organisations that use radioactive materials and create radioactive wastes that are not part of the nuclear sector licensed under NIA65, including hospitals, universities, and industrial undertakings.

SoLA – Substances of Low Activity; among other things, SoLA removes the need for individual authorisation of disposal of some solid radioactive wastes the activity of which is less than 0.4 Becquerels per gram (Schedule 1 activity limits are disregarded for the purposes of SoLA).

Specific Activity – the concentration of radioactivity associated with a material or materials.

Stringer – a string of fuel element assemblies for an AGR.

STUK – the Radiation and Nuclear Safety Authority (Finland).

Supercompaction – a general term which describes the reduction in bulk volume by the application of high external force. It differs from routine compaction methods by using hydraulic equipment capable of exerting forces of 1,000-2,000 tonnes, and the original container (metal drum or box) is supercompacted along with its contents. Waste is often precompacted into steel drums or boxes prior to supercompaction of the drum or box.

TBP – tributyl phosphate. Used as a complexing agent in the solvent extraction of uranium and plutonium from spent nuclear fuel.

Technetium – was the first element to be produced artificially. Since its discovery, searches for the element in terrestrial material have been made. Finally in 1962, technetium-9 was isolated and identified in African pitchblende (a uranium rich ore) in extremely minute quantities as a spontaneous fission product of uranium-38 by B.T. Kenna and P.K. Kuroda. Tests conducted by Southampton University's oceanography centre, found low levels Technetium-9 (Tc-99) in farmed Scottish salmon.

Thermal Reactor – a reactor that uses a moderator. The chain reaction is sustained using 'thermalized' neutrons of lower energy than fast neutrons.

THORP – the Thermal Oxide Reprocessing Plant (at Sellafield site).

Transmutation – a process by which radionuclides are bombarded with neutrons in a reactor or a particle accelerator to convert them into shorter-lived or stable nuclides.

Tritiated – containing tritium (H-3).

Tritium – an isotope of hydrogen (H-3) having a radioactive half-life of about 12 years.

UKAEA – a state-owned nuclear operator largely responsible for the decommissioning of nuclear facilities, including those at Dounreay.

Vitrification – the process whereby liquid high level waste is immobilised as a solid ingot of glass.

VLLW – Very Low Level Waste; wastes with very low concentrations of radioactivity arise from a variety of sources, including hospitals and non-nuclear industry. They contain little total radioactivity and may be disposed of by various means such as with domestic refuse, at landfill sites or by incineration. The method depends upon the nature and quantity of the material to be handled.

VLRM – Very Low Radioactive Material; a radioactive waste classification, proposed by UKAEA for nuclear plant decommissioning and site clean-up purposes, falling at the lower activity end of the LLW range. VLRM incorporates wastes containing up to 40 Bq/g of relatively short-lived beta/gamma activity and long-lived alpha bearing wastes of about 1-2Bq/g. The category is expressly restricted to large-scale arisings of construction wastes from decommissioning and contaminated soil and rock.

Waste Management – the treatment, storage and safe disposal of radioactive materials.

WIPP – the Waste Isolation Pilot Plant (United States).

Zircaloy – an alloy of the element zirconium used for the cladding of nuclear fuel, particularly in water reactors.

Chapter One

Nuclear Waste and Energy

The defining features of the first decade of this century are the defeat of poverty and climate change; both are influenced by the production of energy and waste. Nuclear waste management impacts on both.[1] Nuclear waste from the weapons programme, from research, from the power generation programme, from industrial, agricultural and medical use has been accumulating in the UK over the past half century. Qualified estimates of the amounts that are stored and yet to be treated range from volumes of high and intermediate level radioactive waste[2] that once treated could be accommodated in a volume equivalent to the Albert Hall to much larger amounts from decommissioning existing nuclear facilities. There are varying views on the continuing use of nuclear energy, however a common factor is the need to remove the problem of how to manage radioactive waste. This work is intended to describe the situation of nuclear waste;[3] to identify policy and law that apply in a selection of states but to focus essentially on the UK; to identify the actors and to look to the future.

A European survey of public opinion[4] carried out at the request of the European Commission revealed that eight out of ten of the respondents in 16,155 interviews believed that 'any radioactive waste is very dangerous'. The public perception of threat has been engendered by the general lack of appreciation of the conservative system of radiation protection that has evolved from scientific observation and prediction of the risk of cancer from exposure to low level radiation. The concept of collective dose is based on the system of radiation protection and applied to accident scenarios with remote possibilities, but in the absence of scientific assessment of the balance afforded by the pragmatism that man applies to everyday risks including the risk of cancer from the ever-present background of natural radiation, has added a measure of dread to the public perception of threat. That dread has been exacerbated by the emergence since September 2001 of the possibility of the use of radioactive waste as a terrorist weapon and for waste

---

[1] Parts of this introduction were included in a presentation by the author to *The 9th International Conference on Environmental Remediation and Radioactive Waste Management*, September 21-25, Examination Schools, Oxford, England. Riley, P. (2003), *Policy and Law Relating to Radioactive Waste; International Direction and Human Rights*, ICEM03-4948.

[2] These are defined in Chapter 2.

[3] The term 'nuclear waste' is used to describe radioactive waste; discarded radioactive materials, in some circumstances used nuclear fuel, and radioactively contaminated material and decommissioning waste. All of these categories may be termed radioactive waste and that is used interchangeably with nuclear waste.

[4] European Commission, DG-X Public Opinion Analysis Unit (1999), *Europeans and Radioactive Waste*, Report by INRA (Europe) for Directorate General 'Environment, Nuclear Safety and Civil Protection', Eurobarometer 50.0, p 27.

storage facilities to be seen as terrorist targets. International policy has moved from the comprehensive coverage of nuclear regulation where waste was an integral, but minor player, in the nuclear energy process to separate consideration with nuclear waste requiring specific regulation.

Some would argue that the predicted doubling of world demand for electricity over the next fifty years[5] requires that the gift of nuclear energy that has served developed nations over the past half century must not be wasted. However an obstacle to the development of nuclear energy, the absence of a clear and unequivocal policy regarding the storage and disposal of nuclear waste and the absence of clear regulations based on law, is seen by a significant section of the public as a threat to their rights. Public opposition fuelled by antipathy to the 'command approach'[6] and other fears may cause the demise of nuclear electric power in developed nations and proscribe its use in the developing world.

The commitment to sustainable development was reaffirmed by the representatives of the peoples of the world at the World Summit on Sustainable Development in Johannesburg in September 2002. Amongst the various challenges the Summit specifically resolved to speedily increase access to basic requirements such as clean water and energy; to use modern technology to bring about development and to make sure that technology transfer, human resource development, education and training are deployed to banish forever underdevelopment. Against this background the Summit committed itself to a plan of implementation.[7] The plan acknowledges that eradicating poverty is the greatest global challenge facing the world today. Improved access to reliable, affordable and environmentally sound energy services and resources are a part of this challenge and the use of renewable energy sources, cleaner fossil fuels and hydro power are identified as positive means to achieve it but, except as implied by the phrase 'advanced energy technology', nuclear energy is significantly absent. Concepts that have evolved through the nuclear programme appear in the plan, for example it identifies the necessity to promote the internalisation of environmental costs and the use of environmental impact procedures in development planning and in planning investment in infrastructures. Significantly the plan encourages the development of waste management systems including the technology to recapture the energy contained in waste and perceives a serious potential for environment and human impacts of radioactive waste. In this latter context Governments, taking into account their national circumstances, are encouraged to make efforts to examine and further improve measures and internationally agreed regulations regarding safety, while having in place effective liability mechanisms, relevant to international maritime transportation and other transboundary movement of radioactive material, radioactive waste and spent fuel. Collaboration at all levels

---

[5] Bernard, P. (Printemps 2002) Le nucléaire, une énergie d'avenir, CLEFS CEA – No 46.

[6] The 'command approach' is a phrase used to identify the approach used (hopefully rarely nowadays) to characterise policy made without consultation.

[7] The following is extracted from the advance unedited text of the plan of action of the World Summit on Sustainable Development. See also UN Johannesburg Summit 2002. Highlights of commitments and implementation initiatives, 3 Sep. 2002.

between natural and social scientists and between scientists and policy makers is encouraged to, *inter alia*, promote and improve science based decision making and to reaffirm the precautionary approach.

This careful approach to the development of nuclear energy is evident in the energy policy of the United Kingdom.[8] While in no way encouraging the further development of nuclear power, UK policy is focussing on the removal of obstacles to that development, presumably as a precautionary measure in the context of energy security. A draft Nuclear Sites and Radioactive Substances Bill was issued for consultation in June 2003 based on a White Paper issued a year earlier.[9] It is predicted that within five years the UK will cease to be self-supporting in energy and will be a net importer of natural gas. As reflected in the Summit Plan one of the most significant obstacles to the development of nuclear electric power is the general view that a necessary precursor to further development is to have an acceptable radioactive waste storage and disposal solution or even to have satisfactorily stored and disposed of all existing waste. In the welcome climate of transparency of decision-making, it is a precondition that public opinion must be in favour of any proposed solution for dealing with radioactive waste. High-level waste is largely stored at the nuclear facility site awaiting a long-term solution. The policy of nuclear nations internationally is disparate, however a common factor is the interim nature of the storage of intermediate and high level radioactive waste. Further common factors are public opposition partly due to fear of the unknown, partly from the 'Not In My Back Yard' phenomenon and partly the active opposition of non-government organisations (NGOs).

International Dimension

While far from comprehensive, having been neglected until very recently, control of so-called nuclear waste has in two areas achieved an international dimension. Firstly in an endeavour to attract international attention towards environmental concerns, including the principle of sustainable development, *the Joint Convention on Safety of Spent Fuel Management and on the Safety of Radioactive Waste (the 'Joint Convention')*[10] was adopted in 1997. The *Joint Convention* focuses on safety and was examined in depth at the INLA Congress in Washington[11] where it was noted that, to work, the Convention relies heavily on Contracting States as no new international body is established and relies on the IAEA for its secretariat. The role of the IAEA as stated in the code of practice on transboundary movement

---

[8] DTI and DEFRA (2003), *The Energy White Paper. Our Energy Future – creating a low carbon economy*, (Cm 5761) Feb. HMSO.

[9] DTI (2002), *Managing the Nuclear Legacy – A Strategy for Action* (Cm 5552) July, HMSO.

[10] Kageneck, de A. and Pinol, C. (1998), 'The Joint Convention on the Safety of Spent Fuel Management and on the Safety of Radioactive Waste Management', *International & Comparative Law Quarterly*, Vol 47 Apr.

[11] Cameron, P. (1999), *The Safety of Radioactive Waste Management: new steps forward in the law*, Nuclear Inter Jura, Washington DC.

of radioactive waste,[12] is to collect and disseminate information on the laws regulations and technical standards pertaining to radioactive waste management and disposal, develop relevant technical standards and provide advice and assistance on all aspects of radioactive waste management and disposal, having particular regard to the needs of developing countries.

Secondly in the context of the prevention of pollution and the protection of part of the maritime area against the adverse effects of human activities, *the Convention for the Protection of the Marine Environment of the North-East Atlantic (the 'OSPAR Convention')* entered into force in March 1998 having been signed by the majority of countries bordering the north-east shores of the Atlantic Ocean.[13] The *OSPAR Convention* specifically prohibits the dumping of low and intermediate level radioactive substances including waste and in this case has a Commission made up of representatives of each of the Contracting Parties with duties, *inter alia*, to supervise the implementation of the Convention, to review the condition of the maritime area, the effectiveness of the measures being adopted, the priorities, the need for additional or different measures and to establish at regular intervals its programme of work. The provisions of the *OSPAR Convention* on the arrangements for processing of spent fuel and radioactive waste management will be effective in forcing solutions to nuclear waste management as can be witnessed in the ongoing actions under *the Law of the Sea*.[14] It is probably not the technical aspects of arrangements such as the *Joint Convention* but 'institutional control', the interface with human activities tackled at a national level, which will attract most attention and will be perceived as bearing adversely on human rights.

The European Dimension

The European Court of Justice (ECJ) has recently confirmed the Community's legislative powers in relation to the safety of nuclear facilities[15] despite the technical competence of the national authorities. Taking into account the opinion of the Nuclear Experts Committee, the Commission in November 2002 issued proposals for two Directives;[16] one setting out basic obligations and general principles on the safety of nuclear installations and the other on radioactive waste.

---

[12] IAEA (1990), *Code of Practice on the International Transboundary Movement of Radioactive Waste*. INFCIRC/386 Nov. IAEA Paris.

[13] *The Convention for the Protection of the Marine Environment of the North-East Atlantic* was opened for signature at the Ministerial Meeting of the Oslo and Paris Commissions, Paris, 21-22 Sept. 1992, Ospar Commission. [www.ospar.org]

[14] For example in *Ireland v United Kingdom (International Tribunal for the Law of the Sea, 3 December 2001)* the Tribunal refused to grant a preliminary injunction to permit the operation of the MOX plant at Sellafield. The issue centred on the claim of the Irish Government that the UK's decision to authorise the MOX plant breached certain provisions of the 1982 UN Convention on the Law of the Sea, to which both countries are parties. The Tribunal noted that rights under the OSPAR Convention had a separate existence from those under the Convention.

[15] Judgment of the Court in Case C-29/99 of 10 Dec. 2002.

[16] COM(2002)606.

The latter Directive will require Member States to adopt national programmes for the disposal of radioactive waste, comprising in particular the deep disposal of high-activity waste. Co-operation solutions between Member States are envisaged but no Member State is required to accept imports of radioactive waste from other Member States. The aims of the proposed Directives are to contribute to the establishing of best practice in the management of spent fuel and radioactive waste in the Member States that reflect the fundamental principles of protection of human health and the environment now and in the future, nuclear safety and environmental protection through application of the precautionary principle,[17] public information and where necessary participation as an essential aspect of governance in the radioactive waste sector. Underpinning the protection of individuals, society and the environment from the harmful effects of radiation are *the Basic Safety Standards*[18] and *the Environmental Impact Assessment Directive.*[19]

Human Rights

The *Charter of the United Nations (UN)* declares that the peoples of the UN are determined to promote, *inter alia*, social progress and better standards of life and to those ends to employ international machinery for the promotion of economic and social advancement of all peoples. One of the purposes of the UN is to achieve international co-operation in solving international problems of an economic, cultural or humanitarian character.[20] *The Universal Declaration of Human Rights*[21] confirms that everyone has the right to a standard of living adequate for the health and well being of himself and his family.[22] The governments of the European countries in the *European Convention on Human Rights (ECHR)* and the *European Social Charter* resolve to take certain steps for the collective enforcement of certain rights stated in the *Universal Declaration*. *The European Charter of Fundamental Rights*[23] identifies the right to social security, health care, access to services of a general economic interest and environmental protection. The World Summit in Johannesburg underlines the resolve of nations to convert these rights into reality. A halt to growing starvation and dwindling supplies of drinking water in many parts of the globe could be alleviated by the availability of reliable electrical power and desalination plant. Renewable energy sources are advocated as the solution to the problems of the third-world's shortage of electrical power, nuclear being discounted on the equivocal grounds that it is unsustainable. One of the assumptions by NGOs is that there is no acceptable solution to *the problem* of

---

[17] Stokes, Elen, R. (2003), 'Precautionary Steps: the development of the precautionary principle in EU jurisprudence', *ELM 15 [2003]*.
[18] *Basic Safety Standards Council Directive 96/29/EURATOM* of 13 May 1996.
[19] *Environmental Impact Assessment Directive*. Council Directive 85/337/EEC of 27 Jun. 1985 amended by 97/11/EEC of 3 Mar. 1997.
[20] Charter of the United Nations. Article 1.3.
[21] Adopted by the General Assembly of the United Nations on 10 Dec. 1948.
[22] ibid. Article 25.1.
[23] Universal Declaration. The European Charter of Fundamental Rights 2000/C 364/01 Signed 7 Dec. 2000.

nuclear waste and therefore nuclear electric power is not acceptable on that count alone. The question of safety and economic viability of nuclear electric power is also questioned by NGOs who also see as an implied threat to the development of renewable energy sources, the possibility of a renaissance of nuclear electrical power and fear the consequent diversion of resources away from the development of renewables.

Under the *Aarhus Convention*[24] the public are required to be involved in decision-making;

> In order to contribute to the protection of the right of every person of present and future generations to live in an environment adequate to his or her health and well-being, each Party shall guarantee the rights of access to justice in environmental matters...

It is clear that the public have powers of involvement in decision-making and unless they are satisfied that a sustainable solution to the storage and disposal of nuclear waste is feasible and that governments have accepted those solutions, the development of nuclear electric power will falter and will not be available for the greater good. Sustainable in this sense means a solution that not only satisfies current public opinion but also the safety of future generations.

Factors that Determine Policy

Within this general picture there are a number of vectors that determine the policy that will result in a satisfactory solution to this problem of nuclear waste. These vectors are: technological, including radiological and engineering perspectives; social, including international legislation and public attitudes; and economic, including practical solutions.

Technological

The term technological is used here to mean a combination of science and engineering. An engineered solution can always be found within the rules set down, however, complications arise when the science based rules are not clear and fixed and therefore can be perceived as being manipulable. This is one of the reasons for the perception of nuclear waste as a problem; where there is equivocation and flux in the rules there is the opportunity for ingenuity in the solutions and consequent lack of confidence by the observing public advised by the media. The effect of radiation, particularly low-level radiation is under continuous review and feeds uncertainty not only about the effects but also about the process that leads to regulation. This fluidity is demonstrated by the outcome of the initiative by the chairman of the ICRP to encourage the international radiation protection community to engage in a review of the merits and drawbacks of the current system of radiation protection. The OECD-NEA Committee on Radiation and Public Health (CRPPH) carried out a critical review of the system and noted,

---

[24] The International Convention on Access to Information, Public Participation in Decision-making and Access to Justice in Environmental Matters. Aarhus, Denmark, 25 Jun. 1988. [www.unece.org/env/pp]

inter alia, the desirability of improvement in a number of areas for the International Commission on Radiological Protection (ICRP) to consider, which are discussed in chapter three. It is clear that satisfactory solutions to the radioactive waste question, amongst other things, will not be achieved without these points being taken into account. The question arises as to whether the current process and timescales for their conclusion have both the confidence of the public and the urgency to help with a solution to the problems of the developing world!

Engineering solutions to the storage and disposal of nuclear waste are well within the current knowledge base and should not be a cause for delay provided all the safety concerns are satisfactorily addressed and openly defended. The obstacles to satisfactory conclusion lie more in the area of social science, hence the need for the cooperation between natural and social scientists and policy makers advocated by the Johannesburg Summit.

Social

The *Charter of the UN*, the *Universal Declaration of Human Rights* and the *Aarhus Convention* require the problem of nuclear waste to be resolved in an open and publicly acceptable way and are focussed on human rights and public participation in decision-making. A decision to construct a storage or disposal facility will involve environmental impact assessments, planning permissions and public inquiry all of which give this opportunity for public involvement, although the United Kingdom government has hinted at legislation to curtail or circumvent lengthy inquiries in the case of large infrastructure projects.[25] Public bodies have to make decisions that balance the desires of the few against the needs of the many. Many of the rights guaranteed by the ECHR to individuals are expressly qualified by the needs of wider society and uncomfortable decisions have to be made by those responsible within government. Explaining how the national courts handle the fundamental rights expressed in the Convention, Lord Hope in R v DPP, ex p Kebilene[26] said:

> The questions which the courts will have to decide in the application of these principles will involve questions of balance between competing interests and issues of proportionality. In this area difficult choices may have to be made by the executive or the legislature between the rights of the individual and the needs of society. In some circumstances it will be appropriate for the courts to recognise that there is an area of judgement within which the judiciary will defer, on democratic grounds, to the considered opinion of the elected body or person whose act or decision is said to be incompatible with the Convention.

Equally, a Convention right might allow claims of individuals against the wider public interest to be addressed by providing monetary compensation. In a case

---

[25] The UK Government has scrapped proposals in its planning reforms to abolish conventional public inquiries for major projects and withdraw the public's right to appear at inquiries into local plans.

[26] *R v Director of Public Prosecutions, ex parte Kebilene and others.* [2000] 2 AC 326, 381.

before the European Court of Human Rights (ECtHR),[27] concerning balance between the UK's economic well-being and the applicants' effective enjoyment of their right to respect for their private lives in relation to noise generated by Heathrow Airport, the UK were in violation of Article 8 and Article 13 of the ECHR as UK law did not give an effective remedy for the breach of Article 8. In another case[28] Lord Phillips MR concluded that where community interests were served by the operation of a public authority of a particular undertaking, it may be necessary in achieving the right balance between the individual and community benefit to pay compensation to individuals whose rights are affected.[29]

The question as to whether a policy-maker could also be a decision-maker and remain compliant with Article 6 of the ECHR was challenged and resolved in the affirmative by the House of Lords in *Alconbury*[30] after being challenged in the European Court.

Nevertheless in coming to a decision on a particular application the principle of proportionality will be involved and choices will have to be made between the rights of the individual and the needs of society. A leading issue in examining a decision would be whether the decision-maker had carried out the correct balancing exercise. An inevitable manifestation of the proper application of the principle of proportionality is the general duty to give reasons unless it is disproportionate to do so. A resolution of the Council of Europe Committee of Ministers states:

> Statement of Reasons – Where an administrative act is of such a nature as adversely to affect his rights, liberties or interests, the person concerned is informed of the reasons on which it is based. This is done either by stating the reasons in the act, or by communicating them, at his request, to the person concerned in writing within a reasonable time.

It has been argued that the question of public interest has penetrated behind the decision process.[31] Increased public participation in environmental law through environmental impact assessments[32] and planning regulation and the requirements following the *Aarhus Convention*[33] is evident. The *Aarhus Convention* requires mandatory procedures for public hearings in respect of decisions on specific

---

[27] *Hatton and Others v United Kingdom*, European Court of Human Rights, [2002] 34 E.H.R.R.1 .

[28] *Marcic v Thames Water Utilities Ltd* [2001] 3 AllER 698 and C.A. [2002]Q.B. 1003.

[29] See also, Grecos, M. (2002), 'Human Rights and the Environment', *[2002] 2 Env. Liability 95.*

[30] *R.(on the application of Alconbury Developments Ltd) v Secretary of State for the Environment Transport and the Regions.* [2001] 2 All E.R. 929 (*Alconbury*).

[31] Steele, J (2001), 'Participation and Deliberation in Environmental Law: Exploring a Problem-solving approach', *Oxford Journal of Legal Studies*, Vol. 21, No. 3 (2001), pp 415-442.

[32] Directive 85/337/EEC and Council Directive 97/11/EC.

[33] *Aarhus Convention on Access to Information, Public Participation in Decision-making and Access to Justice*, 25 Jun. 1998; and Directive 90/313/EEC on Freedom of Environmental Information.

activities; it requires States to ensure that due account is taken of the outcomes of this public participation and operates together with public rights of access to information. There are signs that participation is regarded as likely to lead to better decision-making since it is not only a way of handling preferences and choices, it is also deliberative[34] and therefore more validly democratic and a valuable source of knowledge and values. According to the Royal Commission on Environmental Protection's Report, 'Setting Environmental Standards',[35] the public should be involved in setting strategies rather than merely being consulted on already drafted proposals.[36] It was suggested[37] by the House of Lords Select Committee on Environmental Audit that people's values should be incorporated, not only in the eventual decisions reached, but also in the way that policy questions are framed. This should concern

> the values of citizens rather than compromises between interest groups.

Thus participation in the decision-making process leads to assist the achievement of the goal of sustainability.[38] Another aspect of the deliberative value of participation is to release the dual aspects of individuals; firstly as self-interested consumers seeking to satisfy their preferences and secondly as citizens capable of embracing and advancing values that do not reflect their own selfish interests but define the kind of society in which they wish to live.[39] This process of deliberation on an international scale, applied to the wider question of nuclear electric power might well assist in the release of this valuable gift for use in raising the developing world from a state of starvation and thirst.

Economic and Practical Solutions

The storage and disposal of radioactive material provides challenges that transcend traditional economic practices and may have recourse to solutions seen as fanciful today but which may be the norm in future. Abandoned or ignored solutions that are not seen as practical or economic at the time have a habit of reappearing some time later as perfect solutions. In the 19th century chemists distilled petroleum to obtain fuel for oil lamps and they threw away the most valuable fraction, gasoline, as an unfortunate waste product.[40] In 1943, Thomas Watson, CEO of IBM, said; 'I think there's a world market for perhaps 5 computers'.

In the economic field today's practices that are based on rules that favour short-term gain may not apply in the context of the time taken for the decay of the radioactivity of nuclear waste. Involvement of the public may reveal novel

---

[34] According to the National Research Council for America, *Understanding Risk* (1996) 'deliberative' is any process for communication and for raising and collectively discussing issues.

[35] Royal Commission on Environmental Protection (1998), 21st Report Cm 4053 (1998).

[36] ibid. 7.22; 9.77.

[37] Select Committee Report on Environmental Audit (1999), 5th Report, HC Paper 384.

[38] Supra. Steele, J. notes that increasingly public participation has been urged as the best strategy for rebuilding 'trust' in government action on the environment.

[39] Supra. Steele, J. at p 424 quoting M. Sagoff, *The Economy of the Earth*, Cambridge.

[40] Fox, S. (2002), 'A framework for innovation', *Engineering Management Journal*, Aug.

economic and ownership solutions that encourage a positive attitude to the practical answer to both the sustainability of nuclear energy and the storage of discarded radioactive materials, for example, the ownership of the plant that provides heat and power to a community. Systems of operation that are customary today may be superseded by entirely different approaches for example the supply of services by business in future may focus on performance of integrated functions to supply needs as opposed to the supply of individual products and services.[41]

Practical and economic solutions also have international dimensions; concerns must be that the benefit of solutions to the radioactive waste problem contribute to improvement of the third-world situation and do not add to their burdens. Given the appropriate circumstances, radioactive waste and spent nuclear fuel may form the basis for providing future ingenious solutions, for example, perpetual low-level district heating. The use of waste heat from heat generating waste for desalination to provide drinking water on a near perpetual basis under international control must be an idea worth following. It has been reported that Chinese scientists have developed atomic reactors to provide heating and desalinate seawater by burning used fuel from nuclear power stations under normal pressure.[42] A move by Russia to develop floating nuclear power plants[43] may be of great value in future by providing power under the control of an advanced technological authority to coastal states in the developing world.

The Legal Dimension

Proposed solutions to the so-called problem of radioactive waste, technological, social, economic and practical, examples of which are mentioned above, if not limitless go well beyond the bounds of current thinking. It should be the business of legislators to ensure that regulation does not inhibit but facilitates viable and publicly acceptable solutions and in particular to ensure where necessary the amendment of existing law and the generation of new conventions incorporate appropriate new legal concepts. Areas to consider include the regulation of storage, transport and disposal of radioactive waste separately from the regulation of radioactive material destined for uses in industrial, agricultural, medical, military and power applications. The question of liability following the safe securing or disposal of radioactive waste should be addressed in the context of very long time scales in remote, secure locations. The amendment of radiological protection regulations to treat workers and public equally will ease the path to public acceptability. Public participation in decision-making and in the construction and control of nuclear facilities should be considered as a legal right and an obligation of the developer. Finally the encouragement and facilitation of new economic concepts should be a feature of all regulation and control and should be enabled by legislation.

---

[41] For a novel concept see Michaelis, M. *Integrated Performance Systems; the business of the future.* [www.michaelmichaelis.com]
[42] Xinhua News Agency, 20 Jun. 2002. [www.xinhuanet.com]
[43] Brakov, Vitaly. Pravda. Ru 30 Oct. 2002.

Future Development

The development of the system of radiological protection has been a 'bottom up' process where those recommending allowable doses were aware of the potential dangers to themselves; they practised a cautious approach and encouraged those proposing the rules to support adequate margins in regulatory limits. The circumstances at the time of consideration of appropriate dose levels were such that those advising were probably applying measures that today would be seen as obeying the precautionary principle, being unenlightened about the full extent of levels of natural radiation that already existed, and being primarily concerned about the putative effect of radiation on future generations and the need to influence, in a limited sense, the release to the atmosphere of radioactive and radioactive contaminated materials from nuclear explosions. The influence of the media and the Campaign for Nuclear Disarmament (CND) was also a powerful incentive for those at the cutting edge to be seen to practise the precautionary principle. This was quite opposite to the 'top down' process practised even today for pollutants in general where the politicians, acting for the public, were interested in reducing pollutants only when they had already become intolerable and politically unacceptable like the London smogs of the 1950s.

The control of radioactive materials is safe, sound and quite contrary to that promulgated by the NGOs and in media pronouncements in the context of the storage and disposal of radioactive waste. To redress the balance, perhaps it should be more widely disseminated that measures taken as a precaution are of an interim nature and may be adjusted to suit circumstances as they develop. The practice of radiological protection is one of those measures which will be revisited and probably the regulations and practices involving radiation will be adjusted to become less restrictive.

The beneficial use of radiation allows the use of high doses in certain circumstances e.g. the use in medical procedures. In these cases the ALARA (as low as reasonably achievable) practice is replaced by AHARACC (as high as reasonably acceptable, considering the circumstances). In the context of sustainable practices, which must consider the efficient use of resources, it would be advisable to also consider the AHARACC principle. Instead of the relentless pursuit of lower exposure to radiation and lower releases to the environment, where the background levels would not be raised above that naturally occurring, there are circumstances where allowing higher dose rates would be of benefit and save valuable resources. Such an approach in measures for the storage and disposal of radioactive waste might lead to the beneficial use of characteristics of the product such as the decay heat from high-level waste.

Prudently handled and suitably promoted to the public, by involving them in practical and economic solutions and rewarding individuals where they have to make sacrifices for the common good, the gift of nuclear energy may benefit all, particularly the developing world. It will need careful and patient handling in education and in restructuring nuclear legislation and regulation in relation to radioactive substances and nuclear facilities to clarify and simplify to enable a clear understanding of the circumstances.

Waste in Context

Having strayed into the realms of what might be it is necessary to set the scene and to consider nuclear waste in context. Three vectors may determine the treatment of waste: sustainability, environmental laws and energy policy.

The Background

Safety has become the fundamental value of our times.[44] Passions that once were devoted to the struggle to change the world are now invested in trying to ensure that mankind is safe. In the process, the scientist and the engineer are perceived by some of the general public as having been irresponsible developers in the past and a threat to present development and future generations. While the public generally respects scientists, there is also a sense that scientific knowledge is somehow threatening.[45] The implied message of recent European legislation[46] is that engineers are only now being constrained in order to consider the long-term aspects of their decisions concerning the environment. This is far from true and in fact competent engineers have from time immemorial taken into account the long-term effects of their work. One only has to see the edifices of classical times and to read the technical papers of Telford and Brunel to recognise that margins allowing for unknown factors and careful statements describing building features, method statements and safety precautions were accepted as necessary by engineers of past generations. Nevertheless concerns about climate change and the consequent deliberations, in particular Agenda 21,[47] have influenced public policy to search for a sustainable solution to future energy provision, and perversely the role of nuclear energy has been marginalized in this search.

The unique character of the regulation of nuclear facilities, radioactive materials and waste under nuclear law is partly to blame, although it might be said that this exclusive treatment has caused the development of nuclear energy to be favoured unfairly. At a national level nuclear law is guided by international law and soft law emanating from technical and scientific practice, technoscience, in the nuclear field. The synergy of nuclear law and technoscience has achieved a workable system of law but one that suffers public criticism and is characterised as being of an Oedipal nature. Outside the field of nuclear development in the general area of non-nuclear industrial applications criticism of a similar type has been shown to be false. In fact, in Europe a combination of law and technoscience has produced a legal regime of environmental principles and common law practice generally acceptable to the public. Paradoxically, development in the general area of environmental law has benefited from the experience of the progress of nuclear

---

[44] Adapted from Furedi, F. (1996), *The Dangers of Safety*, Living Marxism, pp 16-22.
[45] European Commission (2002), Communication from the Commission to the Council, the European Parliament, the Economic and Social Committee and the Committee of the Regions, Science and Society - Action plan, Luxembourg: Office for Official Publications of the European Communities. [www.cordis.lu/science-society]
[46] Integrated Pollution Prevention and Control Directive 96/61/EC.
[47] UN Conference on Environment and Development (1992), Rio de Janeiro, June.

energy regulation, hindsight and the positive participation of the public through consultation and parliamentary debate.

While all substances are poisonous to any organism in high enough doses, we generally consider toxic substances those that even in small doses have the potential to damage the natural environment and/or adversely affect human health.[48] Risks to human health and the natural environment are seen to be severe when toxic substances bio accumulate, that is as well as having the characteristic of toxicity such substances persist in the environment and are capable of building up in living tissue. Radioactive substances are unique since, as well as having the characteristics of toxic substances in high doses, they are also capable of causing harm to living tissue from a distance by ionising radiation. For various reasons, in particular the association with nuclear weapons, they have the capacity for inducing psychological fears.

To find that death or injury is caused by low-level radiation from a particular source is not straightforward since radiation exists naturally in the environment, radioactive materials are used in industry and medicine and the cancer caused by radiation is indistinguishable from that caused generally. Death and injury by cancer may occur many years after the exposure to radiation. Cancer has many causes, such as chemical exposure, and is a major natural cause of death, killing one fifth of the population. The invisibility of radiation, the manifestation of nuclear energy in the weapon, the much-publicised accidents and the consequent public perception of the radiation risk lead to fear in the minds of the public. A consequence of this fear itself may be the damage to health in the form of psychological damage or nervous shock.

The media influences the views of the man in the street; radiation for many reasons evokes a feeling of dread and is difficult to understand without technical knowledge. The radiation protection system itself leads to concerns that even the smallest exposure to radiation is abnormal and dangerous. It is perceived by the man in the street that low-level radiation from a nuclear facility is more dangerous than from other practices, e.g. disposal of waste in the gas industry,[49] where permitted releases of radioactive substances to the environment are much greater than allowed by regulation of the nuclear industry. A natural conclusion may be that a claimant suffering injury of the type caused by radiation and who had been exposed to radiation, no matter how small a dose, that could be shown to come from a nuclear installation would be awarded damages against the licensee of the site of the installation unless it could be shown that the injury was predominantly caused by another source (radioactive or otherwise).

In the United Kingdom the ALARA principle, 'as low as reasonably achievable', and the term ALARP, 'as low as reasonably practicable', are used in regulations, in conditions in licences, in assessment principles and in guidance notes used in the nuclear industry. In fact the ALARA principle is a cornerstone on which much of radiation protection regulation is based. The words 'reasonably practicable' in

---

[48] Williamson, Richard, L. et al (1993), 'Gathering Danger: The Urgent Need to Regulate Toxic Substances That Can Bioaccumulate'. *Ecology Law Quarterly*, Vol 20 p 604.
[49] Unattributed comment, *Engineering*, May 2002, p 22.

ALARP have an established meaning in UK law and are used extensively in statutes and regulations, in particular *The Health and Safety Act 1974*. The Select Committee of the House of Lords on the European Communities in 1986 concluded that public opinion would play a much larger part in deciding the future of nuclear power than is usual with questions of science and technology and so it is important to industry and the general public for the terms used in legislation to be clear and unambiguous.

Sustainable Development

The sensible use of science and its practice in engineering, medicine and agriculture (technoscience) has enabled mankind to raise its sights from a life which was, for the majority, nasty, brutish and short[50] to one of ease and prosperity for a significant proportion of the western world. The basis of this successful scientific approach has similarities in the legal process and both may be as expressed in the Charter of the Royal Society, 'nullis in verba', take nothing on authority. It is worth noting that in 1663 the Royal Society advised its members to be guided by the facts not the consensus of chatterers. Conclusions based purely on public perceptions whilst they may satisfy political correctness can have disastrous consequences. For example, in the first half of the nineteenth century it was widely accepted that diseases such as cholera were caused by smells from drains and sewers this view being based on crude epidemiological observations. The English physician John Snow[51] and the scientific work of Louis Pasteur finally dispelled this so called Miasmatic Theory in the 1870s. While there may be discrepancies between the perception of law by techno scientific circles and the perception of science by legal circles there is a synergy where the two disciplines work together. Legal principles, statute and the common law allow a platform for that synergy to develop.

The beneficial exploitation of scientific knowledge is not fully accomplished; *inter alia*, the technoscientist, one who combines pure science and practical development, in other words, the engineer, has yet to provide solutions to enable mankind to cope with the enormous tasks of raising the developing world from starvation and to restore and keep the environment clean thereby to enable all life to continue. This is the basis of what is now generally termed sustainable development. The role of the technoscientist is one not without criticism and active opposition. This opposition is not a modern phenomenon; as an example, in medicine the development of the smallpox vaccine from cowpox was strongly opposed and images were evoked of the development in humans with bovine characteristics arising from the vaccination. The development of vaccination, nevertheless, proceeded and today as a direct result smallpox has been eradicated and the lives of millions extended. Today we face opposition to techno scientific

---

[50] Hobbes, Thomas (1651), *Leviathan*, pt.1, ch.13.
[51] The first epidemiological investigation was in 1849 by John Snow who observed that the London cholera epidemic occurred chiefly in the regions served by the Broad Street pump. After the pump was shut down, the epidemic subsided.

developments on many fronts and among the most evocative are nuclear applications and the genetic modification of foods.

The process of using the beneficial output of scientific knowledge continues; reasonable objection is recognised and allowed to influence such use. Harmonious development may be obtained by public participation that may be achieved through education, information and the knowledge that scientific processes are governed by law. The call for strict control of technoscience through legal means is growing. In the USA, the home of extreme consumer caution and massive class-action lawsuits, and in Europe, land of growing bureaucratic regulation, minds are closing against risk. The image of the mad scientist, the memory of the devastation caused by the atom bomb, Chernobyl and the threat of poorly engineered process plants exist to offset the obvious but, for the observer, remote needs of the developing world.

Sustainable Development Laws

In discussing the vision of a sustainable society Michael Decleris notes,[52] 'Agenda 21 ... has united Development Law with Environmental Law'. He then proceeds to identify twelve general principles, which cover all the fundamental problems of relations between man-made systems and ecosystems. The legal significance of principles of law is much debated and criticised as being derived from multi-faceted and ambiguous soft law.[53] Principles are said to proliferate for the reasons that: it is not possible to achieve international environmental regulation by clear and precise rules between states at different stages of development and with disparate economic interests; the world's perception of the environmental crisis and the urgency to find solutions has developed with a speed never before experienced outside of conflict and those principles are necessary in the face of scientific uncertainty in the area of environmental problems. In this context states are more likely to agree more speedily on principles as opposed to detailed prescription and so facilitate decision making within broad direction. The legal significance of a principle may only become clear in its practical application. Binding rules follow the practical formulation of policy and principles. The role of principles is twofold; to provide guidance for courts in the process of interpretation of environmental rules and obligations and advocacy tools for lawyers.

Principles of sustainable development law surface in Conventions and Treaties,[54] have been aggregated into the general principle of sustainable development[55] and

---

[52] Michael Decleris (2000), *The Law of Sustainable Development-General Principles*. A report produced for the European Commission, Office for the Official Publications of the European Communities.

[53] Pradell-Trius, Lluis (2000), *Principle of International Environmental Law: an Overview*, RCIEL 9(2).

[54] These may be summarised as: The right of States to exploit natural resources; Principle 21 of the Stockholm Declaration; The responsibility of States to ensure that the activities within their jurisdiction or control do not cause damage to the environment of other States; *Trial Smelter Case; USA v Canada* 3RIAA(1941); The Principle of Preventative Action; *The Gabcikovo-Nagymaros Case*, [1977] ICJ Rep3; 37ILM 162; The Principle of Good Neighbourliness; Principle 24 of the Stockholm Declaration and Principle 27 of the Rio

have acquired new dimensions as the principles of prevention, intergenerational equity, sustainable use, proportionality or optimisation, the precautionary principle, the principle of justification, the polluter pays principle and the proximity principle.

The combination of the common law and these principles is appropriate for the basis of sustainable development laws, generated by statute, since the regime is dynamic and not merely a static system of legal rules. The influence of nuclear and radiation safety law principles can be clearly identified in these principles. The developing knowledge of the effect of human activity on the environment at an individual level, expanding through local level to continental level, to global and to planetary levels has focused attention on the problems of survival of mankind and of many other forms of life. The environment is, in the perception of some, assumed to have an assimilative capacity and to be a resource the exploitation of which was only limited by the effects of one group of people on another. The environment and species other than human were not seen as being necessary to protect. Attention in the past, therefore, was given to establishing safe levels of contamination that would avoid harm to humans and human activities. This permissive approach has, under the banner of sustainable development,[56] now given way to a series of high-level principles that rule environmental behaviour and may be summarised by the precept; 'economic growth that does not come at the expense of the environment'.

Principles of Environmental Law

The outcome of this higher-level concern over harm to the environment has been to move towards the integration of economic, social and environmental policies, genuine community involvement and the reversal of conditions for establishing liability; in some instances from proof of harm to proof of no harm. Extracting from the principles of sustainable development those principles that are essentially of a political nature, namely; justification, proximity and intergenerational equity, the result is the crystallisation of activities, which may be characterised by a set of principles forming the basis for a global system of environmental law: prevention, precaution, proportionality and the polluter pays. The principle of prevention is the adoption of best available techniques to prevent pollution and, where that is not possible, to follow a precautionary approach. The precautionary principle requires that the risk and environmental impact of normal and accident conditions be assessed, understood and accepted before proceeding. Where it is accepted to proceed with some risk the principle of proportionality should apply, meaning that the effect on the environment under all conditions should be as low as reasonably practicable, social and economic factors being taken into account. Finally, where

---

Declaration; The Principle of Non-Discrimination; 1982 UN Convention on the Law of the Sea, Article 194(4) and 227; and The Principle of Equitable Use and Concerted Management of Shared Natural Resources.

[55] Principle 4 of the Rio Declaration.

[56] Sustainable Development according to Bruntland is 'development that meets the needs of the present without compromising the ability of future generations to meet their own needs'.

the environment is damaged the polluter has a strict obligation to pay for the damage.[57] [58]

The effect of this change of approach has lead to the development of the political agenda in relation to the environment[59] the most notable coming from the Rio Conference[60] in 1992 and the Bruntland Report.[61] At the same time engineers have taken a positive approach by the introduction of environmental management systems.[62] These systems[63] are based on the structure and approach developed for quality management systems and earlier environmental practices of businesses, albeit the latter were mostly carried out on an *ad hoc* basis. Planning law has been amended to ensure that before consent is given, projects likely to have significant effects on the environment are made subject to an assessment with regard to their effects. This has brought about the formal requirement for environmental impact assessment (EIA).[64] The law has developed to become more integrated in relation to the prevention, or where not possible the limitation, of releases of prescribed substances from activities and installations. *The Environmental Protection Act* and the *Pollution Prevention and Control Act and Regulations*[65] have introduced a system of licensing certain industrial processes on the basis of limited permitted releases of pollutants to the environment that includes the air, water and land,[66] which relate to the use, including the effect on the community, of equipment and materials in addition to their effect on the environment. This includes noise, vibration and raw materials consumption, energy efficiency, minimising long distance and transboundary pollution, appropriate protection of soil and groundwater, remediation of contaminated land,[67]

---

[57] Draft Directive on Environmental Liability, COM (2002) 17.

[58] Under the IPPC Regulations a defence against prosecution may be accepted where the polluter can prove that he has used Best Available Techniques.

[59] For example Local Agenda 21.

[60] UN Conference on Environment and Development (1992), Rio de Janeiro, Jun.

[61] Bruntland H.G. (ed) (1987), *Our Common Future*. Oxford University Press.

[62] British Standard 7750; International Standard ISO 14001 and European Union Eco-management and Audit Scheme (EMAS) which have developed from Quality Assurance systems.

[63] ISO 14004 (1996) Environmental Management Systems - General Guidelines on Principles, Systems and Supporting Techniques. BSI 1996.

[64] Environmental Impact Assessment was included in planning law by the *Town and Country Planning (Assessment of Environmental Effects) Regulation 1988* to satisfy the requirements of *EU Directive 85/337/EEC* [OJL 175/40 of 5.7.85] however, the process of EIA was already in operation in the nuclear construction industry and had been in effect in the form of safety cases for some time.

[65] The *Pollution Prevention and Control Act 1999* and the *Pollution Prevention and Control (England and Wales) Regulations 2000*.

[66] Note that the licensing process has applied to nuclear installations since 1965 under the *Nuclear Installations Act 1965*.

[67] A control regime for radioactively contaminated land is currently being established with the powers provided by Part IIA of the *Environmental Protection Act 1990* inserted by section 57 of the *Environment Act 1995*. See DETR consultation paper Control and Remediation of Radioactively Contaminated Land (Feb 98).

accident prevention measures,[68] decommissioning, emission monitoring, waste minimisation and recovery[69] and environmental impact assessment.[70]

This legislation brings forward the concept of best available techniques and will allow, together with regular review and renewal of licenses, the continued ratcheting of the engineering and operation of processes to meet the requirements of developing technology.

Best Available Techniques   Integrated pollution prevention and control requires that the operation of an installation or activity be permitted on the basis of its using the best available techniques for preventing or, where that is not practicable, reducing the emissions from the installation. The 'Best Available Techniques' (BAT)[71] are defined as the most effective and advanced stage in the development of activities and their methods of operation which indicate the practical suitability of particular techniques for providing in principle the basis for emission limit values designed to prevent and, where that is not practicable, generally reduce emissions and the impact on the environment as a whole.

'Available' techniques are those which have been developed on a scale which allows implementation in the relevant industrial sector, under economically and technically viable conditions, taking into account the cost and advantages, whether or not the techniques are used or produced inside the United Kingdom, as long as they are reasonably accessible to the operator. 'Best' techniques are those most effective in achieving a high general level of protection of the environment as a whole and 'Techniques' include the technology used and the way in which the installation is designed, built, maintained, operated and decommissioned. This last statement brings every activity of the engineer under the regulation and consequently the scrutiny of the licensor.

The European Commission, at the time of writing, is in the process of producing BAT Reference documents (BREFs) that will incorporate codes of practice as guidance on BAT for each type of activity or process. These BREFs will require special consideration of technology, use and release of substances, recycling and accident prevention and the timescale, bearing in mind the likely costs and benefits of a measure and the principles of precaution and prevention. Technology means the use of low waste technology; the use of comparable processes, facilities or methods of operation that have been tried with success on an industrial scale and incorporating technological advances and changes in scientific knowledge and understanding. The use and release of substances includes the use of less hazardous

---

[68] Many of the installations covered by IPPC also fall within the Directive 96/82/EC on the Control of Major Accident Hazards (COMAH) that replaced the Seveso Directive 82/501/EEC in Feb. 99.

[69] In accordance with the Waste Framework Directive 75/442/EEC.

[70] A number of installations covered by the *IPPC Directive* also require an EIA under *Directive 85/337/EEC*, the Directives recognise this and a single procedure may be produced to meet the requirements of both.

[71] Pollution Prevention and Control (England and Wales) Regulations 2000, SI 2000/1973 reg. 12(10).

substances; the consumption and nature of raw materials (including water) used in the process and the energy efficiency of the process; the nature, effects and volume of the emissions concerned and the need to prevent or to reduce to a minimum the overall impact of the emissions on the environment and the risk to it. Recycling and accident analysis requires the recovery and recycling of substances and, where appropriate, waste generated and used in the process and the need to prevent accidents and to minimise the consequences for the environment. Programme requirements include the length of time needed to introduce the best available techniques and the commissioning dates for new or existing installations.

Environmental Management Systems In parallel with the evolution of environmental law, stimulated by public concern about the unsustainable use of natural resources and environmental degradation as well as increased industrial regulation, has come the development of environmental management systems (EMS) developed from the quality system approach. Such systems have allowed companies to measure and monitor their environmental performance and to pay attention to public relations. The requirements of environmental management systems are based[72] firstly on commitment and policy which requires that management define the organisation's environmental policy and ensure that it includes a commitment to comply with the relevant environmental legislation and regulations;[73] secondly on planning which includes environmental aspects, legal and other requirements, objectives and targets and environmental management programmes;[74] thirdly on implementation which is the structure and responsibility, training awareness and competence, communication, documentation and document control, operational control, emergency preparedness and response;[75] fourthly measurement and evaluation which means monitoring and measurement, non-conformance and corrective or preventative action, research and audit[76] and finally review and improvement which includes management review.[77] In combination with the regulation of a process, the EMS is a powerful tool which will help to ensure regulatory compliance and in the longer term reduce the need for regulatory control. However, at the time of writing the response from industry has been disappointing.

Proportionality Of the four principles outlined above there is a general understanding of the principle of prevention; the principle of precaution is satisfied by strict adherence to environmental management systems and using best available techniques; the remaining principle to consider is that of 'Proportionality' or 'Optimisation' as it is termed in radiation protection[78] or perhaps more commonly

---

[72] The detail of these five principles may be extracted from ISO 14001.
[73] ISO 14001 clause 4.2.
[74] ISO 14001 clause 4.3.
[75] ISO 14001 clause 4.4.
[76] ISO 14001 clause 4.5.
[77] ISO 14001 clause 4.6.
[78] ICRP Publication 60.

'weighing the odds'. This principle means that if there is to be a risk then it should be as low as is reasonably practicable (ALARP)[79] and will be described in more detail later. The principle as developed through the common law involves both economic considerations and continuous reappraisal of the available technology to reduce risks and releases to below the statutory limits. The term 'reasonably practicable', according to Lord Atkins,[80] implies that a computation be made in which the quantum of risk is placed on the one scale and the sacrifice involved in the measures necessary for averting the risk (money, time or trouble) is placed on the other and if the risk is insignificant in relation to the sacrifice the obligation is satisfied. The definition of BAT together with the guidance provided by the BREFs as described above and properly applied will satisfy the principle of proportionality.

Regulation

The regulation of nuclear facilities overlaps to some degree with the regulation of radioactive material, which is under separate legislation in the UK. Some of the materials discharged from nuclear facilities, for example organic solvents, are regulated under the *Radioactive Substances Act* since at the time those authorisations were granted the *Environmental Protection Act* authorisations for those facilities did not exist. The Environment Agency (EA) has taken increasing interest in the activities on nuclear facilities in recent years and it is apparent from the EA recommendations for future regulation of the disposal of radioactive waste[81] that environmental practices are being taken into operations on nuclear sites. Those practices cover in particular: the use of 'best practicable means' (BPM) to minimise the radioactivity of waste to be disposed under an authorisation; the requirement to introduce management systems to achieve compliance with the limits and conditions of the authorisation and written procedures to carry out 'best practicable environmental option' (BPEO)/BPM assessments[82][83] for all new waste streams.

Energy Policy

The various energy processes via the release of waste, particularly airborne and gaseous waste, have a direct effect on the environment and the atmosphere. This stark fact has ignited international political will, armed with the overarching

---

[79] For an analysis of this term see Peter Riley (1996), 'ALARP and BATNEEC - the synergy of legal regulation and system engineering', *Engineering Management Journal*, Oct. p 237.
[80] *Edwards v National Coal Board* [1949] 1 All AE 743 at 747.
[81] DETR (2000), *UK Strategies for Radioactive Discharges 2001-2020* Consultation Document.
[82] Smith, R. E. (2002), 'Some observations on the concept of best practicable option (BPEO) in the context of radioactive waste management', *Nuclear Energy*, 41, No. 4, Aug. pp 271-181.
[83] Hunt, C. A. (2002), 'Example of a BPEO study at AWE Aldermaston', *Nuclear Energy*, 41, No. 6, Dec. pp 369-373.

principles of sustainable development, namely justification, proximity and intergenerational equity, to seek ways of offsetting the threats to the environment. Concern that had been growing for some years came to a head at Rio in 1992. The World Meteorological Organisation (WMO) and the United Nations Environment Programme (UNEP) established the Intergovernmental Panel on Climate Change (IPCC) in 1988. The United Nations General Assembly (UNGA) adopted resolution 43/53 on 'Protection of global climate for present and future generations of mankind' in the same year. The Johannesburg Summit in September 2002 reaffirmed the commitment to sustainable development.

The first IPCC assessment report confirmed that climate change was a threat; the UNGA responded by launching negotiations on a framework Convention on climate change. The Convention was opened for signature at the United Nations Conference on Environment and Development (UNCED), 'the Earth Summit', in Rio de Janeiro in 1992. The Convention came into force on 21 March 1994. While not analysing the international legislation in great detail it is important to outline the main points from the Climate Change Convention that originated from Rio, the highlights of which are more popularly known as Agenda 21,[84] the main concern being with the limitation of release of gases that may cause changes to the upper atmosphere. Concurrent with the Climate Change Convention are the conventions that are aimed at the protection of the ozone layer from carbon dioxide, methane and substances of nitrogen, chlorine, bromine and hydrogen; and the conventions on transboundary air pollution concerning primarily the emissions of sulphur dioxide.

The United Nations are concerned about the adverse effect of human activity on the atmosphere,[85] particularly from emissions of greenhouse gases (natural and anthropogenic, that absorb and re-emit infrared radiation)[86] and recalling the provisions of previous declarations and resolutions,[87] the possible adverse effects of sea-level rise on islands and coastal areas, particularly low-lying coastal areas,[88] the need to combat desertification and the depletion of the ozone layer[89]

---

[84] United Nations Framework Convention on Climate Change (2003), 'A guide to the Climate Change Convention and its Kyoto Protocol' and a companion booklet 'A guide to the Climate Change Process' may be found on the UNFCCC website. [www.unfccc.int]

[85] UN Framework Convention on Climate Change, signed 9 May 1992, entered into force 21 Mar. 1994. Article 1.1.

[86] ibid. Article 1.5.

[87] Declaration of the UN Conference on the Human Environment adopted at Stockholm on 16 Jun. 1972. General Assembly resolution 44/228 of 22 Dec. 1989 on environment and development; resolutions 43/53 of 6 Dec. 1988, 44/207 of 22 Dec. 1989, 45/212 of 21 Dec. 1990 and 46/169 of 19 Dec. 1991 on the protection of the global climate for present and future generations of mankind.

[88] General Assembly resolutions 44/206 of 22 Dec. 1989 on the possible adverse effects of sea-level rise on islands and coastal areas and 44/172 of 19 Dec. 1989 on the implementation of the plan of action to combat desertification.

[89] *Vienna Convention for the Protection of the Ozone Layer*, 1985 and the *Montreal Protocol on Substances that Deplete the Ozone Layer*, 1987, as adjusted and amended on 29 Jun. 1990.

determined to protect the climate system for present and future generations by agreeing to the framework Convention on climate change at Rio in 1992. The objective of the Convention is to achieve stabilisation of greenhouse gas concentrations in the atmosphere at a level that would prevent dangerous anthropogenic interference with the climate system and at the same time to ensure that food production is not threatened and to enable economic development to proceed in a sustainable manner. In achieving the objectives the parties are guided by the principles of optimisation, precaution, proportionality and sustainable development discussed earlier and manifest in Article 3:

- the need to protect the climate system for the present and future generations on the basis of equity and in accordance with their common but differentiated responsibilities and respective capabilities [proportionality];
- special need of developing countries, particularly those vulnerable to the adverse effects of climate change [proportionality];
- the need to take precautionary measures to anticipate, prevent or minimise the causes of climate change and to mitigate its adverse effects [precautionary principle];
- the promotion of sustainable development [proportionality];
- and the need to promote a supportive and open economic system that would lead to sustainable economic growth and development in all parties [sustainable development].

According to the Convention: to this end, all parties in accordance with their common but differentiated responsibilities and specific priorities, objectives and circumstance undertake a range of commitments that include, identifying and publishing inventories of anthropogenic emissions, programmes to mitigate climate change, promote and cooperate in the development, application and dissemination of information and technology, promote sustainable management, cooperate in the preparation for adaptation of the impacts of climate change, promote and cooperate in research, observation and exchange of information, education, training and public awareness related to climate change.

Further, the parties commit to the adoption of national policies and to take measures on the mitigation of climate change to the objective of the Convention, recognising that the return to earlier levels of anthropogenic emissions of carbon dioxide and other greenhouse gases would contribute to modifying the long-term trends in emissions. The parties are to report periodically information on policies, measures and projected resulting emissions and removal of sinks of greenhouse gases, taking into account best available scientific knowledge. Developed countries are to provide additional financial resources to meet the full cost of developing countries meeting the Article 12 obligations to report national identity of emission sources and sinks, steps taken and other formalities and the transfer of technology to meet the obligations of Article 4.1.

A major stage in the process of satisfying the Climate Change Convention is the Kyoto Protocol of December 1997. The protocol sets specific targets and the way they are to be achieved; each party is required to agree to implement policies and measures according to national circumstances, to limit and reduce carbon dioxide and greenhouse gas emissions. The protocol is not in effect at time of writing and the major player, the USA, is not disposed to sign. The ways to achieve the targets are nevertheless accepted in general and include: enhancing energy efficiency; protection of sinks and reservoirs; promoting forest management, forestation and reforestation; promoting sustainable forms of agriculture; the research of new and renewable forms of energy, carbon dioxide sequestration techniques and advanced and innovative environmentally sound technology; reduction or phasing out of market imperfections in the greenhouse gas emitting sectors that run counter to the objective of the Convention and application of market instruments; encourage reforms which aim at promoting policies that limit or reduce greenhouse gases; taking measures to limit or reduce greenhouse gas emissions in the transport sector; limiting/reducing methane emissions through recovery and use in waste management, production, transport and distribution of energy.

The parties are to cooperate with each other to enhance the individual and combined effectiveness of their policies by sharing experience and exchange of information. Demonstrable progress in achieving these commitments is expected by 2005. The targets for changes in greenhouse gas emissions for each party are based on percentage reductions from that in 1990. For example USA, UK, Finland, Switzerland, Republic of Korea (although not a party) and France each have targets of eight percent. The determination of technical details is delegated to two subsidiary bodies for scientific and technical advance (SBSTA) and for implementation (SBI). A process of trading reductions is allowed by Article 6 of the Convention and the facility to provide financial resources for developing countries to meet their commitments is available on a grant basis operated by the Global Environmental Facility (GEF). The United Nations, its agencies and the IAEA while not party to the Convention may be represented at sessions of the Conference of the Parties as observers.

The Intergovernmental Panel on Climate Change (IPCC), established by UNEP and WMO in 1988, is not an institution of the Convention but it provides important scientific input to the climate change process. It is best known for its comprehensive assessment reports, which are widely recognised as the most credible sources of information on climate change. The First Assessment Report in 1990 helped launch negotiations on the Convention. The 1995 Second Assessment Report galvanised many governments into intensifying negotiations on what was to become the Kyoto Protocol, in particular its statement that 'the balance of evidence suggests ... a discernible human influence on global climate'. The Third Assessment Report, released in 2001, confirmed the findings of the Second Assessment Report, providing stronger evidence of a warming world.

Energy policy as noted by the OECD is under review, the importance of energy to world security is nevertheless manifest in *The Energy Charter Treaty*,[90] which has been in force since 1998 and covers energy trade, investment, transit and energy efficiency. As of 1 January 2002 it comprises 46 countries including the

---

[90] [www.encharter.org] is the Energy Charter Secretariat's website.

European Union. The purpose of the treaty is to establish a legal framework in order to promote long-term cooperation in the energy field and amongst its goals is the commitment to provide open energy markets, and to secure and diversify energy supply. One of its principles is the recognition of the importance of environmentally sound and energy-efficient policies.

A specific *'Protocol on Energy Efficiency and Related Environmental Aspects' (PEEREA)* entered into force together with the treaty on 16 April 1998. The energy sector has a high potential to pollute the environment. Therefore, Article 19(1) commits parties to the treaty to strive to minimise, in an economically efficient manner, harmful environment impacts inside or outside their area from all domestic operations within the energy cycle, taking into account obligations existing under other international agreements and in pursuit of sustainable development. In doing so the parties are exhorted to act in a cost effective manner; strive to take precautionary measures and agree that, in principle, the 'polluter pays' principle should apply. The Article also requires parties to take actions in relation to the promotion of market-oriented price reform and fuller reflection of environmental costs and benefits, the encouragement of energy efficiency, information on sharing environmentally sound and economically efficient energy policies, promotion of environmental impact assessment activities and monitoring, promotion of public awareness on relevant environmental programmes, and R&D of energy efficient and environmentally sound technologies, including the transfer of technology.

The concept of energy efficiency started to develop and gain importance in the aftermath of the first oil crisis in the early 1970s. In this period, energy efficiency became a distinct area of energy policy for most governments of industrialised countries. In formulating their approach to energy policy, governments initially tended to give priority to issues regarding energy security or support in balancing supply and demand. Following the adjustment of energy prices after the two oil crises environmental concerns and industrial competitiveness became driving forces of the energy conservation policies in western countries. It was at this point that energy efficiency programmes came to the forefront, both in terms of their cost-effectiveness and capacity to diminish adverse environmental impacts. In less industrialised countries and in countries with a large amount of domestic energy resources, the impact of the oil crisis was less strongly perceived. Governments in these countries therefore did not consider the creation of a 'culture' of energy efficiency to be a priority. As a result, the ratio of total primary energy supply to GDP in many of these countries is higher than in western countries. Today, for countries in transition towards a market economy, developing countries or industrial countries concerned about changes in the world's climate systems, the concept of energy efficiency has gained great importance. Instruments developed to improve energy efficiency are associated with and support actions oriented towards a cleaner environment, restructuring of economies and higher standard of living. The contribution of improvements of energy efficiency to the security of supply is also an aspect not to be neglected, especially in view of the volatility shown by energy prices in recent years. This is the context in which the Energy Charter process agreed the energy efficiency provisions of the ECT and PEEREA.

The Treaty requires that each party strive to minimise, in an economically efficient manner, harmful environmental impacts resulting from all operations within the energy cycle within its area. Basic principles, such as price formation, liberal trading relations, public awareness and international cooperation are already anchored within the Treaty and have a strong influence on the energy efficient behaviour of an economy. Further, the PEEREA expressly recognises the need to take into account particular national or regional circumstances in developing and implementing policies and programmes in relation to energy efficiency.

A detailed survey and analysis of energy policy internationally is a work on its own. Nevertheless, to give a taste of the extent of activities, the UK, being in preliminary stages of policy development, may be taken as an example. The process started with an energy review[91] that states that in the future the UK will increasingly be dependant on imported gas and oil and is likely to face demanding greenhouse gas reduction targets as a result of international action, which will not be achieved through commercial actions alone. The Review notes that:

> The policy framework should address all three objectives of sustainable development – economic, environmental and social – as well as energy security. Climate change objectives must largely be achieved through the energy system. Where energy policy decisions involve tradeoffs between environmental and other objectives, then environmental objectives will tend to take preference.

> Key policy principles should be: to create and to keep open options to meet future challenges; to avoid locking prematurely into options that may prove costly; and to maintain flexibility in the face of uncertainty. Increasingly policy towards energy security, technological innovation and climate change will be pursued in a global arena, as part of an international effort.

The review states that the UK's future energy strategy should include that: energy security should be addressed by a variety of means, including enhanced international activity and continued monitoring; keeping options open will require support and encouragement for innovation in a broad range of energy technologies; the focus of UK policy should be to establish new sources of energy, which are, or can be low cost and low carbon; the immediate priorities of energy policy are likely to be most cost-effectively served by promoting energy efficiency and expanding the role of renewables. However, the options of new investment in nuclear power and in clean coal (through carbon sequestration) need to be kept open, and practical measures taken to do this. The review concludes that the government should initiate a public debate about sustainable energy, including the roles of nuclear power and renewables and in response the government initiated a public consultation process resulting in the issue of a White Paper on energy policy in February 2003.[92] The White Paper substantially reflects the energy review and takes the objectives a step further by setting out a strategy to achieve a 60 percent reduction in greenhouse gas emissions by 2050 through energy efficiency,

---

[91] The Cabinet Office (2002), *The Energy Review*. A Performance and Innovation Unit Report, Feb. HMSO.
[92] DTI (2003), Our Energy Future – creating a low carbon economy, Cm 5761 Feb. HMSO.

renewable energy sources and security of supplies. A separate study of the role of nuclear energy is promised following public consultation.[93] At the same time the Government is promoting a regional approach to help translate the national targets for renewables into developments on the ground. This involves setting targets for renewable energy, based on an assessment of each region's capacity to generate electricity from all potential renewable sources. In response, as an example of a regional response, the East Midlands established a Regional Energy Steering Group, including representatives of the Region's key stakeholders, to develop a Regional Energy Strategy. This strategy, along with the strategies of all the English Regions, only concerns the achievement of energy efficiency and renewable fuels as a source of energy. Nevertheless, in the United Kingdom, the role of nuclear energy for future needs is said to be significant; in it's response to the Royal Commission on Environmental Pollution[94] the Geological Society noted that as renewable sources cannot, as yet, provide a base load of energy production, we will have to continue to rely on fossil fuels and/or nuclear power for some time to come. Even taking into account externalities that may distort the declared costs of the various energy sources nuclear is a viable form of energy. An example of an externality that is not taken into account in current energy pricing is the impact of coarse particles emitted from traffic and combustion processes on health. This has been the subject of intense study in recent years[95] and the true costs of pollution by traffic and combustion processes are now being revealed. In 1991 the ExternE Project[96] was commenced with the aim of developing a consistent approach to evaluating external costs. The project jointly funded between the Research Directorate of the European Commission and the US Department of Energy is the result of 20 research projects conducted in the past 10 years. The study has assessed the environmental cost from the average UK generating mix. This is estimated as 1.6 pence/kWh for the base year studied (1998). Gas, nuclear and renewables all have lower environmental costs than this value and so the use of these technologies results in net environmental benefits per kWh, as they avoid emissions from more polluting generating technologies.[97] According to the OECD the nuclear industry has accepted responsibility for its emissions, effluents and waste by internalising the corresponding costs, which are borne by the consumers of electricity:

---

[93] ibid para 4.68 p 61.

[94] Response 1013 signed by Dr Ted Nield FGS NUJ, Science and Communications Officer, The Geological Society, Burlington House, London.

[95] DEFRA and DTI (2001), The costs of reducing PM_{10} and NO_2 emissions and concentrations in the UK, Oct. HMSO.

[96] ExternE Core/Transport Project (2000), *External costs of energy conversion-Improvement of the ExternE Methodology and Assessment of Energy-related Transport Externalities.* Final Publishable report, published by the EC DEG Research.

[97] Paul Watkiss (2002), *Establishing environmental externalities, clean generation? Independent perspectives on pollution and waste from electricity generation*, a seminar held on 25 Jun. supported by British Energy.

This internalisation extends fully to waste management, waste disposal and plant decommissioning.   It also applies to the liability in the event of a major accident although the total liability assumed by the industry is capped and governments carry the residual risk.[98]

It should be noted, however, that the potential radionuclide emissions from long-term disposal of nuclear waste are not included although it might be argued that the cost of waste disposal includes measures that internalise such costs.   Public concern is a significant factor and is focused particularly on the question of long-term nuclear waste disposal.   The Geological Society in its response to the Royal Commission on Environmental Pollution report[99] noted:

> Any continued or enhanced role for nuclear power will depend on a safe disposal or storage strategy being demonstrated and implemented whatever the perceived safety of the plants themselves.   The dismissal of the planning application for continued investigation of the Sellafield site as a potential site for a deep repository has left UK policy for the long-term management of intermediate level waste uncertain.   It is essential that any future attempts to select sites for deep disposal must involve a process of widespread consultation, so as to engender sufficiently broad acceptance of the approach to be adopted prior to its implementation.

The importance of the link between continued use of nuclear energy and the management of nuclear waste was reinforced by the RCEP report:

> New nuclear power stations should not be built until the problem of managing nuclear waste has been solved to the satisfaction both of the scientific community and the general public.   Irrespective of the future role of nuclear power, an effective long-term repository needs to be provided to accommodate the wastes that already exist.

This view is supported by the Institute of Public Policy who, in a research paper,[100] argue against new nuclear power construction in the UK because, *inter alia*, there is a continuing lack of progress towards a solution to Britain's long-term radioactive waste management.   Their report argues that,

> ...advocates of new nuclear build are technically correct to say that new nuclear reactors would produce far lower volumes of waste than earlier reactors...but the level of high-level waste would be virtually unchanged.   In this sense it is seriously misleading to claim (as many nuclear advocates do) that the real radioactive waste problem is a cold war legacy...

However, for an alternative perspective, readers should consider the information about the volumes of the different types of radioactive waste that are involved and given in chapter two.

---

[98] OECD-NEA (2000), *Nuclear Energy in a Sustainable Development Perspective*, OECD Paris.
[99] Royal Commission on Environmental Pollution (2000), *Energy - the changing climate* Twenty-second Report, Cm 4749 Jun.
[100] Evans, A. (2003), *The Generation Gap: scenarios for UK electricity in 2020*, Institute of Public Policy Research, Jan. [a.evans@ippr.org].

In considering the contribution of nuclear power to the reduction of greenhouse gases along the path charted by the Kyoto Protocol, the IAEA[101] concludes that on a worldwide basis nuclear power has the potential to reduce emissions in 2010 by about forty percent of the power sector's proportionate share of the required emission reductions. In connection with management of nuclear waste the IAEA points out that while scientific and technical communities generally agree that high-level waste or spent fuel can be disposed of safely in stable geological formations, in developing such facilities, site selection is a major political issue. Countries making progress are USA, Belgium, Canada, Finland, France, Japan, Sweden and Switzerland.

The OECD-NEA in considering sustainable development observes[102] that the aim of nuclear waste practices is to contain all hazardous substances throughout their active life and that while there is no technical urgency to implement long-lived waste repositories it is important to construct such facilities to fulfil the goals of sustainable development, including social acceptance of nuclear energy.

A seminar was organised in 1998 by the European Commission to consider nuclear power in the context of a changing world[103] where it was said that an acceptable solution for the management of nuclear waste is a prerequisite for the renewed use of nuclear power. M. Allegre[104] set the scene for the problem to be solved by defining the wastes and quantifying them. The wastes are short-lived wastes which are no longer harmful after 1000 years even if the initial level of radioactivity is high and long-lived waste which must be isolated from the biosphere for thousands of years to prevent their ingestion or inhalation by any human being. The amounts are cumulative for the whole world by 2020 and are in the region of: 300,000 cubic meters for high-level and long-lived waste and less than one million cubic meters for intermediate-level and long-lived waste. It could be argued that the management and disposal of radioactive waste had become an area on the borderline of science, technology and politics. The following parts of this work examine this position by reviewing the technical aspects and then the political, legal and policy aspects from an international view.

Waste

Mankind has been conscious of the need to protect the environment against waste products from the earliest times, for example[105] the Mohenjo Darro civilisation in India, circa 2500 BC, had a sewer system. Nuclear waste, a product of the 20th century, while having specific characteristics, which will be identified in chapter two and having wider implications than non-nuclear waste, including the

---

[101] IAEA (2000), *Climate Change and Nuclear Power*, Apr. IAEA Vienna.
[102] OECD-NEA (2000), *Nuclear Energy in a Sustainable Development Perspective*, OECD Paris p 52.
[103] European Seminar (1998), *Nuclear in a Changing World*, 14-15 Oct. Brussels.
[104] Nuclear Waste Management XII/0318/98.EN (Volume 1) p 57.
[105] Gorka Gallego (2001), 'Waste Legislation in the European Union', *European Environmental Law Review*, Dec.

perceptions of stakeholders dealt with in chapter four, is considered here in the context of sustainable development and energy policy. Nuclear waste may not be a burden; it has re-usable attributes, which through economic pressures ensure care and preservation.

Internationally the question of nuclear waste and used nuclear fuel has been recognised in the *Joint Convention on the Safety of Spent Fuel Management and on the Safety of Radioactive Waste Management*.[106] The release of nuclear waste to the environment was addressed in the *OSPAR Strategy with Regard to Radioactive Substances*,[107] agreed by the Contracting Parties to the *Oslo and Paris Convention for the Protection of the Marine Environment of the North East Atlantic 1992*, the objective being to prevent pollution of the maritime area from ionising radiation through progressive and substantial reduction of discharges, emissions and losses of radioactive substances. The ultimate aim of the *OSPAR Strategy* is to achieve concentrations in the environment near background levels for naturally occurring radioactive substances and close to zero for artificial radioactive substances. United Nations and OECD Conventions on the liability for damage,[108] on nuclear safety[109] and on the transboundary movement of wastes[110] also influence the management of nuclear waste.

Europe recognised the need to protect the environment by the *Treaty of Rome* amended by the *Single European Act* (art 103r(2)) and the *Maastricht Treaty* that introduced the precautionary principle. The integration of environmental protection into other Community policies was recognised by art 130s(2). The principle of sustainable development was introduced by the *Treaty of Amsterdam*, as was the principle of proportionality (art 174.3). The importance of the promotion of sustainable development was recognised in the *Treaty of Nice*.

Community environmental policy is implemented through environmental Action Programmes. According to *Directive 79/117* the environment comprises the relationship of humans with water, air, land and all biological forms. The Action Programmes have generated a range of principles to establish a high level of protection;[111] precaution;[112] preventative action;[113] self sufficiency and proximity; the polluter pays; common but differentiated responsibility; rectified at source responsibility; subsidiarity; international cooperation; freedom of Member States to adopt more stringent provisions; sustainable development; shared responsibility and proportionality.

---

[106] Adopted at the Diplomatic Conference in Vienna, Austria held between 1 and 5 Sept. 1997.

[107] Paper No. 1998/17, Ministerial Meeting of the OSPAR Commission, Sintra, Portugal, 22-23 July 1998.

[108] *Paris and Vienna Conventions* (see chapter five, International Law).

[109] *Joint Convention on Nuclear Safety 1994* (see chapter five, International Law).

[110] *Basle Convention on the Control of Transboundary Movements of Hazardous Wastes and their Disposal 1989*.

[111] *The Single European Act* Article 100a.

[112] *Maastricht* Article130r(2).

[113] *Basel Convention* Article 4.2.a.

The intent of the European Union waste management policy is the safe disposal of waste and is embodied in the *Waste Framework Directive*,[114] the aim of which is to prevent the generation of waste and to reduce its harmfulness and where that is not possible, to ensure waste materials are reused, recycled or recovered, or used as a source of energy. While radioactive waste is excluded from the scope of the Directive, it is regulated by *Council Directive 92/3 EURATOM*, and is defined as 'any material, which contains or is contaminated by radio-nuclides and for which no use is foreseen'. The phrase 'no use foreseen' is definitive and as there are no rulings on the Euratom Directive from the courts it would appear that it avoids the contradictions of the current state of the case law on waste from the ECJ where the definition of waste turns on the meaning of 'discard', the natural action likely to be taken for a product for which no use is foreseen. Material with low radioactivity would be excluded from control under the *Transfrontier Regulations*[115] and on the face of it would not be caught by other regulatory controls, in particular Council Regulation 259/93,[116] as that regulation excludes radioactive waste as defined in Directive 92/3/Euratom. Because it is clear that nuclear waste is subject to separate European Union legislation, established principles derived from case law on waste generally may influence decisions regarding its storage, recycling, reuse and disposal: it is therefore instructive to consider the case law. The meaning of discard was addressed in the case of *Inter-Environment ASBL/Region Wallone*[117] and the court recognised that it covered both the disposal and recovery of a substance or object. In *ARCO Chemie Nederland Ltd*[118] the ECJ stated that the concept of waste could not be understood as excluding substances and objects that are capable of being recovered as fuel in an environmentally friendly manner and without substantial treatment. The Court acknowledged[119] that recovery or disposal operations were not required before a substance could be controlled waste. Leaving the definition of waste open to further interpretation, the ECJ at the end of the ARCO judgement said;

> waste within the meaning of the directive must be determined in the light of all the circumstances, regard being had to the aim of the directive and the need to ensure that its effectiveness is not undermined.

Nuclear fuel, after passing through a reactor, undergoes many processes including storage, reprocessing and reconstitution as new fuel. It is clear therefore that the meaning of the directive be specific in relation to these various transformations. It may be that, nevertheless, one nation or organisation may wish to deal with used nuclear fuel by treating it as waste while another wishes to use it as feedstock in reprocessing. Within the European Union it is therefore of particular importance

---

[114] *Waste Framework Directive*, Council Directive 75/442 amended by Council Directive 91/156.
[115] Transfrontier Shipment of Radioactive Waste Regulations, SI 1993 No.3031, Section 3(1)(a).
[116] OJ 1996 L59/64.
[117] Case 129/96 [1998] Env LR 623.
[118] Cases 418/97 and 419/97. [2000] ECR I-4475.
[119] A-G's Reference (No.5 of 2000) [2001] ECWA Crim 1077, [2001] 2 CMLR 1025.

that the ECJ recognised in the *Commission of the European Communities v Kingdom of Belgium*[120] that 'it is up to each organisation to take appropriate steps to ensure the disposal of its own waste and therefore the waste must be eliminated as close as possible to the place where it was produced'. In the *Dusseldorf Case*[121] this was modified to state that the principle couldn't be applied to waste for recovery leaving the door open for central reprocessing facilities.

In the context of the *Transfrontier Regulations* the question of what was radioactive waste had to be considered by the Environment Agency for the return of unirradiated MOX fuel assemblies from Japan to Sellafield. Judicial review proceedings were initiated by Greenpeace challenging the EA's decision that MOX was not waste but were subsequently abandoned once the shipment reached the UK.[122]

It has been said[123] that sustainable development entails a holistic approach to the resolution of disputes so that where a dispute arises from a conflict between development and the environment, the principle dictates that the tribunal should not refuse to allow the parties to address the developmental issue in the broad environmental context. Further that sustainable development requires an equitable approach between development and the environment and that disputes can not be resolved by falling back upon the view that ownership confers unfettered rights to use property as the owner chooses, without regard to the interests of others. Viewed in this way, sustainable development becomes a dynamic concept, representing a continuously evolving process encompassing the opportunities constantly created by society to generate human wellbeing for existing and future generations; it takes place because it has to happen in order to fulfil the fundamental need of human beings, which is survival and regeneration.[124]

Nuclear waste must be handled in a sustainable manner so that a reasonable obstacle to the sustainable development of nuclear energy may be removed.

Further Reading

Cameron, P. (1999), *The Safety of Radioactive Waste Management: new steps forward in the law*, Nuclear Inter Jura, Washington DC.
Decleris, M. (2000), *The Law of Sustainable Development-General Principles*, A report produced for the European Commission, Office for the Official Communications of the European Communities, Luxembourg.
Evans, A. (2003), *The Generation Gap: scenarios for UK electricity in 2020*, Institute of Public Policy Research, Jan.

---

[120] *Commission of the European Communities v Kingdom of Belgium,* Case C-376/90; Court of Justice of the European Communities, 1998 ECJ CELEX LEXIS 7666; 1998 ECR I-6153, Nov. 25, 1992, Aug. 02, 2002.
[121] *The Dusseldorf Case*, Case-203/96., Court of Justice of the European Communities, 1998 ECJ CELEX LEXIS 13217; 1998 ECR I-4075, Jun. 25, 1998, Aug. 02, 2002.
[122] Personal communication from Dr W. Leigh.
[123] Vaughan Lowe (1999), International Law and Development, ed. Alan Boyle and David Freestone, Oxford University Press, p 36.
[124] Chaharbaghi and Willis (1999), *Engineering Management Journal*, Feb.

Fox, S. (2002), 'A framework for innovation', *Engineering Management Journal*, August.

Gorka, G. (2001), 'Waste Legislation in the European Union', *European Environmental Law Review*, Dec.

Grecos, M. (2002), 'Human Rights and the Environment', *[2002] 2 Env. Liability 95*.

Hunt, C. A. (2002), 'Example of a BPEO study at AWE Aldermaston' *Nuclear Energy*, 41, No. 6, Dec. 369-373.

IAEA (1990), *Code of Practice on the International Transboundary Movement of Radioactive Waste*, INFCIRC/386, Nov.

Kageneck, de A. and Pinol, C. (1998), 'The Joint Convention on the Safety of Spent Fuel Management and on the Safety of Radioactive Waste Management', *International & Comparative Law Quarterly*, Vol 47 Apr.

OECD-NEA (2000), *Nuclear Energy in a Sustainable Development Perspective*, OECD Paris.

Pradell-Trius, L. (2000), *Principles of International Environmental Law: an Overview*, RECIEL 9(2) 2000.

Smith, R. E. (2002), 'Some observations on the concept of best practicable option (BPEO) in the context of radioactive waste management', *Nuclear Energy*, 41, No. 4, Aug. pp 271-181.

Steele, J. (2001), 'Participation and Deliberation in Environmental Law: Exploring a Problem-solving approach', *Oxford Journal of Legal Studies*, Vol. 21, No. 3 pp 415-442.

Stokes, E. R. (2003), 'Precautionary Steps: the development of the precautionary principle in EU jurisprudence', *ELM 15 [2003]*.

Williamson, R. L. (1993) 'Gathering Danger: The Urgent Need to Regulate Toxic Substances That Can Bioaccumulate', *Ecology Law Quarterly*, Vol 20 p 604.

Government Papers

DFT and DEFRA (2003), *The Energy White Paper. Our Energy Future – creating a low carbon economy*, (Cm 5761), Feb. HMSO.

DTI (2002), *Managing the Nuclear Legacy – A Strategy for Action* (Cm5552) July HMSO.

Chapter Two

Radioactive Waste

This part of the book is given to describing the waste that is termed 'nuclear waste' or more specifically 'radioactive waste' and the circumstances in which it arises. To do this it is necessary to describe in outline the process by which waste is generated and the characteristics of that waste. The ways in which waste is currently handled and future possibilities will be described. The detail that follows is necessarily curtailed; for those wishing to discover more of the technical basis for the design of facilities for the disposal of radioactive waste, two IAEA publications, one on the near surface disposal of low and intermediate level waste[1] and the other on the geological disposal of radioactive waste[2] are recommended reading. The organisations involved in the UK and the future intentions for storage and disposal will be outlined in chapters three and four. The question of what to do with discarded radioactive material is not unique to the UK; the IAEA collects information about radioactive waste management activities and waste inventories in Member States in an internet-based database, Net Enabled Waste Management Database (NEWMDB);[3] it is not intended that this book covers all the countries in NEWMDB and so the discussion below is limited to the USA, the Korean Peninsula, France and Finland only. A brief introduction to nuclear energy is included in Appendix 1.

Sources of Nuclear Waste

There are a range of different types of nuclear waste depending on the origin and history. There is therefore a need to categorise and this will be described later in this chapter, the first objective being to describe the sources of the waste. Uranium is the main source of radioactive material; it was discovered in the mineral pitchblende in 1789 and occurs in most rocks in concentrations of 2-4 parts per million.

Mining[4]

Over half the world's production of uranium is from mines in Australia (22 percent) and Canada (35 percent); of a world supply of 42,180 tonnes of mixed uranium oxide in 2001; 29 percent is from open pits, 40 percent from underground mines, 16 percent from in-situ leaching and 15 percent as by-product. The largest

---

[1] IAEA (2002), *Near Surface Disposal of Low and Intermediate Level Radioactive Waste (LILW)*, IAEA Report No 42, Vienna.
[2] IAEA (2003), *Scientific and Technical Basis for Geological Disposal of Radioactive Waste*, Technical Report Series No. 413, IAEA, Vienna.
[3] [www.newmdb.iaea.org/start.asp].
[4] Briefing papers, Uranium Information Centre, Melbourne, Australia [www.uic.co.au].

mines in 2001 were McArthur River in Canada with 19.4 percent of world production and Olympic Dam in Australia with 10.3 percent. The radioactivity of uranium is very low, comparable with granite, and in most respects the environmental aspects of the uranium mine are the same as those of other metalliferous mining.   Open pits or shafts are excavated, waste rock and overburden is placed in engineered dumps.   The gamma radiation detected by prospecting comes from elements such as radium and bismuth that over geological time have resulted from radioactive decay of uranium.   Dust is suppressed as it represents a potential exposure to radiation.   Following crushing, the ore is ground and processed through a sulphuric acid leach to recover the uranium. The pregnant liquor is then separated from the barren tailings and the uranium is removed in a solvent extraction plant using kerosene with an amine as a solvent. The solvent is then stripped, using an ammonium sulphate solution and gaseous ammonia. Yellow ammonium diuranate is then precipitated from solution by increasing the alkalinity, and then removed by centrifuge. The diuranate is converted in a furnace to uranium oxide product. Uranium is toxic chemically, comparable with lead, and is usually handled with gloves as a sufficient precaution.   The uranium gives off some gamma radiation but less than from a lump of granite.   Process water discharged from the mill process contains trace radium so this water is evaporated and the remaining metals retained in secure storage. Tailings from ore processing are retained in engineered dams.   After the conclusion of mining the tailings are covered with clay and soil to reduce gamma radiation and radon emission rates to levels near those naturally occurring in the region. In the case of in-situ leaching (ISL) the uranium is extracted through boreholes by leaching with weak sulphuric acid plus oxygen or sodium bicarbonate and carbon dioxide.   Uranium (U) is recovered in an ion exchange system, the uranium stripped and precipitated chemically, dewatered and dried.   Apart from groundwater considerations rehabilitation of an ISL mine is by sealing or capping the boreholes and cleaning the surface facilities.

Manufacture of Nuclear Fuel

For all but the early UK reactors that use uranium in its natural form, the next step is to make a useable fuel from the natural uranium by converting the uranium oxide into a gas, uranium hexafluoride, and enriching it by increasing the proportion of the U-235 isotope from its natural level of 0.7 percent to 3 - 4 percent. This enables greater technical efficiency in reactor design and operation, particularly in larger reactors, and allows the use of ordinary water as a moderator. A by-product of enrichment is depleted uranium forming about 89 percent of the original feed. After enrichment, the uranium hexafluoride gas is converted to uranium dioxide that is formed into fuel pellets. These fuel pellets are placed inside thin metal tubes that are assembled in bundles to become the fuel elements for the core of the reactor. For reactors that use natural uranium as their fuel the mixed oxide concentrate simply needs to be refined and converted directly to uranium dioxide. Mixed oxide fuel (MOX) is a term used to describe fuel that has been enriched with plutonium obtained from the reprocessing of used fuel; it is possible and planned to use plutonium from decommissioned nuclear weapons.

Nuclear Power

Over 16 percent of the world's electricity in 2002 was generated from uranium in nuclear reactors. It came from over 430 nuclear reactors with a total output capacity of more than 350 000 megawatts electrical, operating in 31 countries. A further thirty reactors are under construction and another 70 are on the drawing board. Belgium, Bulgaria, Finland, France, Germany, Hungary, Japan, South Korea, Lithuania, Slovakia, Slovenia, Spain, Sweden, Switzerland and Ukraine all get 30 percent or more of their electricity from nuclear reactors. The USA has over 100 reactors operating, supplying 20 percent of its electricity. The UK gets over 20 percent of its electricity from uranium.

Over 200 small nuclear reactors power some 150 ships, mostly submarines, but ranging from icebreakers to aircraft carriers. These ships can stay at sea for very long periods without having to make refuelling stops. In most such vessels the steam generated by the heat of the nuclear reaction drives a turbine directly geared to the propeller.

The heat produced by nuclear reactors can also be used directly rather than for generating electricity. In Russia, for example, steam raised from nuclear heat is used to heat buildings and elsewhere it provides heat for a variety of industrial processes such as water desalination. High-temperature reactors can also be used for industrial processes such as thermo chemical production of hydrogen. In the UK, Japan and France fast reactors have been operated for the development of a breeding process; natural uranium placed around the core of the reactor was irradiated to produce plutonium and other uranium isotopes that could, after reprocessing, be used for reactor fuel. The process that involved cooling the reactor with sodium failed to be an economic proposition as it was prone to unreliable operation and failed to achieve a satisfactory breeding rate.

Radioisotopes

Radioisotopes, radioactive materials, play an important part in the technologies that provide us with food, water and health; they have become a vital part of modern life. Using relatively small special purpose nuclear research reactors to bombard small amounts of particular elements with neutrons produces a wide range of radioactive materials at low cost. For this reason the use of radioactive materials has become widespread and there are now some 280 reactors in 56 countries producing them. In medicine, radioisotopes are widely used for diagnosis and research; radioactive chemical tracers emit gamma radiation providing diagnostic information about a person's anatomy and the functioning of specific organs. Radiotherapy also employs radioisotopes in the treatment of some illnesses, such as cancer. More powerful gamma sources are used to sterilise syringes, bandages and other medical equipment. In the preservation of food, radioisotopes are used to inhibit the sprouting of root crops after harvesting, to kill parasites and pests, and to control the ripening of stored fruit and vegetables. Irradiated foodstuffs are accepted by world and national health authorities for human consumption in an increasing number of countries. They include potatoes, onions, dried and fresh fruits, grain and grain products, poultry and some fish. Some prepacked foods are also irradiated.

In growing crops and breeding livestock, radioisotopes play an important role; they are used to produce high yielding, disease and weather resistant varieties of crops, to study how fertilisers and insecticides work, and to improve the productivity and health of domestic animals. In industry and mining, they are used to examine welds, to detect leaks, to study the rate of wear of metals, and for on-stream analysis of a wide range of minerals and fuels. Most household smoke detectors use a radioisotope (Americium-241) derived from the plutonium formed in nuclear reactors. Radioisotopes are used to trace and analyse pollutants, to study the movement of surface water, and to measure water runoffs from rain and snow, as well as the flow rates of streams and rivers.

Nuclear Weapons

Both uranium and plutonium were used to make bombs before they became important for making electricity and radioisotopes. The type of uranium and plutonium for bombs is different from that used in a nuclear power plant; bomb-grade uranium is highly enriched (>90 percent U-235, instead of about 3.5 percent for nuclear fuel); bomb-grade plutonium is fairly pure (>90 percent) Pu-239 and is made in special reactors.

Reprocessed Uranium

When spent nuclear fuel is reprocessed, both plutonium and uranium are recovered separately. Uranium comprises about 96 percent of that spent fuel. The composition of reprocessed uranium depends on the time the fuel has been in the reactor, but it is mostly U-238. Typically it will have about one percent U-235 and small amounts of U-232 and U-236. The former is a gamma-emitter, making the material difficult to handle, even with trace amounts. The latter, comprising about 0.5 percent of the material, is a neutron absorber which means that if reprocessed uranium is used for fresh fuel it must be enriched slightly more than is required for natural uranium. In the future, laser enrichment techniques may be able to remove these isotopes. As noted earlier, plutonium is used to produce MOX, this may well be significant for using significant stocks of bomb grade material as a fuel and at the same time avoiding the problems of safe disposal.

Depleted Uranium

Every tonne of natural uranium produced and enriched for use in a nuclear reactor gives about 130 kg of enriched fuel (3.5 percent or more U-235). The balance is depleted uranium (U-238, with 0.25-0.30 percent U-235). This major portion has been depleted in its fissile U-235 isotope by the enrichment process. Depleted uranium is stored either as UF_6 or it is de-converted back to U_3O_8, which is more benign chemically and more suited for long-term storage. Every year over 50,000 tonnes of depleted uranium joins already substantial stockpiles in the USA, Europe and Russia. World stock is about 1.2 million tonnes. Some depleted uranium is used to dilute high-enriched (>90 percent) uranium released from weapons programs, particularly in Russia, and destined for use in civil reactors. This weapons-grade material is diluted about 25:1 with depleted uranium, or 29:1 with depleted uranium that has been enriched slightly (to 1.5 percent U-235) to minimise levels of (natural) U-238 in the product.

Other uses depend on the very high density of the metal (1.7 times that of lead) for example, it is well suited as aircraft control surfaces and helicopter counterweights, yacht keels, etc where maximum mass must fit in minimum space. Until the mid 1970s it was used in dental porcelains. In addition, it is used for radiation shielding, being some five times more effective than lead in this role. Also because of its density it is used as solid slugs in armour-piercing projectiles, alloyed with about 0.75 percent titanium it is pyrophoric, so that upon impact about 30 percent of the projectile atomises and burns to uranium oxide dust. It was widely used in the Kuwait war (300 tonnes) and less so in Kosovo (11 tonnes).

Decommissioning

At the end of the useful life of a nuclear facility it will be dismantled and its contents removed. Much of the contents will be waste and some of it radioactive; cement and rubble from shielding; metal from the core and the nuclear fuel. The objective of decommissioning a licensed nuclear site is to return it to a state such that it can be de-licensed.

Accidental Radiation Releases

In the process of handling radioactive material accidents have occurred that have allowed the release of liquid, gaseous and particulate radioactive material from the confines of licensed sites or military establishments or research facilities. Stretching a point, the releases from nuclear explosions could be considered under this heading. These incidents have resulted in areas being contaminated with radioactive material and restrictions placed on access. Remediation of the areas is by removal of radioactively contaminated materials such as equipment used to contain the release, soil, buildings and contaminated groundwater. Certain industries in particular oil, gas and phosphate production accumulate radioactive material as a by-product termed naturally occurring radioactive material (NORM). This has until recently been ignored.

Radioactive Waste

In each type of operation outlined above, waste is generated; radioactive waste material which incorporates radioactivity or is contaminated by radioactive material where the level of radioactivity is measured to be above thresholds set in legislation. Taking mining as an example, the waste left after milling the uranium ore is not radioactive as the level of radioactive material is less than before extraction and not concentrated. On the other hand, material left after evaporation of the water discharged from the mill process contains concentrated amounts of radioactive material, e.g. radium that may have radioactivity above regulatory levels. The measurement of radioactivity is by the rate of release of ionising particles from a given volume of the material. This, however, is not the complete story; ionising radiation can have degrees of energy and the material can be releasing the particles for different lengths of time; generally the more energetic the particle the shorter the time. The combination of these characteristics means that significant heat may be released from some materials. There are three basic types of particle that exhibit different characteristics; an alpha particle is heavy relative to the others, travels only short distances from the material and can be stopped relatively easily by, for example, 1mm of polythene; a beta particle travels a longer distance and a gamma particle even longer. To stop a gamma particle would take about 10mm of steel depending on its particular energy.

Therefore, in taking an economic view of the isolation of radioactive material from the environment these characteristics, heat generation; time to decay and penetrating power dictate the preferred method of isolation. While at present there is no international standard regarding the classification of radioactive waste there is general agreement about categories into which it may be allocated. The different national approaches will be discussed later but for the sake of explanation the system adopted in the UK for management purposes is as follows.

Very Low Level Waste In other words not radioactive waste; it can be disposed of with ordinary refuse because it releases ionising radiation at a rate less than regulatory levels.   Solid material of this type includes some materials from hospitals and the non-nuclear industry.

Low Level Waste Low level waste is potentially radioactive in terms of regulatory levels but not necessarily as individual items since its activity is measured in bulk for operational reasons. It arises wherever radioactive materials are used, mainly as lightly contaminated miscellaneous scrap. The major components of low level waste are metals and organic materials. Metals are mainly in the form of redundant equipment, and organic materials are mainly in the form of discarded protective clothing, paper towels and plastic wrappings.

Intermediate Level Waste Intermediate level waste arises mainly from the dismantling and reprocessing of spent nuclear fuel and from operations and maintenance of radioactive plant. The major components of this waste are metals, with lesser quantities of inorganic flocs and sludge, organic materials, cement and graphite.

High Level Waste High level waste is a heat-generating waste, initially produced as a nitric acid solution containing waste products from reprocessing spent nuclear fuel.

Sealed Sources Radioactive sources sealed in pressure vessel quality, shielded containers and used in medical, pharmaceutical, industrial and academic applications and are classed as intermediate level waste at the end of their useful life.

Decommissioning Waste Decommissioning low and intermediate level wastes are different from operational wastes. They consist mostly of building materials and larger items of plant and equipment. The major components are concrete, cement, rubble, metals and graphite. There are no decommissioning high level wastes as when facilities reach the end of their useful life the nuclear fuel is removed prior to decommissioning. However in an accident situation such as occurred at Windscale in the UK, Three-mile Island in the USA, Chernobyl in the Ukraine and various sites in the old USSR territories, the remains of nuclear fuel are still to be recovered and are treated as high level waste.

Radioactive Discharges[5]

By-products of chemical processes include gases and liquids that have no further use. It is practice to release them to the environment in quantities and concentrations that are accepted by the regulatory authorities as having no deleterious effect. In many instances, before release, they are diluted to achieve acceptable concentrations.

Actual Discharges

Small amounts of radioactive material are discharged as gas and liquid from licensed sites under specific authorisations by the regulatory authority. This very low level waste is from processes that include fuel production, uranium enrichment, nuclear energy production, fuel reprocessing, research, weapons production, naval propulsion and minor applications.

Nuclear Fuel Production and Uranium Enrichment Discharges are related to nuclear fuel production and are principally short-lived decay products of uranium isotopes, tritium and thorium.

Nuclear Energy Production The UK has two power companies that operate nuclear reactors. British Nuclear Fuels plc has seven operating magnox gas-cooled reactors that have radiologically significant liquid discharges of caesium isotopes from leaky fuel elements in cooling ponds, tritium releases and aerial discharges of argon-41. British Energy operates seven advanced gas cooled reactors (AGRs) that release sulphur-35, tritium, cobalt-60, and caesium and aerial discharges of argon-41, and iodine-131. British Energy also operates a single pressurised water reactor where discharges are similar but less than for the AGR.

Spent Fuel Reprocessing Reprocessing plants at Sellafield in Cumbria are operated by BNFL to process magnox and oxide fuels; in France Cogema operate a

---

[5] For details and amounts at 2000 see: DETR (2000), *UK Strategy for Radioactive Discharges 2001-2020*, Environment Agency, June. Proposed decision for the future regulation of disposals of radioactive waste from British Nuclear Fuels plc, Sellafield, Aug. 2002.

reprocessing plant at La Hague in Normandy. Apart from a closed plant at Dounreay these are the only commercial reprocessing plants in the world. The plants separate out the uranium and plutonium from the used fuel and in the process release gaseous and liquid discharges of krypton-85, argon-41, carbon-14, tritium, technetium-99, ruthenium-106, caesium-137, strontium-90, plutonium and uranium.

Research Facilities In the UK the UKAEA operates licensed sites where decommissioning operations are in process. Discharges are very low due to decreasing research activities and are of strontium-90, yttrium-90, caesium-137, cobalt-60, tritium, nickel-63 and iron-55.

Defence Facilities The development, manufacture, maintenance and decommissioning of nuclear warheads is carried out at Aldermaston and Burghfield by the Atomic Weapons Establishment on behalf of the Ministry of Defence. The main discharges from weapons manufacture are tritium, plutonium and uranium. The Royal Navy operates a fleet of nuclear submarines based at Faslane and Devonport. Cobalt-60 and carbon-14 are released into the cooling water of the reactor and in modern designs, leakage from the primary circuit is contained within tanks and the contents disposed of at the naval bases at the time of refitting or decommissioning.

Other Sources (Sealed Sources) The production of radioactive products for the medical, pharmaceutical, industrial and academic sectors result in discharges of tritium, carbon-14 and strontium-35. The production of fertiliser, phosphogypsum, involves the processing of phosphate ore and the consequent discharge of concentrated naturally occurring thorium, radium-226, radium-228, polonium-210 and lead-210. Teaching hospitals use radioactive material for diagnostic and therapeutic purposes and discharge small amounts of radioactivity, mostly tritium and carbon-14, in wastewater and patient's excreta to sewers.

Potential Radioactive Waste

Used Nuclear Fuel[6] An alternative to reprocessing is the direct disposal of used nuclear fuel and final disposal facilities are under construction in Finland and the USA. Should this alternative be pursued in the UK it is envisaged that before disposal the fuel would be stored for some years, probably in dry stores and then conditioned, packed and the chosen disposal followed.

Waste Substitution Used nuclear fuel from overseas is accepted by British Nuclear Fuels Ltd for reprocessing; the products after reprocessing, depending on the contractual conditions, may be returned as new fuel, radioactive material and waste. Intermediate level and low level waste is bulky and it has been agreed in principle that a process of 'waste substitution' could be adopted; this includes

---

[6] OECD-NEA (2000), *Radiological Impacts of Spent Nuclear Fuel Management Options: A Comparative Study*, OECD Paris.

substituting the radioactivity in intermediate and low level waste by the less bulky radioactivity in high level waste. The main advantage of waste substitution is that transport costs would be reduced by an order of magnitude.

Handling Radioactive Waste

Depending on the level of radiation from the waste the preparation for storage will involve different degrees of shielding, methods of handling, transport and storage facilities.

Irradiated Fuel

The terms irradiated fuel, used fuel and spent fuel are used synonymously by different authorities and therefore occur throughout this work. Products of the nuclear reaction build up in the fuel in the reactor and gradually make it less efficient in producing heat; the fuel is slowly 'poisoned' by these products, which is said to 'burn up', and the fuel is removed and replaced by new fuel. In gas reactors in the UK refuelling is carried out with the reactors on load on a continuous basis. In order to have a smooth, sequential operation in the first years of operation, fuel with less than optimum 'burn up' is removed. Pressurised water reactors are periodically shut down to remove the fuel in a concentrated operation over a few days. Re-fuelling shutdowns are synchronised to suit the various requirements of load on the system, type of maintenance and availability of appropriate technicians rather than simply the condition of the fuel. Following removal, the irradiated fuel is stored at the power station to cool awaiting removal for re-processing or long-term disposal. The fuel is stored in cooling-ponds under water, which acts as a cooling medium and a shield. The water is chemically treated to avoid corrosion and to absorb neutrons to prevent criticality. The spacing of the fuel in the cooling ponds and the materials used in the storage racks are arranged so as to have optimum storage capacity with no risk of criticality. The capacity of early PWRs was of the order of a decade's work of nuclear operation. This has been extended so that a storage period equivalent to the lifetime of the reactor is now available. In the UK and France where reprocessing has been accepted, the storage on-site is only long enough for the fuel to cool and to suit operational programs. The fuel is transported to the reprocessing facility in shielded flasks that have been designed and tested to take the maximum credible impact without leaking.[7] In the UK the fuel from the Magnox and AGR reactors follow a similar pattern except that because the material of the outer containment (fuel can) of the magnox fuel element corrodes more rapidly in cooling water than the AGR fuel can, it is taken for reprocessing after only a few months. A separate and older reprocessing plant handles the Magnox fuel and because of operational difficulties and to avoid the need to reduce power at the largest Magnox station at

---

[7] The train test. A good indication of the strength of the casks used in the transport of spent nuclear fuel is the test organised by the British power company CEGB in July 1984 in which a railway engine with carriages, running at full speed, was deliberately crashed against a cask. The cask was not damaged by the collision, except for some minor surface damages.

Wylfa in Anglesey, dry-storage facilities were built to provide one to two years buffer storage. In the USA and Canada dry-storage has also been built as an interim measure to allow the power stations to transfer fuel and continue to operate after the on-site storage ponds reach capacity.

Radioactive Waste

The descriptions and quantities[8] of radioactive waste given in the following sections are taken from the 2001 UK Radioactive Waste Inventory (RWI) commissioned by DEFRA and NIREX to provide information on the status of radioactive waste stocks at April 2001 and forecasts of future arisings in the UK to 2100. The inventory gives details of the known types of waste, the sources, the radioactivity content and the locations. The RWI gives forecasts of the volumes of waste from all UK sources to the end of this century, when packaged, to occupy 2,202,737 cubic meters; a volume just over half the volume of the new English National Stadium at Wembley. The Radioactive Waste Management Committee (RWMAC) has reviewed the inventory in the context of low activity waste.[9] Low Activity Waste (LAW) is a term used by RWMAC to include low level waste as defined below and waste exempted from legislation or specific regulatory action. RWMAC disputes the implied claim that the management of LAW has been solved for the foreseeable future through the availability of the Drigg facility and that EU Directives are likely to have a very significant implication for landfill and incineration plans.

Very Low Level Radioactive Waste   Very low level solid radioactive waste is disposed of with ordinary refuse 'dustbin disposal' by authorisation of the Environment Agency in England and Wales and SEPA in Scotland. Normally such authorisation will specify a maximum of 400 Becquerel (Bq) in any 0.1 cubic meters of waste with no individual item exceeding 40 Bq. These limits may be relaxed by a factor of 10 where the activity arises only from tritium and/or carbon-14. Alpha emitting radionuclides are usually excluded. Changes in disposal practices prompted a review by the National Radiological Protection Board (NRPB) and a report was issued in 1995 reviewing practices from 1987 – 2000.[10] The report concluded that the conditions of authorisation met the radiological standards of the time and represented good regulatory practice. Nevertheless, the Government decided not to encourage greater use of this disposal route because of opposition from local authorities, environmental groups and members of the

---

[8] Annex 1, Table A1.1, Waste volumes from all sources, The 2001 United Kingdom Radioactive Waste Inventory, Main Report, prepared for the DETR and UK NIREX Ltd by Electrowatt-Ekono (UK) Ltd. DEFRA Report DEFRA/RAS/02.004; NIREX Report N/042, Oct. 2002.
[9] RWMAC's *Advice to Ministers on Management of Low activity Solid Radioactive Waste within the UK*, HMSO London.
[10] HMIP Research Report No. DOE/HMIP/RR/95//006. *A Review of the Radiological Implications of Disposal Practices for Very Low Level Solid Radioactive Waste.* HMSO London.

public.[11] The House of Lords Select Committee on Science and Technology in its report on the management of nuclear waste[12] recommended that the Government considers alternatives to landfill disposal that is accepted by local authorities, landfill operators and all those that use landfill disposal.

Low Level Radioactive Waste Waste containing radioactive materials other than suitable for disposal with ordinary refuse but not exceeding 4 GBq/te of alpha or 12 GBq/te of beta/gamma activity can be accepted by controlled burial at dedicated sites. It consists of general rubbish such as used paper towels and discarded protective clothing, lightly contaminated plant and equipment and some materials that have been irradiated arising predominately from the operation of nuclear facilities with some from hospital, universities and industry. In the UK this involves conditioning (compacting and containing the waste in robust but unshielded steel drums) and stacking in concrete lined vaults. The vaults are drained and, as filled, are covered by earth. Facilities in the UK are at Drigg in Cumbria and Dounreay in Caithness; since the 1950s about 1,000,000 cubic meters of low level waste have been placed in these vaults. In the 2001 UK waste inventory it is indicated that 14,452 cubic meters of waste not yet conditioned (to achieve passive safety) and 303 cubic meters of conditioned waste was in storage awaiting disposal. The inventory predicts that 1,508,420 cubic meters of conditioned low level waste will arise from the current operational programme, including decommissioning, to 2100. When packaged this will increase to 1,850,850 cubic meters.

Intermediate Level Radioactive Waste Intermediate level waste arises from reprocessing spent fuel, sludge and clean-up resin from storage pond treatment plants and worn out or decommissioned reactor parts. The major components are metals, organic materials, cement, graphite, glass and ceramics. From 1949 to 1982 over 73,000 tonnes of low and intermediate level waste was disposed of by the UK in the North East Atlantic. Since 1982 intermediate level waste has been stored on sites; the 2001 inventory reports 64,227 cubic meters in storage of which 11,186 cubic meters have been conditioned. Conditioning of intermediate level waste involves containing the waste in stainless steel drums with a resin or cement mix to provide shielding and stabilising the liquid content in a solid form. Facilities for achieving this conditioning exist at Dounreay and Sellafield. As no forward management strategy exists in the UK, proposals for conditioning are put to NIREX, as the expected operator of a future disposal facility, for their endorsement in the form of a letter of comfort. Future conditioned intermediate level waste from all UK sources to the end of the 21st century amounts to 237,021 cubic meters; operational waste includes 119,588 cubic meters from decommissioning. When packaged this will amount to 349,885 cubic meters.

---

[11] Department of the Environment (1995), Review of Radioactive Waste Management Policy, Final Conclusions CM 2919, HMSO.
[12] House of Lords (1999), *Management of Nuclear Waste*, Third Report of the Select Committee on Science and Technology, HL Paper 41, Mar.

The classification and treatment of intermediate level waste in the UK is undecided and therefore can only be defined as that which is not high level waste. The possible options are whether the waste produces heat and/or whether the radioactivity is short or long-lived. The treatment of both intermediate and high level waste is different in other countries; this is demonstrated by example later in this chapter.

High level Radioactive Waste   High level waste is heat generating waste that remains in liquid form from reprocessing nuclear fuel; although it comprises only two percent by volume of the total radioactive waste in the UK it contains over 90 percent of the radioactive content. The liquid is stored in double walled cooled tanks and shielded behind concrete walls. In February 2000 the Health and Safety Executive reported that 1300 cubic meters were stored at Sellafield and 230 cubic meters were stored at Dounreay. In France and the UK liquid is being converted into glass cylinders (vitrification) within stainless steel canisters to remove the risk of accidental leakage of the liquid and to make the waste easier to handle. Government policy in the UK is to leave the vitrified waste in storage for at least 50 years to allow the heat to decline. As with intermediate level waste there is no formal management strategy for high level waste. At 2001 the waste in storage was 2,377 cubic meters not yet conditioned and 342 cubic meters of conditioned high level waste and with future arisings to 2100 the total would amount to 1510 cubic meters. When packaged this will amount to 2,001 cubic meters.

Storage/Disposal Options

In nuclear operating countries worldwide research and development programmes to determine the best options for the storage of high and intermediate level waste have continued. A selection of these is discussed later in the chapter. The main options that have been considered are:

Geological Disposal   Emplacement in geological formations is the preferred option; the types of geological formations that have been considered are those where there is likely to be little or no groundwater flow such as salt domes, clays, shale and granite. Studies have included mined caverns and tunnels both on land or based on land extending under the sea; deep boreholes drilled from the surface and from caverns and tunnels. The option relies on predictable stability of the geological and hydrological conditions over very long time-scales; millions of years.

Indefinite Storage on or Near the Surface   A continuation of the present form of storage that would rely on supervision and could involve continued maintenance. As a solution those who foresee better methods of handling waste in the future, those who see possible future uses and those who reject geological disposal prefer this.

Seabed Disposal Before 1982 intermediate and low level waste in steel containers was dropped from ships (sea dumping) in the sea hundreds of kilometers from shore in water several kilometers deep. Fear of uncontrollable public opposition led to the practice being discontinued. It has since been prohibited under the *Ospar Convention*.[13]

Sub-seabed Disposal This option is to drill into the seabed and place canisters of waste or to fire torpedo shaped canisters into the ocean floor. An international programme on sub-seabed disposal set up by the OECD-NEA concluded that it would be technically feasible and that its impact on human health and the environment could be kept low. However, like the seabed option this is prohibited.

Subduction Zones The canisters of waste would be placed on the ocean floor where one section of the earth's crust is moving under another (Subduction zones) and would move towards the centre of the earth. This option is also prohibited by legislation.

Ice Sheets The idea was to place canisters of high level waste in holes drilled in the Antarctic ice sheet. By melting the ice, the heat generating high level waste packed in suitable canisters would move downwards and the ice would re-freeze over them. The concept was abandoned after preliminary paper studies as it was concluded that there would never be enough confidence in the fate of the waste and there was the potential for releases of radioactive materials to the ocean. The Antarctic Treaty in any case rules out this option.

Ejection into Space For low volume, high active waste the proposition was that canisters would be ejected into space in a spacecraft. The radiological consequences of an accident on launch or early in the trajectory were the prime objection that was reinforced by the Challenger disaster.

Partitioning and Nuclear Transmutation Long-lived radionuclides in high and intermediate level waste after being extracted by chemical means (partitioning) would be irradiated with neutrons in a nuclear reactor or as a target of a particle accelerator to transmute them to shorter-lived radionuclides. Transmutation is also being considered as a way of rendering less potentially harmful plutonium from the military programme. Research and development continues, particularly in France and Japan. It is generally agreed that it is not feasible to deal with existing waste by this process; the technology, if feasible, would form an intrinsic part of the fuel cycle of future programmes.

Synroc Radionuclides would be held within the crystal lattice of a synthetic rock; it could be an alternative to vitrification for stabilisation of high level liquid waste; it is being considered for surplus plutonium from the weapons programme.

---

[13] *Oslo and Paris Convention for the Protection of the North East Atlantic* (see chapter five).

From Theory to Practice

Certain of the nuclear elements (plutonium for example) and the chemicals associated with the output from reprocessing have chemical properties that are toxic and long-lived, as is also the case for hazardous chemical waste, and thus must be taken into account. The difference is radiation from nuclear waste which must be isolated to prevent harm to workers, the public and the environment and to ensure that the radiation bearing materials do not escape and become attached to materials that come into contact with the environment and therefore to man. As with chemical poisons, radiation is long-lived and therefore the method of containment and shielding of the waste must withstand the effects of very long times. Radiation from radioactive materials unlike poisonous chemical elements eventually decreases to zero; some isotopes decay quite quickly, others take a very long time. This decay of radiation is measured by the time taken for the radioactivity to reduce to half the initial level and is termed the half-life of the element.

This quality gives two advantages when dealing with radioactive waste. The intensity of the radiation of a mix of radioactive elements in the waste will reduce with time allowing easier handling. Therefore by waiting for a period of time the handling becomes easier because the heat emission from the material, being a product of the decay process, reduces and the intensity of radiation also reduces. The need for protection over time, in theory, also reduces; however, in the time scale of many of the radioactive elements (plutonium for example) this is purely academic. This characteristic is used in current methods of handling waste; irradiated nuclear fuel from the reactors dwells for a period in storage prior to reprocessing for cooling to allow convenient transport methods. The liquid products of reprocessing are left to cool in shielded tanks prior to being vitrified or subject to cementation. The vitrified waste stored in canisters is stored in cooled and shielded stores awaiting eventual disposal or other use. Some nuclear operators have embarked on this next stage, some are researching to determine the best application and some are waiting to see. A selection of national approaches follows.

United States of America

The world's largest user of nuclear energy in 2000 was the United States (US) with 104 reactors with installed capacity of 97,145 megawatts electrical disposed throughout most of the states.[14] The US for primarily economic reasons decided after 1977 not to reprocess commercial nuclear fuel and retains reprocessing and enrichment plant sufficient only to satisfy its military needs and the manufacture of new fuel. Because of the legal regime between state and federal responsibilities for nuclear and environmental matters, contractual arrangements between the states have been established to allow the central storage and disposal of irradiated nuclear fuel and radioactive waste; those are discussed in a later chapter. The US has a

---

[14] IAEA Bulletin Vol 42, No 3, 2000 Vienna, Austria.

method of classification of radioactive waste that is slightly different from that outlined above. The equivalent of long-lived waste is called transuranic waste; all other wastes, except uranium and thorium mill tailings, are classed as low level waste and are segregated depending on the time over which they remain radioactive. Low level waste, the equivalent to very low level waste, and short lived intermediate level waste is the responsibility of the state, or a grouping of states in a Compact, that have access to surface repositories. Defence wastes are disposed of at private sites.

At present three near surface facilities are operational in the southeast, mid-west and far northwest. A number have been closed that pre-date existing regulations. Not all Compacts use these, some having tried to develop their own facilities against continuous opposition, sometimes with state and federal governments taking opposing sides. Over 100,000 cubic meters of transuranic waste are stored at defence sites around the country. This includes about 160,000 spent fuel assemblies containing 45,000 tonnes of spent fuel. It is planned that all transuranic waste is transported to a repository in southern New Mexico.[15]

The Department of Energy's (DOE) waste isolation pilot plant (WIPP) opened in March 1999 becoming the first US deep geologic repository for the permanent disposal of defence generated transuranic (TRU) waste. The DOE plan is to accelerate the disposal of legacy TRU waste and reduce the risk to the public and the environment. The comprehensive approach to the task is described in 'The TRU waste performance management plan'.[16] The WIPP is located in the Chihuahuan Desert of south-eastern New Mexico and includes disposal rooms mined 2150 ft underground in a 2000 ft thick salt formation that has been stable for over 200 million years. The installation is expected to receive about 37,000 shipments over a 35-year period.[17]

A deep repository is under construction for used nuclear fuel at Yucca Mountain in the Nevada desert, close to the nuclear weapons test site. Prior to obtaining Presidential approval for the start of construction in 2002, the US Department of Energy organised an international peer review of their total system performance assessment by the OECD-NEA[18] and the IAEA[19] between June and December 2001 at the request of the Yucca Mountain Project. The project has an extended history; the first test hole was dug in 1978; in 1982 Congress ordered the development of a permanent national disposal site for waste from commercial nuclear power reactors and the government's nuclear weapons programme. In 1987 Yucca Mountain was designated as the only site to be studied. Following

---

[15] Waste Isolation Pilot Project (WIPP) that began operation in 1999.

[16] US DOE (2002), *The National TRU Waste Management Plan*, Rev3, Aug. Carlsbad Field Office (CBFO).

[17] [www.wipp.carlsbad.nm.us].

[18] OECD-NEA (2001), *The Role of Underground Laboratories in Nuclear Waste Disposal Programmes*, OECD Paris, p 33.

[19] OECD-NEA and IAEA (2002), *An International Peer Review of the Yucca Mountain Project Total System Performance Assessment for the Site Recommendation*, Joint Report, OECD Paris.

that decision, investigations by the department of energy leading to an exploratory facility continued. In February, 2002 President Bush announced plans to seek a permit for the waste site and in July 2002 the Senate overruled objections by Nevada clearing the way for the project to proceed. The licensing process before the Nuclear Regulatory Commission (NRC) is forecast to take four years and construction is expected to complete in 2010. Following that it is planned that 3,200 tonnes a year will be shipped to the Yucca site.

The process of waste processing in the US is surrounded with legal argument and process.   The utilities, having been promised by the government to take commercial nuclear waste by 1989, are being sued for failing to do so.   Six lawsuits filed by Nevada in 2002 have challenged the Yucca project and South Carolina has a disagreement with the government over the storage of defence related plutonium. The plutonium in this latter case is the result of an agreement between the US and Russia to take equal amounts of plutonium from their defence stockpiles and incorporate it in nuclear fuel to be burned in commercial nuclear power stations.   The processing plant is located at Savannah River in South Carolina and the plutonium is to be shipped there from Rocky Flats Arsenal in Colorado. The Yucca Mountain Project is nevertheless proceeding and involves the design of waste packages for transport to and installation in horizontal shafts into the mountain 300 meters above the water table and shielded from natural dripping of ground water from fractures. Fractures have never been observed and so the design of the packages may prove to be too conservative.[20] The US NRC regulations[21] require that the design allow the retrieval of the used fuel under certain circumstances.   The OECD-NEA Radioactive Waste Management Committee have considered the question of reversibility and retrievability from geologic disposal and have concluded, *inter-alia*, that because of the large margins of passive safety built into an engineered geologic repository, no circumstances have been identified that would require urgent retrieval of waste.[22]

France

Nuclear energy is the main source of electrical power in France comprising in 2000 75 percent of the installed capacity at 63,103 megawatts electrical from 59 nuclear power stations. France also has a nuclear defence programme. Radioactive waste generated in France is similar to that produced in the US but characterised slightly differently from that described generally above and specifically in the US.[23] The waste is divided into categories; very weak activity (*tres faible activite or TFA*), or weak activity (*faible activite*), (A-wastes) medium activity (*moyenne activite*), (*B-*

---

[20] International Peer Review ref. 19 at p 39.

[21] US *Nuclear Waste Policy Act* (see chapters three and six).

[22] OECD-NEA (2001), *Reversibility and Retrievability in Geologic Disposal of Radioactive Waste*, OECD Paris, p 38.

[23] The information that follows is from the journal of the CEA, CLEFS and CEA No 46 Spring 2002.

wastes) equivalent to intermediate level waste and high activity (*haute activite*) and (*C-wastes*) equivalent to high level waste. Used fuel is mostly reprocessed.

TFA waste comes mostly from decommissioning and will amount to about 250,000 cubic meters by 2020 and one to two million cubic meters in total. Some of the material will be recycled and some placed in dedicated facilities managed by ANDRA the national agency for nuclear waste. Waste held by the French Atomic Research Agency (CEA) is stored at Cadarache (Bouches-du-Rhone) where regulations limit the activity to between 10 and 100 Bq/g for alpha emitters.

A-wastes are from nuclear facilities consisting of protective clothing, filters and resins and from medical and industrial users. They are characterised by beta and gamma radioactive materials with half lives of less or equal to 30 years or where the radiation is negligible after 300 years. The waste will amount to about 500,000 cubic meters by 2020 and comprises about 90 percent of the total volume of nuclear waste. It is stored in surface facilities; one at le Centre de la Manche is full and one at le Centre de l'Aube is in operation. Regulatory limits are such that at the end of the operational phase, when no longer under surveillance, at 300 years alpha emissions will be no greater than 370 Bq/gm. Another facility is being developed for long-lived low activity materials, e.g. graphite and radium, that will comprise about 15,000 cubic meters by 2020.

B-wastes with a half-life of greater than 30 years and activity of greater than 3,700 Bq/gm without significant heat generation from fuel fabrication and reprocessing and from research establishments are stored in interim-storage at the nuclear facilities. The waste will amount to about 60,000 cubic meters by 2020. Solid B-wastes are stabilised in bitumen and the liquids in cement. The final disposal of B-waste is being developed as required by French environmental law.[24]

C-wastes have a half-life of greater than 30 years and are fission products from reprocessing. These are the principal source of radioactive waste in terms of activity and will constitute about 5,000 cubic meters in 2020. In 2002 France has about 200 cubic meters of C-waste. When encased in glass (vitrified) they will be stored similarly to the arrangement for B-waste.

France has been studying deep disposal of B and C-waste since the 1970s but instigation of four sites was suspended in 1987 as a result of public opposition. Following a government review, the law referred to above was instituted in 1991 that set out the framework for research and development on the management and disposal of wastes over a 15-year period. The framework requires at least two potential repository sites with underground laboratories to be established in agreement with local communities. A decision on the chosen site is required by 2006. In 1998 the government announced that an underground laboratory is to be constructed in clay at Bure en Meuse; a centre for research into reversible emplacement of waste underground in clay is to be considered at Gard near Marcoule. A search was commenced for a third site in granite in the Vienne region but abandoned in 2000 following adverse public reaction in the areas. Construction of the first shaft in clay is underway and being monitored by local

---

[24] Code de l'environment, la loi 91-1381 du 30 decembre 1991 ('loi Bataille').

information commissions. A local public interest group has the equivalent of about £6 million to allocate to various local projects.

Used fuel is not considered as waste in France and is reprocessed. Plutonium is the most important radionuclide (about 670 tonnes will be generated by 2070) and it is envisaged that this will be incorporated as MOX in new fuel. However, this is probably not sufficient to satisfy all requirements and alternative programmes are being researched.[25] Three actinides, americium, curium and neptunium and two fission products, technetium and iodine 129, can be transformed to elements with shorter lives or non-radioactive elements by transmutation after separation from used fuel. The optimum method of transmutation is currently being researched.[26] For the future this also offers the possibility of producing elements with useful industrial characteristics.

Finland

The four Finnish nuclear power plant units, Loviisa 1 and 2 and Olkiluoto 1 and 2 generated 32 percent of the electricity consumed in Finland in 2001 with an installed capacity of 2,656 megawatts electrical. From the information available at the end of 2002, apart from the US, Finland may have the most advanced programme for the final disposal of nuclear waste of all the countries operating nuclear power plants. In 2002, the Finnish Parliament approved the construction of a further nuclear power plant[27] and was able to do so based on the evidence of a positive solution to the final disposal of nuclear waste. At the beginning of the 1980s, final disposal of spent fuel was included in the plans for the Olkiluoto Nuclear Power Plant. From the Loviisa Plant, spent fuel was returned to the Soviet Union/Russia until 1996. The Amendment to the *Nuclear Energy Act,* however, stipulates that spent fuel generated in Finland be handled in Finland. For this task Posiva Oy, was established; an organisation owned by Teollisuuden Voima Oy (60 percent) and Fortum Power and Heat Oy (40 percent), the power companies who are responsible for nuclear waste management. Posiva is responsible for the characterization of sites for final disposal of spent fuel, for the construction and operation of the final disposal facility and the decommissioning of the final disposal facility. The following details are extracted mostly from the Posiva annual report of 2001.[28]

Operating Waste

Operating waste consists of low level radioactive waste and intermediate level radioactive waste generated in the operating and servicing of a nuclear power plant. Operating waste is produced in the nuclear power plant's process water

---

[25] supra CLEFS-CEA No 46 at p 45.

[26] ibid p 45.

[27] On 24 May 2002 the Finnish Parliament ratified the Government's decision to proceed with a new nuclear power unit and the building of a final repository for spent fuel.

[28] Posiva Oy (2001), *Nuclear Waste Management of the Olkiluoto and Loviisa Power Plants*, Annual Review [www.posiva.fi].

purification systems and by service and repair activities. Low level waste includes protective plastic sheets, tools, protective clothing and towels used in service work. Intermediate level waste consists of the ion-exchange resin used to purify the process water. In Olkiluoto, the total amount of operating waste generated annually is 150-200 cubic meters, half of which is low level waste and the other half intermediate level waste. Loviisa generates a total of 100-150 cubic meters of operating waste every year. Low level waste is compressed into 200-litre drums. Material that cannot be compressed is packed into either steel or concrete containers. Intermediate level waste from the ion-exchange resins is solidified in drums. Olkiluoto uses bitumen and Loviisa cement as solidifying agent.

Final Disposal of Low and Intermediate Level waste

The waste is first stored in the power plant buildings and then in separate interim stores for low and intermediate level waste. From the interim stores, the waste is transferred into the final disposal repository. The repository in Olkiluoto has been operational since 1992, and in Loviisa since 1997. In Loviisa, the solidification and final disposal of ion-exchange resins will be started within the next few years. Until then, the resins are stored in casks located within the power plant facility. In both Olkiluoto and Loviisa, the disposal repository silos are excavated inside the power plant area in the bedrock at a depth of 70-100 meters. The operating waste is transported to the repository on special vehicles along a transport tunnel. When the repository is decommissioned, the tunnel and shaft will be closed. The repositories do not require monitoring after they have been decommissioned. The radioactive elements contained in the waste remain in the bedrock and over the time will decay to a harmless level. At Olkiluoto by the end of 2001 operating waste amounted to 4102 cubic meters of which 3671 cubic meters was in the repository; at Loviisa operating waste totalled 2427 cubic meters with 1031 cubic meters in the repository. The repository at Olkiluoto has a dedicated section for non-nuclear radioactive waste, for example, sealed sources. Waste from unsealed sources used, for example, in hospitals are stored at the place of origin until the radioactivity decays to a very low level where it can be disposed of as normal waste.

Very Low level Waste

In Finland very low level waste is exempt from regulatory control and is either deposited in engineered dumps on site or handed over to local authorities to be processed as refuse. Ion-exchange resins contain a large proportion of liquid that is non-radioactive and at Loviisa the cement-based solidification plant approved in 2001 is designed to remove radioactive caesium leaving the liquid to be disposed as very low level waste and so reducing the radioactive waste to a very much smaller volume.

Decommissioning

In the Olkiluoto power plants decommissioning will not start for a period of 30 years after the plant has been closed down. This delay period ensures that the short-lived nuclide in the structures decay which will reduce the amount of radioactive waste that requires final disposal. According to the decommissioning plan for the Loviisa power plant units, decommissioning of the structures will start immediately after the operation of the plant ceases. Both in Loviisa and in Olkiluoto the decommissioning waste will be stored in facilities that are constructed as an extension of the operating waste repository.

Used/Spent Fuel

Used or spent fuel (the terms are interchangeable) is treated as radioactive waste in Finland and, in 2001, Parliament approved the start of a rock characterisation facility as the first stage of the project for the final disposal facility to be built at Olkiluoto. In the meantime the fuel is stored at the power station sites; at Olkiluoto by the end of 2001 the fuel assemblies in interim store amounted to 5274. The interim store has a capacity to store 30 years worth of operational spent fuel and can be enlarged if necessary. Until 1996 the used fuel from Loviisa was returned to Russia. The change of Finnish law[29] forced the expansion of storage capacity on site that was achieved by denser stacking and can be further expanded. At the end of 2001 the store contained 2335 fuel elements.

Final Disposal of Spent Fuel

The Finnish nuclear power plants generate a total of about 2600 tonnes of spent fuel during their 40 years of service. The spent fuel will be encapsulated at the final disposal site designed to accommodate over 1500 final disposal canisters for which about 15 km of underground tunnels will be excavated. The network of tunnels, running down to a depth of several hundreds of meters, will cover an area of some tens of hectares. The tunnels mined in the bedrock will not restrict later use of the land area above them for other purposes. Above the tunnels, on the ground surface, an encapsulation plant will be built. In this encapsulation plant the spent fuel rod assemblies will be packed into metal canisters of double construction made of nodular cast iron, enclosed in a watertight 5 cm thick stainless copper shell. The canisters will be packed and sealed and their tightness tested on the filling line in the encapsulation plant inside thick concrete walls. The plant is designed so that no radiation in excess of regulatory levels can be emitted to the environment from the encapsulation plant even in the case of a failure on the packing line resulting in the fuel rod assemblies being damaged. The canisters will be lowered in a lift to the underground final disposal repository that will consist of tunnels excavated at a depth of hundreds of meters at 25 m distance from each other and connected by transport tunnels. Apart from the canister transfer shaft, the facility will be connected to the ground surface by a personnel shaft and a working shaft. The canisters will be placed in holes drilled at the bottom of the repository tunnels, spaced at a few meters from each other. The canisters will then be surrounded with bentonite clay, which expands when it absorbs water. The clay will prevent direct water flow to the surface of the canister and will protect the canister against minor bedrock movements. The Posiva Safety Case will claim that the rock isolates the fuel from the environment; by emplacing the canisters deep in

---

[29] Amendment of the Nuclear Energy Act to retain all spent fuel in Finland.

the bedrock, the nuclear waste will be isolated from any events taking place on the ground surface and will prevent unintentional penetration by man into the final disposal facility; the bedrock will create mechanically and chemically stable conditions in the final disposal repository and restrict the amount of water coming into contact with the final disposal canisters. The research results obtained so far indicate that groundwater movement is minimal inside the rock at a depth of hundreds of meters. The water is also almost oxygen-free so that its corrosive influence on both the canisters and the spent nuclear fuel will be negligible. The Safety Case will claim that if the spent fuel for some unforeseeable reason should come into contact with the groundwater, the materials dissolved from it would be trapped in the bentonite and the bedrock round the canisters. The bedrock will stop any possible radiation emitted from the waste canister, but it is claimed that this is not the primary reason for burying the nuclear waste in a depth of several hundred meters: a solid rock course of just of few meters would be enough to dampen the radiation to the level of natural background radiation. When the last canisters have been placed in the repository, the encapsulation plant will be decommissioned, the tunnels filled with a mixture of bentonite and crushed stone and the shafts leading to the repository will be closed. It is claimed that the final disposal repository will require no monitoring after it has been decommissioned and after decommissioning, the use of the land above, covering 40 hectares, will not be restricted by the repository tunnels.

The spent fuel will be transported to the encapsulation plant at the final disposal site by road and/or rail. For transfer into the interim store, the fuel rod assemblies are currently packed into transport casks of solid, impact-resistant construction. The purpose of the cask is to act as shielding against radiation emitted by the spent fuel and to protect the assemblies against damage during the transfer. Transport casks of the same massive type will be used when transporting the spent fuel from the interim stores in the plant area to the final disposal site. In the power plant the cask, filled with fuel rod assemblies and tightly sealed, will be lifted by a crane onto a transport base mounted on the carriage of a truck supported in the horizontal position with strong shock absorbers mounted at the ends of the cask and covered with a weather guard. For road transport special carriages hauled by a heavy-duty truck will be used and in rail transports an easy-to-load deep-loading carriage will be used.

In practice, the safety of the final disposal of spent nuclear fuel is based on several technical and natural barriers that prevent and slow down the release of radioactive materials from the final disposal repository into the bedrock and into the organic nature. These barriers include the solid state of the spent fuel, the double construction of the final disposal canister and the bentonite clay in which it will be enclosed. The final barrier will be formed by hundreds of meters of rock between the final disposal repository and the natural environment.

Korea

The Korean Peninsula has been divided at about the 38th parallel, into north and south regions since the war of 1953. For the purposes of this work north and south will be treated separately although there are positive connections and hopefully a chance of reconciliation from a developing political situation.

The Democratic Republic of Korea (North Korea)

Little is known about the practices used for radioactive waste storage and disposal in North Korea since the question of nuclear development is the subject of intense political concern; this is discussed in the next chapter. Intelligence reports and rumour indicate that it is probable that small amounts of plutonium[30] and enriched uranium have been separated using a research reactor and so it is reasonable to assume that radioactive waste must exist but in what form and where stored are kept secret. A joint north/south project, supported by Japan and the US is underway to construct two 1000 megawatt pressurised water reactors by the Korean Peninsula Energy Development Organisation. The project design is based on the power stations operating in South Korea and so it is reasonable to expect that the practices for storage of used fuel and radioactive waste will also be based on the practice and plans of South Korea. In 1997 a representation to the UN was made by South Korea to halt the export from Taiwan of 200,000 barrels of radioactive waste to North Korea.[31]

The Republic of Korea (South Korea)

South Korea at 2002 has 16 operating reactors giving nearly 13,000 megawatts electrical that provide over 40 percent of their electrical generation. There are a further four reactors under construction and five planned.[32] Radioactive waste and spent fuel are stored at the power station sites pending a successful search for a disposal site[33] planned for 2008 and a centralised interim spent fuel store planned for 2016. Radioactive waste is classified into two categories; high level waste that contains alpha-emitting radionuclides of longer than 20 years in excess of 4000 Bq/gm and generates heat in excess of 2 kilowatts per cubic metre and low and intermediate level waste. In reality high level waste only applies to spent fuel in South Korea, as reprocessing is not carried out. Reprocessing is, however, an option for the future as the long-term storage of spent fuel is on an interim basis, it is recoverable and storage is planned only for a period in the region of 50 years.[34]

---

[30] Hwang Jang-jin, Korea Herald 28 Oct. 2002.

[31] UN, Economic and Social Council, 4 Apr. 1997 E/1997/2- - A/S - 19/8.

[32] Kim, Jeong-Mook, *Management of Radioactive Waste Generated from Nuclear Power Reactors in Korea*, IAEA-CN-78/104.

[33] Lee, Sang, Don (1999), *Law and Policy of Nuclear Waste Management in Korea*, Nuclear Inter-Jura, Washington.

[34] Kim, Hho Jung (2002), Director of Regulatory Research Division, Korea Institute of Nuclear Safety, personal communication Jun.

Low and Intermediate Level Waste

Low and intermediate level waste is, other than high level waste, all radioactive waste above that which may be exempted from regulatory concern i.e. where it would result in radiation dose to any individual no greater than 0.01mSv/yr and a collective dose of no greater than 1 person Sv/yr. Pending the construction of a final disposal facility, low and intermediate level waste are stored on the site where they are generated except for waste from sources other than nuclear facilities that are collected and stored in a dedicated interim facility. Prior to its discharge, gaseous waste is either held in gas decay tanks or filtered through charcoal delay beds. Liquid waste from process and floor drains is filtered and evaporated, the solids remaining are fixed with paraffin; distilled water is demineralised, diluted and discharged to the sea and laundry waste is neutralised, filtered and discharged to the sea. The discharges are monitored and if higher than the regulatory limit are returned for further treatment. High-speed centrifuges, selective ion exchangers and reverse osmosis are being considered for the future. Solid waste is packed into metal drums, concrete drums and high integrity containers. The existing storage capacity is for 99,900 drums with 58,574 drums in storage at 2001. The life of the present storage has been extended by improving facilities and the introduction of new technologies to dry and compact the waste thus reducing the output of drums from 550 per year in the early 1990s to 172 in 1998. A fuel repository in near surface or rock-cavern locations is forecast to be in operation by 2008.

Spent Fuel

Spent fuel from pressurised water reactors is stored in the spent fuel pool, the water being demineralised and cooled; spent fuel for the Heavy Water Reactors is kept in a pool and also in dry silos. The storage capacity in the country can cater for 9,803 tonnes of uranium with 5,385 tonnes already in storage at 2001.

European Union Classification System for Radioactive waste

National systems of classification of radioactive waste are similar and the present methods of handling waste and used fuel use similar processes and procedures based generally on the advice from the IAEA. However, it can be seen from the examples of national practice outlined above that even over the small sample described there are significant differences in detail. A system based on the IAEA classification has been proposed for use in the European Union in conjunction with national systems. This system differs from the present system in operation in the UK; firstly by the introduction of categories for transitional waste that will decay within a short period of storage to unrestricted clearance levels and secondly by the division of low and intermediate level waste into categories of short-lived and long-lived waste. This proposed system presents difficulties where the waste is mixed with radionuclides with different half-lives. The dose resulting from contact with radionuclides is not related to their half-life and the toxicity of radionuclides of similar half-lives are not necessarily the same, so while classification on the basis lifetime would be an advantage for storage the safety aspects would have to be the same.

Next Steps

The USA and Finland have embarked on programmes of deep disposal of used fuel and high level waste; France and the UK reprocess used fuel and are researching the long term/final disposal alternatives for intermediate and high level waste and South Korea is taking interim measures. These examples cover the reasonable alternatives known at this time, however, changes to the radiological protection rules and to national policies may well be the cause of modification. The OECD has stimulated a review of the radiological protection system. Public participation in the solutions proposed in the UK may reveal different approaches to the siting and construction of disposal facilities and the practical experience in Finland and the USA may well reveal new approaches to the storage and disposal of used fuel. The existing and projected amounts of radioactive waste from all sources and used fuel is under control in safe systems for at least the next century and possible much longer, the notable exceptions being unacceptable practices mainly adopted by nuclear weapons nations in the cold war, for example disposing of waste and military equipment in potentially accessible locations. Proposed final systems of disposal will be in place in the next fifty years. The risk that remains is the deliberate destruction of facilities without concern as to the effects. While the design of facilities is in most cases sufficiently robust to withstand overt action, deliberate military action, such as the destruction of the Bushehr reactor by enemy firepower in Iran in 1987 and the risk of clandestine action remain a danger. The question of policy and stakeholder attitudes will continue to be a major influence on the progress to future arrangements and are discussed in the following chapters. Nevertheless those arrangements can be seen to be based on a sound foundation and do not need to be hurried.

Further Reading

DEFRA (2002), *UK Strategy for Radioactive Discharges 2001 – 2020*, June, DEFRA Publications, London.

Department of the Environment (1995), *Review of Radioactive Waste Management Policy, Final Conclusions*, Cm 2919, HMSO London.

House of Lords (1999), *Management of Nuclear Waste,* Third Report of the Select Committee on Science and Technology, HL Paper 41, March.

IAEA (2002), *Near Surface Disposal of Low and Intermediate Level Radioactive Waste (LILW)*, IAEA Report No 42, Vienna.

IAEA (2003), *Scientific and Technical Basis for Geological Disposal of Radioactive Waste*, Technical Report Series No. 413, IAEA, Vienna.

OECD-NEA (2000), *Radiological Impacts of Spent Nuclear Fuel Management Options: A Comparative Study*, OECD Paris.

Chapter Three

International and Government Policy

Until recent years national policies specifically designed for regulating radioactive waste have been effectively non-existent. Waste has been seen as a part of the nuclear process with adequate control through the legislation and regulation covering radioactive materials and nuclear facilities and dominated by the physics of materials, the behaviour of the particles that make up atoms and their interaction with the environment and people. In the last decade public concern has focussed on the question of radioactive waste to the extent that failure to have a sound and open policy threatens continuing use of nuclear energy at a time when other indigenous fuels are running out. This chapter will identify the organisations that influence governments and will summarise the state of policy by relating the current situation in the five selected countries; the USA, France, Finland, Korea and the UK.

Supra-national Influences

Science

Underpinning the policy adopted by nations throughout the world are the recommendations of the International Commission on Radiological Protection (ICRP) that has roots back to 1928 and is a non-profit organisation that provides general guidance on the use of radiation sources. Its recommendations cover all aspects of protection against ionising radiation and form the basis for radiation safety throughout the world.[1] Since it is ICRP's advice that is used almost without exception by the International Atomic Energy Agency in its standards and guidance on the use of radiation it is important to have an understanding of ICRP organisation. To this end Appendix 2 includes the Convention of the ICRP and a review of its history, mode of operation, concepts and current policies. The appendix briefly touches upon the objectives of the Commission's recommendations; the quantities used; the biological basis of the Commission's policy; the quantitative basis for its risk estimates; the structure of the system of protection; some problems of interpretation and application in that system; and the need for stability, consistency and clarity in the Commission's recommendations.

Development of International Control

After the Second World War, western nations came to see the development of nuclear energy as essential to the continuing development of mankind to enable the replacement of fossil fuels. The early attempts by the USA to internationalise the

---

[1] Valentin, Jack (1999), *What if? ICRP Guidance on potential radiation exposure*, IAEA Bulletin, Vol 41 No.3 1999, Vienna, Austria.

promotion of nuclear energy were not successful. The Acheson-Lilienthal Report in 1945, which led to the Baruch Plan,[2] advocated an international agency;[3] 'to which should be entrusted all phases of the development and use of atomic energy'. This proposal was, however, frustrated by East/West non-co-operation. The development of the peaceful use of atomic energy was forced into independent national development following the *US McMahon Act (1946)*. The Act prevented the dissemination of information about the research leading up to the explosion of the atom bomb. In 1953 when it was clear that states other than the US were making independent moves in bomb development and peaceful uses, the spirit of co-operation was rekindled by the Eisenhower initiative.[4] From this developed the International Atomic Energy Agency and the Conventions concerning the non-proliferation of nuclear weapons and the liability for nuclear damage in the case of a nuclear incident in a nuclear installation. Following the Eisenhower initiative three international organisations were formed: the International Atomic Energy Agency (IAEA) by the United Nations; the Nuclear Energy Agency (NEA) by the Organisation for Economic Co-operation and Development (OECD) and EURATOM now embodied in the European Union (EU).

The International Atomic Energy Agency (IAEA)

The International Atomic Energy Agency (IAEA) serves as the world's foremost intergovernmental forum for scientific and technical co-operation in the peaceful use of nuclear technology. Established as an autonomous organization under the United Nations (UN) in 1957, the IAEA represents the culmination of international efforts to make a reality of US President Eisenhower's proposal in his Atoms for Peace speech before the UN General Assembly in 1953. He envisioned the creation of an international body to control and develop the use of atomic energy. Today, the Agency's broad spectrum of services, programmes, and activities is based on the needs of its 134 Member States. At the end of 2000, the number of staff members in the Secretariat was 2,173 with 912 in the Professional and higher categories and 1,261 in the General Service category. IAEA financial resources fall into two categories: the regular budget and voluntary contributions. The Regular Budget for 2001 amounts to US$ 230 million. The target for voluntary contributions to the Technical Co-operation Fund for 2001 was established at US$ 73 million.

The mission of the IAEA being somewhat less powerful than envisioned in 1953 requires it to act:

- as an independent intergovernmental science and technology based organization with the United Nations to serve as the global focal point for nuclear cooperation;

---

[2] Baruch, Bernard (1946), Speech at the United Nations, 14 June.
[3] US State Department Publication 2498. Report on the International Control of Atomic Energy, Mar. 1946.
[4] United Nations. Atoms for Peace, UN General Assembly, Eighth Session, 1954.

- to assist its Member States, in the context of social and economic goals, in planning for and using nuclear science and technology for various peaceful purposes, including the generation of electricity, and facilitate the transfer of such technology and knowledge in a sustainable manner to developing Member States;
- to develop nuclear safety standards and, based on these standards, promote the achievement and maintenance of high levels of safety in applications of nuclear energy, as well as the protection of human health and the environment against ionizing radiation;
- to verify through its inspection system that States comply with their commitments under the Non-Proliferation Treaty and other non-proliferation agreements, to use nuclear material and facilities only for peaceful purposes.

While it is recognised that the IAEA is the product of compromise[5] and rather than being a body with responsibility for international management of nuclear power has a facilitating mission, the events in Iraq, North Korea and the threatened terrorist action with radioactive materials (the dirty bomb) are influencing international views to strengthen the Agency's role. The role of the UN inspectors to a limited extent transcend sovereignty in relation to radioactive materials and nuclear facilities that may well include waste facilities.[6] The need for integrated control structures from the global regime to the national operator will undoubtedly become, once again, a distinct possibility.

The Organisation for Economic Co-operation and Development (OECD)

The Organisation for Economic Co-operation and Development (OECD) was created by the Convention on the OECD, signed in Paris on 14 December 1960 and came into force on 30 September 1961. The Nuclear Energy Agency (NEA) was established on 20 April 1972. The member countries of the OECD together with the Commission of the European Communities take part in the work of the NEA: the primary objectives being to promote co-operation between the members in the safety and regulatory aspects of nuclear development, and in assessing the future role of nuclear energy as a contribution to economic growth. The NEA works in close collaboration with the IAEA, with which it has concluded a Co-operation Agreement to achieve its objectives.

The NEA considered the liability issues raised by the disposal of nuclear substances in the context of waste management and decontamination of nuclear installations in 1983. It was agreed by the NEA experts that the definition of 'nuclear installation' in the Paris Convention should include waste disposal facilities; but other arrangements may be needed for the post closure phase.[7]

---

[5] Birnie, P. W. and Boyle, A. E. (1992), *International Law and the Summit*, Clarendon Press, Oxford.
[6] Scheinman, L. (2001), *Transboundary Sovereignty in the management of nuclear material*, IAEA Bulletin, Vol. 43, No. 4, Vienna, Austria.
[7] OECD-NEA (1984), *Long-term Management of Radioactive Waste. Legal, Administrative and Financial Aspects*. OECD, Paris, pp 86-88.

An objective of the OECD is to assist Member countries in the area of radioactive waste management, developing safe management and disposal strategies for spent fuel, long-lived waste, and waste from the decommissioning of nuclear facilities by:

- ensuring the exchange of information and experience and increased understanding of management of long-lived waste, spent fuel and decommissioning waste;
- elaborating waste management strategies, including regulatory approaches;
- increasing scientific and technical knowledge for the management of radioactive waste;
- enhancing co-operation with non-member countries with a view to promoting safe waste management practices and addressing current waste management concerns.

The European Atomic Energy Community (EURATOM)

The *Treaty establishing the European Atomic Energy Community* (Euratom Treaty) is one of the founding treaties of the European Union. The Treaty was originally drafted in the 1950s and addresses the issues in the field of nuclear power that were relevant at that time. These include radiological protection of the work-force and the public, the supply of uranium for the developing nuclear power sector, the safeguarding of this fissile material to prevent it from being used for unauthorised military purposes and general aspects such as research and dissemination of information. Under the provisions of the *Euratom Treaty*, the European Commission acquired the status of a supranational regulatory authority in three areas: radiological protection, supply of nuclear fissile materials and nuclear safeguards. Radiological protection is relevant to the operation of all facilities handling radioactive substances, whether they are nuclear power plants, radioactive waste stores/disposal facilities or institutions outside the nuclear power sector such as research centres and hospitals. In all these facilities, certain EU-wide limits to radiation exposure must be respected. However, the *Euratom Treaty* makes no specific mention of aspects such as operational safety of nuclear power plants and radioactive waste storage or disposal facilities. This is probably because at the time the Treaty was drawn up, these were not major concerns. As a result, these aspects of nuclear industry regulation have become the responsibility of National Authorities in the individual Member States. Nevertheless, research activities on the long-term storage of nuclear waste and transmutation (or incineration) has proceeded under EU direction.[8] A draft Directive on the management of spent nuclear fuel[9] and a proposal for a Council Directive on the control of high activity sealed sources[10] are evidence of a growing involvement by the EU. These proposals are being adopted at a time when the Community's

---

[8] See European Institutions press release IP/03/189, Brussels 5 Feb. 2003.
[9] Euratom(2002), Draft proposal for a Council Directive (Euratom), European Commission.
[10] COM (2003) 18 final, 24 Jan. 2003.

legislative powers with regard to the safety of nuclear facilities have been confirmed by the Court of Justice.[11]

As will be seen international organisations such as the IAEA and the OECD-NEA have, through their efforts, resulted in a certain standardisation at the qualitative level of the design, operational and maintenance aspects of nuclear installations. Several international conventions have helped to establish a culture of best practice amongst the Member States of these organisations (which include all the EU Member States).

Development of Policy

International Commission on Radiological Protection

The ICRP started life as a scion of the International Society of Radiology and according to its constitution members are chosen on the basis of their recognised activity in the fields of medical radiology, radiation protection, physics, health physics, biology, genetics, biochemistry, biophysics and other disciplines relevant to the objects of the Commission, with regard to an appropriate balance of expertise rather than nationality. The executive committee of the International Society of Radiology are kept informed of changes to the membership of the Commission. The work of the ICRP as outlined in Appendix 2 and as demonstrated by the list of publications and recommendations, can be seen to come from a strong radiation user base. It is not the intention of this work to examine the details of the system of radiation protection, however, the following summary may help those who do not wish to delve into the detail by wider reading. The latest ICRP recommendations are expressed in Publication 60[12] and characterise activities that involve radiation exposure into practices that add radiation exposures or risks (*Practices*) and activities that can decrease the overall exposure by removing the source of radiation, modifying the pathways or reducing the number of exposed individuals (*Intervention*). For Practices the system of protection recommended is:

- no practice involving exposures to radiation should be adopted unless it produces sufficient benefit to the exposed individuals or society to offset the radiation detriment it causes (*Justification*);
- in relation to any particular source within a practice, the magnitude of individual doses, the number of people exposed, and the likelihood of incurring exposures where these are not certain to be received should be kept as low as reasonably achievable, economic and social factors being taken into account (*ALARA or Optimisation*) and

---

[11] Judgement of the Court in *Commission of the European Commission v Council of the European Union, Case C-29/99* [http://curia.eu.int/jurisp/].

[12] ICRP (1991), *1990 Recommendations of the ICRP*. Publication 60. Annals of the ICRP 21(1-3).

- the exposure of individuals resulting from the combination of all the relevant practices should be subject to dose limits, or to some control of risk in the case of potential exposures. These are aimed at ensuring that no individual is exposed to radiation risks that are judged to be unacceptable from these practices in any normal circumstances (*Limitation*).

The ICRP purports to be concerned to evolve and modify its output and meet new challenges by both internal initiatives[13] and from international bodies.[14] In the former, the chairman of the ICRP proposed a series of ideas for simplifying the system of radiation protection in line with societal needs. However others[15] have pointed out that no new scientific information that would call for a major revision is available and the basic needs of protection have not altered. Nevertheless, the emphasis has changed to warrant the consideration of long-time periods of nuclear waste disposal and environmental issues. The OECD through the Committee on Radiation and Public Health (CRPPH) has reviewed specific aspects of the current system of radiation protection, extracts being as follows:[16]

- Clarity and coherence; 'one of the most important characteristics of any new or modified system of radiation protection should be a high level of self coherence';
- Justification; 'the ICRP should give full consideration in the future to the roles and interactions between justification (with a small 'j') and optimisation principles';
- Triviality; 'the utility and necessity of the concept of "triviality" in the context of radiation protection regulation should continue to be discussed. Regulations are in fact "concerned" with all exposures, however one may judge that some low levels of exposure do not require regulatory actions';
- Zero Release; 'Thus, how optimisation, dose constraints, "zero release" and triviality applied within the process of authorisation for release should be re-examined in future';
- Public Protection; 'The CRPPH feels that one way to move towards better understanding of the system of radiation protection is to better highlight the distinctions between the various stages of protection of public welfare' and 'The role of the radiation protection expert (as scientist, as regulator, or as decision maker) needs to be redefined, and effective methods of involving stakeholders need to be developed';

---

[13] Clarke, R. H. (1999), 'Control of low level radiation exposure: time for a change', *J. Radiol. Prot.* Vol.19 No.2, 107-115.

[14] OECD-NEA, (2002), *A Critical Review of the System of Radiation Protection, The Way Forward in Radiological Protection*, An Expert Group Report, OECD Paris.

[15] Jensen, P. H., Paile, W. and Salo, A. (2002), Views expressed in the Nordic countries on the suggested modifications to the ICRP approach [www.nsfs.org/irpa_nsfs.html].

[16] OECD-NEA (2000), *First reflections of the OECD-NEA's CRPPH*, NEA2628, OECD Paris.

- Protection of the Environment; 'the rationale for making or for not making recommendations should be more thoroughly and openly discussed by the ICRP and other stakeholders';
- Optimisation; 'practical guidance is needed to better apply the principle of optimisation';
- Collective Dose; 'Clear, objective operational guidance for the valid application of collective dose is important'; and
- Dose Limits; 'In today's societal context, the transparency of recommendations is as important as the numerical values of dose limits and is essential to foster stakeholder confidence in the entire system of radiation protection'.

The ICRP is considering revising its recommendations, with a view to publication in 2005, to use the controllability of sources to provide a simpler scale of protection levels similar to the methods used to control other non-radioactive pollutants and so offering the potential for an integrated pollution policy. In the meantime, the CRPPH formed an expert group on the evolution of the system of radiation protection (EGRP) with terms of reference to, *inter alia*, identify the areas of the current system of radiological protection that are, in their opinion, most in need of further elaboration. The EGRP reported four significant areas on which to focus improvement:[17] that a simplified approach, based on a process of authorization involving interested parties as appropriate should be considered; de-emphasising, or eliminating, various terms would result in a greatly simplified, more coherent and understandable system; that clear distinctions should be made between the scientific aspects of risk assessment, the social aspects of risk evaluation and management and the regulatory aspects of risk management; and the relationship between justification and optimization should be thoroughly explored and clearly explained. The EGRP report advocates a modern system of radiological protection that should fit within a common policy framework with the management of other carcinogenic risks. The sources of radiation would be characterised in terms of exposure and protective action to facilitate the identification and social acceptance of the radiological protection action. The proposal has been 'road tested' by various case studies covering the range of likely activities from reactor discharges to hospital waste incineration[18] and it has been concluded that, *inter alia*, a system of characterisation would serve as a tool for triggering stakeholder involvement and that it would remove some of the terminological confusion of the present system.

As yet the dichotomy between Practices and Intervention has not been decided for the various categories of waste. For example, used fuel storage could be treated as an Intervention thus avoiding the strictures of the system of protection for Practices, whereas used fuel being reprocessed would class as a Practice. The jury is still out!

---

[17] OECD-NEA (2002), *The Way Forward in Radiological Protection. An Expert Group Report*. OECD [http://www.nea.fr/htm/rwm/reports/2002/nea3685-way-forward.pdf].
[18] Osborne, R.V. and Turvey, F.J. (2003), *A New Approach to Authorisation in the Field of Radiological Protection, The Road Test Report*. OECD-NEA Paris.

The International Atomic Energy Agency

In 1955 the General Assembly of the United Nations established the Scientific Committee on the Effects of Atomic Radiation (UNSCEAR) in response to widespread concerns regarding the effects of radiation on human health and the environment. At that time, nuclear weapons were being tested in the atmosphere, and radioactive debris was dispersing throughout the environment, reaching the human body through intake of air, water and foods. The Committee was requested to collect, assemble and evaluate information on the levels of ionizing radiation and radionuclides from all sources (natural and produced by man) and to study their possible effects on man and the environment. The Committee is comprised of scientists from Argentina, Australia, Belgium, Brazil, Canada, China, Egypt, France, Germany, India, Indonesia, Japan, Mexico, Peru, Poland, Russia, Slovakia, Sudan, Sweden, United Kingdom, and the United States of America. The UNSCEAR Secretariat, which gives the Committee the necessary assistance in carrying out its work, is located in Vienna; it consults with scientists throughout the world in establishing databases of exposures and information on the effects of radiation. The Committee produces detailed reports to the General Assembly, which are increasingly used by organizations and individual scientists as sources of information. The reports review exposures from natural radiation sources, from nuclear power production and nuclear tests, exposures from medical radiation diagnosis and treatment, and from occupational exposure to radiation. They include detailed studies on cancer induced by radiation, on the mechanisms of the development of cancer and the body's repair systems against it, on the risks of hereditary diseases induced by exposure to radiation, and on the combined effects of radiation and other (for instance chemical) agents. Important consideration is also given to the assessment of the radiological consequences of accidents, such as the Chernobyl accident.

In the field of radioactive waste management the IAEA encompasses three elements:[19] committing to legally binding international agreements among States; establishing globally agreed waste safety standards; and providing for the application of those standards. *The Joint Convention on the Safety of Spent Fuel Management and on the Safety of Radioactive Waste Management (The Joint Convention)* adopted in 1997 was facilitated by the IAEA. International waste safety standards have been established with the active involvement of Member States. Radioactive Waste Safety Standards (RADWASS) were issued in the 1980s and the Principles of Radioactive Waste Management were issued in 1995; the latter formed the technical base for the Joint Convention. The IAEA strategy for the application of the RADWASS is focussed on:

- the systematic exchange of information;
- support and co-ordination of R&D;

---

[19] González, A.J. (2000), 'The Safety of Radioactive Waste Management. Achieving internationally acceptable solutions', *IAEA Bulletin*, Vol. 42, No. 3, pp 5-18. Vienna, Austria.

- promotion of education and training;
- providing co-operation and assistance programmes; and
- providing assistance to Member States.

IAEA waste safety standards[20] include the safety of disposal waste; dischargeable waste and residual waste. Waste technology standards include the handling, processing and storage of waste; waste disposal; technology and management aspects of decontamination and environmental restoration and technical co-operation. It can be seen that although the IAEA has little direct power in dictating policy relating to radioactive waste management, through its wealth of experience, expertise, standards and its global contact it has significant influence over national policies.

OECD-Nuclear Energy Agency

The OECD-NEA to achieve its goals, established the Radioactive Waste Management Committee (RWMC) as an international committee made up of senior representatives from regulatory authorities, radioactive waste management agencies and research and development institutions. The purpose of the committee is to foster international co-operation in the field of radioactive waste management among the OECD Member Countries. The main tasks of the RWMC are:

- to constitute a forum for the exchange of information and experience on waste management policies and practices in NEA Member countries;
- to develop a common understanding of the basic issues involved, and to promote the adoption of common philosophies of approach based on the discussion of the various possible waste management strategies and alternatives;
- to keep under review the state-of-the-art in the field of radioactive waste management at the technical and scientific level;
- to contribute to the dissemination of information in this field through the organisation of specialist meetings and publication of technical reports and consensus statements summarising the results of joint activities for the benefit of the international scientific community, competent authorities at national level and other audiences generally interested in the subject matter;
- to offer, upon request, a framework for the conduct of international peer review of national activities in the field of radioactive waste management, such as R&D programmes, safety assessments, specific regulations, etc.

As mentioned above the NEA through its committees and expert groups is actively co-operating with the ICRP in revising the system of radiological protection to make it more easily understandable and to involve stakeholders in authorisations where appropriate. On a biennial basis the Radiation and Radioactive Waste Management Division of the OECD-NEA prepares the NEA Nuclear Waste

---

[20] [www.iaea.org/ns/rasanet/standards/WASSAC.htm].

Bulletin.[21] The Bulletin gives concise information on current activities, policies and programmes in 18 NEA Member countries and three international organisations. It provides biennial updates of progress in the development of technologies for the management and disposal of radioactive waste and reports of the status of radioactive waste management in each country. The OECD, therefore, provides the facility for members to take the work of the IAEA together with their national efforts in the field of radioactive waste management to a forum of international deliberation.

Euratom

Euratom has a number of tasks including research into and development of the peaceful use of nuclear energy, the drawing up of uniform safety standards, the creation of a common market for nuclear energy equipment and an adequate supply of nuclear energy. It is also responsible for ensuring that nuclear materials are not used for unlawful purposes such as the production of nuclear weapons. The institutions common to the European Community, the Council, Commission, the European Parliament and the Supply Agency created by the *Euratom Treaty* are responsible for implementing the Treaty. Euratom plays an active role in international initiatives, having concluded many international agreements with third countries or international organisations, such as the International Atomic Energy Agency (IAEA) with the *Convention on Nuclear Safety*. The Euratom Safeguards Office, for its part, is responsible for ensuring that within the European Union nuclear materials are not diverted from their prescribed use and that the safeguards to be applied by the Community under an agreement with a third country or international organisation are observed.

The Euratom Supply Agency acts under the supervision of the European Commission, which issues directives to it, possesses a right of veto over its decisions and appoints the Director-General. Two fundamental objectives of the *Euratom Treaty* are to ensure the establishment of the basic installations necessary for the development of nuclear energy in the Community, and to ensure that all users in the Community receive a regular and equitable supply of ores and nuclear fuels. The Euratom Supply Agency, operative since 1960, is the body established by the *Euratom Treaty* to ensure this supply by means of a common supply policy based on the principle of equal access to sources of supply. It has legal personality and financial autonomy. The *Euratom Treaty* gives the Supply Agency the right of option to acquire ores, source materials and special fissile materials produced in the Community and an exclusive right to conclude contracts for the supply of such materials from inside the Community or from outside. In order to be valid under Community law, supply contracts must be submitted to the Supply Agency for conclusion. The Supply Agency and the Commission pursue the objective of long term security of supply through a reasonable diversification of supply sources and the avoidance of excessive dependency on any one supply source, and ensure that in a context of fair trade, the viability of the nuclear fuel cycle industry is

---

[21] OECD-NEA (2001), *Update on Waste Management Policies and Programmes* Nuclear Waste Bulletin No 14 – 2000 Edition, OECD Paris.

maintained. The broad lines of the policy were published in the Agency's Annual Report for 1997. The ECJ in the *KLE-Case* have confirmed its legality.[22]

In the 1950s, when the *Euratom Treaty* was drawn up, there was little concern about the wastes produced by the operation of nuclear power plants. Certainly no one foresaw that the management of radioactive waste would play such a crucial role in the future of the nuclear sector or in the energy/environment debate. Consequently, there is only a very limited reference to this subject in the Treaty. Nonetheless, the present Community activities grew out of the application of Chapter I of the Treaty (Promotion of Research) and to a lesser extent Chapter II (Dissemination of Information). Although these activities were carried out by DG XII (Research) and the JRC (Joint Research Centres) the priorities in the radioactive waste debate shifted from research to ones of implementation. As a result, DG XII became increasingly involved in aspects of policy and strategy as well as pure research. Eventually, in the early 1990s, the non-research activities were transferred to DG-Environment (then DG-XI), thus stressing the importance of principles of protection of man and the environment. More recently, following a re-organisation of the Commission's nuclear safety activities in late 2000, these activities are now located within DG-Energy & Transport (TREN), though these same overriding principles of protection of man and the environment remain at the forefront of the Commission's policies. DG-TREN retains responsibilities in the fields of radioactive waste management policy and nuclear installation safety. Radiation protection, for which there is an extensive Community 'acquis' under the *Euratom Treaty* and derived legislation, remains under the general responsibility of DG-Environment.

The activities of DG-TREN in the field of radioactive waste continued to be guided to a large extent by a legal basis, the Community Plan of Action in the Field of Radioactive Waste prepared many years earlier in DG XII[23] and by an Advisory Committee made up of experts nominated by the Member States that had been closely involved in DG XII's activities. However, the Plan of Action is now effectively at the end of its mandate and as described below, the Commission's services are currently preparing new policy initiatives in this field.

An integral part of the Commission's activities within the Community is setting up and encouraging co-operation, co-ordination and information exchange between the various bodies and organisations involved in radioactive waste management. Good contacts are maintained with the regulators and legislators, the waste management organisations, the nuclear industry, international bodies and non-governmental organisations. The Commission holds the chair of the Club of Agencies a high level group of European national radioactive waste management organisations and the secretariat of the Forum of Radioactive Waste Regulators an ad-hoc group of EU regulators involved in radioactive waste issues.

---

[22] *Kernkraftwerke Lippe-Ems GmbH v. E.C. Commission* [2000] 2 C.M.L.R. 489 ECJ (1st Chamber).
[23] Initially in 1980 and renewed on 15th Jun. 1992 by Council Resolution 92/C 158/02. A later Council Resolution dated 19th Dec. 1994 94/C 379/01 helped to define the Community strategy in this field.

The Commission's activities are also increasingly oriented towards the major problem areas of radioactive waste management. These include, in particular, the various issues related to geological disposal of high level or long-lived radioactive waste. Stimulating and raising the level of the debate on such topics as siting, safety cases, environmental impact assessments, public involvement, information and acceptance form an important part of the activities. Another key area of the activities concerns the policy related to decommissioning of nuclear installations and the management of the associated waste, destined to become increasingly important in the years ahead.

In the past the Commission has funded studies and projects on many aspects of radioactive waste management that have usually been carried out by external contractors. Topics covered include financing schemes for storage and disposal of radioactive waste, management of used radioactive sources, management of wastes from outside the nuclear sector with enhanced concentrations of natural radionuclides, the importance of environmental impact assessment and the production of a CD-ROM on the management of radioactive waste in the EU[24] together with an allied website. Official Commission documents in this field include the communication and fourth report from the Commission on the present situation[25] and the Commission recommendation on a classification system.[26] This recommendation is that:

- the Member States and their nuclear industry adopt a common classification scheme for national and international communications purposes;
- the scheme should be used for providing information on such waste to the public, national and international institutions and other interested organisations.

In November 2000 the Commission issued a green paper on energy[27] that stressed that a satisfactory solution for the waste issue has to be found with maximum transparency. The Commission's final report[28] indicates the requirement for precise deadlines for the introduction of more effective waste disposal systems at national level. This together with concerns about sustainable practices, the threat of terrorist action and encouraged by public opinion identified by an EU wide survey[29] caused to be issued, at the time of writing, a draft Directive on nuclear waste.[30] Priority is given in the draft to the geological burial of waste as the safest

---

[24] [www.europa.eu.int/comm/energy/nuclear/CDROM].

[25] COM (98) 799 [www.europa.eu.int/comm/environment/docum/98799sm.htm].

[26] SEC (1999) 1302 final, 1999/669/EC, Euratom; OJL324, 16/12/1999, p23.

[27] European Commission (2001), *Towards a European strategy for the security of energy supply*, COM (2000) 769, 29 Nov. 2000,Office for Official Publications of the European Communities.

[28] COM(2002) 321 final, 26 Jun. 2002.

[29] 2001 Europeans and Radioactive Waste Eurobarometer no. 56. [www.europa.int/comm/energy/nuclear/pdf/eb56_radwaste_en.pdf].

[30] Draft proposal for a Council Directive (Euratom) on the management of spent nuclear fuel and radioactive waste.

method of disposal known at present. A timetable is set by the draft directive for a decision on burial sites for high level waste by 2008 and to have the site operational by 2018. For low level waste disposal arrangements it is proposed that they must be ready by 2013. The different categories of solid radioactive waste are explained in the Commission Recommendation on a classification system.[31] The draft is fashioned on principles that ensure the protection of individuals, society and the environment from the harmful effects of ionising radiation underpinned by the *Basic Safety Standards for the protection of workers and the public*,[32] the Community system of supervision and control of international shipments of radioactive waste[33] and the environmental impact directive[34] and amendment.[35] The draft concludes that disposal in deep geological formations can isolate wastes from man and his environment for very long periods and is the best available option for long term management of many of the more hazardous forms of waste. Other forms of management of radioactive waste must also continue to be pursued such as the technologies for minimising the quantities. The Commission notes that Member States must be encouraged to continue to cooperate in common areas of research and technological development and proposes to the Council the setting up of a joint undertaking under *Chapter 5 of Title II of the European Treaty* to manage funds and organise the research in which industry and Member States would participate on a voluntary basis. While encouraging self-sufficiency of Member States the Commission also encourages collaboration between them and suggests that regional approaches and sharing of facilities might have advantages. It is noted in the draft Directive[36] that a crucial aspect of the programme towards implementation is open and comprehensive public information and involvement with respect for the 'Polluter Pays' principle.

It is expected that the Directive will become final by the end of 2003 and become law in Member States within a reasonable period following.[37] Within the EU the problems of different approaches to the management of radioactive waste and the different definitions of waste identified in chapter two of this book should become harmonised with the implementation of this Directive reinforced by the Commission's proposal to adhere to the terminology of the *Joint Convention*.[38] One such approach is the position regarding naturally occurring radioactive materials (NORM), which is tactfully dealt with in Article 3 of the draft by excluding it but leaving the option for it to be included by Member States. Nevertheless, a firm approach is demonstrated by the issue of a proposed Council Directive on the control of high activity sealed radioactive sources.[39]

---

[31] SEC(1999) 1302 final.
[32] Basic Safety Standards for the protection of workers and the public Council Directive 96/29/EURATOM of 13 May 1996.
[33] Council Directive 92/3/Euratom of 3 Feb. 1992.
[34] Council Directive 85/337/EEC of 27 Jun. 1985.
[35] Council Directive 97/11/EEC of 3 Mar. 1997.
[36] Explanatory Memorandum Para. 5 Conclusions p8.
[37] Draft Directive Article 9.1.
[38] COM(2001) 520 final, 15 Oct. 2001.
[39] COM (2003) 18 final, 24 Jan. 2003.

Environmental radioactivity surveillance is required under Articles 35-37 of the *Euratom Treaty* and while monitoring is still an important function, not least for the provision of information to the public, it is no longer predominantly concerned with health protection as the present state of the environment is quite different from that anticipated at the time of signing the Treaty.[40] Nuclear installations have managed to keep discharges of radioactivity so low as to cause non-trivial exposure of the population only for limited reference groups in the proximity of the installation the levels of radioactivity elsewhere, dominated by fallout from weapons testing of the 1960s and Chernobyl deposition of 1986, being not significant.[41]

Research programmes are a significant part of the EU activity. The 5th Framework programme in the field of nuclear energy [1998-2002] in the area of safety of the fuel cycle aims at developing a sound basis for policy choices on the management of spent fuel, radioactive waste and decommissioning. The research focuses on waste and spent fuel management and disposal, partitioning and transmutation and decommissioning of nuclear installations.[42]

Outside the Community, the Commission is involved in activities to alleviate the problems of radioactive waste management in the EU applicant countries of Central and Eastern Europe and in the New Independent States (NIS). This involvement stemmed partly from the Council resolution of 1992, which stated 'it is important to develop co-operation between the Community and third countries, in particular those of central and eastern Europe including the republics of the former Soviet Union, in the field of the management and storage of radioactive waste...' In very general terms, these activities had the overall objective of raising the level of safety of radioactive waste management in these regions towards the level in the EU. In the NIS, owing to the extent of the problems and the limited resources, activities were restricted to identifying and describing the problems and possibly pointing the way towards a solution. Nonetheless, the Commission's services in DG-Environment played an important role in publicising and raising the political profile of problems in a number of areas – especially in north-west Russia and around Chernobyl and Mayak. In the candidate countries, though the radioactive waste problems are not of the same magnitude as in the NIS, the level of safety is generally still below that in the EU. The activities in this region aim to build up further the safety culture, to establish the necessary contacts and generally to improve the radioactive waste management infrastructure, all in preparation for the accession of these countries to the EU.

---

[40] Janssens, A., Hornung-Lauxmann, and Hunter, G. (2002), 'Environmental radioactivity surveillance under the Euratom Treaty', *Nuclear Energy*, 41, No. 5, Oct. 339-346.
[41] For details see: Smith, J. (2002), 'Assessment of the radiological impact of routine discharges from EU nuclear sites', *The e-bulletin (Radiological Protection Bulletin)* No. 2 Dec. [www.nrpb.org/publications/bulletin/no2/article2.htm].
[42] See European Institutions press release IP/03/, Brussels 5 Feb. 2003.

National Policies

Of the selection of countries chosen here to demonstrate radioactive waste practices, policies and law three, the UK, France and Finland, are also members of the EU. It is therefore convenient to deal with them at this point immediately following the policy emanating from the international organisations and the EU. The policies of Korea and the USA will follow.

United Kingdom Government Policy

Sponsorship of the civil nuclear industry and accountability to Parliament for civil nuclear safety in Great Britain rests with the Secretary of State for Trade and Industry. Environment Ministers are accountable to Parliament for radioactive waste policy in England. Radioactive waste policy is devolved to the Scottish Executive and the Welsh Assembly Government (WAG). However, the Secretary of State for Trade and Industry remains accountable for the safe management of radioactive wastes kept or stored at licensed nuclear sites in England, Wales and Scotland. The Secretary of State for Work and Pensions is responsible for the sponsorship of the the the Health and Safety Commission (HSC) and the Health and Safety Executive (HSE), and accountable to Parliament for radiation protection matters as well as general health and safety at work issues throughout Great Britain. The Department of Health and the territorial health departments have general responsibility for public health. The Food Standards Agency (FSA) is a non-ministerial department, and is a statutory consultee to the Environment Agency (EA) and the Scottish Environment Agency (SEPA) on discharge authorisations. The FSA monitors radioactivity in food and holds the principal responsibility for any radioactivity in food in the UK.

The UK Government's review of radioactive waste management policy (the 1995 Review)[43] is framed within the context of international guidelines and regulations and identifies the ICRP, IAEA, OECD-NEA, Euratom, the *OSPAR Convention*, Sustainable Development and Agenda 21. The responsibility for radioactive waste management is shared between the Government, the regulators and the producers of waste with the Government being responsible for overall policy. The development of policy was set in motion in 1976 by the Flowers Report[44] and is currently shared in Government between the Department for Environment, Food and Rural Affairs, the National Assembly for Wales and the Scottish Executive. The HSC was set up by *HSWA74* as the overarching body that sets the policy framework for health and safety regulation. The HSC's duty is to: assist and encourage people to promote health and safety at work; make arrangements to carry out and publish research and provide training and information in connection with health and safety at work; ensure that people are kept informed of, and adequately advised on, matters relevant to health and safety

[43] Department of the Environment, (1995), *Review of Radioactive Waste Management Policy*, Final Conclusions, Cm 2919 July, HMSO London.
[44] Royal Commission on Environmental Pollution (1976), *Nuclear Power and the Environment*, Sixth Report, (Cmnd 6618) HMSO London.

at work; submit proposals for the making of regulations. The HSE is the second body set up by *HSWA74* and comprises three persons appointed by HSC with the approval of the Secretary of State. The Executive's duty is to enforce the relevant statutory provisions where it is the enforcing authority; to exercise on behalf of the HSC such of the HSC's functions as HSC directs; and to give effect to any directions given to it by HSC (except that HSC cannot give the Executive any directions as to enforcement in a particular case). Civil servants who are known collectively as the HSE assist the Executive. These civil servants include nuclear installation inspectors. HSE is responsible for enforcing legislation on health and safety at work and in particular, in relation to spent fuel and radioactive waste management, for the operation of the nuclear site-licensing regime. Within HSE, the responsibility for regulating the nuclear industry has been delegated to its Nuclear Safety Directorate (NSD), NSD includes HM Nuclear Installations Inspectorate (NII) and it is NII that carries out the licensing and day-to-day regulation of the nuclear industry. Licensing powers are delegated to HSE's Director of Nuclear Safety, who is also Her Majesty's Chief Inspector of Nuclear Installations. This delegated authority from the Executive gives the Chief Inspector the power to issue, add conditions to, and revoke nuclear site licenses.

The Government is advised by independent committees:

- The Radioactive Waste Management Advisory Committee (RWMAC) – an independent body of experts established in 1978 in response to a recommendation in the Flowers Report. The committee includes experts in nuclear, academic, medical, research and lay interests and is a source of independent advice on matters of civil radioactive waste management.[45] At the time of writing a new Committee on Radioactive Waste Management (CoRWM) is being formed.[46]
- The Advisory Committee on the Safety of Nuclear Installations (ACSNI) – set up in 1977 to advise the Health and Safety Commission (HSC) and Government on matters affecting the safety of nuclear installations. It has a Chairman, 12 members appointed by the HSC and nominated members from the Confederation of British Industry (CBI) and the Trades Union Congress (TUC).[47]
- The Ionising Radiations Advisory Committee (IRAC) – advises the HSC on matters concerning protection against exposure to ionising radiations. The Committee consists of 18 members from the TUC, CBI, Local Authorities, Government bodies and professional bodies with an interest in radiation protection.[48]

---

[45] [www.defra.gov.uk/rwmac].
[46] DEFRA News Release, 26 March 2003.
[47] [www.hse.gov/nsd].
[48] [www.hse.gov.uk/foi/openirac.htm].

- The National Radiological Protection Board (NRPB) – was created by the *Radiological Protection Act 1970* to give advice, to conduct research and to provide technical services in the field of ionising and non-ionising radiations.[49]
- The Committee on Medical Aspects of Radiation in the Environment (COMARE) – set up in 1985 with terms of reference to assess and advise government departments and devolved administrations on the health effects of natural and man made radiation in the environment and to assess the adequacy of the available data and the need for further research. Members of the committee are appointed by the Chief Medical Officer for their medical and scientific expertise from universities, research and medical institutes.[50]
- The Nuclear Safety Advisory Committee (NuSAC) – provides a technical forum in which nuclear safety issues and any proposals that might impact on nuclear safety can be considered in as open and independent a manner as possible. Its terms of reference are: to advise the HSC, and when appropriate Secretaries of State, on major issues affecting the safety of nuclear installations including design, siting, operation, maintenance and decommissioning which are referred to them or which they consider require attention; and to advise the HSC on the adequacy and balance of its nuclear safety research programme.

Regulation The Department for Work and Pensions (DWP) sponsors the HSE. However, the Secretary of State for Trade and Industry is answerable to Parliament for nuclear safety in England, Wales and Scotland. The HSE provides factual information to the Minister on matters of nuclear safety regulation, but the Minister is not responsible for HSE's nuclear regulatory actions. In addition, HSE maintains lines of communication with DEFRA, notably the Radioactive Substances Division, to ensure that the nuclear safety implications of environmental policy and vice versa are properly considered. The EA is sponsored by DEFRA and WAG. On radioactive waste matters it works closely with the Radioactive Substances Division of DEFRA, the Department of Health (DoH) and WAG. It also maintains lines of communication with Department of Trade and Industry (DTI). The Scottish Executive sponsors the SEPA. On radioactive waste matters it works closely with the Scottish Executive Environment and Rural Affairs Department, the Radioactive Substances Division of DEFRA and the DoH. It also maintains lines of communication with DTI. Concordats or Memorandums of Understanding (MOUs) exist between the regulators and the FSA. In addition, the FSA acts as statutory consultee to both EA and SEPA under *RSA93*. Regular liaison meetings take place between EA, SEPA and FSA. The DTI has a number of policy roles in respect of the nuclear industry. These include responsibility for energy policy generally (including the role of nuclear power), prescribing the activities that should be subject to the nuclear licensing regime, nuclear emergency planning, nuclear security and safeguards, international treaties and the *Convention on Nuclear Safety*, and the international nuclear liability regime. It is also responsible

---

[49] [www.nrpb.org.uk].
[50] [www.doh.gov.uk/comare/comare.htm].

for those parts of the UK civil nuclear industry still owned by the Government (this includes BNFL). In carrying out its responsibilities, DTI when appropriate, seeks technical factual information on safety related matters from HSE and advice on environmental issues from the environment agencies through DEFRA. HSE's independence as a regulator is ensured under *HSWA74*, where HSE is given direct responsibility for the enforcement of the nuclear safety regulatory system. The environment agencies are responsible, as appropriate, to DEFRA, WAG, the SE, or the Department of the Environment Northern Ireland (DOENI) to provide the environmental protection regulatory system.

The regulation of radioactive waste under *RSA93* is the responsibility of the EA and the SEPA. The management of radioactive waste on nuclear licensed sites is regulated by the NII. To avoid potential conflict of interest relating to the regulation of nuclear safety and radioactive waste and the disposal or discharge of radioactive waste from nuclear licensed sites the Director General of the HSE and the Chief Executive of the EA signed in July 2000 a memorandum of understanding on matters of mutual concern at nuclear sites licensed by the HSE in England and Wales;[51] it was updated in April 2002. Arrangements made between SEPA and HSE in March 2002 are fundamentally similar. The memorandum sets out the respective roles and responsibilities and how they will be co-ordinated to achieve the goals set. Ministry of Defence (MOD) sites are excluded from statutory regulation under *RSA93*; however, those sites operated by civilian contractors are subject to statutory regulation. The MOD's radioactive waste management practices are subject to periodic review by RWMAC. The nuclear industry that is the subject of regulation is considered in chapter four of this book.

In July 2003 the Government announced that Nirex was to become independent of industry. Since Nirex are not a licensed site nor are they authorised under the *RSA* there is no formal interface with either the NII or the EA, however, at the time of writing proposals are in hand to regularise the position.[52] Increasingly policy on the future of radioactive waste will be influenced by Nirex, overseen by RWMAC and as far as the plans for ILW by the CoRWM that is currently being formed.

Policy UK radioactive waste management policy reflects and is reflected in the IAEA's Safety Standard[53] and is described in the 1995 Review as follows:[54]

> 50. Radioactive waste management policy should be based on the same principles as apply more generally to environmental policy, and in particular on that of *sustainable development*. Most societies want to achieve economic development to secure higher standards of living, now and for future generations. They also seek to protect and enhance their environment, now and for their children. Sustainable development tries to reconcile these two objectives. A widely quoted definition of this concept is 'development that meets the needs of the present without compromising the ability of

---

[51] [www.hse.gov.uk/policy/memorand.htm].
[52] Newstead, S. (2003), *Developments in UK Regulation of Nuclear Wastes* ICEM03-4707, Oxford.
[53] IAEA, Establishing a National System for Radioactive Waste Management.
[54] Cm 2919 pp 14-15.

future generations to meet their own needs.' This principle is outlined at greater length in *Sustainable Development –the UK Strategy* (Cm 2426), which also sets out the following supporting principles: decisions should be based on the *best possible scientific information* and analysis of risks; where there is uncertainty and potentially serious risks exist, *precautionary* action may be necessary; ecological impacts must be considered, particularly where resources are *non-renewable* or effects may be *irreversible*; *cost implications* should be brought home directly to the people responsible-*the polluter pays principle*.

51. More specifically, and consistent with the above, radioactive wastes should be managed and disposed of in ways which protect the public, workforce and the environment. The radiation protection principles and criteria adopted in the UK and applied by the regulatory bodies are designed to ensure that there is no unacceptable risk associated with radioactive waste management. In defining these principles and criteria and in their application by the regulators, it is recognised that a point is reached where additional costs of further reductions in risk exceed the benefits arising from the improvements in safety achieved and that the level of safety, and the resources required to achieve it, should not be inconsistent with those accepted in other spheres of human activity.

52. Within the approach outlined in the foregoing two paragraphs: (1) the *Government* will maintain and continue to develop a policy and regulatory framework which will ensure that: (a) radioactive wastes are not unnecessarily created; (b) such wastes as are created are safely and appropriately managed and treated; (c) they are then safely disposed of at appropriate times and in appropriate ways; so as to safeguard the interests of existing and future generations and the wider environment, and in a manner that commands public confidence and takes due account of costs; (2) the *regulators*, including in future the Environment Agencies, have the duty to ensure that the framework described above is properly implemented in accordance with their statutory powers; (3) within that framework, the *producers and owners* of radioactive waste are responsible for developing their own waste management strategies, consulting the Government, regulatory bodies and disposal organisations as appropriate. They should ensure that: (a) they do not create waste management problems which cannot be resolved using current techniques or techniques which could be derived from current lines of development; (b) where it is practical and cost effective to do so, they characterise and segregate waste on the basis of physical and chemical properties and store it in accordance with the principles of passive safety (i.e. the waste is immobilised and the need for maintenance, monitoring or other human intervention is minimised) in order to facilitate safe management and disposal; (c) they undertake strategic planning, including the development of programmes for the disposal of waste accumulated at nuclear sites within an appropriate timescale and for the decommissioning of redundant plant and facilities. These programmes should be acceptable to the regulators and discussed with them in advance. The producers and owners of radioactive waste are responsible for bearing the costs of managing and disposing of the waste, including the costs of regulation and those of related research undertaken both by themselves and by the regulatory bodies. They should cost radioactive waste management and disposal liabilities before these are incurred and make appropriate financial provisions for meeting them. They should regularly review the adequacy of these provisions.

The nervousness expressed by the Government in the 1995 Review relating to site selection was justified in 1997 when the Secretary of State for the Environment upheld Cumbria County Council's refusal to grant Nirex Ltd planning permission for a Rock Characterisation Facility (RCF), an excavation to investigate the characteristics of the rock in the proposed location of a proposed deep disposal facility at Sellafield.

Following the rejection of Nirex's planning application, the House of Lords Select Committee on Science and Technology took evidence to January 1998 and released a report in March 1999.[55] The Report concluded, *inter alia*, that phased disposal in a deep repository is feasible and desirable, but the present policy is fragmented and that any future policy for nuclear waste will require public acceptance. It was recommended that a Nuclear Waste Management Commission be established charged with the development of a comprehensive strategy.

Nearly two and a half years later the Government responded by issuing a consultation document[56] that has in effect opened the subject of radioactive waste management to national debate. The paper proposes a plan of action:

- Stage 1 – to consider responses to the consultation and to plan the next stage. 2001-2002. This stage was partially completed by the issue in July 2002 of a summary document.[57]
- Stage 2 – research and public debate, to examine the different options and recommend the best option (or combination). 2002-2004.
- Stage 3 – further consultation seeking public views on the proposed option. 2005.
- Stage 4 – announcement of the chosen option, seeking public views on how this should be implemented. 2006.
- Stage 5 – legislation if needed. 2007.

The consultation is only for solid waste, it takes no account of liquid and atmospheric discharges. The paper does raise the question as to how spent fuel and plutonium should be treated as part of the waste management strategy.

In July 2002 a report was issued on the responses to the consultation that proposes a review of waste management options with a new independent body to oversee the review and to make recommendations on the options that achieve long-term protection for people and the environment.[58]

In its response to the consultation RWMAC commented that the management of solid waste is only one element in the UK's radioactive waste problem. A policy for the control of liquid and gaseous radioactive discharges and the clean up of radioactively contaminated land also needed to be brought to fruition. They

---

[55] House of Lords Select Committee on Science and Technology (1999), *Management of Nuclear Waste Report*, HL Paper 41, HMSO, London.
[56] DEFRA, the Scottish Executive and the Welsh Assembly (2001), *Managing Radioactive Waste Safely, proposals for developing a policy for managing solid radioactive waste in the UK*, Sept. DEFRA.
[57] DEFRA, the Scottish Executive and the Welsh Assembly (2002), Managing Radioactive Wastes Safely, summary of responses to the consultation, Sept. 2001 – Mar. 2002, July, DEFRA.
[58] DEFRA, Next steps on managing radioactive waste announced, 29 July 2002.

comment that there is a need for all these policy elements to fit together and be based on a clear and consistent set of principles applied uniformly to all sites (nuclear and non-nuclear) that manage radioactive waste. RWMAC cautioned the Government against changes to the planning system that might prejudice an open, staged approach.

The House of Lords Select Committee on Science and Technology made the point that since the terrorist attacks of the 11th September 2001 the question of storage above or below ground had been clarified by the event. It was now a clear priority to concentrate on the single realistic option of deep geological storage or disposal and to consider the removal of materials in existing surface stores to below ground locations. In July 2003 the Government announced that Nirex was to be made independent of industry.

It would appear therefore that the UK is set on a course with a timetable of events such that for solid high level radioactive waste a decision will be possible by 2007, within the target of 2008 set by the EU draft directive.

Radioactive Discharges In July 2002 the Government issued a strategy for radioactive discharges[59] that describes how the UK will implement the agreements reached at the 1998 Ministerial meeting, and subsequent meetings, of the OSPAR Commission with regard to radioactive substances. The strategy was limited to liquid discharges; aerial discharges will be addressed in future issues. Following a consultation process it was modified in some instances and in others the points were addressed in the text. A policy base has been set for future reviews of discharge authorisations and a strategic framework has been set for radioactive discharges from UK installations to 2020. The aims of the strategy are:

- the progressive and substantial reduction of radioactive discharges and discharge limits;
- progressive reduction of human exposure to ionising radiation arising from radioactive discharges such that a representative member of a critical group of the general public will be exposed to an estimated dose of no more than 0.02mSv/yr. from liquid discharges to the marine environment made from 2020 onward; and
- progressive reduction of concentrations of radionuclides in the marine environment resulting from radioactive discharges such that by 2020 they are close to zero.

The UK Government's view is that unnecessary introduction of radioactivity into the environment is undesirable, even at levels where the doses to human and non-human species are low and unlikely to cause harm. The Welsh Assembly issued guidance notes on the discharge of radioactivity for consultation in October 2002.[60]

---

[59] DEFRA (2002), *UK Strategy for radioactive discharges 2001-2020*, July [www.defra.gov.uk/environment/radioactivity/discharge/strategy/summary.htm].
[60] Statutory Guidance on the Regulation of Radioactive Discharges to the Environment [www.wales.gov.uk/subienvironment/topicindex-e.htm].

The adoption of environmental law principles is evident in the strategy's attention to the progressive reduction of discharge limits and discharges through the application of Best Practicable Means (BPM). It is also noted that it is anticipated that the established nuclear law principle of ALARP (As Low As Reasonably Practicable) will reduce discharges sufficiently to achieve the object of the OSPAR Strategy. The overall strategy is also guided by the environmental law principles of the 'polluter pays'[61] and the 'precautionary principle'.[62]

Contaminated Land and Other Liabilities According to RWMAC,[63] within the UK there are no formal Government policies or standards for remediation of radioactively contaminated land, either on or off nuclear sites. The outcome of the 1998 Government consultation has never been declared. Further, in their advice on the Ministry of Defence's arrangements for dealing with radioactively contaminated land,[64] RWMAC observed that the Government appears to be relying on the planning system to remediate the land to a standard appropriate to the proposed new use and conclude that it is not appropriate to do so. RWMAC note[65] that it is important to determine the precise implications of new or emerging EU Directives that could potentially affect the availability of disposal routes. These include the *Landfill Directive*[66] and the *Water Framework Directive*[67] in respect of landfill sites and the *Waste Incineration Directive*[68] and the *Landfill Directive* in relation to incineration facilities. Apart from nuclear sites there are sites that handled radioactive materials before 1963, the year that *RSA60* came into force, which include uranium mines, civilian and defence luminising works, medical applications of radium, electronic component manufacturing works, thorium/uranium metal processing, uranium munitions and armour manufacture, gas mantle production, the phosphate industry, mining, heavy mineral sand processing, gasworks, coal-fired power stations and landfill sites. The intention expressed in the 1998 consultation was to establish a control regime with powers provided by Part IIA of the *EPA90* inserted by the *Environment Act 1995*. In the absence of feedback on consultation, the solution to potential interfaces between the EA and Local Authorities and the treatment of pollution of controlled waters under the *Water Resources Act 1991 for* England and Wales and the *Control of Pollution Act 1974* for Scotland is unknown.

The lack of definition of remediation policies leads to speculation about future clean-up requirements and volumes of waste that could be generated and have to be managed. Without a full and integrated policy that deals with all radioactively

[61] *OSPAR Convention* Article 2 (a).
[62] European Council of Ministers Resolution, Nice, Dec. 2000.
[63] RWMAC (2003), *Advice to Ministers on Management of Low Activity Solid Radioactive Wastes within the UK*, March, DEFRA Publications.
[64] RWMAC, *Advice to Ministers on the MOD's Arrangements for Dealing with Radioactively Contaminated Land*, Annex 5.
[65] RWMAC 2003 para 12.
[66] 1999/31/EC.
[67] 2000/60/EC.
[68] 2000/76/EC.

contaminated areas there is, *in extremis*, significant risk that lightly contaminated materials may be excavated, treated and moved from one location only to create a similarly contaminated area in another location. The *status quo* on licensed sites is that contamination is governed by conditions in the site licence or by improvement notices under the *HSWA74* and the *IRR98*. Contamination entering the ground water or being released would be governed by an authorisation under *RSA93*. Accidental release off site would be treated as a breach of the authorisation. The risk of setting precedents or inconsistent decisions for non-nuclear sites is apparent.

RWMAC has called for the management regime to be predicated on appropriate risk-based criteria,[69] taking account of accepted principles of radiological protection. It has also commented on the existing system of RSA93 EOs[70] and recommended that it be placed on a 'properly rationalised, sound, scientific and easily operable basis'.[71] In particular RWMAC see a need for rational and transparent clarification of how the set of EOs would apply to policy on and standards for, facility decommissioning and site clean-up activities, including the use of particular disposal routes, recycling and free release. The outcome of policy in this area will significantly affect estimated levels of LLW and VLLW arisings. In the case of some facilities holding back decommissioning final stages by 100 years after shutdown could halve the estimates of LLW that will need to be managed. Similarly the standards of remediation of contaminated land will affect estimated quantities of waste to be managed.

The Environment Agency made public its guidance on the characterisation and remediation of radioactively contaminated land in May 2002 even though, according to RWMAC, it is of limited value since there is no Government policy in the area of contaminated land.[72] Contaminated land is only one of the elements of the management of historic liabilities for which the Government has proposed remedial action.[73] The *Energy Act 2004* to restructure the nuclear industry[74] was issued in July 2004, it included for a Nuclear Decommissioning Authority to manage the facilities that will remain Government responsibility.

It can be seen from this review of the influences on UK radioactive waste policy that, at the time of writing and probably at the time of publication, policy is in a state of flux. Updating the 1995 Review will only be possible when legislation setting up both the Waste Management Authority and the Nuclear Decommissioning Authority is effective.

---

[69] RWMAC 2000 para 4.27.

[70] Exemption Orders under SoLA (Substances of Low Activity Order).

[71] RWMAC 2000 para 4.28.

[72] RWMAC (2000), *Problems of Small Users of Radioactive Materials*, Annual Report Sept. DETR.

[73] DTI (2002), *Managing the Nuclear Legacy: A strategy for action*, White Paper Cm 5552, July, HMSO.

[74] The *Draft Nuclear Sites and Radioactive Substances Bill* became law as *The Energy Act 2004* following intense debate in Parliament and modification, including measures for the development of renewable energy, in July 2004 .

France

The pressure of French public opinion in the late 1980s caused a reassessment of the plans for the disposal of radioactive waste resulting in public hearings and a firm policy in 1991 backed by an Act of Parliament.[75] This allowed the continuation of existing practice of storing the short-term and medium-term high level and long-lived radioactive waste, after conditioning, in specially designed buildings on site pending a long-term solution. The *Act* also defined a programme of research into the long-term management of high level and long-lived radioactive waste and establishes a national radioactive waste management agency, ANDRA, publicly owned under the Ministers of Environment, Research and Industry.[76] The decree identifies three research areas:[77]

- Area 1 – research into the separation and transmutation of radioactive waste. This will be undertaken by the French Atomic Energy Commission (CEA);
- Area 2 – feasibility studies into retrievable and non-retrievable disposal in deep geological formations by ANDRA; and
- Area 3 – studies relating to waste conditioning and long-term storage by CEA.

ANDRA is charged with reporting in time to allow the Government to take a decision on the chosen repository by 2006 following evaluation by a national commission that includes at least two international experts.

The legislation provides for the establishment of an underground laboratory for the purposes of research,[78] however, commencement of the project in granite is subject to the opinion of an Evaluation Committee on a report from a mission of three people designated by the Ministry of Economy, Finance and Industry and the Secretary of State for Industry. The mission will initiate consultations with elected representatives, associations and the public.[79] The decree implements the creation of a local information and monitoring committee and authorises ANDRA to install and operate an underground laboratory in clay on the territory of the commune of Burse (Meuse). It was reported in September 2003 that ANDRA had not been able to establish a facility in granite and in order to meet the timetable was relying on information from experience in Sweden, Switzerland and Canada where underground rock characterisation facilities exist.[80]

---

[75] *Law 91-1381 of December 30, 1991* relating to research on the management of radioactive waste, known as '*loi Bataille*' after its originator.
[76] ibid Article 13.
[77] ibid Article 4.
[78] ibid Article 6.
[79] *Decree 99-686 of 3rd August 1999* to implement Article 6 of the Act of 30 December 1991 relating to research on radioactive waste management (1999).
[80] Tarbourini, Jaques presenting a paper on behalf of ANDRA by Mouroux, B. et al (2003), *The Disposal of HLL Waste in a Granitic Formation: The Status of Research in France*, ICEM03-4818, Oxford.

The management of the disposal of low and intermediate level waste at the Aube Center in Soulaines-Dhuys is by ANDRA. The importation of foreign waste is prohibited, however this does not apply to the import of spent fuel for reprocessing as the waste produced must be re-exported with the reprocessed fuel. ANDRA is charged with the annual production of a report detailing the state and location of all radioactive waste on French territory.[81] The Government has additionally asked ANDRA to study the management options for very low level waste.

Regulation The regulation of radioactive waste facilities is subject to the supervision of the Office of Nuclear Safety (ASN)[82] and the Institute for Radiation Protection and Nuclear Safety (IRSN).[83] The ASN is responsible to Ministers in charge of the Environment, Industry and Health for the regulation of nuclear safety and radiological protection of workers, the public and the environment against risks in the field of nuclear and radiological activities including radioactive waste management. The *Law on Environmental Health and Safety* created the IRSN[84] by the merger of the Institute for Protection and Safety (IPSN) and the Office of Radiological Protection (OPRI) and made it responsible to the Ministers of Defence, Environment, Industry, Research and Health. The IRSN has no regulatory responsibility but is responsible for research into risk in the field of ionising radiation in industry, medicine and from naturally occurring radiation in the areas of: the safety of nuclear installations and defence establishments; safety of the transport of radioactive materials; protection of man and the environment against ionising radiations; the control of nuclear weapons materials and the protection of installations and transport against theft and misuse of materials and sabotage.

This division of responsibilities keeping regulation separate from the technical aspects ensures a degree of transparency in the control of nuclear facilities and ionising radiations. It is interesting to note that there is no mention in the French documents of the ICRP, the French appearing to rely only on IAEA guidance.

Radioactive discharges The release of liquid and gaseous effluent and water samples from major nuclear establishments are subject to individual authorising orders and must include as a minimum general requirements which concern:[85]

- limits and technical requirements applicable to water samples and liquid and gaseous releases;
- the means of analysis, measurement and control of authorised activities, as well as the supervision of their effects on the environment;

---

[81] 9th edition of the Observatory Report, 20 Nov. 2002.

[82] [www.asn.gov.fr].

[83] [www.irsn.gov.fr].

[84] *La Loi sur l'AFSSE (Agence Française de Sécurité Saintaire Environmental).*

[85] Order setting out General Technical Rules on the Limits and Conditions governing Samples and Waste subject to Licensing, carried out by Major Nuclear Installations (1999).

- controls carried out by the Board for Protection against Ionising Radiation and State services;
- provision of information to the public.

It appears that the French arrangements are such that they will meet the requirements of the draft EU Directive given public acceptance of the solution and no serious problems with the chosen site for the final disposal facility.

Finland

Nuclear power facilities in Finland are of Russian design and while the licensed operators are responsible for the care of radioactive waste, stored at the operating power plant as described in chapter two, until 1996 spent fuel was returned to Russia. However, that was changed by the *Amended Nuclear Energy Act*[86] that stipulated that spent fuel generated in Finland be handled there. An expert organization, Posiva Oy, owned by the nuclear power operating companies, 60 percent Teollisuuden Voima Oy (TVO) and 40 percent Fortum Power and Heat, was formed for the task. Posiva is responsible for the characterization and later for the construction and operation of sites for the final disposal of spent fuel.

Regulation of the use of nuclear energy in Finland is based on the *Nuclear Energy Act* and the *Radiation Act*.[87] The Radiation and Nuclear Safety Authority of Finland (STUK) sets safety requirements and verifies compliance with them. In the field of nuclear waste STUK assesses the content, quality and comprehensiveness of the plans, research and development work concerning waste management, including final disposal, with the objective of permanently isolating nuclear waste from the biosphere. The use of ionizing radiation is licensed by STUK in accordance with the *Radiation Act* and includes safety requirements assessment, advance inspection of plans, approvals, licences, statements, inspections, radiation dose monitoring and reports. Underpinning the regulatory process is a broad foundation of research into the levels of radiation, the effects of radiation and the prevention of hazards caused by radiation. The effectiveness of STUK in this field has been positively evaluated by the IAEA following their inspections in 2000. In accordance with the *Nuclear Energy Act* the input of STUK is decisive in government decision making in matters relating to nuclear energy.

An application was made to the Government in May 1999 for a decision to allow Posiva to proceed with the final disposal project for spent nuclear fuel and to construct an underground rock characterization facility at Olkiluoto in the municipality of Eurajoki. After considering this application, the Government made a favourable policy decision to construct the facility on the basis that the prerequisites for the decision had been met, the preliminary safety assessment of STUK supported the project and the municipality of Eurajoki were in favour of the

---

[86] *Nuclear Energy Act (990/87)* issued on December 11, 1987, Section 6a, 29 Dec. 1994/1420.
[87] *Radiation Act (592/91)*.

decision. To achieve this situation a series of public hearings were held as prescribed by the *Nuclear Energy Act* and a clear majority of the people of Eurajoki was seen to be willing to accept the building of the final disposal facility at Olkiluoto. A nationwide poll was also conducted and 92 percent of Finnish adults supported the disposal of nuclear waste in Finland, with 78 percent in support of the application for a policy decision to continue with preparations for the final disposal facility in Eurajoki. The municipal council voted 20 to 7 in support of proceeding with the project. The Government voted 10 to 6 in support of the project and in accordance with the *Act*, the Finnish Parliament ratified the decision as being in accordance with the overall interests of Finnish society. In the preliminary debate the matter was subject to eight parliamentary committees; the committees heard over 100 experts representing interest groups, trade unions, industrial stakeholders, community, scientific and non-government organizations. On a free vote on ratification or rejection Parliament voted 107 against 92 in favour of ratification.

The democratic process proceeds throughout the project. Citizens have the opportunity to express their opinions on the alternatives and environmental impact as detailed in the environmental impact assessment required by law and the planning implications contained in the regional plan, master plan and local or town plan. Further decisions will be required throughout the project; according to the *Law on Nuclear Energy*,[88] the Council of State must invite the councils of the proposed and neighbouring municipalities, the representatives of regional and central government to submit their statements on the project. A construction permit, later an operating licence and transport permits for radioactive materials will be required.

Korea

Occupation of the Korean peninsula by the Japanese in 1913, after over 1000 years of united Korean rule over a country extending to the Chinese/Manchurian border, ended in 1945 and was replaced by an ideological struggle between the forces of communism and liberalism. The struggle was halted by the stark reality of geographical and ethnic division following the suspension of armed conflict that at one time teetered on the brink of world war and the use of nuclear weapons. Since 1953 the peninsula has been divided, north and south at approximately latitude 38 degrees north (38th parallel), with the nations of the Democratic Peoples Republic of Korea (DPRK) on the northern side and the Republic of Korea (ROK) to the south. Difficult though it is to believe of a homogeneous people, there has been no contact other than by clandestine incursion and the occasional skirmish for nearly fifty years when moves towards opening the border were made in 1994 following initiatives arising from agreement concerning nuclear materials. Since 1953 the northern nation has followed totalitarian, communist principles under the

---

[88] *Nuclear Energy Decree (161/1988)* issued on 12 Feb. 1988 as amended by decrees of 26 Mar. 1993 (278), 25 Aug. 1994 (794), 16 Jun. 1995 (881), 20 Jun. 1996 (473), and 20 Dec. 1996.

leadership of a dynasty lead in the first place by the national hero in the struggle against Japanese occupation, Kim Il Sung, and after his death in 1994, his son Kim Jong Il.[89] The southern nation has followed an Asian version of the western model of democracy. International nuclear power politics has been a predominant factor in the separate development of the Korean nations and at the time of writing in early 2003 is probably the world's second most important political issue with the possible extreme outcomes of, on the one hand, a resumption of the suspended conflict and on the other an opening to peaceful cooperation with the possibility of reunification of the Korean peninsula.

Democratic Peoples Republic of Korea (DPRK)

Following the suspension of armed conflict in 1953 the regime in the north under the leadership of Kim Il Sung was supported by the USSR and to a lesser extent by China. Electrical power requirements were met by coal fired and hydroelectric power stations which had previously provided the requirements of the whole peninsula; the south existed following partition in 1953 with electrical power supplied from US warships docked in the southern city of Busan. The availability of adequate power supplies and the comfort that the defence of the north was underwritten by the USSR gave no apparent need for the development of nuclear energy and the north concentrated on building a strong military force using conventional weapons trained on the south. Until the late 1970s the north was seen as the hawk to the southern dove; a strong conventional army with plentiful supplies from its communist benefactors and with weapons stationed at the 38th parallel only 30 km from the southern capital, Seoul. Only the presence of a 40,000 strong UN force in the south, predominantly US manned, and the restraining hand of the USSR fearing nuclear conflict prevented a resumption of war. Political changes in the USSR in the late 1980s caused support for the DPRK to become less secure and this coupled with the success of the south in its industrial expansion, by then underwritten by adequate electrical power with a significant nuclear content, lead to the identification of nuclear ambitions in the north. The nuclear aspirations of the southern leader,[90] Park Chung Hee democratically elected but by questionable methods, also became obvious in the mid 1970s and could be seen by the north as potentially threatening.

The nuclear activities of the north first came to the surface in 1977 with the signature of an agreement with the IAEA[91] that allowed the monitoring by IAEA inspectors of a Russian supplied 2MW research reactor and a 0.1 MW critical assembly at Nyongbyong.[92] The Non-Proliferation Treaty (NPT) was signed by the DPRK on 12 December 1985 and in May 1988 the IAEA commenced

[89] Goodman, P. S. (2003), 'Brinkmanship:A Family Trait', *Washington Post Foreign Service*, 6 Jan. [www.washingtonpost.com].
[90] Associated Press (2003), 'S. Korea Once Tried to Build Nuclear Arms', *New York Times*, 3 Jan.
[91] INFCIRC/66 type Safeguards Agreement, INFCIRC/252.
[92] Bermudez, J. S. (1991), James Intelligence Review, Sept., p 406.

inspection of the 2MW reactor. A safeguards agreement in compliance with the NPT was ratified in 1992.[93] After protracted and sometimes erratic progress[94] the extent of the nuclear programme in the DPRK was revealed and following a meeting between Kim Il Sung and President Carter of the US, agreement was reached that was endorsed by the UN Security Council on 4 Nov. 1994 to allow IAEA inspection of all the declared nuclear sites that included the 2MW research facilities, a 5MW gas-graphite reactor, a 50MW and 200MW gas-graphite reactor under construction, two reprocessing lines and two nuclear waste facilities. Coupled with this was the agreement by the US to help replace the gas-graphite reactors with two 1000 MW light water reactors (LWRs), the supply of 5000,000 tons per year of heavy oil fuel to make up for the reduced supplies from Russia following the break-up of the USSR and a nuclear weapons free zone in the Korean peninsula. The DPRK was to remain in the NPT and was to allow the implementation by the IAEA of an NPT safeguards agreement.

The safeguards agreement was implemented and construction of the gas-graphite reactors ceased but problems that included limiting access of inspectors to examine radioactive waste lead to the suspicion that materials were being diverted for secret reprocessing. Progress in the construction of the LWRs was delayed, fuel oil deliveries were delayed and in 2002 the US identified the DPRK as a 'rogue state'. At the time of writing, January 2003,[95] the inspections of the nuclear facilities have been suspended and the DPRK has acknowledged that it has a programme to enrich uranium for nuclear weapons in breach of the NPT, the Agreement with the US, the Safeguards Agreement and the joint north/south declaration on the demilitarization of the Korean peninsula. The DPRK announced its withdrawal from the NPT effective from 11 January 2003. Since that time to July 2003, the Republic of Korea and the US have made diplomatic advances and further threats have been made on both sides; the continuation of the LWR project is in doubt and the DPRK is proceeding to produce weapon grade materials.

Republic of Korea (ROK)

At the time of suspension of the north/south conflict in 1953 the Republic of Korea (ROK) had virtually no electrical power capacity as the main sources of electrical power were located north of the 38th parallel. Imported coal, oil and LNG fuelled the first generation of power stations built with US and European assistance. Education and research into nuclear energy was commenced in 1964 with a low power TRIGA reactor. In 1971 construction of the first commercial nuclear power station was started with a 600MW pressurized water reactor and by 2001, 16 power

---

[93] INFCIRC/403 NPT Safeguards Agreement, 10 Apr. 1992.

[94] For details see [www.iaea.org/worldatom].

[95] For a detailed chronology of events from 1985 see: Reuters Newsdesk (2003), 'Nuclear diplomacy on North Korea since 1985', 7 Jan., Reuters Foundation [www.alertnet.org/thenews/newsdesk/SEO142891].

reactors were in operation with 4 under construction and 4 planned to start construction by 2003.[96]

The Atomic Energy Commission (AEC) is the decision making body on policy and the utilization of nuclear energy; it is composed of members of government, academia and industry and is chaired by the Prime Minister. Research and development and regulatory and licensing activities are the responsibility of the Ministry of Science and Technology (MOST). The construction and operation of nuclear power stations, the supply of nuclear fuel and the management of low and intermediate radioactive waste is the responsibility of the Ministry of Commerce and Industry (MOCIE).[97] Within MOST are the Nuclear Safety Commission (NSC), the Korea Institute of Nuclear Safety (KINS)[98] and the Korea Atomic Energy Research Institute (KAERI),[99] which in turn includes the Technology Centre for Nuclear Control, the Training Centre and the Cancer Centre Hospital. Professional and business societies include the Korea Atomic Industrial Forum,[100] the Korea Radioisotope Association,[101] the Korea Society for Non-destructive Testing, the Korea Society for Nuclear Medicine[102] and the Korea Nuclear Energy Foundation.[103]

Nuclear Energy Policy has four primary objectives: firstly to enhance the stability in energy supply by promoting nuclear energy as a major source of domestic electricity generation; secondly to achieve self-reliance in a nuclear reactor and proliferation-resistant nuclear fuel cycle technology through comprehensive and systematic nuclear energy research and development; thirdly to foster nuclear energy as a strategic export industry by securing international competitiveness through the advancement of atomic energy technology, on the basis of active participation and initiatives of the civil sector and fourthly to play a leading role in the improvement of human welfare and the advancement of science and technology by expanding the use of atomic energy technology in agriculture, engineering, medicine, and industry, and by enacting basic research of nuclear technology.

In order to achieve the objectives of the long-term nuclear energy policy, the Government established a legal basis in January 1995 to formulate the Comprehensive Nuclear Energy Promotion Plan (CNEPP) every five years through the amendment to the *Atomic Energy Act*. The CNEPP includes long-term nuclear policy objectives, basic directions, sector-by-sector objectives and a budget and investment plan. The *Atomic Energy Act* stipulates that the Minister of Science and Technology and the heads of the concerned Ministries shall formulate sector-

---

[96] For details see chapter two and Korea Ministry of Science and Technology (MOST) [www.most.go.kr].
[97] [www.mocie.go.kr].
[98] [www.kins.re.kr].
[99] [www.kaeri.re.kr].
[100] [www.kaif.or.kr].
[101] [www.ri.or.kr].
[102] [www.ksnm.or.kr].
[103] [www.okaea.or.kr].

by-sector implementation plans for those areas under their jurisdiction every five years in accordance with the CNEPP and shall establish and implement annual action plans according to the sector-by-sector implementation plans. The first CNEPP was formulated in June 1997 and as of July 2001 the Government has formulated the second CNEPP which includes an implementation plan for five years from 2002 to 2006, and a direction to nuclear energy policy towards the year of 2015. Included in the 10 promotion areas of the CNEPP is Radioactive Waste Management. After transfer of responsibility for radioactive waste management from the MOST to MOCIE in January 1997, a new radioactive management plan was proposed by MOCIE and approved by the AEC in September 1998. According to the new plan, a low- and intermediate level radioactive waste (LILW) repository will be constructed by 2008 and spent fuels will be stored at each nuclear power plant site until interim storage facilities are constructed in 2016. Site selection and notice to the public is planned to be completed by 2003, and land purchasing by 2005.

United States of America (US)

Radioactive materials including radioactive waste are regulated in the US under the *Nuclear Waste Policy Act*[104] by Federal Agencies, the Nuclear Regulatory Commission and States. The Department of Energy (DOE) is responsible for the development of permanent disposal capacity for spent fuel and other high level radioactive waste[105] including radioactive waste relating to nuclear weapons production and certain research facilities. The Environmental Protection Agency (EPA) is responsible, *inter alia*, for developing environmental protection standards to evaluate the safety of a geologic repository.[106] The EPA also has responsibilities for ensuring standards of air and water. The Nuclear Regulatory Commission (NRC) is an independent agency established by the *Energy Reorganisation Act* of 1974 which assigned the regulatory work to the NRC but does not include the regulation of defence facilities. The NRC's mission is to regulate the US civilian use of radioactive materials, to ensure adequate protection of public health and safety, to promote the common defence and security and to protect the environment. This covers three main areas: reactors; *Atomic Energy Act* materials and radioactive waste. Regulation includes the development of regulations to implement the EPA safety standards and licensing, transportation, storage and disposal of nuclear materials and waste, and decommissioning of nuclear facilities. The Centre assists the NRC for Nuclear Waste Regulatory Analyses (CNWRA) that is federally funded and was established in 1987 to resolve technical and regulatory issues related to a geologic repository for high level nuclear waste.

Individual States usually regulate sources of radiation not covered by the NRC but some States have agreements with the NRC to regulate some radioactive

---

[104] Nuclear Waste Policy Act of 1982, as amended by Public Law 97-425, 96 Stat. 2201, 7 Jan. 1983.
[105] [www.ymp.gov/].
[106] [www.epa.gov/radiation/yucca].

materials within their borders.   Under the *Atomic Energy Act*[107] the NRC is permitted to make agreements with States to turn over regulatory authority for radioactive materials to the State; a State that has signed an Agreement with the NRC under which the State regulates the use of byproduct, source and small quantities of special nuclear material within that State is called an 'Agreement State'. Usually Agreement States regulate all sources of radiation except reactors and large quantities of special material. Currently 32 States have Agreements.[108] Certain locations within Agreement States may be subject to exclusive federal jurisdiction where NRC retains regulatory authority over Atomic Energy Act Materials. These areas include protected areas of nuclear reactors, most American Indian reservations and certain areas on military bases. The NRC and the States have a programme for the regulation of *Atomic Energy Act* materials through which the NRC provides technical support to the State and maintains a database of regulatory information. Communications between the NRC and Agreement States is facilitated by the Organisation of Agreement States and the Conference of Radiation Control Programme Directors.

The NRC's regulatory powers may be summarized under five main heads:

- developing regulations and guidance for applicants and licensees;
- licensing or certifying applicants to use nuclear materials or operate nuclear facilities;
- overseeing licensed operations and facilities to ensure that licensees comply with safety requirements;
- evaluating operating experience at licensed facilities or involving licensed activities;
- conducting research, holding hearings to address the concerns of parties affected by agency decisions and obtaining independent reviews to support regulatory decisions.

Radioactive Materials   The use of regulated materials under the *Atomic Energy Act of 1954*, AEA Materials, includes Special Nuclear Material (SNM), Source Material and Byproduct Material. SNM is defined by Title 1 of the *Act* as plutonium, uranium-233 or uranium enriched in the isotopes uranium-233 or uranium-235 (fissile material). These isotopes do not occur naturally but can be formed in nuclear reactors and extracted chemically. The NRC regulates two gaseous diffusion enrichment plants operated by the US Enrichment Corporation. No commercial plutonium reprocessing plant is currently licensed by the NRC for operation. SNM is only mildly radioactive but it includes fissile material that in concentrated form are the primary materials of an atomic bomb. In concentrated quantities these materials are defined as 'strategic special nuclear materials' (SSNM). The NRC regulates the peaceful use of SNM through licensing and oversight of licensed operations.

---

[107] *Atomic Energy Act of 1954* as Amended in (NUREG-0980).
[108] [www.hsrd.ornl.gov/nrc/rulemaking.html] for details of State regulations and legislation.

Source Material is either the element uranium that has not been enriched or the element thorium that can result from the milling and concentration of uranium from ore, or generated in the process of refining ores mined for other elements. Source Material can also arise in the reprocessing of spent nuclear fuel, although no commercial reprocessing is currently licensed in the US, and as depleted uranium which contains lower amounts of uranium-235 following extraction for enrichment. The NRC regulates the use of source material through licensing and oversight of licensed operations. Currently at January 2003 the source material regulations are undergoing revision to make them more risk informed. The NRC operates a collaborative rulemaking forum, RuleForum, in a Web environment to allow public comment.[109] [110]

Byproduct Material[111] is radioactive material, except special nuclear material, produced or made radioactive by exposure to radiation in the process of producing or using special nuclear material, examples being materials with self luminous properties and materials used in medical procedures. Byproduct material is regulated by the NRC under 10CFR Part 30; certain quantities and concentrations are exempted from regulation. Byproduct material is also waste and tailings, generated in the process of extracting uranium and thorium from the ore,[112] and is regulated by the NRC under 10CFR Part 40. States with Agreement State status can retain authority over byproduct material.

Waste Disposal Three low level waste disposal facilities are operating in the US: Barnwell in South Carolina, licensed by the State to accept class A, B and C waste from all US generators except those in Rocky Mountain and Northwest compacts; Hanford in Washington State licensed by the State to accept class A, B and C waste from Rocky Mountain and Northwest States and Envirocare in Utah, licensed by the State to accept class A waste, which generally contains lower concentrations of long lived half-life radioactive material than class B and C wastes, from all regions of the US.

Policies governing the permanent disposal of high level radioactive waste are defined in the *Nuclear Waste Policy Act* that specifies the disposal of high level waste to be underground in a deep geologic repository and that Yucca Mountain, Nevada as the single candidate for characterization as a potential repository. The legality of this *Act* has been challenged in the Courts as will be seen in chapter five.

Spent Fuel Most spent fuel is stored in specially designed pools[113] at the individual reactor sites. If pool capacity is reached, storage may be moved to above ground

---

[109] NRC regulations may be found in Title 10, Energy, of the Code of Federal Regulations (CFR) Chapter 1, Parts 0-199.

[110] [www.ruleforum.llhl.gov/].

[111] *Atomic Energy Act as Amended* 1978 Section 11e(1).

[112] ibid Section 11e(2).

[113] [www.nrc.gov/waste/spent-fuel-storage/pools.html].

dry storage casks.[114]   Within the US each year about 3 million packages of radioactive materials are shipped. Regulating the safety of these shipments is the joint responsibility of the NRC and the Department of Transport (DOT).[115] Within the DOT the office of Hazardous Materials Safety[116] is responsible for coordinating a national safety programme for the transport of hazardous materials by air, rail, highway and water.

Legacy Waste Legacy waste is the term given to transuranic waste (TRU) created in the nuclear research programme, the weapons production and test programme and the decommissioning of facilities associated with those programmes. The DOE is committed to honouring the federal government's obligation to clean up legacy waste and is in the process of moving waste from 27 sites located throughout the US to the Waste Isolation Pilot Plant in New Mexico. The details of the plans for the complete disposal of legacy waste are described in the national TRU waste management plan.[117]   The EPA inspects and audits the TRU waste sites; the status of inspections is notified to the DOE by letter.[118]

Decommissioning Decommissioning is defined as the removal of a facility or site from service and reduction of residual reactivity to a level that permits the release of property for unrestricted or restricted use and termination of the licence. Most of the 300 licences that are terminated each year are routine and require little, if any, remediation.   More complex decommissioning activities are required for nuclear licensed sites.

Interaction between Nuclear Regulation and Environmental Protection[119]

Both the NRC and the EPA have commitments to protect public health and safety and the environment and in order to establish a basic framework for the relationship of the agencies in the decommissioning and decontamination of licensed sites they entered into a memorandum of understanding (MOU). The MOU identifies the interactions and principles relating to the operations of the two agencies when the EPA is operating under the *Comprehensive Evaluation Response, Compensation and Liability Act (CERCLA)* and the NRC licensed sites undergoing decommissioning.

Interstate Compacts

The *Low Level Radioactive Waste Policy Act*[120] provides for and encourages States to develop compacts for jointly managing radioactive wastes. It is recognized that

---

[114] [www.nrc.gov/waste/spent-fuel-storage/dry-cask-storage.html].

[115] [www.nrc.gov/materials/transportation.html].

[116] [www.hazmat.dot.gov/].

[117] US DOE (2002), *The National Waste Management Plan*, Rev 3, August, Carlsbad Field Office (CBFO).

[118] TRU Sites Approval Status [www.epa.gov/radiation/wipp/status.htm].

[119] [www.nrc.gov/reading-rm/doc-collections/news/2002/mov2fin.pdf].

[120] *Low level Radioactive Waste Policy Act* Title 42 U.S.C. sec. 2021.

the management of low level radioactive waste is handled more efficiently on a regional basis. As an example, the State of Illinois and the Commonwealth of Kentucky entered into such a compact[121] an extract for illustration being as follows:

> (a) It is the policy of the party states to enter into a regional low level radioactive waste management compact for the purpose of: (1) Providing the instrument and framework for a cooperative effort; (2) Providing sufficient facilities for the proper management of low level radioactive waste generated in the region; (3) Protecting the health and safety of the citizens of the region; (4) Limiting the number of facilities required to manage low level radioactive waste generated in the region effectively and efficiently; (5) Promoting the volume and source reduction of low level radioactive waste generated in the region; (6) Distributing the costs, benefits and obligations of successful low level radioactive waste management equitably among the party states and among generators and other persons who use regional facilities to manage their waste; (7) Ensuring the ecological and economical management of low level radioactive waste, including the prohibition of shallow-land burial of waste; and (8) Promoting the use of above-ground facilities and other disposal technologies providing greater and safer confinement of low level radioactive waste than shallow-land burial facilities. (b) Implicit in the congressional consent to this compact is the expectation by the Congress and the party states that the appropriate federal agencies will actively assist the compact commission and the individual party states to this compact by: (1) Expeditious enforcement of federal rules, regulations and laws; (2) Imposition of sanctions against those found to be in violation of federal rules, regulations and laws; and (3) Timely inspection of their licensees to determine their compliance with these rules, regulations and laws.

Although only three operating low level radioactive waste facilities exist at this time, most of the US States have entered into arrangements which as of January 2003 included 12 compacts.[122]

Summary

Policies relating to the management of nuclear waste including spent fuel are based on a common source applied to suit national aspirations. The connection between a publicly accepted solution to the storage and disposal of nuclear waste and the continuation of the nuclear power programme is clear and is demonstrated by the public acceptance of the Finnish programme. The pragmatic approach of the UK Government, through UK Nirex, is best summarised in the following statement demonstrating the transformation forced by past failures:[123]

- the waste exists and must be dealt with in an ethical manner;
- legitimacy is the key to public acceptance of any attempt to solve the waste issue; and

---

[121] Central Midwest Interstate Low level Radioactive Waste Compact 211.859.

[122] Compacts believed to be in effect may be viewed at: [www.ssl.csg.org/compactlaws/cenmid.pdf].

[123] Murray, C. et al (2003), *Legitimacy as the Key: The Long-term Management of Radioactive Waste in the UK*, Session 29 – National and International EM Programmes, ICEM03, Oxford, Sept.

- credible options and a new political will allow, and indeed, compel this generation to deal with it.

Further Reading

Birnie, P. W. and Boyle, A. E. (1992), *International Law and the Summit*, Clarendon Press, Oxford.

Clarke, R. H. (1999), 'Chairman ICRP, Control of low level radiation exposure: time for a change', *J. Radiol. Prot.* Vol 19 No 2, pp 107-115.

González, A. J. (2000), 'The Safety of Radioactive Waste Management. Achieving internationally acceptable solutions', *IAEA Bulletin*, Vol. 42, No. 3, pp 5-18. Vienna, Austria.

Janssens, A., Hornung-Lauxmann, L. and Hunter, G. (2002), 'Environmental radioactivity surveillance under the Euratom Treaty', *Nuclear Energy*, 41, No. 5, Oct., 339-346.

Jensen, P. H. Paile, W. and Salo, A. Views expressed in the Nordic countries on the suggested modifications to the ICRP approach [www.nsfs.org/irpa_nsfs.html].

OECD-NEA (2002), A *Critical Review of the System of Radiation Protection, The Way Forward in Radiological Protection*, An Expert Group Report, OECD Paris.

Scheinman, L. (2001), 'Transboundary Sovereignty in the management of nuclear material', *IAEA Bulletin*, Vol. 43, No. 4. Vienna, Austria.

US DOE (2002), *The National Waste Management Plan*, Rev 3 Aug. Carlsbad Field Office (CBFO).

Government Papers

DEFRA, the Scottish Executive and the Welsh Assembly (2001), *Managing Radioactive Waste Safely, proposals for developing a policy for managing solid radioactive waste in the UK*, Sept. HMSO London.

DEFRA, the Scottish Executive and the Welsh Assembly (2002), *Managing Radioactive Wastes Safely, summary of responses to the consultation*, Sept. 2001 – Mar. 2002, July, HMSO London.

DEFRA (2002), *UK Strategy for radioactive discharges 2001-2020*, July.

DEFRA (2002), *Managing the Nuclear Legacy: A strategy for action*, White Paper, July, Cm 5552 HMSO London.

Department of the Environment (1995), *Review of Radioactive Waste Management Policy, Final Conclusions*, July Cm 2919, HMSO London.

Draft Nuclear Sites and Radioactive Substances Bill, Jun. 2003.

House of Lords Select Committee on Science and Technology (1999), *Management of Nuclear Waste Report*, HL Paper 41, HMSO, London.

Chapter Four

Attitudes and Influences of Stakeholders

Waste and energy are intricately connected as shown in the first chapter. The sources and amounts of radioactive waste and the policies at international and national levels have been identified in the second and third chapters respectively. While much of what happens to radioactive waste has been dictated by the command approach of decide, dictate and defend, there is now a growing acceptance that civic interests have to be identified and accepted by the public. However, public interest is not limited to the opinion only of the vocal minorities. Elected bodies, associations, non-government organisations, educational institutions, manufacturing and construction companies as well as the man on the Clapham omnibus have a vital interest in freedom from pollution and secure energy. This chapter identifies the stakeholders in radioactive waste, those with a role to play in the process, and examines various aspects of their views. However, the views and reactions of stakeholders are affected by the supervening influence of science, ethics, ingenuity and risk.

Supervening Influences

Stakeholder attitudes are influenced by developments in science and by the concerns related to scientific investigation and experimentation. The ethical aspect of experimentation is of concern to a wide range of the public and public attitudes have a direct influence over projects and practices that are founded on the associated science. These attitudes may be inflamed by the activities of pressure groups resulting in potential scientific advances being curtailed, a prime example being the pressures of animal rights considerations on the development of pharmaceutical products. The ingenuity involved in the practical application of the scientific idea is of concern in a society seeking immediate perfection; the necessary trial and error associated with achieving the near perfect solution may be seen as failure. Innovation involves risk and newly recognised risks are not easily measured against everyday risks. Security of our way of life and the means of ensuring its continuity and improvement are threatened by the fear of what might happen as well as the threat imposed by forces outside the individual's control.

The desire to maintain the status quo has become manifest in the moves toward sustainable development that, in turn, has enabled both the recognition of unsustainable processes and novel approaches to potential solutions. Finally, fate has its place; the unforeseen can change future plans for good or bad. Nevertheless, precautionary processes can anticipate, arm and enable the avoidance of adverse effects of future uncertainties. When certainty becomes more obvious the precautionary process may be seen as wise and reinforced or transient and unnecessary in the known circumstances.

Science and Society

Science includes all public and private activities of a scientific and technological nature, including social sciences. The term society covers all citizens and their associations, as well as businesses and public authorities. According to Philippe Busquin, Member of the European Commission and Commissioner for Research;

> ...while scientists still enjoy the trust of Europeans, only half of the Europeans consulted said that they were interested in science and many of them consider themselves to be poorly informed.

Examples abound to show that knowledge, in particular science, technology and innovation, are indispensable. Every day, scientific and technological progress contributes innovations essential to our quality of life and international competitiveness.[1] Scientific cooperation is also often an important factor in dialogue between countries.[2] However, there are indications that the immense potential of achievement is out of step with citizens' current needs and aspirations, such as peace, jobs, security and sustainable development of the planet. European attitudes to science give a mixed picture,[3] ranging from confidence and hope to lack of interest in scientific activities or even fears regarding some of their impacts. Eighty percent of Europeans believe that science will one day conquer diseases such as cancer or AIDS, and scientists enjoy a high level of public confidence, to the extent that 72 percent of the respondents said they would like politicians more frequently to use expert advice in making their choices. Despite these expectations and the climate of confidence, the same survey also shows that Europe's citizens do not always have a very positive perception of science and technology, and that science is remote for some sections of the population. Industrial hazards and ethical issues are widely highlighted in the media, raising questions and reinforcing the public's desire for progress to be more closely monitored. Some people feel that science and technology are changing their lives too quickly and young people no longer find studying science and scientific careers sufficiently attractive. Together with demographic trends, this potentially affects the labour market where industry has difficulties in recruiting the engineers and scientists needed.

The Ethical Dimension in Science and the New Technologies

The rapid pace of scientific and technological progress can give rise to serious ethical questions of concern. These questions may also have potential implications for future generations. Society is a rich cultural tapestry, made up of divergent ethical, religious, historical and philosophical backgrounds. While respecting these cultural differences, it is vital to make research functional and clearly supported by members of the public. The freedom of science and ethical considerations in

---

[1] European Community (2000), *Innovation in a knowledge-driven economy*, COM (2000)567, Sept. Brussels.
[2] European Commission (2001), *The International Dimension of the European Research Area*, COM(2001)346, June, Brussels.
[3] An opinion poll 'Europeans, science and technology' was conducted at the Commission's request in the fifteen Member States between 10 May and 15 June 2001.

research as expressed in the *EU Charter of Fundamental Rights*[4] should be respected and implemented, where possible. Several international organizations (governmental and non-governmental such as the Council of Europe, the European Science Foundation, UNESCO, WHO, the World Medical Association, FAO and others) are actively promoting ethics in science and research. The OECD – NEA in the context of the management of long-lived radioactive waste issued in 1995 a collective opinion on the ethical and environmental basis of geological disposal.[5]

Ingenuity

The ingenuity of the engineer has always been backed where practicable by the use of standards and verification by test following the well-established philosophy of hypothesise, synthesise and verify. The engineer naturally uses the improvement achievable in designs by the application of new scientific knowledge, primarily about materials. The term 'reasonably practicable' is not only a term of art used in the legal arena, but one that defines the engineering objective. However, legal regulation is necessary for the want of three elements in the engineering regime; a law licensing the engineer, a comprehensive, legally enforceable system of codes and standards and the constraint on industry only to use the licensed engineer. In the absence of such a system it should not be surprising that there are practicing engineers who are not competent, engineers working outside their remit and some even having a nihilistic attitude. Hence there is the need for regulation. Regulation is necessary also to ensure that the start up, continuing use and operation of engineered processes are used in the way they were designed to operate. However, it is only in recent times that the disciplines of the engineer have been reflected back on him by statutory regulation. A developing knowledge of materials, knowledge of the effect on human health of chemicals and a better understanding of the mechanisms of the environment has enabled the regulation of activities that affect health and safety initially through the *Factories Acts* in the UK in the early part of the century leading to the *Health and Safety at Work Act* of recent times. The problems of a polluted atmosphere have been similarly successively regulated over time through the *Public Health Act*, the *Alkali Act*, the *Clean Air Act*, the *Control of Pollution Act*, the *Environmental Protection Act and* the *Environment Act*. At the same time international concern has forced regulation of the marine environment and the major source of marine pollution, the rivers, through various European Directives and the *United Kingdom Merchant Shipping Act* and the *Water Resources Act 1991*. The development of land also has an effect on all aspects of the environment and regulation has been instituted by the Town *Planning Acts* from the early part of this century through to the *Town and Country Planning Act 1990*. Even more recently, European legislation has forced the integration of pollution laws with a holistic approach to regulate releases across all the environmental media in place of the case by case approach of previous regulation dealing with air, water and land in separate regimes and under separate

---

[4] Charter of Fundamental Rights of the European Union, OJ C 364/01, 18 Dec. 2000.
[5] OECD-NEA (1995), *The Environmental and Ethical Basis of Geological Disposal of Long-Lived Radioactive Waste*, OECD Paris.

regulatory bodies. The requirement of environmental impact assessment has also been introduced for significant projects by the insistence of European law.

Risk Perception

Key factors that influence public perception of risk are trust in regulations, norms and standards; locally based experts being seen as more reliable than those from outside. Where the local community is not adequately involved decisions are more suspect. Risks that are under personal control and that offer some immediate benefit are acceptable, for example smoking a cigarette and experiencing that soothing and relaxing effect or driving a car and experiencing the exhilaration of speed. In contrast risks that are remote but with a catastrophic potential are of a greater concern, to the extent of dread, than incidents with a large actual number of fatalities but scattered in time, such as road deaths and deaths from lung cancer. The public is concerned about the complexity of explanations of radiation and its potential risk, centralised control, no obvious needs and no perceptible benefit. The memory remains of a visit to a nuclear facility in 1958 at Calder Hall; the eerie feeling of something that could not be touched or felt but that might have been present, radiation, made scarier by the metronomic click of the instrumentation. If only low-level radiation caused one to itch it would seem less fearsome. The reality of radiation doses from various sources of exposure compared with the perception of what that exposure might mean demonstrates the gulf between perception and fact; the earth's crust gives a dose in microsieverts per year of 7,000 in Cornwall but in Sydney, Australia of between 160 and 900; the dose per year at sea-level from cosmic radiation is 260 microsieverts, from a medical X-ray 200, an airline flight of 1,000 miles is 10, living in a stone building is 70, a coal fired power station within 50 miles is 0.3, a nuclear station within 50 miles is 0.09 and a smoke detector in the house is 0.08.[6] In fact the radiation dose an individual would experience from living within 50 miles of a nuclear power station is one third of that from a coal fired power station and if he lived in certain parts of Cornwall he would experience 70,000 times more from the naturally occurring radiation than from a nuclear power station if he lived, for example, in Somerset.

Perhaps greater involvement in the decision-making will bring familiarity with the facts; the reality for the proponent of nuclear power is that irrationality cannot be brushed aside, that's how people are. It's now accepted that public involvement in decision-making about major projects is desirable, the era of 'big brother' knowing best has passed. Greater exposure to the necessary decision-making and the facts behind the alternatives will engender rational outcomes; equally exposure to public views will ensure more sound institutional attitudes. Matters that have previously been minimised will be examined and the fears about technical inadequacies, bias in information, vested interests of the authorities and the NGOs, personal ambition and interests might be exposed and addressed fairly. In the UK it is proposed that participation will be achieved through the mechanism of opinion polls, focus groups, citizen panels, issue forums and consensus conferences; issues

---

[6] McHugh, J. et al (2002), *The Way Forward in Radiological Protection. An Expert Group Report*, OECD 2002.

to be addressed later in this chapter. The use of the internet and the interaction with digital maps by the use of Global Information Systems (GIS) will allow public exploration and experiment with the available data and information sources such as the location of power sources, demand and distribution at national, regional and local levels. This should foster a higher degree of trust and transparency. Experts will no longer decide for the public but with the public.

Public Acceptance of Risk and Uncertainty

Innovation improves our quality of life, and is essential for economic growth. However, it can also raise uncertainties and concerns, and can bring new hazards to health and the environment. Scientific work is then needed to address these issues and to help identify and assess the risks posed by these hazards, and to reduce uncertainties. There is rarely a simple answer to the question 'is it safe?' It is known that a variety of risks must be faced in everyday life. Some risks are taken voluntarily others simply cannot be avoided. Not only is the likelihood of harm considered when assessing whether something is 'safe' but also factors such as the likely benefits and the existence of alternatives. 'Science is not a matter of certainties but of hypotheses and experiment'[7] but 'Taking some risk is indeed a necessary condition for progress'[8] and according to the UK House of Lords[9]

> ...admitting to uncertainty does less harm than trying to conceal it ...The public should be kept informed...This may involve delays and difficulties, but in the long run openness is the best policy.[10]

In most situations risk and uncertainty cannot be eliminated, they must be managed by an acceptable process. The traditional process relies on the advice of independent experts. However, the public is currently in no mood to place uncritical trust in experts. It is the hidden risk of which the public is suspicious; risk without choice; risk for the profits of another or because of lack of attention and laziness the risk that leads to litigation.[11] The concept of independence is problematical; when assessing what science says, regard may be had to where opinion comes from and who paid for it. However, according to Sir Aaron Klug,[12]

> If we are not to lose the public services of commercially aware expert scientists, we will need to proceed by the route of establishing panels whose expert members, collectively, represent a balance between the main sets of interests at stake.

Alternatively, the same objective may be achieved by across the board review of regulation and application of science by making industry-wide regulations involving experts from the various branches of science. Sponsorships and

---

[7] The Royal Commission on Environmental Pollution (2000), *22nd Report*. Cm 4749 June p 442.
[8] Sir Aaron Klug (1999), Royal Society Anniversary Address.
[9] House of Lords Science and Technology 3rd Report.
[10] Royal Society (1999), Anniversary address.
[11] Liability Risk and Insurance. Feb. 2001, Issue 127.
[12] Royal Society (1999), Anniversary Address.

affiliations must be openly declared and must not be assumed to colour the quality or outcome and the whole process must be subject to peer review.

The fear of climate change is a paradigm of risk and uncertainty that is occupying the minds of scientists and lawmakers. In summarising the findings of the Intergovernmental Panel on Climate Change (IPCC) meeting of November 2000,[13] it was stated that without action to limit greenhouse gas emissions the Earth's climate would warm at a rate unprecedented in the last ten thousand years. Policymakers are faced with responding to the risks posed by anthropogenic emission of greenhouse gases in the face of significant uncertainties and they will have to decide to what degree they want to take precautionary measures. In the body of his presentation,[14] Robert T. Wilson maintained that significant reductions in net greenhouse gas emissions are technically, and economically, feasible by energy supply and demand, agricultural, forestry, and waste management measures. Also he believed that, subject to satisfactorily addressing safety, environmental and other concerns, increased use of nuclear energy would have a part to play. The UK Royal Commission on Climate Change appears to endorse that position but adds significant qualifications:

> Nuclear power could continue to play an important role in reducing UK greenhouse gas emissions. We do not, however, accept the arguments of those who hold that it is indispensable. We do not believe public opinion will permit the construction of new nuclear power stations unless they are part of a strategy which delivers radical improvements in energy efficiency and an equal opportunity for the deployment of other alternatives to fossil fuels which can compete in terms of cost and reduced environmental impact.

The International Atomic Energy Agency view[15] is that the best chance for sustainable development lies in allowing all energy supply options to compete on a level playing field on the basis of cost effectiveness, environmental protection and safety. However, in the absence of accepted monetary value being given to environmental externalities it is not possible to agree the level and consequently bias exists in the form of taxes and acceptance of some forms of embedded atmospheric, land and water pollution. Before renewable sources of energy are practicable nuclear energy is necessary in the near future in order to reduce the amount of carbon dioxide released to the atmosphere. The problem is that the public having been told by the technologists of the possible dreadful outcomes of radiation releases and in the absence of similar predictions for alternative scenarios, they are not disposed to accept a nuclear future. It is the fearsome statistics that frighten the public; statistics that are not based on scientific certainty but on epidemiological prediction. The in-built precautionary nature of the public defers to a seemingly safer alternative.

Risk governance, embracing risk identification, assessment, management and communication has become a crucial but often highly controversial component of

---

[13] Presentation of Robert T. Wilson (2000), Chair, Intergovernmental Panel on Climate Change, 13 Nov.

[14] ibid. Part III-Approaches to mitigate climate change.

[15] IAEA (2000), *Climate Change and Nuclear Power*, Nov. IAEA, Vienna.

public policy. In recent years the European Union has dramatically overhauled its risk assessment and risk management processes in the areas of consumer health and food safety. Regulatory measures in these areas are founded on scientific advice from committees based on the principles of excellence, independence and transparency.[16] The Union has established general principles and requirements of food law and the European Food Safety Authority laying down principles of food safety.[17] The Commission has also set out its approach to the use of the Precautionary Principle,[18] suggesting guidelines for risk management when faced with scientific uncertainty, and stating general principles always to be applied in risk management.[19] In all areas ways should be examined to provide for a more dynamic interface and better communication between risk managers, risk assessors and those carrying out the underpinning scientific research. Risk governance should be opened to debate and scrutiny; for example what are the costs and benefits, how are they to be measured and how safe is 'safe enough'.

Uncharted Fate

While precautionary steps may be taken about recognisable fates there is no certainty about the outcomes. In an address to the Japanese Atomic Industrial Forum,[20] Hans Blix noted that Japan was among the few countries that have consistently and successfully tamed the atom to use in medicine, in agriculture and above all to give a substantial and independent energy base for its growing standard of living and its fast expanding industry. He noted that important elements were the privilege of early demilitarisation and determined use of peaceful nuclear power. He went on to say that the spectre of nuclear war between great powers, which haunted the world ever since bombs fell on Hiroshima and Nagasaki, was at last losing its grip on the world. How fragile this utopian view! Terrorist threats in the form of dirty bombs using radioactive materials and 'rogue nation' threats to manufacture nuclear weapons now take the place of the mutually assured destruction threat of the cold war. At the time of writing, Mr. Blix is deeply involved in countering the latter. Economic uncertainty, the potential nuclear threat from North Korea (DPRK) and a series of occurrences at nuclear sites in Japan have combined to engender a less confident view of the nuclear scene there. At the time of writing it has become apparent that the threat from the DPRK has induced Japan to reconsider its nuclear weapon free status.

---

[16] Communication on consumer health and food safety (1997), COM (1997) 183.
[17] Regulation (EC) No 178/2002 of the European Parliament and of the Council of 28 Jan. 2002.
[18] Communication from the Commission on the Precautionary Principle (2000), COM (2000) 1 Feb. Brussels.
[19] Proportionality, non- discrimination, consistency, examination of the benefits and costs of action or lack of action, examination of scientific developments.
[20] Blix, Hans (1994), Opening Session of the Japan Atomic Industrial Forum, 13 Apr. IAEA, Austria.

Engaging the Public

The public wants to see a level playing field. According to a Select Committee[21] public confidence in scientific advice to Government has been rocked by a series of events and many people are uneasy about the huge opportunities presented by areas of science, which seem to be advancing far ahead of their awareness and assent. There are many things that we know for certain, however, where science is advancing rapidly much is uncertain. A recognised problem is the scientific assessment of the safety or environmental effects of new technology; while science from some quarters and for some purposes enjoys public confidence, other kinds of science and scientist are rated very low. In the former category can be cited renewable technology with nuclear power falling into the latter category. The Select Committee found that people's attitudes show the robust common sense people usually bring to bear on technology if they have a fair degree of information.[22] Current research[23] suggests that the public understands uncertainty well, on the basis of everyday experience and use common sense to interpret and evaluate what they hear about technological advances. Where there is secrecy the field is wide open to allegations of conspiracy and cover up.[24] Policy makers therefore face the challenges of recognising peoples' values, seeing that they are understood and brought into the debate and policy making, which comes near enough to satisfying the values of enough people to command support. The Committee concluded that policy makers would find it hard to win public support, or even acquiescence, on any issue with a science component, unless the public's attitude and values are recognised, respected and weighed in the balance along with scientific and other factors. Public consultation is a time consuming but necessary operation, which has been found to be successful in controversial projects where previously, more direct methods, had failed.[25] The process involves genuine consultation and takes the form typically of a community advisory forum, a public information programme, focus groups consisting of members of the public chosen at random and a questionnaire survey. For this process to work in a high technology situation there must not be a confusion of rules and regulations between the conflicting activities or processes. It is important, therefore, that a holistic attitude be adopted on matters that cross boundaries and which might otherwise be treated as separate issues. Hence a nuclear project, to have a chance to be accepted by the public, must be considered alongside the alternatives and against the same

---

[21] House of Lords (1999), *Management of Nuclear Waste*, Third Report of the Select Committee on Science and Technology, Session 1998-9, Mar. HMSO London.

[22] ibid paragraph 2.10.

[23] Irwin and Wynne (eds) (1996), *Misunderstanding Science*. Cambridge University Press.

[24] ibid paragraph 2.45.

[25] For example, work on consensus building in Hampshire (UK) began in 1993 after the collapse of a large incineration project in Portsmouth; advisory fora were set up, made recommendations and public meetings were held. Most of the forum members recognised that energy from waste incineration would be a necessary component of the waste strategy and planning applications for two incinerators were submitted. ENDS Report Sept. 1999, Issue No. 296.

economic rules and sustainable development laws. The decision must be made without the influence of crooks, cowboys and men of straw.

Technology has a poor image in the perception of a risk-averse public yet the risks, for example fuel poverty, associated with not taking advantage of technological solutions, in particular the provision of clean nuclear energy, are greater than the actual risks of the technological solution. According to Hans Blix:[26]

> If the wastes from burnt fossil fuels could be managed and disposed of as safely as the waste from nuclear power our global environment would not be endangered. It is the wastes from burnt coal, oil and gas – not the waste from nuclear power plants – that cause acid rains and greenhouse gases. These wastes are so voluminous that they cannot be contained and buried. Sites for the ultimate disposal of these wastes are not selected. They are our atmosphere and the surface of our earth.

To resolve this dilemma it is necessary to engage governments and the public in an open manner and to open to a balanced public debate all the solutions that contribute to a sustainable future. Principles leading to a rational management of man's approach to future development have been distilled from environmental, development and health and safety practice and are recognised at an international level. The combination of law and principles could be the mechanism to bring together the current fragmented approach to development under a unified set of sustainable development laws. An international dimension may be necessary, using the paradigm of nuclear law to co-ordinate the necessary change to national legal systems, but this is for the next chapter.

International Influences

Stakeholder influence has been recognised by international bodies. For the purposes of illustration a cross section of alternative views are taken to represent a range of international influences. The OECD, who represent a variety of national views, the World Association of Nuclear Operators' (WANO) representing the utilities, the International Nuclear Law Association (INLA), bringing a legal dimension, the Uranium Institute, Greenpeace and Friends of the Earth are considered below.

OECD – Nuclear Energy Agency

The Nuclear Energy Agency under the mandate of the Radioactive Waste Management Committee (RWMC) created a forum on stakeholder confidence to share experience in addressing the societal dimension of radioactive waste management, to explore means of ensuring an effective dialogue with the public and to consider ways to strengthen confidence in decision-making processes. From early discussions of the forum it was clear that exchanges between nuclear energy institutions and the public had developed from the rigid mechanisms provided by

---

[26] Blix, supra.

the law to a more complex interaction with a broader, more realistic view of decision making encompassing a range of actors.

Where public concern over a particular risk is not reflected in government policy (for example, in emerging technologies such as genetic modification) the Government and regulatory bodies are pressurised to act. However, the information to the public may be incomplete or misleading and may be sensationalised in the media. This is pressurising governments to improve their processes of decision-making. In the case of radioactive waste management the needs of stakeholders in the vicinity of a proposed repository are now being considered after experiencing delayed or aborted programmes due to inattention to public concerns. In Finland as detailed in chapter three, the process has been to the advantage of the nuclear operators.

One lesson learned by the regulatory authorities, although probably obvious to others, in such dialogue with the public is that they should remain neutral and refrain from the temptation to educate the public about nuclear energy since it could be misinterpreted as promotional. As noted in chapter one, technical complexities regarding exposure to radiation that have been developed by a fairly closed circle of academics and scientists, confuse the public and lead to suspicions. A positive result of public exposure to the process of regulatory development is that the process is being re-examined and the NEA is considering, *inter alia*, whether the radiation protection system should be treated differently from that for other hazards and toxic agents.

An expert group of the NEA[27] identified four priority areas and it is interesting to see that in three of them it is obvious that social considerations are taken into account:

- Numerical guidance: dose levels and intervention levels. It was noted that social considerations of unacceptable and tolerable risk were involved in ICRP recommendations and should in future be expressed in terms of international consensus and social judgment.
- Concepts of regulatory control, exemption and triviality. The word triviality was considered to be more socially divisive than useful.
- Justification and optimisation.
- Decision making versus decision aiding. It was noted that those that are worried should be involved in the decision making process. It is important that the decision maker not be perceived as the expert or the decision aider and the decider but that he be perceived as taking all factors, not just technical issues, into account in arriving at a decision.

It is clear that it has been recognised in the nuclear field that there is a need to obtain a thorough understanding of the policy and decision-making process and the roles of the various participants and to do this it is necessary to identify and

---

[27] Supra McHugh.

analyse the key social and political values and behaviour patterns that affect scientific, technical and economic decision making.

A further example of NEA concern is demonstrated by the outcomes from the forum on stakeholder confidence held in August 2000[28] where the Deputy Director, S. Thompson, noted:

> ... the NEA has an obligation to take up the challenges of understanding the needs of stakeholders and to provide a neutral forum where experiences can be exchanged and analysed and lessons can be drawn.

Speakers from a number of countries expressed the views of institutional stakeholders and although by no means the totality of the discussed matters some of the common points, for illustration of the thrust of the discussions, were:

- Management programmes have often included substantial public information and consultation efforts in their initial phases. However, these do not elicit massive response. Only when programmes move into a site-specific phase do non-technical stakeholders appear to take an active interest. It is thus a challenge to find ways of involving stakeholders early.[29]
- Independence, competence and effectiveness are essential for public confidence in the regulator. The regulator's role and responsibilities must thus be clearly defined, and separated from nuclear energy policy and promotion.[30]
- Each partner needs to have a clearly defined and well-communicated role both for the national dialogue and under the EIA *(Environmental Impact Assessment)* framework.[31]

In the context of the changing environment for waste management programmes it was said that in a field project people could contribute very effectively to planning if they are allowed to participate continuously in small groups over a period of about a year.[32] In contrast, development projects are rejected when stakeholders have not been actively involved in creating them and developed a sense of responsibility for them.[33] A social psychologist, an outside observer of the proceedings of the conference, noted that attendees seemed to embrace a broader, more realistic view of decision in society, far removed from the technocratic position seen at the beginning of the decade;[34]

> There was recognition that the existing consultation mechanisms are probably insufficient or sometimes inadequate, and that it is a real challenge for organisations and individuals to find new manners of communicating and receiving input. Each attendee

---

[28] OECD-NEA (2000), *Stakeholder Confidence in Radioactive Waste Disposal*, Workshop Proceedings, 28-31 August, Paris.
[29] ibid. Hooper, A. UK Nirex, p 8.
[30] ibid. Niles, A. Federal Ministry of Environment, Germany, p 9.
[31] ibid. Carlsson, T. Mayor of Oskarshamn (Sweden), p 10.
[32] ibid. Ipsen, D. University of Kassel, Germany, p 13.
[33] ibid. Kuri, O. Posiva Oy, Finland, p 15.
[34] ibid. pp 22-23.

appeared to be ready to rise to that challenge and curious about opportunities to learn. Members appeared to agree that democracy includes an extensive system of players and that power is necessarily shared.

In another study[35] the NEA surveyed the results of opinion polls in six[36] of the seventeen OECD member countries where nuclear energy is produced[37] and found that although energy prices, price stability and security of supply were generally acknowledged the main concerns were safety, radioactive waste management and disposal and the adequacy and reliability of information provided to the public on nuclear safety especially in the case of a major accident and on the local impacts of radioactive waste management. Two major areas considered in the study are public attitudes to risk and public involvement in decision-making.

World Association of Nuclear Operators (WANO)[38]

With the prime objective of ensuring that never again would there be a nuclear accident of the type and scale of the accident at Chernobyl in 1986 WANO was formed in 1989. The organisation unites all the nuclear electricity operators in the world in 34 countries including Taiwan and Cuba who are not members of the IAEA. By the exchange of operating experience it facilitates the highest standards of safety and operation and it provides a performance indication programme for all reactor designs that also allow a measure of how well reactors are managed. Information is published on the performance, radiation exposure of workers automatic shutdowns and incidents. However, it does not publish information on releases to the environment of radiation or on the amounts of radioactive waste created.

International Nuclear Law Association (INLA)[39]

At an international level INLA's objectives are to arrange for and to promote studies and the acquisition of knowledge of legal problems related to the peaceful use of nuclear energy, in particular the protection of man and his environment, to help promote the exchange of information among members and to cooperate on a scientific basis with similar associations and institutions. The association operates through working groups and a bi-annual congress that meets on a rotational basis in member countries. The working groups cover safety and regulation, nuclear liability and insurance, international nuclear trade, radiological protection, waste management and radioisotopes.

Greenpeace

Born out of protest against nuclear weapon testing by the US in 1971 in Alaska, Greenpeace continued to oppose the tests by the French at Maruroa in 1973 and

---

[35] OECD-NEA Secretariat (2000), *Society and Nuclear Energy: Towards a Better Understanding*, OECD Paris, p 109.

[36] Finland, France, Germany, Japan, United Kingdom and United States.

[37] 10,000 reactor years of worldwide experience.

[38] [www.wano.org.uk].

[39] [www.aidn-inla.be].

Soviet nuclear testing in 1982. In 1987 it launched a campaign against the US weapons tests at sea, in 1989 it prevented a Trident II missile test and in 1990 delayed a British test in the Nevada desert. Greenpeace has clearly established an anti-nuclear war position on an international level and influenced the establishment of the Test Ban Treaty in 1995. Its opposition to nuclear weapons has been supplemented by its total opposition to all things nuclear and claims to have been instrumental, by implication, in the London Dumping Convention's ban on ocean dumping of radioactive waste in 1993 and the Ospar Convention's resolution in 1998 to phase out radioactive discharges to the seas. Greenpeace has campaigned against radioactive waste disposal since its filming of the dumping of radioactive waste in the North Atlantic in 1978. In 1980 Greenpeace protested against the shipment of radioactive materials from Japan and in 1983 and 1987 it attempted to stop the discharge of very low-level liquid waste from Sellafield by attempting to block the discharge pipe. The latter exercise incidentally resulted in the prosecution of BNFL.[40]

Greenpeace has invested in research into pollution and supports the Greenpeace International Laboratories at the School of Biological Sciences at Exeter University. However, a scan of their published material, going back to 1995 while revealing extensive work on chemical pollutants and general environmental principles such as precaution and management of risk has nothing on low-level radiation. Despite the lack of scientific argument in relation to the release of low-level radioactive waste, Greenpeace claims to have successfully aided the shelving of plans for a 'Nuclear Waste Dump' in 1997. The public appeal of Greenpeace and its apparent credibility in its nuclear waste campaigning is probably its spectacular prominence in the anti-nuclear weapons campaigning and humanitarian efforts against whaling and the release of CFCs. The sabotage of Rainbow Warrior, the anti-nuclear test ship, by the French navy in Auckland harbour in 1985 added greatly to public sympathy for the organisation. Similarly its association with the children of Chernobyl gave it significant humanitarian credibility. Its involvement in reversing the perfectly safe and sensible plan to dispose of the Brent Spar oil platform and its activities in 2001 at the Vandenburg airbase in California against Star Wars missile tests have, however, harmed its credibility in the eyes of the thinking public. Similarly the occupation of the Sizewell 'B' nuclear station in 2002 to protest against presumed government policy on nuclear power while revealing security failures demonstrated an irresponsible, pretentious attitude in their campaign management. Greenpeace methods can be bold, media attracting and dangerous; the methods appeal to the bravado in people; they appeal to the animal loving instincts and they appeal to the desire for peace in people's nature. While in some circumstances such as chemical pollution the organisation appears to have a good scientific understanding of the issues, in others such as GM Foods and radioactive waste they appeal to people's emotions and are light on scientific backing for their views. Greenpeace has, nevertheless, raised awareness and caused both government and industry to focus attention on public information and opinion.

---

[40] Chapter six.

Friends of the Earth (FoE)

Friends of the Earth operates locally, nationally and internationally and claims to have scored 'many remarkable victories on behalf of the threatened world', having since 1971, saved hundreds of wildlife havens, won protection for endangered species, halted unnecessary and damaging road schemes, blocked unsafe plans for nuclear waste dumping, and achieved the passage of five Acts of Parliament – to name just a few! They claim to get the facts right; to expose environmental destruction and related social injustices; to propose positive solutions – and show how solving environmental problems will help solve economic and social problems; to pursue campaigns over the long term; to cover a wide range of issues; to work at all levels – locally, nationally and internationally; to increase awareness and understanding and offer opportunities for everyone to get involved.

The views of FoE on nuclear energy are, however, intransigent and are expressed in the following extract from their website of September 2000:

> In November at The Hague in the Netherlands, the next meeting of the UN Framework Convention on Climate Change will be held. It will take decisions that may decide the future of the nuclear industry. Due to the combined effects of Chernobyl and appalling economics the nuclear industry has been stagnating for years. However the need to curb climate change by cutting carbon dioxide emissions has been seen by the nuclear industry as a potential lifeline, as nuclear power plants do not emit carbon. Some Governments have accepted this rhetoric. Friends of the Earth believes that the real solution lies with renewable energy and energy efficiency and that nuclear power – with its intrinsic accident risks, radiation risks and production of highly dangerous nuclear waste which we don't know what to do with – cannot be part of the solution to climate change.

The following view on nuclear waste management gives no quarter:

> Nuclear power produces long-lived radioactive wastes for which no disposal route has been found. The Royal Commission on Environmental Pollution stated: 'We must assume that these wastes will remain dangerous and will need to be isolated from the biosphere for hundreds of thousands of years. In considering arrangements for dealing safely with such wastes man is faced with timescales that transcend his experience.' Despite having had over forty years to deal with the problem created, no repository for high level wastes has been established anywhere in the world. Forty years' research has only demonstrated the failure of the idea that nuclear waste can be 'disposed of' underground, without leaking back into the environment and threatening the health of future generations. The fact there is no disposal facility is a result of this failure. In 1997 the UK Government rejected the nuclear industry's plan to begin building a nuclear dump because of the appalling science that was put forward to support the plan. That same year the British Government Panel on Sustainable Development reported; 'the options for handling radioactive waste, and the danger that nuclear waste might contribute to the proliferation of nuclear weapons, are all issues which warrant urgent consideration at the highest international level'.

While both of the quotations above are correct it is the view of this work that they give a one sided view, and they are views not facts, and in particular seem to accept without the same rigorous criticism they make of nuclear energy the view that known renewable sources of energy will provide for the needs of the third world.

National Influences

Other than government bodies considered in the previous chapter, stakeholders may be grouped in categories covering utilities and industry, non-government organisations including professional bodies and the man in the street. As the organisations within these categories are broadly similar regardless of their national bases the United Kingdom is considered as representative of all nations supporting the nuclear business and so the discussions below are so limited.

Utilities and Industry

Prior to denationalisation of many aspects of the electrical power industry in the UK, the UK Atomic Energy Agency led the development of nuclear energy for both defence and civil aspects. Early devolution separated the isotope development and production by Amersham International, the nuclear fuel production and reprocessing by British Nuclear Fuels Limited (BNFL) and technical aspects by AEA Technology. The privatisation of the electrical supply industry led to the formation of British Energy (BE) that took over the business of Nuclear Electric, a government owned company that had been operating part of the nuclear power station fleet built up since the mid-fifties under The Central Electricity Generating Board (CEGB). The part not taken by BE, the early design of reactor based on the Calder Hall reactors that were primarily built to make plutonium from natural uranium, have been operated on behalf of the government by BNFL. These magnox reactors, so called because the fuel was natural uranium encased in a magnesium alloy can have on-load refuelling and so avoid the necessity to shut down to exchange fuel elements. The magnox reactors built from the late fifties to the early part of the seventies were a significant part of the generating capacity and were seen as a hedge against a recurrence of an oil shortage; they were indispensable to government action in the miners strikes of the late seventies. The design of the fuel element was, however, not suited to long-term storage and therefore reprocessing is essential. At the time of writing the government is in the process of separating responsibility for the magnox reactors, the research facilities of the UKAEA and facilities owned by the Ministry of Defence into a single Nuclear Decommissioning Agency (NDA)[41] funded by a separate statutory account[42] and so releasing BNFL to manufacture and reprocess fuel for the balance of the UK reactors and export as a separate but profitable business. The final disposal of all radioactive waste and the continuation of all reprocessing is subject to government consultation following suspension of previous plans to build an underground repository under the leadership of Nirex a company owned by UKAEA, BE and BNFL.

---

[41] Cm 5552 April 2003.
[42] DTI Press release p/2003/228, 3 April 2003.

United Kingdom Atomic Energy Agency (UKAEA)[43] The development of nuclear energy was pioneered in the UK by the UKAEA a government owned organisation incorporated in 1954 and funded by the Department of Trade and Industry. It is now responsible for managing the decommissioning of the facilities used for research and development at sites at Dounreay, Windscale, Risley, Harwell, Culham and Winfrith and the magnox reactors at Berkley in Gloucestershire, Trawsfynydd in Wales and Hunterston in Scotland. The future operation of the UKAEA is subject to government plans for the management of civil liabilities in the UK. Nuclear waste is held at its sites in varying quantities and is recorded in the Nirex waste directory;[44] at Dounreay a vitrification facility to encapsulate high-level waste in glass is being built. The gasified waste will be stored on site until a final disposal facility is available as will intermediate-level waste which is conditioned for long-term storage. Low-level and decommissioning waste is stored on site at Dounreay; for other sites the waste is transferred to the BNFL disposal facility at Drigg on the Sellafield site. Public involvement in the plans for decommissioning the sites is being pursued by participation and consultation via the website.

British Nuclear Fuels (BNFL) Around the world BNFL employs around 23,000 people, its prime activity being the nuclear fuel cycle. Nuclear fuel is manufactured from mined uranium ore by enrichment with uranium recovered by spent fuel reprocessing. Recovered plutonium is also mixed with uranium to form a mixed oxide fuel (MOX) that is used in reactors in Germany and Japan. Fuel waiting reprocessing is stored and waste from reprocessing is conditioned awaiting final disposal. Through its ownership of Westinghouse Electric Company, BNFL has a portfolio of technology, products and services including nuclear plant services, maintenance, instrumentation and control, plant design and construction. Environmental services are provided by BNFL to continue decommissioning and waste management projects around the world. BNFL is also responsible for the management of six operating magnox reactor power stations and two undergoing decommissioning through its government services group. The future of this group and the reprocessing of magnox fuel are subject to government plans for the future management of its civil nuclear liabilities. At BNFL sites local liaison committees operate and through its stakeholder dialogue programmes the company interfaces with unions, academia, regulators, local councils and campaign groups to inform the decision making process. By 2002, working groups facilitated by The Environment Council and about 450 individual stakeholders had addressed waste management of liquid and aerial discharges, spent fuel management options and recommendations for dealing with plutonium.

British Energy (BE)[45] Formed by the privatisation of Nuclear Electric in 1996 BE has electricity generating capacity comprising seven advanced gas-cooled reactors (AGRs) at power stations at Hinckley Point, Hunterston, Dungeness, Heysham,

[43] [www.ukaea.org.uk].
[44] Nirex (2003), The 2001 United Kingdom Radioactive Waste Directory, DETR.
[45] [www.british-energy.com].

Hartlepool and Torness and one pressurised water reactor (PWR) power station at Sizewell with a total generating capacity of 9,600 MWe. BE also owns a 2,000 MWe coal fired power station at Eggborough, purchased in 2000. In 1997 BE expanded internationally forming a joint venture, AmerGen, with PECO Energy of Philadelphia, which owns one PWR and two boiling water reactor (BWR) power stations. In May 2001 BE leased the Bruce power station in Ontario, Canada. At the time of writing in March 2003 BE has experienced cash flow shortfalls and has obtained government loans to continue operations. The problem was first identified in July 2002 and was said by BE to be due to loss of income due partly by unplanned outages, high fixed costs (including the fuel contracts with BNFL), the reduction in wholesale electricity prices which had fallen by 35 percent over the previous two years, onerous power purchase contracts, uncertainty in the decommissioning costs in excess of its decommissioning fund and fuel liabilities not included in contracts with BNFL. The price to be paid by BE for government financial assistance is to restructure[46] to include the disposal of the AmerGen interest in the US and in Canada the Bruce lease. It is proposed that the liabilities for decommissioning and the historic liabilities for used fuel will be met by a Nuclear Liabilities Fund operated by the government and will comprise the decommissioning fund, ongoing contributions from BE of 65 percent of its net cash flow and bonds to the amount of £250 million from BE. Agreements with BNFL regarding fuel related services are being revised. Greenpeace who sought leave to proceed for judicial review and then withdrew to seek annulment of the European Commission approval in the European Court has challenged this rescue plan on the grounds that the government had not obtained prior approval of the loan. Part of Greenpeace case is along the lines that nuclear energy is not essential to the electricity system in the UK as the system currently has 25 percent overcapacity and as nuclear provides only 20 percent it is not essential to the economy of the UK. In July 2004 Parliament passed the *Energy Act 2004* to deal with the legacy of nuclear facilities and waste (see chapter seven). During its passage through Parliament the EU Commission launched an inquiry against Community guidelines into the restructuring of BE, proposed in the Bill.[47] The FoE released information, confidential to the Commission and BE, that purports to show that the restructuring would benefit BE in excess of £4 billion.

NIREX With the agreement of the government Nirex was set up in the early 1980s by the nuclear industry to examine safe, environmental and economic aspects of deep geological disposal of radioactive waste. To carry this out Nirex had begun looking for a suitable site in 1987, which led in 1991 to investigation work being concentrated on a site near Sellafield. Nirex wanted to develop an underground rock characterisation laboratory to find out more information about the suitability of the site. However, planning permission was refused, and following a public inquiry, the application was rejected. Nevertheless, Nirex continues to advise

---

[46] Press Release (2002), British Energy plc Announcement of Restructuring, RNS Number 4177E, 28 November.
[47] EU Institutions Press release (2003), IP/03/1082, 23 July, Brussels.

producers of radioactive waste on how they should package the waste so that it would be suitable for deep disposal, should that be the final method of disposal and issues letters of comfort or letters of advice (Loc/LoA); monitors the processes of the producers to check procedures and records; sets standards for radioactive waste packaging; produces on behalf of the Department of the Environment an updated public record of the quantities and types of radioactive waste that exist in the UK; continues to develop an understanding of the options for dealing with radioactive waste; and discusses with a wide range of organisations the common issues, scientific, technological and environmental, including the development of an understanding of the requirements for public acceptability.

In common with BE and BNFL, Nirex has recognised the need to promote dialogue and debate as a step towards building consensus as to how to manage the UK's radioactive waste and talking and listening to as many organisations and individuals with a stake in the disposal as is possible. To provide a snapshot of stakeholder views Nirex commissioned a review of their mission statement and objectives, their performance against them and the content of their policies on transparency, corporate responsibility and environment.[48] In the transparency policy Nirex made a commitment to give their stakeholders access to and influence on its work programme. Nirex perceives that each group of stakeholders has different levels of direct experience and knowledge and so wants to engage in the debate at different levels and to cater for this, different techniques are used, coordinated and tailored to understand the needs of the stakeholders. To enable members of the public to engage with issues relating to radioactive waste management Nirex has commissioned internet questionnaire and discussion groups; focus groups on radioactive waste management, people's issues and concerns about radioactive waste; a citizens panel on partitioning and transmutation; questionnaires on radioactive waste management and discussion groups on issues related to Nirex's phased disposal concept. Nirex also attends meetings including the nuclear free local authorities; communities that live close to radioactive waste stores; the nuclear industry; the IAEA; the OECD-NEA; the International Association for Environmentally Safe Disposal of Radioactive Materials; the British Nuclear Energy Society (BNES) and the British Nuclear Industries Forum (BNIF).

In July 2003 the Government announced that Nirex was to become independent of industry.

Amersham plc The producer of radioactive isotopes in the UK is Amersham, a company that employs 9,500 people worldwide, with sales of £1.6 billion in medical diagnostics and life sciences. The company has two businesses, Amersham Biosciences that develops integrated systems and solutions for research, drug development and manufacture and Amersham Health, a pharmaceutical provider of diagnostic and predictive imaging products, services and related therapeutic products. The company was formed in 1997 from Amersham

---

[48] Environment Resources Management, An Independent Stakeholder Review of Nirex, July 2001 [www.ermuk.com].

International UK, Pharmacia Biotech (Sweden) formed in 1874 and Nycomed (Norway) founded in 1911. Amersham International had its origins as a government facility in 1940 and by the end of that year had produced 35 grams of radium. In 1946 Amersham became a national centre for the development and manufacture of radioactive materials and in 1949 became the Radiochemical Centre owned by the UKAEA; it was privatised and became Amersham International in 1982. The products used for research and the therapeutic products contain radioactive materials; emissions to air and wastewater are regulated and low-level waste is disposed of at nationally licensed sites. Intermediate-level waste and short-lived radioactive materials are held and stored on site. A programme of volume reduction of waste originally intended for sea disposal but halted by the government in line with international agreement has resulted in an 8:1 volume reduction of waste stored.

Nuclear Related Industry Research, development, design, project management, manufacturing and construction industries are another category of industrial stakeholder in the nuclear and radioactive waste field. It is beyond the scope of this work to give details of the organisations involved, however, the British Nuclear Industries Forum (BNIF)[49] represents over 60 of them and is a source of further detail. BNIF was formed in the early 60s and is the trade association, information and representative body for the British civil nuclear industry. Its objectives are to influence the climate of public and political opinion in favour of nuclear energy as part of a sustainable balanced energy policy and to promote commercial performance of the UK nuclear industry by assisting and supporting member companies to develop their business. Research is carried out at a number of universities and specifically at The National Physical Laboratory.[50] All industrial and research stakeholders have a direct interest in both the commercial activities involved in the generation, storage and disposal of radioactive waste and in the health of their employees that are in contact with radioactive materials.

Non-Governmental Organisations (NGOs)

The international bodies Greenpeace and Friends of the Earth have national and local branches that carry through the ideals of the parent bodies; they also give succour and support to bodies set up for specific campaigns. A search of the Radwaste Org. database[51] revealed over 750 NGOs worldwide with an interest in radioactive waste, 33 in the UK, over 200 in the US, 39 in France, 6 in Korea and 2 in Finland. A typical example was CANSAR, the campaign against nuclear storage and radiation. CANSAR is a resident based non-political group dedicated to addressing the threats to the Health and Safety of the people of Plymouth and South East Cornwall from nuclear radiation and pollution arising from the operations carried out at the Devonport Royal Dockyard by the MoD and DML – Devonport Management Limited (subsidiary of Brown and Root/Halliburton of the

---

[49] [www.bnif.co.uk].
[50] [www.npl.co.uk/npl/rad].
[51] [www.radwaste.org/ngo.htm].

USA). It was formed in May 2000 in response to news of plans to increase the discharge of nuclear waste into the river Tamar by 700 percent and to store up to 26 nuclear reactor components from redundant submarines on land in the centre of Plymouth. It has a small resident based committee formerly of Keyham residents against air pollution who ran a successful campaign against South West Water and Devonport Royal Dockyard. CANSAR has forged links with other groups such as WDC, Greenpeace, CND, Green Party, DIG, NTS, Nuclear Free Local Authorities and has mounted a legal challenge to:

- Stop the Environment Agency from issuing a license to DML to increase tritium discharge into river Tamar by 700 percent.
- To force 'Justification' onto DML / MoD.
- Protect the human rights of local people and the next generation.

Its method is to hold regular committee meetings; to work with the media to raise public awareness; to speak to other residents' groups starting new CANSAR cells and to try to research cancer statistics to be able to prove that Plymouth is already a cancer 'black spot'.

Individual Stakeholders

Individual Stakeholders are considered here in three categories, the general public, the professionals and employees at nuclear facilities. While many are critical of some of the activities of non-governmental organisations (NGOs) there are two aspects for which they must take credit: the environmental organisation for bringing attention and interest of governments and nuclear organisations to the need to consult, involve and take notice of the general public and in the case of the professional non-governmental representative bodies such as the Institution of Electrical Engineers, the Royal Geographical Society, the British Nuclear Energy Society and the Trades Unions in representing to their respective members a reasonably balanced view of both the scientific, technological and social aspects of the management of nuclear waste.

General Public

While workers and professionals through their representative bodies are generally well informed of the technical and social aspects of radiation and nuclear waste the same cannot be said of the vast majority of the general public. For all but the budding scientist, the education system has failed to give the public an understanding of the nature of radiation and so views of potential hazards delivered from the protagonists and antagonists of the peaceful use of nuclear energy, are accepted or rejected based on views other than from a firm grasp of the scientific background. The views, such as for example, that 'we don't trust the Scientist but we trust that he has told us it is unsafe' are coloured by mistrust of those failing to deliver past promises, a well broadcast example being, 'that power from the atom would be too cheap to meter' and from concerns about cancer from exposure to radiation regardless of the actual levels that the public could be exposed to. According to Government research,[52] the public believe that the effects of radiation are long lasting and people struggle with the concept of a 'half-life'; the invisibility of radiation helps create a sense of insidiousness – it exists beyond the senses and perhaps no one really understands it – or perhaps the reality is such that there is a conspiracy to keep the facts secret; from failure in the past for governments to act to reduce pollutants in the environment;[53] from well advertised accidents and insufficient public explanation of the precautionary measures taken; the dichotomy of risk denial and catastrophic accidents that are exemplified in the acceptance of road transport risks with the deaths from accidents in the thousands and the rejection of rail transport with the occasional single accident with tens of deaths. This absence of accurate knowledge and understanding is not limited to the nuclear issue: public grasp of the causes and possible remedies for climate change is sparse; the cost in terms of environmental damage of the alternative energy forms is limited.[54]

In January 2000 the OECD convened a workshop to discuss the range of issues surrounding the evolution towards a democratisation of knowledge and of decision-making process.[55] Some of the key issues emerging from the Workshop were:

- the need to foster mutual trust between the radiation protection community and society as a whole;
- to develop context-specific approaches;
- the development of innovative approaches including openness and inclusiveness;
- to focus on developing procedures so that if there is ultimately an agreement to disagree, all outcomes will merit respect;
- the clarification of the respective roles of experts and political actors with regard to advice and decision making;
- a proper understanding of the nature of scientific rationality, that science produced knowledge not certainty;
- that circumstances will change, whether in terms of the state of scientific knowledge or of societal attitudes and expectations; and
- the encouragement of mutual learning where all concerned are able to learn from their interactions.

---

[52] DEFRA (2002), Benchmarking Public Opinion on the Management of Radioactive Waste (MRWS/02.007), DEFRA/RA/02.012, July p 7.
[53] Environmental Data Services (2001), 'Data on dioxins in eggs kept under wraps for years' *ENDS Report 319*, Aug.
[54] House Reporter (2001), 'EC costs environmental damage of power industry', *Environment News Briefing*, 2 Aug., p 4.
[55] OECD-NEA (2001), *Policy Issues in Radiological Protection Decision Making*, Summary of the 2nd Villigen Workshop, OECD Paris.

The pressures caused by environmental groups and particularly the failure of NIREX in the UK to gain approval of their plan to commence a rock characterisation project as a precursor to deep geological storage/disposal of radioactive waste that resulted in the hiatus in forward movement of management of radioactive waste since 1997 in the UK must be contrasted with the positive momentum in the USA and Finland described in chapters two and three. This failure was in the most part due to poor preparation in public information and consultation that appears to have been remedied in the last two years. Acting on the House of Lords Select Committee Advice[56] NIREX looked outside the circle of nuclear proponents and commissioned advice from independent sources[57] [58] and the Government initiated consultation in 2001.[59] The UK Centre for Economic and Environmental Development (UKCEED)[60] in May 1999 was responsible for organising and managing the UK National Consensus Conference on Radioactive Waste Management (a panel of 15 citizens), it was reconvened to contribute their views on the DEFRA consultation paper in their capacity as informal members of the public. Summarizing the panel's response to the DEFRA consultation paper:[61]

> As far as public consultation is concerned, the Panel agrees that the consultation process will only work if the information given to the public is accepted as accurate, objective and complete by all interested parties (paragraph 6.2 of the DEFRA consultation paper). The Panel believes that this relies critically on a general increase in the basic levels of public awareness of radioactive waste management and the issues involved. In all of this, the most important comment the Panel wishes to make is about the need for openness, honesty and transparency – and the need for policy makers to be seen to be listening.

To reinforce the process of public consultation DEFRA commissioned a programme of research among the general public that found, *inter alia*:[62]

> **Radioactivity** was poorly understood, and while medical experience had made its existence familiar, it was linked more readily to harm than to benefits to life. Except among a small minority, spontaneous awareness of radioactive waste was low and understanding slight and often inaccurate. Discussion revealed higher levels of awareness, mainly drawn from media, often items related to Chernobyl, but also to Sellafield. Concerns, once they surface, were mainly about the possible effects of

---

[56] House of Lords (1999), *Management of Nuclear Waste*, Third Report of the Select Committee on Science and Technology, Session 1998-9, March, HMSO London.
[57] Nirex News Release (2000), *Nuclear Waste? No thanks!* What's New 27 Oct.
[58] Hunt, James and Simmons Peter (2001), *The Front of the Front End: Mapping Public Concerns about Radioactive Waste Management Issues*, Nirex News Release, What's New, 19 April.
[59] DEFRA (2001), *Managing Radioactive Waste Safely, Proposals for developing a policy for managing solid radioactive waste in the UK*, DoE. HMSO London.
[60] UK CEED is an independent charity founded in 1984.
[61] DEFRA (2002), *Reconvening of the Consensus Conference to Consider DEFRA's Consultation Paper: Managing Radioactive Waste Safely* (MRWS/02.006), DEFRA Report No: DEFRA/RAS/02.002, April.
[62] Benchmarking Public Opinion on the Management of Radioactive Waste (MRWS/02.007), DEFRA/RA/02.012, July 2002. p 2.

leakages/explosions, including (in the wake of September 11th 2001) those resulting from terrorist action.

Radioactive waste, seen as entirely man-made, was thought to derive mainly from 'the nuclear industry', from nuclear weapons and sometimes from medical or industrial application. Few understood nuclear power in any detail and reprocessing was rarely understood. Attitudes to the nuclear industry and to the problems of nuclear waste tended to be conditioned by individual attitudes to political and scientific authority. Regulation of the industry was seen as mainly a government matter and there was some vague awareness of agencies involved.

Most felt a need to understand nuclear waste better, though some preferred not to, from fear and sense of impotence. All potential sources of information were seen as flawed to some degree and it was felt that, ultimately, individuals should judge for themselves. The new information seemed both alarming and depressing as radioactive waste emerged as a perilous legacy lacking an evident solution. Highly active waste dominated perceptions, but all levels of radioactive waste appeared threatening.

All current strategies for the storage/disposal of radioactive waste were seen as unsatisfactory. Discussion tended to modify initial suggestions that <u>highly active waste*</u> be sent into space or given deep disposal underground to a sense that it should be stored securely but accessibly on site, both to avoid transportation and to allow monitoring and, potentially, treatment. Similar strategies were proposed for <u>medium active waste</u> and also for the longer-living elements of <u>lightly active waste,</u> though there were concerns about the demands on land for stores. The discussion of <u>barely active waste</u> mainly provoked concern that its level of activity would increase through accumulation over time.

The reprocessing industry and the nuclear power industry should be abandoned, immediately or in the case of the latter, possibly once alternatives – wind, sun and wave technologies – had been further developed. Current levels of power usage should be reviewed and technologies to neutralise radioactive waste should be developed. Cost should be secondary in consideration.

The public should be involved in radioactive waste management decisions – along with government and industry specialists and **NGOs** – because of the dire implications of the problem for the future and to provide a curb upon any vested interests. Non-specialists might produce insights in a forum where specialists had yet to succeed, but many felt inadequate or under-motivated for involvement. Those involved – and the population in general – should be educated in the subject matter and all useful channels should be employed, including the education system and the entertainment industry.

The current Government review was seen variously as a heartening sign of seriousness of intent and as an alarming confirmation of the gravity of the problem and the lack of solutions. Despite a wide sense of 'tokenism' there were calls to extend its scope and to internationalise it.

Recommendations flowing from the research are methodological and include possible modifications to the sample and to the stimuli used in the interviews. They do not include any specific implications for the conduct of the Review.

* The adjectives 'highly, medium, lightly and barely' were used to make comprehension easier for the respondents rather than use adjectives 'high, intermediate, low and very low' used by the UK nuclear fraternity.

At the time of writing the UK Government is in the process of setting up a new Committee on Radioactive Waste Management (CoRWM) to review the options for safely managing long-lived radioactive waste and recommend a strategy to the UK Government and the devolved administrations for Scotland, Wales and Northern Ireland.[63] As part of its work, CoRWM will launch a programme of research and debate involving the public and stakeholder groups across the UK, to ensure that its strategy is sound, can win public confidence, and can be implemented.

Professionals

Engineering Institutions, the Society for Radiological Protection, the British Geological Society, the British Nuclear Energy Society, and the UK Environmental Law Association are examples of representative bodies that provide information and facilities for the professional individual in the UK. These organisations have contact with and exchange information with similar bodies in all other countries. As well as providing information and unsolicited opinion and advice they are consulted by governments on specific matters relating to their professional competence.

As an example of the role and function of a professional body, the Institution of Electrical Engineers (IEE)[64] is a Registered Charity, founded in 1871 and is the largest professional engineering society in Europe. The IEE has a worldwide membership of just under 130,000, men and women. The Institution represents the profession of electrical, electronic, manufacturing and systems engineering and related sciences; acts as the voice of the profession in matters of public concern and assists Government to make the public aware of technological issues; sets standards of qualifications for professional electrical, electronics, software, systems and manufacturing engineers; accredits degree courses in subjects relevant to electrical, electronic, manufacturing and information engineering at universities and colleges around the world; accredits professional development schemes for engineering graduates; awards scholarships, grants and prizes; issues regulations for the safe installation of electrical and electronic equipment and takes a leading part in the formulation of national and international standards; provides an extensive range of lectures, meetings, conferences, seminars, residential vacation schools and publications; sets standards for the professional conduct of its members; assists Government to make the public aware of technological issues; offers guidance on best practice in professional development; operates a Career Advisory Service to give advice and assistance to members on various aspects of career development; operates a Learning Resources Service to provide details of potential professional development activities provided by both the IEE and other organisations; operates a computer-assisted information service, Inspec, which has the world's largest computerised database in the English language in physics, electro technology, computer science and control engineering and provides

---

[63] DEFRA News Release (2003), Chairperson and Members sought for new radioactive waste task force, 26 March.

[64] [www.iee.org.uk].

business and technical information on electrical, electronic, IT and manufacturing subjects.

As an example of unsolicited involvement in the question of radioactive waste management the Geological Society and the British Geological Survey convened an open meeting of professional geoscientists and other interested individuals in February 1999 to consider the geo-scientific issues which impact on concepts and solutions for radioactive waste management.[65] Sixty persons attended in an individual capacity. The attendees comprised academics, scientists, consultants and contractors, including those with experience of working in the UK and overseas, geoscientists who had represented environmental groups on radioactive waste management issues and persons employed in the regulatory and waste agencies. The meeting discussed, in both plenary sessions and four syndicate groups, a series of significant questions concerning the design and delivery of a sound waste management policy. Each session was asked to produce statements covering current geo-scientific knowledge and capacity. Consensus was not sought directly; the meeting was asked also to identify those issues about which little consensus existed in the event, there was almost no technical disagreement. The meeting noted that the UK has radioactive waste arising from over fifty years of involvement with both military and civil nuclear programmes. It concluded that the current plans for long-term management arrangements for these wastes are unsatisfactory and that it should be our aim to manage the waste so as to minimise any hazard far into the future.

Employees in the Nuclear Industry

As with many other areas of newsworthy items, employment in the field of nuclear energy and nuclear waste comes to the public attention on a sporadic and often alarmist and sophistic way through the media. Satirical programmes such as 'The Simpsons' have instilled in the minds of sectors of the public an image of the nuclear worker as almost imbecilic. In fact the nuclear worker is generally well qualified and well informed. The nuclear industry has a good record of employee relations and health. In particular the industry monitors the health of its employees as part of the radiological protection programme and regularly publishes statistics regarding personnel safety including exposure to radiation. Accidental exposure to radiation in excess of the dose restriction levels rarely occur but where they do it is reported to the Health and Safety Executive and when damage is caused to an individual the individual is compensated in accordance with a procedure and scale agreed between the companies and the trades unions. The careful handling of radiation doses allows, for example, British Energy (BE)[66] to claim that during 2001 over 97 percent of the people working on their sites received a lower dose at work than the average dose received by members of the public in the UK from natural background sources of radiation. No one in BE in 2001 was permitted to exceed the Company Dose Restriction level of 10 mSv while working on their sites

[65] Summary statement of an open meeting of professional and other interested individuals, Geological Society of London and the British Geological Society, 29 March 1999.
[66] [www.british-energy.com].

against a legal limit of 20 mSv. British Nuclear Fuels (BNFL)[67] claim similar standards for 2001 with only three employees receiving a dose of over 10 mSv and with an average exposure of 0.11 mSv. In 2001 Nycomed Amersham[68] average employee exposure was less than 5 mSv worldwide with fewer than two percent receiving doses in excess of 15 mSv, no employee in 2001 received a dose of greater than 20 mSv. In one of the US pharmacies in 2000 an incident occurred resulting in a total dose of 27 mSv to an employee. The maximum individual dose in the UK was 7.7 mSv. In general the employees in the nuclear industry are statistically healthier than the general average; Sir Richard Doll in 1965[69] noted this phenomenon to be probably due to the 'healthy worker effect'.

People Generally

From the above discussion it may be seen that the public involved in the management of nuclear waste may be considered in three categories: those who have a stake in the nuclear industry and are aware of it; those who have a stake in it and are not yet aware of it; and those with neither a stake or an interest in nuclear energy. The first category is polarised into those for and those against, the endeavour in finding an acceptable solution to the final disposal of nuclear waste is to find common ground and to work towards agreement. Here the involvement of the public is further categorised into the man in the street, the employee and the aggressive opposition.

Since the mid 1950s the attitude of the nuclear industry has made a radical turnaround from one of 'we know best – the public when suitably educated will understand' to one of dialogue by consultation and agreement as demonstrated by the brief outline of the major industrial players of the previous section. A 'trust me' society has transformed to a 'show me' society, best expressed by the editor of a publication supported by BE[70] as follows:

> Conflict in the energy field has been exacerbated by adversarial science, not least over the role of nuclear energy. One form is to doubt the independence of the official findings; another is to present alternative studies with results and implications that differ from the official ones. Companies should not view such perceptual problems as being without substance. It is necessary to recognise how to deal with circumstances where others use alternative, perhaps equally valid, ways to form different perceptions. Irrational reactions cannot be brushed aside. The sensible way is to acknowledge and address public emotions and the deeper concerns therein. The process of building trust means involving stakeholders in decision-making.

> Stakeholder dialogue is one of a number of effective forms of engagement. It is a flexible and deliberative process seeking to find common ground and build agreement out from this area. Both the interests and needs of the parties concerned inform it. The structured format means people confront issues and related perceptions rather than each

---

[67] [www.bnfl.com].
[68] [www.amersham.co.uk].
[69] Doll, Sir Richard (1988), *Healthy Worker Effect*, Imperial Cancer Research Fund Cancer and Epidemiology and Clinical Trials Unit, Radcliff Infirmary, Oxford.
[70] Laughton, M. (2002), Editor, 'Clean Operation?' supported by British Energy, p 6.

other. The problem is that many contentious issues cannot be resolved using this approach, e.g. building or not building new plant. In this case other key decision makers are called upon to adjudicate between two positions, often using the law; however hopes that contentious elements will be handed to the Government who will then simply 'tell' people what they are going to get are as naive as they are misplaced.

On the other hand, despite excellent progress in the development of stakeholder dialogues, thorny issues remain unresolved. Examples are the local opposition to wind farms, biomass or waste burning plants and the whole nuclear issue. Here the Government has an important role to play in influencing public opinion where a decision whether to bring forward for a new nuclear build will lie with the commercial sector, but where answers lie also in the debate over economic instruments as a means of compelling the market to internalise environmental cost, particularly carbon emissions, and in bringing to public perception the very real issues connected with long-term affordability and security of supply.

The writer while taking classes on nuclear law has confirmed the latter point and in trying to show students already conditioned against nuclear energy that there are both sides to the argument. In engaging stakeholders in dialogue there is the opportunity to identify mutual gains and to confront issues. This is most important where matters of risk and risk perception are concerned. Risk perception as discussed earlier is shaped by the amount of control involved. The BE publication reinforces this view:[71]

> Consequently concerns about proximity to a particular facility may be mitigated if people have the opportunity to discuss them openly and maturely. Concerns can even be completely allayed if, after discussion, an alternative corporate proposal emerges with negligible effect on the area.

> Stakeholder discussions may require sharing data and establishing or interpreting particular 'facts'. The sense of control can genuinely be heightened and the adversarial science trap avoided if joint fact-finding is used. Here the stakeholders address what information is needed and why, who might be an acceptable provider for all parties and how should the fact-finding be funded. This means that subsequent discussions can then productively focus on the implications of the information.

Education of the interested man in the street, by involvement and some control over the direction of the moves toward a solution seems to be the vogue and certainly in the process followed in Finland to proceed with a new nuclear power plant it has worked as reported in the previous chapter.

Further Reading

Doll, Sir Richard (1988), *Healthy Worker Effect*, Imperial Cancer Research Fund Cancer and Epidemiology and Clinical Trials Unit, Radcliffe Infirmary, Oxford.
European Commission (2000), *Innovation in a knowledge-driven economy*, COM (2000)567, Sept. Brussels.
House of Lords (1999), *Management of Nuclear Waste*, Third Report of the Select Committee on Science and Technology, Session 1998-9, March, HMSO London.

---

[71] ibid p 60.

McHugh, J et al (2002), *The Way Forward in Radiological Protection*. An Expert Group Report, OECD Paris.

NEA Secretariat (2000), *Society and Nuclear Energy: Towards a Better Understanding*, OECD Paris, p 109.

Renn, O. (1988), 'The Role of Risk Communication and Public Dialogue for Improving Risk Management', *Risk, Decision and Policy*, Vol 3, No. 1, Routledge, London.

Renn, O. and Levine, D. *Credibility and Trust in Risk Communication, Communicating Risks to the Public*, Kluwer Academic Publishing, Dordrecht, Netherlands.

The Royal Commission on Environmental Pollution (2000), 22nd Report. Cm 4749 (June).

Wynne, B. (2000), Public Participation in Scientific Issues: What is the recent fuss about and how should we address it? Public Consultation in Science, British Council Lecture, Amsterdam, Netherlands.

Chapter Five

Sources of Law Relating to Nuclear Waste

The Background[1]

The rules for the regulation of ionising radiation and nuclear technology are a product of the synergy of technoscience and law. The development of the use of ionising radiation has proceeded along with the perception of risk and the consequent constraints to ensure the minimum of risk commensurate with the benefits of proceeding. Less than 100 years ago the science of radiation was new and the benefits of its application were variable. Information accumulated regarding the benefits and risks from the beneficial use of X-rays in medical diagnostic procedures and in the fashionable use in cosmetic applications such as the treatment for acne. The only way to discover the effect of radiation was through example supplemented by theoretical experimentation. Risks were identified and slowly understood; firstly deterministic effects of high doses of radiation were recognised and sensible precautionary limits to exposure were set. Latterly stochastic effects of small doses were predicted and by epidemiological investigation effects were projected to large populations. Precautionary limits were set to ensure the total avoidance of deterministic harm and to be well below dose levels at which the risk of stochastic harm to all but a very small proportion of the population was perceived. This has been an exercise of technoscience that is still in process. The regulation of radiation releases to the worker and to the population were obviously in the interests of the technoscientist who was the first in line for exposure and so margins except in the case of accidents were adequate in the circumstances of the knowledge available. In the case of accident, limiting precautions such as shielding, remote handling and evacuation to limit the dose have been developed by the technoscientist. Because the public were not affected by radiation except in the unlikely event of an accident releasing radioactive material they were not involved in such decision-making. The problem is now that as the wider public perceives that it is affected by radiation and that a self-interested minority made the decisions, they do not trust the processes.

Recognition of the possible hazards of radiation became public with the explosion of the atom bomb. Since that time statutory regulation has developed under the influence of four vectors; the need to control radioactive materials; the protection of workers and the general public from harmful effects of radiation; the safeguarding of materials and the means of manufacturing materials for nuclear weapons and, finally, environmental protection. Criminal law ensures the

---

[1] Riley, Peter (2002), 'Nuclear Energy; a sustainable future?' Engineering Management Journal, Vol.12 No. 2, April, p 97.

enforcement of regulations in the case of limits to exposure to radiation under non-accident conditions; the limiting values are those determined by technoscientific procedures outlined above. In the case of breach of regulatory limits, penalties and compensation are governed by statute. Public interest was invoked as a reason to introduce the licensing of nuclear facilities, strict (or absolute) liability of the operator, backed by a financial limit, compulsory insurance and Government responsibility in excess of those provisions.[2] In the 1950s, in the face of threats to the availability of fossil fuels, the need to develop peaceful uses for nuclear energy to supplement the sources of energy at risk of diminution and deliberate withdrawal was seen to be in the public interest. It was also seen to be necessary to encourage developers by enabling them to limit their exposure to the financial effects of perceived potential damage to property and persons. To offset these obvious advantages to the potential developer the requirement to show negligent behaviour in the case of a nuclear accident in a nuclear facility was removed and replaced by a strict liability for such damage. The operator became strictly liable; a claimant would not have to prove negligence in the case of a nuclear incident. This freezing of the common law could have lead to the ossification of the law, regulation and practices set by technoscientist. However, the practices of the technoscientist were imbued with common law principles, in particular the concept of reasonableness. This concept introduced the requirement to ensure that whatever the radiation dose or release levels set down in regulations, authorisations and licenses, the operator would be obliged always to endeavour to reduce the dose levels to a reasonably achievable level. The introduction of reasonableness meant that the operator always must be aware of the circumstances of current knowledge of the effects of radiation and the most modern measures available to reduce exposure to radiation. The technoscientist has the obligation to ensure that such knowledge and measures are available to the operator. This reasonable approach satisfied the development of the technology and has influenced the development of the more general laws of environment and health and safety.

The Question of Risk

Throughout this chapter and the following chapter the word risk is liberally used. Risk is according to the New Oxford Dictionary of English, 'the possibility that something unpleasant or unwelcome will happen'. In its explanation of the basis for decisions about the regulation of risk[3] the HSE notes that the conduct of human affairs does not divide into black and white terms such as 'safe' and 'unsafe' and the word risk implies there are degrees of safety. Four vectors, as outlined above, direct the basis of regulation: health and safety, liability for damage, safeguards and environmental law. Two of these vectors, health and safety and environmental law involve the balancing of the risk of harm of carrying out an operation against

---

[2] Paris and Vienna Conventions on third party liability in the field of nuclear energy (see below).
[3] HSE (1999), *Reducing Risks, Protecting People*, Health and Safety Executive, Dec. HMSO London.

the wider benefits of that operation and in doing so numerical targets are used. In the case of health and safety in the UK the HSE have developed a philosophy based on the tolerability of risk and ALARP that is concerned with the exposure to radiation of the workforce and members of the public by normal operation of a nuclear facility and from all possible accident scenarios. The philosophy also takes account of wider issues such as societal risk, changing values and expectations of society, court judgments and wider principles of good regulation.[4] Upper limits of tolerable risk, from normal operation, are set by existing Basic Safety Limits (BSLs). The BSL for members of the public (expressed in terms of maximum allowable radiation dose) is lower than the BSL for the workforce; below the BSL, doses must be reduced to levels that are As Low As Reasonably Practicable (ALARP). Each BSL is complemented by a BSO (Basic Safety Objective) that is lower than the BSL; the ALARP requirement also applies below the BSO level but the regulator does not normally require the licensee to devote excessive resources to demonstrate that below the BSO the risk is ALARP. For possible accident scenarios there are different BSLs. For members of the public the risks of death per year implied are: BSLs from normal operation 5×10^{-5} and from accidents 10^{-5} and BSOs from normal operation 10^{-6} and from accidents 10^{-7}. These levels of risk have been determined by the HSE based on the risk of death from any industrial activity of 10^{-4} per year[5] that also corresponds to an individual's risk of death by road accident in the UK. The Hinckley Point C public inquiries[6] proposed that a tolerable upper limit to risk of death to an individual member of the public from the operation of the proposed PWR should be 10^{-5} per year subject to the condition that the risk was ALARP. The HSE also defined a broadly acceptable level of risk: a level considered small by comparison with other generally accepted risks and such that, provided precautions are taken and benefit is to be gained, the level of risk posed by an activity does not worry or cause the individual to change behaviour. The level of 10^{-6} per year corresponds to an individual's risk of death by electrocution in the home. This level concurs with the findings of the Royal Society who judged that very few people would commit their own resources to reduce further an annual risk of death 10^{-6} per year.[7]

The link between radiation dose and risk is made by using a risk factor used by the ICRP[8] and endorsed by the NRPB which associates a dose of 1 mSv to a suitably mixed population with an average risk of death of 5×10^{-5} per year. The BSOs and BSLs mentioned above provide standards against which the NII can make judgments on the Safety of the plant. Using the ICRP factor doses of 1mSv and 0.02 mSv can be estimated to result in the risk of death of 5×10^{-5} and 10^{-6} per year respectively. An accident sequence with an assessed frequency of 10^{-6} per year (once in 1,000,000 plant years) is called a design basis accident. The HSE

---

[4] ibid p 38.
[5] HSE (1992), Tolerability of risk from nuclear power Stations, HSE Books.
[6] Barnes, Michael QC (1990), *The Hinckley Point C Public Inquiries*. A Report, HMSO London.
[7] Royal Society (1983), Risk Assessment: Report of a Royal Society Study Group, London.
[8] ICRP (1990), *Publication 60*, London.

requires that it should be demonstrated that a design basis accident would result in no significant dose to persons off the licensed site. These calculations, however, take no account of people's real behaviour, which may include self-evacuation or of countermeasures that would be implemented to protect them in the event of an accident. Taking into account these real factors the HSE conclude that the risk of death to any individual living close to a nuclear plant that conforms to current safety principles from all accident scenarios would be at or near the 10^{-6} level.

Environmental protection is through the control of radioactive discharges that are limited by their predicted effects. Conformity with a maximum exposure level to the public of 1mSv per year is suggested by a constraint that the dose to members of a critical group from the activities of a site should be below 0.5 mSv per year.[9] A critical group level of 0.02 mSv per year being a lower level of optimisation below which the regulators would not seek to secure future reduction proves that the operator was using Best Practicable Means (BPM) to limit releases. Using the ICRP recommended risk factors the 0.5 mSv per year represents a risk of 2.5×10^{-5} per year and the 0.02 mSv per year a risk of 10^{-6} per year. The UK is committed to the OSPAR Sutra statement[10] and consequently has set a target to reduce radioactive discharges such that a representative member of the UK general public will not be exposed to a mean dose of more than 0.02 mSv per year as a result of authorised discharges to the marine environment from the year 2020 onwards.

The Law Relating to Nuclear Facilities and Radiation in General

The basis of the law in this area is the radiological protection system recommended by the ICRP and described in detail in Appendix II. To remind readers the following is an extract from the appendix:

The Biological Basis of the Commission's Policy

There are two types of harmful radiation effects to be protected against. High doses will cause inevitable harm, the *deterministic effects*, which do not appear if the dose does not exceed a *threshold value*. The primary protection policy is then to prevent high doses. Both low and high doses may cause *stochastic*, i.e. randomly occurring, effects (cancer and hereditary disorders). At low doses, of the order of those caused by natural sources of radiation, these effects will occur only with a small probability, which is judged by the Commission to be in proportion to the dose. This proportionality (the linear, non-threshold dose-response relationship) has characteristics that facilitate the administration of radiation protection. For example, it makes it possible to consider each source and exposure separately from other sources and exposures – the probability of harm per unit dose will always be the same. However, the probabilistic nature of the stochastic effects makes it impossible to make a clear distinction between 'safe' and 'dangerous', a fact that causes problems in explaining the control of radiation risks. The major policy implication of a non-threshold relationship for stochastic effects is that some finite risk

[9] Department of the Environment (1995), Review of Radioactive Waste Management Policy. Final Conclusions, July, Cm 2919 HMSO.
[10] Ministerial Meeting of the OSPAR Commission (1998), *OSPAR Strategy with Regard to Radioactive Substances Paper No. 1998-17*, July, Sutra, Portugal.

must be accepted at any level of protection. Zero risk is not an option. This leads to the basic system of protection which has three components – (1) the justification of a practice, which implies doing more good than harm, (2) the optimisation of protection, which implies maximising the margin of good over harm, and (3) the use of dose limits, which implies an adequate standard of protection even for the most highly exposed individuals. A simple proportional relationship also has some important practical implications. It allows – (a) doses within an organ or tissue of the body to be averaged over that organ or tissue, (b) doses received at different times to be added, and (c) doses received from one source to be considered independently of the doses received from other sources. These practical aspects are of overwhelming importance in radiological protection because of the complexity of the dose distributions in both time and space and because of the ubiquitous presence of natural sources of radiation. The Commission makes a distinction between what it calls *practices* and *intervention*. A practice is a human activity that is undertaken by choice but which increases the overall exposure. For that reason, practices have to be controlled so that additional doses are appropriately restricted. Intervention is an action against radiation exposures that already exist, for the purpose of reducing the exposures. Both practices and intervention are justified when they cause more good than harm.

The forces of law that constrain those who deal with radiation, the operators of nuclear facilities in particular, may be represented by four vectors of legal regulation which are broadly summarised as legislation relating to health and safety, liability for damage, safeguards in support of the non-proliferation of nuclear weapons and environmental law. The form of the law relating to radiation and nuclear facilities has been shaped primarily by health and safety considerations and the liability for accidental damage; non-proliferation of nuclear weapons and the regulations relating to safeguards has to a large extent been fitted in alongside security, operational and quality procedures. Nevertheless, the ICRP recommendations are the bedrock of radiation regulation and while dose limits may be understood in regulatory terms, the question of justification and optimisation are peculiar to nuclear law.

Justification and Optimisation of the Use of Radiation

According to the ICRP system of protection, practices involving the exposure to radiation should follow the general principles of justification, optimisation, dose and risk limits. Failure to follow any of these principles could be considered to be a breach of the duty of care and the basis of a prima facie case against the user in negligence. Such a case could not easily be contested where dose limits were exceeded. In some States of the US and in the UK there is precedent to show that the failure to follow the principle of optimisation would be a breach of the duty of care and whilst the failure to follow the principle of justification and the failure to meet risk limits as a basis for establishing a breach of the duty of care has not been tested in the courts there are many opportunities to exercise legal minds.

Justification

According to the New Oxford English Dictionary 'to justify' is to prove to be right or reasonable. Article 6(a) of the *Basic Safety Standards Directive (80/836/Euratom)* States that each activity resulting in an exposure to ionising radiation shall be 'justified' in advance by the advantages which it produces. The origin of this principle is an ICRP recommendation[11] that States that no practice involving exposures to radiation should be adopted unless it produces sufficient benefits to the exposed individuals or to society to offset the radiation detriment it causes. Thus the exercise of justification will involve weighing the benefits arising from the activity against the radiation detriment it produces, but it is not necessary to show that the activity is the best option available. The limits to the process and application of justification are being tested in the English courts. Although there is no requirement under the *Radioactive Substances Act 1993(RSA93)*, the judicial decision in *R v Secretary of State for the Environment, ex p Greenpeace*[12] has highlighted the requirement to interpret the UK legislation in accordance with *Euratom Directives*. In this case, which was in relation to the grant of a radioactive waste disposal authorisation for the THORP reprocessing plant, Potts J held that the principle set out in Article 6(a) of the Basic Safety Standards Directive should be read into the *RSA*. As a result of the judgment of Potts J, a 'justification' exercise of this type must be applied to every consideration of an authorisation of radioactive waste discharge under sections 13 and 16 of *RSA93*. According to a report by the UK HSE,[13] justification of types or classes of practice is a Government activity. The requirement for a site-specific justification in *Directive 80/836/EURATOM* has been superseded by the requirement in Council *Directive 96/29/EURATOM* that came into force in 2000 by the justification of a generic type or class of practice. In the case of *R (on the application of Friends of the Earth Ltd and Greenpeace Ltd.) v Secretary of State for the Environment, Food and Rural Affairs and another*,[14] Collins J. concluded that once it had been determined that a process (the manufacture of MOX) was justified, that exercise would not have to be undertaken again, unless there was new evidence, if any other site was proposed. In the case of *R (on the application of Marchiori) v Environment Agency*,[15] Turner J noted that a correct interpretation of the IRCP recommendations did not bear out the applicants' argument that design, manufacture and decommissioning were separate processes requiring separate

---

[11] ICRP Publication 60, paragraph 112.
[12] *R v Secretary of State for the Environment, ex p Greenpeace* [1994] 4 All ER 352, [1994] 4 All ER 352.
[13] HSE on behalf of DEFRA (2003), National Report on conformance with the obligations of the Joint Convention on the Safety of Spent Fuel Management and on the Safety of Radioactive Waste Management, May, E24 p 22. HMSO London.
[14] The Court of Appeal heard the appeal on 27 and 28 Nov. 2001 and delivered the judgment on 7 Dec. 2001.
[15] [2001] EWHC Admin 267, [2001] J.P.L. 1438 appeal dismissed [2002] EWCA Civ 3, [2002] Eu.L.R. 225.

justifications. Expert evidence amplified the EA's view that justification could sensibly be considered only on the basis of the operation as a whole. The question of whether 'sunk' costs should be considered in examining the economic aspects of the justification of a process has been raised in the context of MOX manufacture in the UK[16] and it was decided in the Court of Appeal that in the economic assessment of MOX manufacture such costs could properly be disregarded but the decision was restricted to a situation where the generic practice in question would be confined to the operation of a single plant.[17]

Optimisation

According to the NRPB[18] the choice of the words 'as low as reasonably achievable economic and social factors being taken into account (ALARA)' shows that the fundamental aspect of the ALARA requirement is a balancing of the benefit of radiation dose reduction, with its health and social implications, against the overall cost of the resources, and of any additional harm included in achieving that reduction. The NRPB says that ALARA does not require everything possible, or technically feasible, to be done to reduce doses without consideration of the cost or of the magnitude of the benefit from dose reduction.

The question of failure to follow the principle of optimisation, or the ALARA principle[19] has been tested in the US. Following the accident at Three Mile Island the Court held[20] that the duty of care owed to the plaintiffs is measured by whether the defendants released radiation in excess of the levels permitted by the code of federal regulations rather than the ALARA regulations and is measured at the boundary of the facility and not the amount of radiation to which each plaintiff was exposed. However in another case[21] the court ruled that ALARA was the standard by which the duty of care should be determined; the defendant must demonstrate that the release/exposure was as low as reasonably achievable and it is for the jury to decide if it had been achieved.

In the context of the storage and disposal of radioactive waste in the UK the Radioactive Waste Management Advisory Committee (RWMAC)[22] recommended to the Secretary of State for the Environment that it would be desirable to find a

---

[16] Administrative Court, 15 Nov. 2001 ELM 13 [2001]6 p 276, ENDS 323 Dec. 2001.
[17] Leigh, W. J. (2003), 'The Principle of Justification: the Application of the Principle to the Manufacture of MOX Fuel in the UK.' *Nuclear Law Bulletin* 71 Vol 2003/1. OECD Paris.
[18] NRPB (1986), Advice given by the NRPB in compliance with the Direction of the Health Ministers dated 9 August 1977 in relation to radiological protection standards. NRPB ASP 9, para 3, Mar., Chilton.
[19] ALARA - As Low As Reasonably Achievable. For a rigorous analysis of the principle of optimisation see: Lochard, Jacques and Boehler, Marie-Claude (1993), 'Optimising Radiation Protection-the ethical and legal bases.' *Nuclear Law Bulletin* 42.
[20] 67F.3d1103.
[21] *James v Southern California Edison Co.* District Court for the Southern District of California. D.C. No CV-94-01085-NAJ. and 94F3d651 US App. LEXIS 37542.
[22] Radioactive Waste Management Advisory Committee (1984), Fifth Annual Report, Jun. Appendix C p 40 para 5.

principle more readily operable in law than the obligation recommended by the ICRP[23] that discharges of radioactive waste should be contained so that exposures be 'as low as reasonably achievable taking economic and social factors into account' (ALARA). It was their view that by applying to those discharges the principle 'as low as reasonably practicable' (ALARP) the regulations and certificates of authorisation would have the backing of the common law and that the application of ALARP as it applies to the actual discharge would be fully under the control of the licensee in contrast to the ICRP recommendations of the principle of ALARA which refers to exposures, i.e. the doses to individuals and communities, which are removed from the point of discharge and therefore will be affected by circumstances not under the direct control of the licensee.[24] Having thus made a recommendation that would be enforceable the RWMAC added to the recommendation that discharges: ... should be reduced to a level which is 'as low as reasonably practicable' by using the 'best practicable means' thus moving to a standard which in law would be interpreted more strictly than 'reasonably practicable'. According to Selwyn:[25]

> 'So far as is practicable'; 'best practicable means' is a high standard but not an absolute one. If something is practicable it must be done; if the best practicable means are required, then it is up to the person on whom the obligation is placed to find the best practicable means, and to constantly bring his knowledge up to date. However, it is not practicable to take precautions against a danger which is not known to exist, although once the danger is known, it becomes practicable to do something about it (*Cartwright v GKN Sankey Ltd*). The test is one of foresight, not hindsight (*Edwards v National Coal Board*). The standard of practicability is that of current knowledge and invention (*Adsett v K and L Steel Founders and Engineers Ltd*). Once something is found to be practicable, it is feasible, and it must be done, no matter how inconvenient or expensive it may be to do it. The burden of proof to show that it was not practicable to do something, or to do more than was in fact done, is on the person upon whom the obligation is placed (in civil proceedings) and upon the defendant or accused in criminal proceedings. (*HSWA* Section 40)

It would appear that by taking the route of 'best practicable means (BPM)' the RWMAC recommendation would then satisfy the requirement 'As low as technically achievable' (ALATA).[26] On the basis of evidence presented at the Sizewell 'B' Power Station public inquiry[27] the DOE, an Authorising Department, appear to have a different view. In a paper 'General Principles Governing the

---

[23] ICRP Publication 26.

[24] House of Commons (1986), *Radioactive Waste*, First Report from the Environment Committee, January HMSO, para 143.

[25] Selwyn (1999), Law *of Health and Safety at Work*, 8th Ed. Croner Publications, p 61 para 1.101.

[26] Webb, G.A.M. (1986), *Development of ALARA - philosophy and practice*. Institution of Nuclear Engineers Symposium, Sept.

[27] Sizewell B Inquiry (1984), Evidence DOE/P/2(ADD 3), Sept. DOE.

Setting of Control Limits on Radioactive Discharges to the Environment'[28] it is said that:

> What constitutes BPM (best practicable means) may vary from one site to another and will change from time to time for a given plant according to local circumstances.... For example, practicable has been defined as meaning reasonably practicable having regard amongst other things to local conditions and circumstances, to the financial implications and to the current state of technical knowledge...Should disagreement arise.... as to what constitutes BPM.... to the satisfaction of the Inspector the matter can be referred to the Courts with whom the final decision rests.

Although the BPM philosophy has developed through the pollution legislation route and ALARP has developed through the health and safety route it is implied in the DOE evidence to the Sizewell Inquiry and by RWMAC in their advice to the Minister that both practices would be judged using the tests established in *Edwards v NCB*.[29] In the later case of *Cartwright v GKN Sankey Ltd*[30] it was said that:

> What the occupiers have to do under Section 4(1) they have to do 'so far as is practicable'. Under (Factories Act 1961) Sec.63 (1) and (previously under Sec.47 (1)) they have to take 'all practicable measures' and in particular 'when the nature of the process makes it practicable' provide exhaust appliances, etc. In neither case is the word 'practicable' qualified by 'reasonable' or 'reasonably' as it often is elsewhere in the Act. .... Plainly the standard required of occupiers under these sections is a high and strict one, though 'practicable' qualifies it to some extent and reduces the duty below what would otherwise be an absolute one.

In the Court of Appeal in *Adsett v K and K Steel Founders and Engineers Ltd*[31] Singleton L J said:

> In deciding whether all practicable measures were taken one must have regard to the state of knowledge at the material time, and, particularly, to the knowledge of scientific experts.

In support of the DOE and RWMAC interpretation that practicable means reasonably practicable it could be argued that under the *Control of Pollution Act 1974* according to s72 'best practicable means' does mean 'reasonably practicable'; s72 of the Act States:

> In that expression 'practicable' means reasonably practicable having regard among other things to local conditions and circumstances, to the current state of technical knowledge and to the financial implications.

However, it is quite clear that this interpretation of the definition is strictly limited to Part III of the *Act* that deals only with noise. The words of s72 (1) limiting the definition to 'this part of this *Act*' also limit the definition to the *Control of*

---

[28] DoE and MAFF (1985), Disposal Facilities for Low and Intermediate Level Radioactive Waste, Report on a Consultative Exercise on the Draft Principles for the Protection of the Human Environment, HMSO London.

[29] [1949] 1 All E.R. 743.

[30] [1972] 2 Lloyds Rep 242.

[31] [1953] 2 All E.R. 320.

Pollution Act (1974) only. The Government's statement[32] that radioactive waste does not fall within the *Control of Pollution Act 1974* adds strength to this conclusion that 'best practicable means' (BPM) is not to be qualified as 'reasonably practicable'.   Therefore it would appear that the Government is prepared in future to have the means by which radioactive waste is controlled and released to the atmosphere or sea or stored, judged by a standard which requires that once a measure is found to be practicable, if feasible it should be implemented no matter how inconvenient or expensive it may be. This view seems to be shared by the House of Commons Environment Committee[33] in their conclusion regarding discharge limits where they refer only to the principle of ALARA and to BPM in setting discharge limits below a ceiling which will satisfy the dose limits[34] (i.e. the dose which might be received by a critical group).   No mention is made of the ALARP principle. The Committee further recommend that once discharge limits are set reference to ALARA or BPM in the Certificate of Authorisation should be deleted.   The current view of the HSE[35] is that in the UK, the policy on the regulation of radioactive waste discharges and disposals is governed by two optimisation concepts: BPEO and BPM. If BPEO and BPM are applied to a set of processes, facilities and methods of operation, then it is considered that radiation risks to the public and the environment will conform to the ALARA principle. BPEO[36] is about the optimisation of waste management options (for example, apportionment of waste disposal between environmental media) with respect to its environmental impact, whereas BPM is about the continual optimisation of the management of individual waste streams.

In the *Health and Safety at Work Act 1974 (HSWA74)*, part of the 'ALARP' term 'so far as is reasonably practicable' occurs throughout the Act. In a guide to the Act, the Health and Safety Commission (HSC) state, 'Although none of the expressions are defined in the Act, they have acquired meanings through many interpretations by the courts'.

The position in common law is that, *prima facie*, a measure that is practicable is reasonably practicable. This may be modified according to the test in *Edwards v National Coal Board*,[37] where Asquith L J said:

> 'Reasonably Practicable' is a narrower term than 'physically possible' and seems to me to imply that a computation must be made by the owner in which the quantum or risk is placed in one scale and the sacrifice involved in the measures necessary for averting the risk (whether in money, time or trouble) is placed in the other, and that, if it be shown

---

[32] Supra Disposal Facilities.

[33] Supra House of Commons First Report p xxiii para 155.

[34] SI 1875 No 1333 Health and Safety. Ionising Radiations Regulations 1985.

[35] HSE on behalf of DEFRA (2003), National Report on conformance with the obligations of the *Joint Convention on the Safety of Spent Fuel Management and on the Safety of Radioactive Waste Management*, May, B20 p 8.

[36] Smith, R.E. (2002), 'Some observations on the concept of best practicable environmental option (BPEO) in the context of radioactive waste management', *Nuclear Energy*, 41, No.4, Aug. 271-281.

[37] [1949] 1All E.R. 743 at 747.

that there is a gross disproportion between them – the risk being insignificant to the sacrifice – the defendants discharge the onus on them. Moreover, this computation falls to be made by the owner at a point in time anterior to the accident.

In criminal proceedings it is for the accused to prove that it was not reasonably practicable for him to do more than was in fact done to satisfy the requirement. He can establish this by the burden of proof, i.e. on the balance of probabilities. Finally, because the requirement of reasonableness is an objective one, it is for the court to decide as a question of fact based on the evidence whether or not something was reasonably practicable.

The saving grace of nuclear power is that it would be possible to operate on the basis of zero emissions. This has not yet been accepted, there are still releases to the environment and there is still the possibility of accidental releases. Nuclear and radiation practices having contributed to the development of environmental law must show that the industry continues to respect the concerns of the public in respect of the environment by demonstrable support of environmental law principles.

Environmental Law[38]

Environmental law is a body of law that has developed in parallel with nuclear and radiation law; some would say that environmental regulation has, to some extent, been shaped by the experience of the technological, legal and social developments in nuclear and radiation applications. Until the late seventies and the influence of the Brundtland Report[39] the laws that we now term environmental law were probably not seen as a coherent body of law. Environment concerns were dealt with incidentally; for example the *Clean Air Act* was introduced in England after the effects of dirty air were made painfully obvious by the great smog of the early 1950s that killed thousands of Londoners. Similarly industry, including the nuclear industry was tarred with the same brush; it dealt with problems as they arose as demonstrated by the practice of waste disposal. The environment was seen as having an assimilative capacity and was a resource to be used. Deep trenches under the seas were seen as being sufficiently removed from human contact to serve as dumping grounds for low-level radioactive waste. The eventual leakage of radioactive contaminated material from deteriorating or damaged containers should it happen, was not seen as a problem for current generations nor even a serious problem for future generations on account of the low level of radiation from the disposed material, the radioactive decay and the likely slow and diluted leakage which would ensure that any radioactivity from the released material would be lost against the natural radiation background. The problem was that scientific proof was lacking, that arguments in support of the practice were not convincingly presented, such arguments came after the practice had been in operation for some time and that the logic of the arguments was easily destroyed

---

[38] Riley, Peter (2000), The Precautionary Principle and its Practice, *Engineering Management Journal*, Vol. 10 No. 6, Dec. p 281.
[39] Brundtland, H.G. (Edair) (1987), *Our Common Future*. Oxford University Press.

once the thinking public became aware of the practice. Public concern has been expressed about the effect of released radiation on animals, insects, bacteria and plant life. Radiation protection systems have concentrated on the protection of humans; the ethical considerations about aspects of the use of radioactive material such as the disposal of radioactive waste[40] focus on the effects on humans. The implication must be that it is considered that life in general will be protected if practices with radioactive material are organised to ensure human safety. A hypothesis that has yet to be verified and one that assumes we have more knowledge about the environment than we really have; the practice is still being tested!

It may be said that environmental law as a coherent body of law came of age at the Rio Conference[41] with the *Rio Declaration of Principles (Agenda 21)* which relate to the prevention of pollution and the protection of the environment. In the context of potentially polluting processes the alliteration of Ps define a set of principles, Prevention, Precaution, Proportionality and the Polluter must pay. By prevention of harmful polluting releases to the environment and measures to prevent accidental releases, the effects of an activity are confined to that activity and the environment is protected. Prevention therefore can only operate where the nature and effects on the environment of all releases from a process are known and controllable. However, since full knowledge is ephemeral a decision to proceed with a process will always be subject to doubt. In the absence of full knowledge it may be acceptable to proceed on a precautionary basis. This was recognised in principle 15 of Agenda 21:

> In order to protect the environment, the precautionary approach shall be widely applied by States *according to their capabilities*. Where there are threats of serious or irreversible damage, lack of full scientific certainty shall not be used as a reason for postponing *cost-effective measures* to prevent environmental degradation (parenthesis by author).

The principle of precaution was taken into European Law by the *Maastricht Treaty*:

> Community policy on the environment shall aim at a high level of protection *taking into account the diversity of situations in the various regions of the Community*. It shall be based on the precautionary principle and on the principles that preventative action should be taken, that environmental damage should as a priority be rectified at source and that the polluter should pay. Environmental protection requirements must be integrated into the definition and implementation of other Community policies[42] (parenthesis by author).

---

[40] OECD-NEA (1995), The Environmental and Ethical Basis of Geological Disposal, OECD Paris.
[41] United Nations Conference on Environment and Development (1992), Rio de Janeiro, June.
[42] Title XVI of EC Treaty, Article 130r.

The relevance of the precautionary principle in English law was raised in the case of *Duddridge*[43] [44]where the issue was whether the Secretary of State, in declining to take specific measures to limit the level of electromagnetic field from power lines, had acted unlawfully in the light of the precautionary principle. The question was raised but not, in the writer's opinion, answered as to whether the precautionary principle was intended to apply to long-term harm to the environment itself rather than damage to human health from transitory environmental conditions. It was decided by the Judge that *Article 130r of the EC Treaty* only lays down principles upon which Community policy on the environment will be based and so specific obligations, at whatever level, will be identified in subsidiary legislation, Directives and Regulations. It is to be expected that as with the Integrated Pollution Prevention and Control Directive[45] specific reference will be made to Article 130r in the preliminaries of all environmentally related legislation emanating from Europe and so the precautionary principle will therefore apply to all aspects of environmental law. Elen Stokes notes[46] that European case law insinuates an elevation of the status of the precautionary principle beyond a pure policy tool to a legally binding norm and whilst it is undoubtedly growing in significance, it simultaneously generates growing confusion and scepticism.

Nuclear and radiation matters in Europe are subject to the *Euratom Treaty*, for example the *Basic Safety Standards Directive*[47] and so not directly subject to the principles identified in the EC Treaty but it is probably only a matter of time before the two treaties are harmonised on the question of environmental law. The construction and operation of a nuclear facility is, however, subject to environmental impact assessment under the *Council Directive 85/337/EEC* and so must take account of the principles of environmental law. In an ongoing series of cases in the Supreme Court of Ireland[48] the plaintiffs, the citizens of Ireland and the European Union, claim that British Nuclear Fuels plc in not carrying out an environmental impact assessment before establishing a nuclear fuel reprocessing plant at Sellafield (Thorpe) is in breach of its obligations under the *EC Treaty* and in contravention, inter alia, of the precautionary principle contrary to Article 130r of the *Treaty*. Although these Irish cases are ongoing it should be noted that a similar approach was made in England in 1994. That case[49] was also about Thorpe. It was a judicial review of the Secretary of State's decision to grant an authorisation for the discharge of radioactive waste to the sea and air from the Sellafield site. Potts J. concluded in that case that the Thorpe project predated the

---

[43] R v Secretary of State for Trade and Industry ex p Duddridge [1995] Env L.R. 151.

[44] Hughes, D.J., 'The Status of the Precautionary Principle in Law' *[1995] 7JEL224.*

[45] Council Directive 96/61/EC of 24 Sept. 1996 O.J.L 257 10 Oct 1996.

[46] Stokes, Elen R. (2003), 'Precautionary steps: the development of the precautionary principle in EU jurisprudence', *ELM 15[2003]1.*

[47] Council Directive 96/29/Euratom of 13 May 1996 laying down the basic safety standards for the protection of health of workers and the general public against the dangers arising from ionising radiation (O.J.L 159, 29.6.1996).

[48] An early case was *Short v BNFLplc* where the issue of jurisdiction was determined.

[49] *R v Secretary of State for the Environment and others ex parte Greenpeace Limited and others.* [1994] Env L.R. 401, [1994] 4 All ER 352.

Environment Impact Assessment Directive 85/337 and so Ministers were therefore not under a legal duty to provide an environmental impact assessment. However, he expressed his satisfaction that the information provided by BNFL and made available for consultation by the Inspectorate and the Ministers met the substantive requirements of the Directive.

In the extracts from Agenda 21, and the *Maastricht Treaty* quoted above parts have been parenthesised; these phrases describe limits to the strict application of the principles of prevention and precaution implying their relaxation to enable their implementation within the capabilities of the different regions of the European Union and limited to cost effective measures. This brings into play the third principle, that of proportionality or as it is known in the radiation field 'optimisation'.

The final principle that the polluter must pay is specifically identified in the *Maastricht Treaty* and has been accepted from the outset of nuclear liability legislation in respect of damage arising from a nuclear incident as a strict and absolute obligation of the nuclear facility operator and Governments.

The Precautionary Principle

It can be seen therefore that the precautionary principle is an intrinsic and pivotal part of a system of environmental protection principles that have been accepted by the United Nations, built into European law and which through directives and national legislation are part of English law. The principle has been described by six basic concepts:[50] *preventative anticipation*, a willingness to take action in the absence of scientific proof of evidence of the need for the proposed action; *safeguarding of ecological space* or room for manoeuvre as a recognition that margins of tolerance should not even be approached, let alone breached; *proportionality of response or cost effectiveness of margins of error* to show that the selected degree of restraint is not unduly costly; *duty of care, or onus of proof on those who propose change*, this raises profound questions over the degree of freedom to take calculated risks, thereby to innovate, and to compensate for possible losses by building in ameliorative measures; *promoting the cause of intrinsic natural rights*, the notion of ecological harm is widened to include the need to allow natural processes to function in such a manner as to maintain the essential support for all life on earth; *paying for past ecological debt*, precaution is essentially forward looking but there are those who recognise that in the application of care, burden sharing, ecologically buffered cost effectiveness and shifting the burden of proof, there ought to be a penalty for not being cautious or caring in the past.

This academic view that the scope of the precautionary principle covers both the long-term environmental harm and the damage to human health. How then does nuclear and radiation law and its practice stand against these concepts? As mentioned above, in many ways the nuclear experience has probably been the

---

[50] O'Riordan, Timothy and Cameron, James (1994), *Interpreting the Precautionary Principle*. Earthscan Publications, London.

paradigm for the development of the principles outlined here. The only failings are that the light was hidden under a bushel of secrecy and that methodology and technology having moved on, the actions taken could in hindsight have been different. Let us take the six concepts elucidated above and consider a typical nuclear project engineered before such concepts were formally recognised as a basis for the precautionary principle of environmental law.

Preventative anticipation and the safeguarding of ecological space can be seen in operation in the decisions to contain the nuclear reaction, to create a pressure boundary and to provide secondary containment to guard against the possibility of accidental escape of radioactive materials beyond the primary boundaries. The provision of shielding in anticipation of future activities, the storage of irradiated fuel in shielded and accessible facilities which preserve options without harming the environment are actions in the absence of definitive knowledge of the way ahead. The safety case and design basis show anticipatory actions.

Proportionality of response etc. is implicit in the ICRP philosophy of optimisation in radiation protection as manifest in the *Basic Safety Standards*. Through the process of setting safe levels of radiation exposure which are well below the levels at which stochastic harm is seen to occur and then endeavouring to reduce them to levels below that to as low as reasonably achievable (ALARA) by design and operation is also evidence of safeguarding ecological space. The 'reasonably achievable' character of ALARA also satisfies the requirement of proportionality.

A duty of care and the reasonable demonstration of the analysis of risks by following the process of environmental impact identification and assessment, building a safety case, setting standards and design basis for a nuclear facility and taking account of the effects on the environment as well as analysing possible accident scenarios and their consequences through design processes such as HAZOP analyses allows ameliorative measures to be seen to be built into design and procedures.

By satisfying the precautionary principle as outlined above the concept of promoting the cause of intrinsic natural rights of man is also satisfied. Radiation protection philosophy, as mentioned above, appears to take the view that if man is protected then so is all other forms of life. Finally some of the assumptions made and actions taken in the design, construction and operation of nuclear facilities have not been correct and some of the actions taken have not been under the necessary strict control outlined above, particularly in the military area, thus resulting in personal pain and some expensive and time consuming efforts to remedy the effects. The penalties are being paid in costly reclamation. Where the damage extends to other than the operator or the Government the licensed operator is strictly liable for the damage. It is clear that the polluter is paying for past ecological debt.

In Practice

Implied into the precautionary principle is the presumption that systems will exist to identify and remedy failure to take the steps necessary to satisfy the principles of environmental law, in particular the precautionary principle, and that such systems, responses, recommendations and actions are open to scrutiny by the general public. Such systems operate at policy levels and licences to construct, commission, operate and decommission nuclear facilities are granted. At the 'sharp end' the implementation of the policy is by introducing limiting conditions into licences; operations are performed against regulations, radioactive material is used, stored and disposed only with authorisations under limiting conditions. Many of the conditions and regulations are about activities well upstream of the occurrence that might release pollution. Such conditions and regulations may involve activities at the design, manufacture and construction stage of a project; they may involve updating of procedures or the routine testing of a plant component. Observance of the conditions and regulations are monitored by procedures and by regulatory agencies and findings are reported. This is the precautionary principle in practice and can be demonstrated by a few examples that although they represent specific failures, do provide evidence of an ongoing intention by operators to support the precautionary principle and by the regulatory authorities to monitor, recommend the punishment of failures and report the findings.

In August 1997 the failure to correctly translate design basis information into emergency operating procedures at Indian Point 3 was reported.[51] The NRC said that this failure represented a significant regulatory concern because it was indicative of inadequate controls to properly incorporate design basis information into procedures and it represented a breakdown in control of licensed activities. The precautionary principle can be seen in operation at three levels in this instance: the requirement to identify potential safety issues through design basis information; the licence requirement to incorporate design basis information into operating procedures and the identification by the inspection team of failures in that process. The failure did not cause actual pollution; nevertheless the NRC proposed that the potential polluter pay a $55,000 fine. In June 1998 the NRC reported violations of their requirements concerning cooling water flow in the high-pressure safety injection system at Waterford, Louisiana.[52] The failure to notify NRC of a failure to show by design analysis adequate cooling flow was in breach of regulations and a fine of $110.000 was proposed. A penalty of $55,000 was proposed in February 1999 for the failure of the operator of River Bend, La[53] to promptly identify and correct design deficiencies in the compressed air system that controls the emergency diesel generators thereby creating substantial uncertainty as to the capability of the generators to perform their intended safety functions. Washington DC Hospital were the subject of an NRC proposed fine of $5,500[54] for the temporary loss of a nuclear powered pacemaker containing 2.8 curies of plutonium 238, as well as failure to make a timely report and failure to provide adequate training and instruction to staff. The examples are not confined to the USA; the

---

[51] US Nuclear Regulatory Commission (NRC) News Announcement 1 - 97 - 108 20 Aug. 1997.
[52] NRC RIV 98 – 23, 18 Jun. 1998.
[53] NRC RIV 99 – 03, 2 Feb. 1999.
[54] NRC Report 1 - 99 – 23, 1 Apr. 1999.

Environment Agency in England monitors the operation, *inter alia*, of nuclear facilities. The precautionary principle was seen to be in operation when BNFL were penalised for not responding to the need to provide improved protection for a pipeline carrying potentially radioactive contaminated liquid over a bridge.[55] BNFL were fined £20,000 for failing to take action to prevent corrosion and failing to assess whether settlement of the bridge could cause the pipe to crack.

The level of detail published and the stage at which action is taken must satisfy even the most ardent anti-nuclear activist. Most national regulatory bodies now follow the IAEA/OECD recommendations for reporting nuclear events on a scale of 0–7.[56] Events identified at levels 0 and 1 are clearly in the region that represents precautionary action. As well as identifying potential failure modes, taking steps to design systems to prevent the failure, carrying out reviews, inspections and tests, the system of reporting failures and making assessments of their severity itself is a precautionary step. In summary it can be seen that the precautionary principle as well as operating at the policy level and project approval level is manifest in the regulation of nuclear facilities and users of radioactive materials at many subsidiary levels of activity, namely: identification of safety issues; design to incorporate measures to prevent occurrences; procedures to incorporate design basis information; test procedures; analysis and reporting of test results; handling of radioactive materials and instruction and training of staff. The obligations to perform these activities are embodied in regulations, are open to public scrutiny and policed by regulatory authorities.

It has been said that the impossible burden of the continuing attempt to demonstrate that a particular level of pollution is safe is destroying scientific credibility. While the dearth of toxicity information for more than three quarters of the thousands of chemicals currently in use[57] may support that contention for the chemical process industry the wealth of information about the effects of various levels of radiation in the nuclear and radiation using industry gives the lie to this statement. Furthermore the ease of detection and measurement of radiation have allowed dose limits to be set and monitored and for a system of protection based on the ICRP recommendations to operate successfully. The measure of its success is the health and longevity of the majority of people who work in and live near to nuclear facilities. The precautionary principle of environmental law is seen to operate at policy levels and in practice in the field of nuclear and radiation operations. Public opinion is probably the greater hurdle for the nuclear industry but given the continuation of the control and the openness of reporting and recognition of the need to respect the total environment, this will eventually soften.

---

[55] ENDS Report 276 Apr. 1997 p 44. Whitehaven Magistrates found that BNFL were in breach of their authorisation contrary to section 13(1) of the Radioactive Substances Act 1993.

[56] International Event Scale. IAEA, OECD.

[57] Percival, R. Miller, A. Schroeder, C. and Leope, J. (1992), *Environmental Regulation: law, science and policy*. Little, Brown & Co., Boston.

To ease this process the convergence[58] of the regulation of radiation and nuclear facilities with that of the utility and process industry under the principles of environmental law will continue to allow rational-decision making and will continue to assist the development of environmental law.

International Law

Conventions and International Provisions

A network of obligations arising from international conventions and agreements to which the United Kingdom is a party and has an effect on the management of radioactive waste in the U.K. includes:

The Paris Convention on Third Party Liability in the Field of Nuclear Energy (1960); amended by protocols of 1964 and 1982;

The Convention concerning the Protection of Workers against Ionising Radiations (1960);

The International Convention for the Future Safety of Lives at Sea (1960);

The Vienna Convention on Civil Liability for Nuclear Damage (1963); amended by the protocol of 1997; (the United Kingdom is a signatory but has not ratified);

The Brussels Convention on Third Party Liability in the Field of Nuclear Energy (1963); amended by protocols of 1964 and 1982;

The Treaty on the Non-proliferation of Nuclear Weapons (1968);

The Brussels Convention relating to Civil Liability in the Field of Maritime Carriage of Nuclear Material (1971);

The Convention on the Prevention of Marine Pollution by Dumping of Wastes and Other Matter (London Dumping Convention) (1972);

The Convention on the Physical Protection of Nuclear Material (1980);

The Convention on Assistance in the case of a Nuclear Accident or Radiological Emergency (1986);

The Convention on Early Notification of a Nuclear Accident (1986);

The 'Ospar Convention' for the Protection of the Marine Environment of the North East Atlantic (1992);

The Convention on Nuclear Safety (1994);

The Joint Convention on the Safety of Spent Fuel Management and on the Safety of Radioactive Waste Management (1997);

The Convention on Supplementary Compensation for Nuclear Damage (1997);

The Aarhus Convention on Access to Information, Public Participation and Access to Justice in Environmental Matters (1998); and

The Convention on Environmental Impact Assessment in a Transboundary Context (Espoo) (1991).

---

[58] See Radiation Protection Today and Tomorrow. OECD (1994) at p 7 where it refers to the closer integration of the management of radiation risks with that of other hazardous substances or situations.

Whilst these Conventions are most directly applicable to radioactive substances handled and produced by nuclear installations, some aspects of them are relevant to the use of radioactive substances in other industries. *The Paris Convention on Third Party liability in the Field of Nuclear Energy (1960)* sought to harmonise for the first time the basic laws applying to the liability incurred for damage caused by nuclear incidents involving nuclear fuel and radioactive products or waste arising from land-based nuclear installations. The main principles of the *Paris Convention* are the absolute and exclusive liability, without proof of fault, of the operator of the nuclear installation concerned; long legal limitation periods and the obligation to cover liability by insurance or other financial security arrangements. Austria, Luxembourg and Switzerland have not ratified the Convention.

The *Vienna Convention on Civil Liability for Nuclear Damage*, signed in 1963, is based on the same principles as the Paris Convention but unlike the *Paris Convention* the *Vienna Convention* has a worldwide application. The principles of the *Vienna Convention* include provisions as to absolute and exclusive liability of the operator of a nuclear installation similar to those contained in the *Paris Convention*, although this liability is limited in time and in money – and the obligation to cover the liability with an appropriate financial guarantee.

There is a *Joint Protocol to the Paris and Vienna Conventions (1988)* that provides for a mutual extension of the operator's liability under the Paris and Vienna systems. *The Brussels Supplementary Convention to the Paris Convention of 1963* created a mechanism whereby the amount of compensation for victims of nuclear accidents could be increased through public funds; Austria, Luxembourg and Switzerland signed the *Convention* but have not ratified it. *The Paris and Brussels Supplementary Conventions*, which were revised in 1982 through the adoption of two protocols, increased the compensation payable as provided for by the *Brussels Supplementary Convention*. In September 1997, two new international instruments in the field of nuclear liability were adopted under the aegis of the IAEA. The first was the *Protocol to Amend the Vienna Convention on Civil Liability for Nuclear Damage* signed by 15 States but ratified by only four of the five required for the Convention to enter into force. The second was the *Convention on Supplementary Compensation for Nuclear Damage*, a new instrument for giving extra compensation to victims of a nuclear accident, over and above the amounts provided for in the *Paris and Vienna Conventions* signed by 13 States but ratified by only three of the five required for the *Convention* to enter into force. The Contracting Parties to the *Paris Convention* have begun to consider ways of amending that Convention.

Concerns about the discharge of radioactive effluent into seas and rivers and the dumping at sea of solid radioactive waste has prompted other treaties, for example the *Oslo Convention on Waste Dumping at Sea (1972) and the Paris Convention on the Prevention of Marine Pollution from Land-Based Sources (1974)*. This second treaty, in particular, requires signatories to take account of the available technology in order to minimise radioactive discharges from nuclear reprocessing plants. The *1972 Oslo Convention and the 1974 Paris Convention* are now effectively replaced by the *Ospar Convention on the Protection of the North Sea and North-East Atlantic*, which was signed in Paris in September 1992 and ratified by all parties by March 1998. The *Ospar Convention* prohibits the disposal at sea of all radioactive wastes but France and the UK retained the option to resume dumping after a period of 15 years. In February 1994, the UK Government announced an indefinite ban on the disposal at sea of low and intermediate-level radioactive wastes following the Consultative Meeting in 1972 of the *London Convention on the Prevention of Marine Pollution by Dumping of Wastes and Other Matter* (the disposal of high-level waste was already prohibited by the Convention), whilst stating that it would be ready to reappraise its decision if scientific opinion changed. The UK Radioactive Discharges Strategy[59] was published in July 2002. This sets out how the UK intends to meet its *Ospar* obligations agreed[60] at Sintra, Portugal in 1998 by ensuring that, by 2020, discharges, emissions and losses of radioactive substances are reduced to levels where the additional concentrations in the marine environment above historic levels, resulting from such discharges, emissions and losses, are close to zero.

Ireland brought a claim before an arbitral tribunal established under the *Ospar Convention* in which the allegation was made that the UK breached Article 9 of the *Ospar Convention* by refusing to supply Ireland certain information relating to the economic case for a new Mixed Oxide Fuel Plant (MOX Plant) at BNFL's plant at Sellafield.[61] In rejecting Ireland's claims, the Tribunal confirmed: the information Ireland sought was not information on the state of the maritime area or on activities affecting or likely to affect the maritime area; accordingly, it is not information of the sort that Parties are required to make available under the *OSPAR Convention*; Ireland's claim that the United Kingdom has breached its obligations under the convention by refusing to provide the requested information did not arise.[62]

Ireland also brought a claim before an arbitral tribunal established under the *1982 UN Law of the Sea Convention (UNCLOS)* in which the claim was made that the operation of the new MOX Plant at Sellafield will amount to a violation by the UK of obligations under *UNCLOS* to protect and conserve the marine environment, to take all necessary measures to prevent, reduce and control pollution, and to ensure that activities under its jurisdiction and control do not cause any damage by pollution to Ireland and its environment.[63] Because of its concerns about whether it had the jurisdiction to hear it the *UNCLOS Tribunal* suspended the case taking note in particular of the fact that the European Commission is contemplating infraction proceedings against Ireland over Ireland's submission of matters that appear to be of European Community law to legal procedures other than those provided for under the Treaties of the European Communities. Ireland subsequently made a

---

[59] DEFRA (2002), UK Strategy for Radioactive Discharges 2001–2020, July, HMSO London.

[60] Ministerial meeting of the OSPAR Commission (1998), *OSPAR Strategy with regard to Radioactive Substances Paper no. 1998-17*, 22-23 July, Sintra, Portugal.

[61] Isted, Jonathan (2003), Novel developments in the use of international law to oppose nuclear activities, INLA Congress, April, Cape Town.

[62] The Tribunal's award can be found at the website of the Permanent Court of Arbitration at [www.pca-cpa.org/].

[63] Supra Isted.

wide-ranging request for a number of provisional measures. All of the requests were rejected by the Tribunal which stated that Ireland had not established that 'serious' harm would be caused to the marine environment by operation of the MOX Plant and pointed out that 'The Attorney General for Ireland, in opening the case, had accepted that ...the level of discharges from the MOX plant ... were not of a significant magnitude....'.[64] These recent actions by Ireland against the UK under *OSPAR* and *UNCLOS* illustrate how neighbouring non-nuclear States can use public international law to attempt to curtail nuclear activities. The meaning of 'pollution of the marine environment' in *UNCLOS* will be crucial here. The claim in private law in the Irish courts[65] shows that plaintiffs in non-Paris Convention countries can attempt to bring actions in their own courts under their own laws to seek compensation against nuclear operators for alleged harm and other remedies.

The Chernobyl accident prompted concerns about international co-operation on nuclear safety. After negotiations involving a number of governments, the IAEA *Convention on Nuclear Safety* was agreed in Vienna in September 1994. The obligations contained in the Convention are based on internationally accepted nuclear safety principles covering siting, design, construction operation, safety assessment and emergency procedures. A Diplomatic Conference convened by the IAEA in September 1997 adopted the *Joint Convention on the Safety of Spent Fuel Management and on the Safety of Radioactive Waste Management.*

Despite the substantial number of treaties which have been signed during the past 30 years, international regulation of the safety of nuclear power is still criticised for failing to provide sufficiently tight and comprehensive control over what, in the view of many, constitutes a major transboundary environmental risk. Alan Boyle observed[66] that international regulation of the safety of nuclear power and its potential environmental impact is amongst the weakest examples of the regulation of major ultra hazardous transboundary environmental risks. He quoted:

- minimal assurance of common standards;
- limited information standards;
- governments' unfettered discretion to determine their own safety.

In the context of potential jurisdiction questions in the event of a nuclear accident in a member state of the EU[67] a particular difficulty is the lack of an effective international policing organisation and the provision for only limited international inspection. The large measure of discretion as to the implementation of standards and obligations left to national governments recurs as a constant theme. For example although the *1968 Non-Proliferation Treaty* makes it obligatory in practice for parties to accept non-proliferation of nuclear weapons safeguards

---

[64] DTI Press release P/2003/383 2 July 2003.
[65] See ref 48.
[66] Boyle, Alan E. (1989), *Nuclear Energy and International Law: An environmental perspective*, (1989) British Yearbook of International Law Vol. LX.
[67] Galizzi, Paolo (1966) 'Questions of Jurisdiction in the event of a nuclear accident in a member state of the European Union' (1966) JEL Vol. 8 No 1 p 71.

through bilateral agreements with the IAEA and to allow periodic compulsory Agency inspection for the purpose of verification, no comparable attempt has been made to enforce common adherence to the IAEA's health and safety standards. After the Chernobyl accident a UN review group recommended that the IAEA should promote better exchanges of information among States on safety and accident experience, the development of additional safety guidelines and the enhancement of the IAEA's capacity to perform safety evaluations and inspections on request.   The Chernobyl incident has undoubtedly provoked wide-ranging international discussion on the adequacy of the existing regimes on nuclear safety, liability and notification arrangements. The negotiation of a number of treaties has followed.   Whether these measures prove to be adequate will be an important element in the public and political acceptance of future developments in the nuclear energy sector worldwide.

The *Aarhus Convention on Access to Information, Public Participation and Access to Justice in Environmental Matters* was opened for signature in June 1998. The Convention may be seen as opening up important opportunities in environmental enforcement through challenges in law to the substance of decisions as well as the objective of '...fair, equitable, timely and not prohibitively expensive' access to justice.   The Convention also seeks to provide a legally enforceable right to information rather than the more limited concept of 'freedom of information'. This is also reflected in the EUs proposal to revise *Directive 90/313* published in July 2000.   The proposal seeks to extend information access beyond public agencies to bodies such as utility companies.

The *Convention on Environmental Impact Assessment in a Transboundary Context (Espoo, 1991)* entered into force on 10 September 1997; it stipulates the obligations of Parties to assess the environmental impact of certain activities at an early stage of planning. It also lays down the general obligation of States to notify and consult each other on all major projects under consideration that are likely to have a significant adverse environmental impact across boundaries. A Protocol on Strategic Environmental Assessment (SEA) was established by the second Meeting of the Parties to the Espoo Convention, in February 2001 and an Extraordinary Meeting of Partners to the Convention, held on 21 May 2003 during the Ministerial 'Environment for Europe' Conference (Kiev, Ukraine), adopted the Protocol, 35 countries, together with the European Community, signed the SEA Protocol in Kiev on 21 May 2003.   The Protocol also applies to the *Aarhus Convention.* Article 4 of the Protocol requires each Party to ensure that a strategic environmental assessment is carried out for, *inter alia*, plans and programmes which are prepared for energy and waste management and listed in annex 1 and 2 that require environmental impact assessment under national legislation. Article 7 requires an environmental report to be prepared and Article 8 requires opportunities for timely and effective public participation, including NGOs, to express opinion on the draft plans or programmes and the environmental report. Where the implementation of the plan or programme has significant transboundary environmental or health effects the affected party is to be notified. Annex 1 lists, *inter alia*, nuclear reactors above one kilowatt and installations solely designed for the enrichment of nuclear fuels or for the reprocessing of irradiated nuclear fuels or for the storage, disposal and processing of radioactive waste. Annex 2 includes nuclear power stations including their dismantling or decommissioning.

European Law

Regulations have been made under the *Euratom Treaty* providing for inspections of national facilities and for the application of Euratom safeguards. These safeguards apply to all Member States. They may be compared with the separate IAEA safeguards system for non-nuclear weapon Member States. Verification agreements that ensure the compatibility of both systems came into force in 1977/1978 and provide for the wider application of the *Non-Proliferation Treaty Safeguards* and for co-operation between the European Atomic Energy Community and the IAEA. Articles 30 and 31 of the *Euratom Treaty* provide for the Commission to lay down certain basic standards for the protection of the health of workers and the general public from the dangers of ionising radiation. These standards cover maximum permissible doses, maximum permissible exposures and contamination and principles governing health surveillance (see the *Basic Safety Standards Directive* below). Particular objectives of the radiological protection standards developed by the Community are that exposure to ionising radiation should be 'justified by the advantages which it produces' and should be kept 'as low as reasonably achievable' (the 'ALARA' principle). It should also be noted that in the field of environmental and public health protection the *Maastricht Treaty* and the *Single European Act* have substantially increased the powers of the EU. Another important provision of the *Euratom Treaty* is Article 34, which concerns 'dangerous experiments' in the nuclear field. Such experiments can only take place after the Member State in question has taken 'additional health and safety measures on which it shall first obtain the opinion of the Commission' and the consent of the Commission is required where the effects of such experiments are liable to affect the territories of other Member States. The Commission is also entitled under Article 35 to a right of access to these facilities to determine their operative efficiency. Article 37 provides for Member States to produce data that relates to any plan for the disposal of radioactive waste. This makes it possible to determine whether the implementation of such a plan is liable to result in radioactive contamination of the water, soil or airspace of another Member State. The Commission is then required to give an opinion. Although this opinion is non-binding, the Court of Justice in *Saarland and Others v Minister for Industry, Posts and Telecommunications and Tourism and Others*[68] having held that the opinion must be sought prior to final authorisation of such an activity, also ruled that the Member State must accord the opinion the most searching examination and consideration.

A Commission opinion issued under Article 37 follows a standard format. The main issues it must address include; the distance between the nuclear facility and the nearest territory of another Member State, discharge limits for liquid effluents

---

[68] EU: Case- 187/87; OJ 1987 C188/8.

in the case of (a) normal operations and (b) accident situations; the water body receiving the effluents, and where appropriate, the desirability of these neighbouring States concluding bilateral or multilateral agreements concerning, for example, joint regulation of the conditions governing routine discharges of radioactive waste into an international river. A number of bilateral agreements in fact already exist in respect of the siting of nuclear facilities close to international borders. In December 1990, the Commission issued a recommendation on the application of Article 37 to Member States, specifying the information that must be supplied. Since 1987 the opinions of the Commission under Article 37 have been published in the Official Journal of the European Communities.

Article 38 empowers the Commission in cases of emergency to issue a Directive requiring a Member State to take all necessary measures to prevent infringement of basic standards relating to levels of radioactivity. The Community, in seeking to safeguard health, has the power to lay down other safety criteria for nuclear operations, such as the transportation and management of radioactive waste. However, because of the strong sense of national interest that a number of Member States still entertain in relation to both their civil and military nuclear programmes, the EU has not yet been able to develop a comprehensive or strong role in regulating the European nuclear industry. In particular, the Commission has no enforcement powers and only minimal consultative powers in respect of siting of nuclear installations, the storage of nuclear waste, the valuation of different types of reactor and the setting of permissible discharge levels for radioactive effluents. In these wider areas national policy remains the determining factor.

EU Measures

The Basic Safety Standards Directive   The authorisation and the subsequent operation of a nuclear installation and similar plant are governed by Community law, namely by the *Directive on Basic Safety Standards.*[69] The Directive is based on the ICRP Publication 60.   This safety standard provides the basis for a Community policy on radiation protection that applies to any activity that may involve a risk to the population, to workers and to the environment caused by radiation or radioactive contamination.   For example, Article 45(4) of the *Basic Safety Standards Directive* provides that in the event of accidents each Member State shall stipulate measures to be taken by the competent authorities and surveillance procedures with respect to the population groups that are liable to receive a radiation dose in excess of the dose limits laid down in the Directive, and the necessary resources both in personnel and in equipment to enable action to be taken to safeguard and maintain the health of the population. These measures may, if necessary, be taken by one Member State jointly with other Member States. Quantitative dose limits for various categories of workers and for members of the public are laid down and Article 6 specifies a set of wide principles including ALARA, on which EU approaches to dose limitation should be based.

---

[69] *96/29/Euratom* adopted on 13 May 1996.

A recent case in the Court of Justice[70] relating to safety standards for the health protection of the general public and workers against the dangers of ionising radiation was brought against Belgium by the Commission. The Commission considered that Belgium was infringing certain Articles of the *Basic Safety Standards Directive* relating to occupational exposure to ionising radiation. The case concerned the imposition by Belgium of stricter standards in respect of the exposure to radiation of apprentices aged between 16 and 18. The Court of Justice held, firstly, that whilst the specified dose limits were based on the ICRP guidelines these guidelines did not constitute absolute norms but were simply guidelines and the principle that governs dose limits in the principle of optimisation of protection. Having regard to the objective of the Directive, the Court of Justice considered that, had legislation intended to prohibit a higher level of protection in individual Member States, it would have expressly indicated this in its provisions.

The *Basic Safety Standards Directive* contains some provisions that concern medical exposure and these are supplemented by the more detailed requirements of the *Medical Exposures Directive*[71] that replaced the *Patient Protection Directive*.[72]

Environmental Impact Assessment The *Directive on the Assessment of the Effects of Certain Public and Private Projects on the Environment*[73] applies to nuclear power stations, other nuclear reactors and installations solely designed for the permanent storage or final disposal of radioactive waste. It also applies to installations for the production or enrichment of nuclear fuels, for the reprocessing of irradiated nuclear fuels and for the collection and reprocessing of radioactive waste if the relevant Member State considers that characteristics of these installations so require. The Directive requires the carrying out of an environmental impact assessment by relevant national regulatory bodies before consents to proceed with projects of this sort are granted. However, projects serving national defence purposes are exempt, as are those that are approved by a specific act of national legislation. In addition, Member States can exempt projects in whole or in part from the provisions of the Directive. The dismantling or decommissioning of nuclear power stations and other nuclear reactors, installations designed for the final disposal of irradiated fuel and installations designed for the final disposal of radioactive waste became subject to the Directive's provisions in 1997.[74]

The Council formally adopted the *Strategic Environmental Assessment (SEA) Directive*[75] on 5 June 2001. The purpose of the *SEA-Directive* is to ensure that environmental consequences of certain plans and programmes are identified and assessed during their preparation and before their adoption. The public and

---

[70] *Commission of the European Communities v Kingdom of Belgium*, Case C-376/90, [1992] ECR I-6153.

[71] 97/43/Euratom.

[72] 84/466/Euratom.

[73] 85/337/EEC.

[74] Council Directive 97/11/EC of 3 Mar. amended Directive 85/337/EEC, 1997 OJL73.

[75] 2001/42/EC, OJL197 of 21 July 2001, p 30.

environmental authorities can give their opinion and all results are integrated and taken into account in the course of the planning procedure. After the adoption of the plan or programme the public is informed about the decision and the way in which it was made. In the case of likely transboundary significant effects the affected Member State and its public are informed and have the possibility to make comments which are also integrated into the national decision making process.

Intra-EU Movement of Radioactive Materials and Waste

The completion of the single market in the EU and the abolition of border controls present complications in monitoring the shipment of radioactive waste and radioactive substances in general. There are presently two principal EU instruments in this domain: a *Regulation on Shipments of Radioactive Substances within the European Community*[76] which came into force in July 1993 and now also applies to shipments of substances other than radioactive waste; and a *Directive on the Supervision and Control of Shipments of Radioactive Waste between Member States and into and out of the Community*[77] which the United Kingdom has implemented through the *Trans-frontier Shipment of Radioactive Waste Regulations 1993*[78] which came into force in the UK on 1 January 1994. The Regulation applies to shipments of radioactive substances between Member States whenever the quantities and concentrations of radioactive material exceed the levels laid down in the *Basic Safety Standards Directive*. The Regulation stipulates that controls of shipments of radioactive substances must be performed 'as part of the control procedures applied in a non-discriminatory manner throughout the territory of the Member State'. The Directive applies to shipments of radioactive waste between Member States, as well as into and out of the EU, in the same circumstances as the Regulation. The Directive sets out rules on applications for authorisation of shipments within the EU to the competent authorities of the Member States. Any conditions required by those authorities may not be more stringent than those laid down for similar shipments within their own territories and must also comply with existing international agreements. There are special rules governing shipments of radioactive waste into and out of the EU territory.

Emergency Measures and Provisions

Following the Chernobyl accident, the EU adopted a Regulation[79] that stipulated maximum permitted contamination levels of foodstuffs for a period of time after the incident. This Regulation was twice extended before being allowed to lapse. There are also several Regulations that lay down maximum permitted radioactivity levels for foodstuffs and feeding stuffs in the case of a nuclear accident or any

---

[76] Euratom 1493/93.
[77] 92/3/Euratom.
[78] 1993 SI 1993 No 3031.
[79] 1707/86/EEC.

other case of radiological emergency.[80] *The Council Decision on Community arrangements for the early exchange of information in the event of a radiological emergency* was issued in 1987.[81] This established a rapid information exchange, ECURIE, which is based on a system set up by IAEA. A Resolution was also adopted in 1987 on the introduction of *Community Cooperation on Civil Protection.*[82] It provides, in particular, a guide to civil protection in the EU including a list of liaison officials from the Member States and the Commission who are required to hold meetings to organise 'regular authorised simulation exercises' and to work towards better use of the data banks that exist in the civil protection field. In 1995 the Commission published a proposal for a Decision establishing a Community Action Programme in the field of Civil Protection. In Addition, the *Directive on Informing the Public about Health Protection Measures in the Event of a Radiological Emergency*[83] defines the content of the information to be provided to the population under normal circumstances and in the case of an emergency. A system entitled the International Nuclear Event Scale classifies nuclear events at seven levels. The Chernobyl incident, for example, registered at level 7.

Sealed Sources

A large number of incidents involving the loss of control of sealed sources have been reported over the last 50 years. Some have resulted in excessive radiation exposure of members of the public, while others have led to widespread environmental contamination as a result of sources finding their way into metal scrap destined for recycling. There is also the threat of disused sources being used for malicious purposes. A European Directive is currently in draft on the control of high activity sealed sources. This will require EU Member States to have in place regulatory systems for the authorisation of practices involving sources. Before issuing such an authorisation, the relevant competent authority must ensure that adequate arrangements exist for the safe management of sources, including when they become disused sources. These latter arrangements may provide for the transfer of these sources to the supplier or to a recognised installation, or an obligation for the manufacturer or supplier to receive them. In addition, financial provision must have been made to cover the cost of managing disused sources safely, including the eventuality of the holder becoming insolvent or going out of business. Under the provisions of the new Directive, all high activity sealed sources manufactured in or entering the EU will have to be marked with a unique identification number. The holder will be required to maintain records on the nature and location of each source and any transfer to another holder notified to the competent authority. At the termination of use of a source, the arrangements for its management as a disused source must be implemented without undue delay. Where

---

[80] Commission Regulation Euratom 770/90 and Council Regulation Euratom 2218/89, amending Council Regulation Euratom 3954/87.
[81] 87/606/Euratom.
[82] 87/C76/01.
[83] 89/618/Euratom.

a use is foreseen for a disused source, for instance through recycling or reuse, any shipment of that source between EU Member States is subject to the notification/declaration process detailed in European Regulation 1493/93.[84]

National Laws

International Conventions, in particular *The Law of the Sea* and the *Ospar Convention* have limited the freedom of States in the management of radioactive waste. In response to pressures from *OSPAR* Member States BNFL sought permission of the UK HSE to re-route the future production of a key radioactive liquid process stream, Medium Active Concentrate (MAC), at Sellafield. In the long term this will significantly reduce radioactive discharges into the environment. The modification to re-route new MAC was a key part of the Environment Agency's decision on the future regulation of Technetium-99 discharges from Sellafield. The Agency's decision acknowledged the need for the proposed re-routing to be subject to HSE permission. Currently, arisings of MAC from Magnox reprocessing are sent to the Enhanced Actinide Removal Plant (EARP), where the bulk of the radioactivity is removed, before discharge to the Irish Sea. The intended modifications will route future MAC to storage in the highly active storage tanks and subsequently to vitrification. BNFL has had to demonstrate to HSE that a modification to the process and operations can be done safely and will have no detrimental effects on either the high level waste storage or the vitrification plants. The outcome of this decision will be to significantly reduce the level of discharges of radioactive Technetium-99 (which EARP is unable to remove) and other radioactivity from future MAC arisings into the Irish Sea.

Further Reading

Barnes, Michael QC (1990), The Hinckley Point C Public Inquiries. A Report, HMSO London.

Boyle, Alan E. (1989), *Nuclear Energy and International Law: An environmental perspective*, British Yearbook of International Law Vol. LX.

Department of the Environment (1995), *Review of Radioactive Waste Management Policy. Final Conclusions,* Cm 2919, July, HMSO London.

Department of the Environment (2002), *UK Strategy for Radioactive Discharges 2001 – 2020*, July, DEFRA London.

Galizzi, Paolo (1966), 'Questions of Jurisdiction in the event of a nuclear accident in a member state of the European Union'. *JEL* Vol. 8 No 1 p 71.

HSE (1992), *Tolerability of risk from nuclear power Stations,* HSE Books, London.

HSE (1999), *Reducing Risks, Protecting People*, December, HMSO London.

HSE on behalf of DEFRA (2003), National Report on conformance with the obligations of the Joint Convention on the Safety of Spent Fuel Management and on the Safety of Radioactive Waste Management, May HMSO London.

Hughes, D.J. 'The Status of the Precautionary Principle in Law' [1995] 7JEL224.

---

[84] Council Regulation (Euratom) No 1493/93 on shipments of radioactive substances between Member States, O.J. L 148, p 1-7.

Isted, Jonathan (2003), *Novel developments in the use of international law to oppose nuclear activities*, INLA Congress, April, Cape Town.

Leigh, W. J. (2003), 'The Principle of Justification: the Application of the Principle to the Manufacture of MOX Fuel in the UK'. *Nuclear Law Bulletin* 71 Vol 2003/1. OECD Paris.

Lochard, Jacques and Boehler, Marie-Claude (1993), 'Optimising Radiation Protection - the ethical and legal bases', *Nuclear Law Bulletin 42.*

OECD-NEA (1995), *The Environmental and Ethical Basis of Geological Disposal*, OECD, Paris.

O'Riordan, Timothy and Cameron, James (1994), *Interpreting the Precautionary Principle.* Earthscan Publications, London.

OSPAR Strategy with Regard to Radioactive Substances, Paper No. 1998-17, Ministerial Meeting of the OSPAR Commission, Sutra, Portugal, July 1998.

Riley, Peter (2000), 'The Precautionary Principle and its Practice', *Engineering Management Journal*, Vol. 10, No. 6, Dec., pp 281-287.

Riley, Peter (2002), 'Nuclear Energy; a sustainable future?' *Engineering Management Journal*, Vol. 12, No. 2, April, pp 97-104.

Royal Society Study Group (1983), *Risk Assessment*, Royal Society Report, London.

Smith, R.E. (2002), 'Some observations on the concept of best practicable environmental option (BPEO) in the context of radioactive waste management', *Nuclear Energy*, 41, No.4, Aug., 271-281.

Stokes, Elen, R. (2003), 'Precautionary steps: the development of the precautionary principle in EU jurisprudence', ELM 15[2003]1.

Chapter Six

National Nuclear Laws

Nuclear waste practices and policies in five selected States are described in earlier chapters. Each of the five States have in place nuclear legislation to enable the regulation of facilities, materials and waste that, in the case of the US and UK have developed together with technological development and have contributed to sources of law that are described in the previous chapter. In the divided peninsula of Korea the law has developed in the south to accommodate an intensive programme of power station building based on US, UK and French technology under US licence arrangements and international safeguards. In the north, where until the early 1990s the technology was Russian and regulation followed the Russian model of technologically based rules, to enable the use of US, EU and Japanese technology and equipment the western model of regulation has been imported for a specific project. The influence of European Law can be seen in the development of the laws of both the UK and France. In Finland a fresh approach has been initiated by two major influences; a clean break from the Russian control over the supply and disposal of nuclear fuel and the need to convince the public of the sense in using nuclear energy to prevent energy poverty from limiting economic development. The close examination of the laws relating to nuclear waste in the five selected States demonstrates these diverse aspects but at the same time demonstrates a general consistency between the States' laws.

Nuclear Law in the United Kingdom

The use of nuclear energy and the manufacture of nuclear materials are controlled by the licensing of the facilities, the regulation of the use and storage and the authorisation of the disposal of radioactive materials. The manufacture, use, storage and disposal are also monitored, or safeguarded, to prevent the unauthorised use of nuclear materials. Radiation is released to the environment and is controlled by a system of dose limits that have been determined from experience of the harm caused by accidental radiation exposure, medical treatment and nuclear weapons. Assessment principles have evolved to allow the assessment of licence applications. The safety submissions in the licence application are assessed in the context of the plant design causing the lowest reasonably achievable exposure of workers and public to radiation. The use, storage and disposal of radioactive materials appears to be subject to the same rules, however on close inspection the measures taken in this context err towards what is practically or technically achievable. In a rigorous review of UK practice[1] the HSE

---

[1] HSE on behalf of DEFRA (2003), *National Report on conformance with the obligations of the Joint Convention on the Safety of Spent Fuel Management and on the Safety of Radioactive Waste Management*, May, HMSO London.

submission to the first review meeting of the Contracting Parties to the *Joint Convention on the Safety of Spent Fuel Management and on the Safety of Radioactive Waste Management (the Joint Convention)* considers each of the *Joint Convention's* obligations and explains how the UK meets them.

The *Paris Convention* was accepted by the participating States as a basis for continuing with the peaceful development of nuclear energy. The States agreed to establish laws to replace other statutory and common law liabilities in the area of law applying to the consequences arising from the operation of nuclear facilities. The common law remedies in the field of negligence, nuisance and breach of statutory duty for the consequences of damage arising from a nuclear incident would no longer apply. A strict liability regime was incorporated into the law of the United Kingdom by the *Nuclear Installations Act 1965 (NIA65)*. The keeping, use, storage and disposal of radioactive materials both on and off the site of a nuclear installation are controlled under the *Radioactive Substances Act 1993(RSA93)* and the *Health and Safety at Work Act 1974 (HSWA74)*. The European Community also requires that ionising radiations be controlled; their requirements have been incorporated into the *HSWA74* by the *Ionising Radiations Regulations 1999 (IRR99)*.[2] The powers to protect nuclear facilities and materials from terrorist and other action is given in the various *Atomic Energy Authority Acts*. The effect of low levels of radiation is not direct; not everyone who is exposed to a low level of radiation will suffer noticeable damage. '...if radiation itched, the legal response would be very different'.[3] An assessment of risk is made when deciding to use radiation, for example when deciding to treat a patient with X-rays the effect on the patient and the operator must be balanced against the benefit of the treatment. The effects of radiation can be avoided by shielding the operator, however at some point it is necessary to optimise the amount of shielding for economic reasons. The size and complexity of the equipment may become uneconomic and the exposure to radiation may be small in relation to the radiation present due to natural sources. The laws relating to nuclear energy all require that this balancing of effects against economic cost be taken into account in the licensing and operation of nuclear facilities and in the use, storage and disposal of radioactive materials.

Health and Safety

Under the *HSWA74*, an employer is required to ensure so far as is reasonably practicable that he does not cause harm either to his employees or to other people either on or off the site (s2 and s3). The basic objectives of the control of use and disposal of radioactive materials stem from a White Paper, *The Control of Radioactive Wastes*,[4] published in 1959, and from *European Council Directive*

---

[2] IRR99 Ionising Radiations Regulations 1999 SI 1999 No. 3232.
[3] For a view of civil liability of the nuclear industry see; Maria Lee (2000), 'Civil Liability of the Nuclear Industry', *Journal of Environmental Law* Vol 12 No 3.
[4] Cmnd. 884.

96/29/EURATOM, the Directive on Basic Safety Standards (BSS)[5] and are implemented in the *IRR99[6]* made under *the HSWA74.* The basic objectives are:

> that all practices giving rise to radioactive wastes must be justified, i.e. the need for the practice must be established in terms of its overall benefit.[7] NB. Questions of justification do not apply to military defence installations;[8] radiation exposure of individuals and the collective dose to the population arising from radioactive wastes shall be reduced to levels which are as low as reasonably achievable, economic and social factors being taken into account; and the average effective dose equivalent from all sources, excluding natural background radiation and medical procedures, to representative members of a critical group of the general public shall not exceed 1m Sv in any one year.

The *IRR99* are the controlling regulations for work with radiation and apply to the use of X-rays as well as to work on power reactors. In the *IRR99* a radioactive substance is defined as any substance that contains one or more radionuclides whose activity cannot be disregarded for the purposes of radiation protection. This part of the regulations was interpreted in the Approved Code of Practice, issued by the Health and Safety Executive (HSE) as including;

> examples (which) have low activity concentration but are often involved in dusty processes and may create an internal radiation hazard from inhalation.... (or) there may be an external radiation hazard from bulk storage of such materials and (a)nother test, which may be applied if the use of the substance would create, because of its radioactivity, the need for a supervised area to be designated....

The regulations set down rules for all work with ionising radiations under all circumstances and require the employer to notify the HSE of all work or changes to work with ionising radiations other than work carried out on a licensed site, this exclusion being to avoid unnecessary duplication since Her Majesty's Nuclear Installations Inspectorate (NII) will have already been notified by the licence application, s6 (1)(b). A prior risk assessment of work with ionising radiations is necessary s7 (1). Every employer is obliged to restrict, so far as is reasonably practicable, the extent to which his employees and other persons are exposed to radiation, s8 (1), by engineering systems and controls and working practices, s8 (2). The regulations set down the means of control of the working area, s16 and s18, and the designation of classified persons, the requirement for Radiation Protection Advisors and qualified persons, s13. The employer is also responsible under s20 and s21 to measure and keep records of the dose absorbed by employees. The medical surveillance of employees and arrangements for the protection of certain susceptible employees is also required. Rules for the control of radioactive substances, s27, accounting, s28, keeping, s29, the monitoring of radiation and

---

[5] O.J. L 159, 29 Jun. 1996.
[6] Ionising Radiations Regulations (IRR99) SI 1999 No. 3232.
[7] The principle of justification is discussed in Tromans S., *The Law of Nuclear Installations and Radioactive Substances*, (1997).
[8] *R v Environment Agency ex parte Marchiori and NAG Ltd* (High Court 29 March 2001) [2001] Env L.R. 47; [2001] J.P.L. 1438, see also ENDS Report 315 April 2001 p 60/1. Appeal dismissed Court of Appeal [2002] EWCA Civ 3; [2002] Eu L.R. 225.

dose assessment, s21, s22, the investigation of exposure to radiation, s25, and the notification of certain occurrences, s30, are also required. A number of significant changes have been brought about by the *BSS Directive* including:

- the definitions of quantities and units and weighting factors to follow ICRP 60;
- extended scope to include work activities involving exposure to natural sources of radiation;
- a distinction has been made between radiation protection principles applied to 'practices' and 'interventions';
- radiation principles are applied to practices in a more rigorous manner through an improved definition of the justification principle, a strengthening of the optimisation principle by introducing the concept of dose constraints and the setting of lower dose limits (limitation principle) in order to take account, firstly, of the most recent estimates of the risk of cancer arising from the exposure to ionising radiation and secondly of the complex notion of health detriment; and
- the concept of potential exposure has been introduced.

The *BSS Directive* deals with the preparation of emergency plans for sites and rail transport operations using or carrying radioactive substances (Articles 48 to 52) and are implemented by the *Radiation (Emergency Preparedness and Public Information) Regulations (REPPIR)* in force from Summer 2001.[9] *IRR99* and the *Ionising Radiation Regulations (Northern Ireland) 2000*[10] also implement *Council Directive 90/641/Euratom*[11] on the operational protection of outside workers exposed to the risk of ionising radiation during their activities in controlled areas. Outside workers are persons undertaking activities in controlled areas designated by an employer other than their own.

Prosecution

Under the *HSWA74* it is an offence to contravene regulations, however, the NII says that as a policy it does not prosecute for every breach, only where:

> employers or others concerned appeared deliberately to have disregarded the relevant regulation or where they have been reckless in exposing people to hazards or where there is a record of repeated infringements.[12]

Therefore even though in an accident at Sellafield where a worker was exposed to plutonium mist caused by an accident to a valve, and received twice the legal limit of exposure to radiation, the NII did not prosecute. In contrast the Factory

---

[9] Radiation Protection News issue 19 May 2001.
[10] *The Ionising Radiation Regulations (Northern Ireland) 2000*, SR 2000, no. 375.
[11] Outside Workers Directive 90/641/Euratom, O.J. 1990 L 349/21.
[12] New Scientist, 1 Oct. 1987, p 23.

Inspectorate prosecuted the company Tele-Trading Ltd[13] in breach of the *Ionising Radiations Regulations 1985* the precursor to the *IRR99:*

> Tele-Trading Ltd employed evening workers (twelve were children) to dismantle telephones to remove luminous betalights which contain tritium gas with about seventy thousand million Becquerels of radioactivity and which could be easily released to the environment by damage to the glass container. It transpired that Tele-Trading had embarked on the work with a total lack of appreciation of the hazards. The company pleaded guilty to charges of being in breach of the Regulation 6(1) – restriction of exposure of employees to radiation (ALARA), Regulation 11 – provision of written rules, Regulation 12(a) – provision of information, instruction and training and Regulation 12(d) – women to be informed of the importance of advising their employer of pregnancy.

The lack of knowledge about the task they had undertaken was, perhaps, the main difference between the Tele-Trading case and the BNFL case. In a similar case in Brazil,[14] which was associated with a scrapped radiotherapy machine, cesium-137 caused ten people to be exposed to a lethal 10 Sv of radiation killing five of them.

Licensing and Liability

The absolute and exclusive liability of the operator of a nuclear installation under the *Paris Convention* is implemented in the United Kingdom by the *NIA65* amended by the *NIA69* and by *Part II of the Energy Act 1983*. It has three main objectives: to control nuclear installations by licensing, s1 to s6; to impose duties, s7 to s11 and to provide for compensation for a breach of duty, s12 to s21. The NII on behalf of the HSE administers s1 to s6 of the *Act*. Under s1 no one (except the Government) is allowed to operate a nuclear installation without a site licence. Nuclear site licences granted under s1 of the *NIA65* are required for: all nuclear reactors, including experimental reactors (but excluding those used in ships and aircraft); other nuclear power plants; plants engaged in the nuclear fuel cycle (e.g. uranium enrichment, fuel preparation and fuel assembly and storage plants); sites and plants for storing and reprocessing radioactive waste; and radioactive waste depositories. Licences can only be granted to corporate bodies and are not transferable, s3. Regulatory control of operations on the site is through a set of conditions attached to the licence s4(1). NII has considerable freedom to attach whatever conditions it judges appropriate s4(2) and s4(3) and therefore has flexible means of control over the construction of plants and their operation on the site.

Assessment of Nuclear Installations for Licensing   A central and key element during the design process is the analysis of possible accidents on the spent fuel or reprocessing facility. This covers all significant sources of radioactivity associated with the plant and all planned operating modes. The analysis starts with a list of initiating faults, including internal and external hazards, and faults due to personnel error that have the potential to lead to any person receiving a significant dose of radiation. A radiological analysis is performed for fault sequences, which could

---

[13] Radiation Protection Bulletin No 81 Aug. 1987 NRPB pp 15, 16.
[14] Nucleonics Week Vol 28, No 41, 8 Oct. 1987.

lead to the release of radioactive materials, to determine the maximum effective dose to persons on or off the site. The fault sequences are normally grouped and a 'bounding case' for each group is specified that takes account of the demands made on the safety system. The fault analysis process leads to the determination of the Design Basis Accidents (DBAs) for the nuclear installation. These accidents are drawn from the fault analysis but do not include initiating faults that are determined to be very improbable. The analyses of DBAs are done on a conservative basis and assume the worst normally permitted configuration of equipment and unavailability for maintenance, test or repair. For each design base fault sequence or bounding case, which leads to a release of radioactive material, the radiological analysis determines the maximum effective dose to a person outside the site. The design basis analysis establishes the minimum safety system requirements for each initiating fault and also identifies the operator's administrative requirements.

The site licence is usually issued in stages; the first stage, linked to planning permission, is granted for construction only. The operator takes the risk that he will be able to convince the NII during construction, by issuing a safety report, that the reactor should proceed to generate power. The route to full power is via stages, each stage being preceded by the issue of a licence; the first stage, for example, would be a licence to load nuclear fuel on the successful completion of engineering test runs. The NII make an assessment of the safety case made in a licence application and in so doing use judgments based on the reasonable practicability of the safety measures proposed. The construction, commissioning, operation and decommissioning of any nuclear installation which is granted a nuclear site licence is carried out by the licensee under the strict supervision and control of the NII. Before the licence is issued, prospective licensees are required to provide the NII with a preliminary safety report (PSR) to demonstrate to the NII's satisfaction that in principle the licensee is capable of constructing and operating the proposed facility to an acceptable standard of safety. A pre-construction safety report (PCSR) is then prepared which is based on the detailed design. It gives a design description and a comprehensive Statement of the safety case that enables the safety features of the facility to be identified and its safety significance assessed. As the development proceeds the NII identify points at which they require further information on particular nuclear safety aspects of the project before issuing consent to proceed. Consent to commence construction of the facility depends upon a satisfactory outcome of the NII's review and assessment of the PCSR.

NII have developed a set of safety assessment principles (SAPs)[15] to help them to assess the safety reports. They review prospective licensees' proposals within this framework of principles and they are used at the conceptual stage of a project, and during its design, development, manufacture, construction and operation to eventual decommissioning. The SAPs are also used in the assessment of proposals for modification to operating plant. The SAPs are framed to ensure that a design safety submission shall show that in normal operation radiation exposures of

[15] HSE (1992), *Safety Assessment Principles for Nuclear Plants*, HMSO London [www.hse.gov.uk/nsd/saps.htm].

persons on and off the site of the facility will not exceed the limits recommended by the International Commission on Radiological Protection (ICRP)[16] and set down in the *EEC Directive of 13 May 1996*.[17] The majority of the SAPs are engineering (or deterministic) principles. In creating a design there are many choices to be made. Each choice involves to a greater or lesser extent the use of judgment in technical, scientific or commercial issues. Probabilistic Safety Analysis (PSA) is part of a methodical accident analysis process that produces numerical estimates of the risk from the plant. It provides a comprehensive logical analysis of the potential for things to go wrong on the plant and the role played by the safety provisions. PSA enables weaknesses in the design to be identified, anticipated and remedied at an early stage. In addition, it can be used to reconcile the calculated risks against the licensee's criteria and against the relevant SAPs. It provides evidence that confirms the plant is balanced, that is, that no particular class of accident or feature of the plant makes a disproportionate contribution to the overall risk.

Not all of these judgments are concerned directly with safety, but most will influence its achievement. The deterministic SAPs provide inspectors with guidance on what to look for when judging the ALARP arguments in a safety case. They represent HSE's view of good nuclear engineering practice. They point to the provisions that in HSE's view would lead to a safe plant. PSA acts as a crosscheck on the level of safety achieved, so that the PSA and deterministic SAPs are complementary. In carrying out an assessment the Inspector judges the extent to which the design safety submission shows conformity with the following principles:[18]

> No person shall receive radiological doses in excess of the appropriate dose limit as a result of normal operation. Doses to individual persons shall be kept as low as is reasonably practicable. Having regard to the foregoing, the collective dose to persons on and off the site resulting from operation of the nuclear installation shall be kept as low as is reasonably practicable. All reasonably practicable steps shall be taken to prevent accidents. All reasonably practicable steps shall be taken to minimise the consequences of any accident.

As an example, to guide the assessor in judging the extent to which the fundamental principles have been satisfied, assessment levels are given as fractions of the dose limits set by the ICRP and as advised by the National Radiological Protection Board (NRPB).[19] It is stressed in the SAPs that these assessment levels are not to be taken as targets for designers and operators whose duties are to reduce risks to as low a level as is reasonably practicable.

---

[16] ICRP Publication 60.

[17] EEC Council Directive 96/29/EURATOM of 13 May 1996 Amending Directives on Ionising Radiation Safety Standards, O.J. L159/1 and O.J. L314/20.

[18] Supra, Safety Assessment Principles.

[19] Advice given by the NRPB in compliance with the Direction of the Health Ministers dated 9 Aug. 1977 in relation to radiological protection standards. ASP 1 to 9. The NRPB was created by the Radiological Protection Act 1970 and is responsible for, inter alia, advising government departments and statutory bodies on the acceptability of standards recommended or proposed by international bodies and on their application in the UK.

Site Licence Conditions Spent fuel and reprocessing facilities are prescribed under
NIA65 and are therefore subject to HSE's nuclear licensing regime, however, a
waste disposal or storage facility not on a licensed site, not being prescribed, would
not be. The accumulation, storage, and disposal of radioactive substances are
subject to authorisation by the EA under *RSA93*. In the event of high and
intermediate level waste facilities being located outside licensed sites licensing
processes similar to those of the HSE for licensed sites would be adopted. Indeed
this approach is implied from Statements made by the EA[20] concerning joint
working arrangements in the event of future possible development of an eventual
repository. HSE's standard nuclear site licence conditions contain detailed
requirements for documentation and reporting. The NII may impose a wide range
of conditions on a site licence *NIA65* s4 (1) and the NII has an on-going obligation
to review these conditions in the light of any relevant representations that may be
made by organisations such as trade unions representing workers on the side s4 (4).
The nuclear site licence may also be varied at any time to exclude parts of the site
which no longer need to be licensed s3 (6) or may be totally revoked s5 (1).
During construction, conditions may be imposed requiring the licensee to provide
the NII with design information that it considers necessary and to submit for
approval whatever quality control system is in operation. Other matters covered by
conditions during construction may be the inspection and testing of components
and the setting up of a plant commissioning committee. Conditions will later be
added concerning authorised personnel, the preservation of records, radiological
protection control, the storage of nuclear fuel, accumulation of wastes and the
preparation of emergency reports. The NII supervises the construction and
commissioning of new plant and equipment on a step-by-step basis. The site
licensee can only move on to the next relevant stage of development after the NII
has been satisfied on technical grounds that this is appropriate and has issued a
formal licence instrument permitting it to be done. As a matter of practice the NII
liaises with the Environment Agency (EA) on plant development questions relating
to radioactive waste discharges and waste management systems generally. *RSA93*
was amended by *EA95* so that the EA is the regulatory body for authorisations in
respect of premises in England and Wales and the SEPA is the regulatory body for
Scotland. The Radiochemical Inspectorate in the Environment and Heritage
Service (EHS) is the regulatory body for authorisations in respect of premises in
Northern Ireland. Inspectors from these agencies check compliance with the
conditions and limitations in authorisations granted under *RSA93* and have a range
of enforcement powers.
  Once the plant becomes operational, the conditions invariably require the setting
up of a permanent safety committee. They also make provision for the plant to be
shutdown regularly to permit detailed examination and testing of components and a
search for common faults. After the examination, consent to operate the reactor

---

[20] Newstead, S. (2003), *Developments in UK Regulation of Nuclear Wastes*, ICEM03-4707,
Oxford.

again must be obtained from the EA.[21]   Site licence conditions may also require the maintenance of an efficient system for monitoring ionising radiations from anything on the site, or from anything discharged on or from the site.   This monitoring, in the case of stations operated by the nuclear generating industry, is extended in some cases to points up to 20 miles from the station. The programme may start up to a year before the station begins operation, to provide a point of reference. The results are reported to the Department of the Environment (DoE) and DEFRA (which also carry out their own monitoring exercises). The NII is also entitled to recover the costs of nuclear safety research that it sponsors from nuclear site licensees and applicants.   The *Nuclear Reactors (Environmental Impact Assessment for Decommissioning) Regulations 1999*[22] require HSE to consult the public before it gives its consent to the commencement of dismantling and decommissioning of power reactors. Conditions may be imposed relating to the process of decommissioning, the demolition methods employed and the disposal of the materials on the site.   Further, prior to decommissioning, as installations approach the end of their design life, NII will conduct a long-term safety review of the plant.   The licensee has a duty to keep copies of the conditions that are contained in a schedule to the licence posted on the site s4(5).

A Challenge to the Licensing Process In evidence to the Sizewell 'B' Inquiry the Friends of the Earth (FOE) argued that the NII were wrong in their approach to licensing nuclear facilities. They argued that s7 of the *NIA65* imposed an absolute duty to achieve a certain standard of safety, namely that no occurrence on a licensed site involving nuclear matter causes injury to any person or damage to any property other than that of the licensee. They argued that the site licence should only be granted if this standard of safety could be guaranteed. They contended that a decision by NII to grant a nuclear licence for Sizewell in accordance with their SAPs, which were based on the 'as low as reasonably practicable' (ALARP) principle and the qualified safety requirements of the *HSWA74*, would be null and void since the s7 duty was absolute, not being qualified by such phrases as (ALARP). FOE contended that the use by the NII of the SAPs was therefore *ultra vires* and a decision to grant a site licence based on them would be null and void. NII argued that s7 did not specify a standard of safety; there could be no breach of duty under s7 before injury or damage occurred; the possibility that a breach of duty might occur in the lifetime of a nuclear station was not a breach of duty under s7 and that s7 provided no guidance on the level of risk to be attained throughout the lifetime of an installation.   NII contended that it was inconceivable that Parliament intended a licensee to design, construct and operate a plant to a standard that would prevent injury and damage arising from an unforeseeable natural event. In conforming to the principles of statutory interpretation, NII's alternative construction of s7 was simply giving rise to a course of action in the event of an unforeseen occurrence. The NII argued that s4(1) of the *NIA65* empowering the

---

[21] For the purposes of this work, EA, unless specifically noted includes SEPA and EHS.
[22] Nuclear Reactors (Environmental Impact Assessment for Decommissioning) Regulations 1999, SI 1999, No. 2892.

imposition of conditions on the grant of a site licence in 'any accident.... or emergency' and s22 which requires 'dangerous occurrences' to be reported were irreconcilable with the FOE's construction of s7 as imposing a standard of safety that no occurrence causing injury or damage should occur. NII submitted that if Parliament had intended s7 of the *NIA65* to create standards of safety it would have been listed in Schedule 1 of the *HSWA1974* as a relevant statutory provision to be enforced by the HSE under s18(1) of the Act.

At the public inquiry into the construction of the Sizewell B power station, Sir Frank Layfield decided that for the purposes of the inquiry s7 of the *NIA65* did not set a standard of safety against which the CEGB's design principles must be assessed. He concluded that if the construction of s7 advanced by the FOE was correct, *NIA65* s2 consent for Sizewell B could not be granted unless the CEGB could demonstrate that no occurrences involving nuclear matter and no ionising radiations emitted from anything on the site or waste discharged on or from the site would cause injury to any person or damage to any property other than the licensee's. If the FOE's construction of s7 were to be accepted the safety standards governing the entire nuclear industry would need to be reassessed. Following the Secretary of State for Energy's decision to grant consent to the construction of the Sizewell B nuclear power station, the Friends of the Earth sought leave to apply for judicial review of the decision. After being refused at first instance on the grounds that the application had not been made promptly, the Court of Appeal considered the case.[23] Sir John Donaldson rejected the application and although he accepted that s7 of the *NIA65* bound the Secretary of State to impose conditions designed to secure that an accident did not occur, it was not addressed to the issue of a licence. He said:

> .... in my judgment it is unarguable that he (the Secretary of State) was bound by Section 7 to impose conditions which were designed to have the effect that no such accident, occurrence or damage as it mentioned there could ever occur. His approach is not fettered by Section 7, which, whatever it may mean, is addressed to a different point.

According to Sir Ralph Gibson L J, Parliament did not by s7 of the *NIA65* impose on the Health and Safety Executive or the Nuclear Installations Inspectorate the duty of requiring proof by the applicant for a licence that the proposed power station would be designed and operated so that no occurrence would ever happen. Furthermore the Secretary of State was not prevented from granting consent unless satisfied that the grant of a site licence would be based upon such proof; Sir George Waller concurred. It seems, therefore, that since none of the judgments disputed the FOE interpretation of s7 the true meaning of the *NIA65* could be argued in a different context, for instance during later stages of a licensing process. In the event Sizewell B was completed without further challenge.

The Balance of Benefit and Risk in Licensing   Notwithstanding the ICRP recommended dose limits, the dose equivalent is to be kept to a level which is as low as is reasonably achievable, with economic and social factors being taken into

---

[23] Re Friends of the Earth [1988] JPL 98 (CA).

account (ALARA). According to the NRPB[24] this choice of words shows that the fundamental aspect of the ALARA requirement is a balancing of the benefit of radiation dose reduction, with its health and social implications, against the overall cost of the resources, and of any additional harm included in achieving that reduction. The NRPB says that ALARA does not require everything possible, or technically feasible, to be done to reduce doses without consideration of the cost or of the magnitude of the benefit from dose reduction. The NII's SAPs make use of the phrase, 'as low as is reasonably practicable' (ALARP), a term that is fundamental to the *HSWA74* and qualifies the general duties placed on employers. The phrase has been defined in the Court of Appeal in *Edwards v National Coal Board (1949)*.[25] In the House of Lords in *Marshall v Gotham*[26] according to Lord Reid the definition of 'reasonably practicable' was distinguished from 'practicable'. Therefore in the context of licensing the ALARA principle and the ALARP principle are identical. Sir Frank Layfield took this view in the report on the Sizewell Inquiry where he said,[27] 'For present purposes I regard the ALARA and ALARP principles as indistinguishable in effect'. He also warned of the possibility of inconsistent approaches by different regulatory bodies and the threat of relentless increase in safety standards, with little regard to the economic aspects involved.

Emergency Plans Licence conditions invariably also include an obligation to provide for an emergency plan and, at least in installations operated by the nuclear generating industry, these plans are exercised annually. The plan typically outlines the duties of fire control bodies, first aid, rescue and the monitoring of radiation within and in the vicinity of the station. These plans must also be capable of extension to deal with events resulting in large releases of radionuclides, even though the basic design philosophy is intended to make such accidents improbable. Emergency plans also depend on co-operative action between the site operator's staff, the local authorities and the emergency services, co-ordinated as in any civil emergency by the police who are specifically responsible for any evacuation of the local population that may be called for. In the early stages of a major accident at a United Kingdom site, responsibility for advising the police on off-site countermeasures lies with the site operator. Within a few hours, the operator should have established an Off-Site Centre, some way from the site, at which a wider range of regional and national organisations would be represented to provide advice and assistance as required. Central Government would appoint a Government Technical Adviser (GTA) to co-ordinate the advice from these bodies, which would include the DoE and DEFRA (or equivalents in Scotland and Northern Ireland), plus the NII and the NRPB. Each of these bodies would be supported by its own headquarters emergency organisation. The radiological protection aspects of emergency plans require an early assessment of the

---

[24] op cit NRPB ASP 9, para 3, March 1986.
[25] [1949] 1 All ER 743 at 747.
[26] [1954] 1 All ER 937 at 942.
[27] Layfield, Sir Frank *Sizewell B Inquiry*, Ch 7, p 11, para 7.51.

magnitude and nature of the release, its dispersion in the environment, and the doses that might arise. The countermeasures that might be taken to avoid exposure of the public would depend on the projected levels of dose that would otherwise be received. Article 45 of the *BSS Directive* requires that in the event of an accident each Member State shall stipulate 'intervention levels' and measures to be taken by the competent authorities and surveillance procedures with respect to the population groups that are liable to receive a dose in excess of the dose limits. In August 1977 the NRPB was given a directive by the Secretary of State for Social Services, which made it responsible for specifying Emergency Reference Levels (ERLs) of dose criteria for limiting doses to the public in the event of accidental exposure to radiation. The NRPB is also responsible for recommending levels of dose equivalent at which countermeasures would be introduced to produce some positive overall benefit when a release of radioactive material or the generation of ionising radiation fields is or may become uncontrollable, as after an accident, to limit any resulting exposure of the public. Such countermeasures would include sheltering in houses, prohibition or limitation of access to particular areas, evacuation of the affected population, control of food supplies and, in the special case of the release of the isotopes of iodine, administration of tablets containing stable iodine. The site operator would carry out measurements of dose rates and activity concentrations in air and other media in the vicinity of the site. DEFRA would undertake comprehensive monitoring of foodstuffs in the affected area and would extend its routine monitoring programme to provide information on a wider basis. The NRPB would make an independent assessment of the radiological impact, and would provide suitable advice to the GTA and to Central Government. The NRPB would also co-ordinate monitoring of the environment on a national scale, to provide reassurance to people living in unaffected areas and to enable the full impact of the accident to be assessed. Although accidents occurring overseas are by their nature likely to have lower radiological impact on the United Kingdom than equivalent accidents occurring within the country, the Government completed in 1993 the implementation of the National Response Plan to deal with the consequences of overseas nuclear accidents. This set up a network of automatic gamma-ray dose rate monitoring stations and an emergency response system together known as RIMNET (Radioactive Incident Monitoring Network). In the event of an overseas accident being notified or detected, this system will provide information on dose rates throughout the United Kingdom. It is operated by DEFRA and provides facilities for the collection and analysis of radiological monitoring data, necessary for the response to a nuclear accident. It also provides communications systems for distributing data summaries and Government information and advice bulletins.

The *Radiation (Emergency Preparedness and Public Information) Regulations 2001 (REPPIR)*[28] implement in the UK the articles on intervention in cases of radiation (radiological) emergency in the Euratom BSS Directive. They aim to protect members of the public from a radiation emergency that could arise from

---

[28] The Radiation (Emergency Preparedness and Public Information) Regulations 2001, SI 2001, No. 2975.

work with ionising radiation. A radiation emergency is an event that is likely to result in any member of the public receiving an effective dose of 5 mSv during the year immediately following the emergency. REPPIR establishes a framework of emergency preparedness measures to ensure that members of the public are properly informed and prepared, in advance, about what to do in the unlikely event of a radiation emergency occurring, and provided with information if a radiation emergency actually occurs. REPPIR formalises into regulations emergency planning arrangements with local authorities. The regulations do not replace existing nuclear site licence conditions but operators of licensed sites who comply with those conditions will satisfy equivalent provisions in REPPIR. A guide to REPPIR[29] was published in January 2002. IRR99 also require the preparation of contingency plans (Regulation 12) to restrict any exposure that arises from an accident both to the employees and to others, including emergency services personnel, who may be affected by it. The accident assessment and the reasonably practicable steps flowing from it provide the platform from which to build the plan. An air crash on a nuclear installation is a particular hazard that is provided for in the Air Navigation (Restriction of Flying) (Nuclear Installations) Regulations 1988.[30] These Regulations restrict flying in the vicinity of certain specified nuclear installations where the Secretary of State considers it necessary in the public interest. The Government Advisory Committee on the Safety of Nuclear Installations, which keeps under general review safety measures at licensed sites, monitor, in particular, emergency exercise procedures.

Liability for Injury and Damage

In compliance with the agreement under the *Paris Convention*, s7 (1)(a) of the *NIA65* imposes a strict duty upon the licensee in the event of an occurrence causing injury to any person or damage to any property of any person other than the licensee on the site (whether or not he is at fault). Once damage is proved to have resulted the licensee is absolutely liable. Similarly under s7 (1)(b)(ii) the licensee is liable for damage caused by waste even though it was not discharged intentionally or negligently. The liability under s7 (1)(b)(i) for damage caused by radiation on the site from non-nuclear matter, e.g. industrial X-ray apparatus, is on the face of it less strict; the source of ionising radiations must have been 'caused or suffered' to be on the site by the licensee. So in the improbable event of the licensee not having brought on or allowed on site the source of radiation and not being aware of its presence he would not be liable under the *NIA65* for damage caused by its emissions. This could pose real problems where contractors have such radioactive sources for non-destructive testing purposes. However, the licensee would be hard pressed to show that he was operating a secure site with controlled access and yet was unaware of the presence of radioactive materials.

---

[29] HSE (2001), *A Guide to the Radiation (Emergency Preparedness and Public Information) Regulations*, HMSO London.
[30] Air Navigation (Restriction of Flying) (Nuclear Installations) Regulations, SI 1988 No 1138.

Constructively all materials are on site with the licensee's permission therefore he would be strictly liable for an emission caused by any material on the site.

Injury includes nervous shock which may range from non-actionable anxiety to recognisable psychiatric illness and is discussed in chapter seven,[31] but an employee who is denied employment elsewhere because he has suffered an excessive dose of radiation but who is not ill, has probably not suffered physical injury within the Act and would not be able to claim compensation. *The Congenital Disabilities (Civil Liabilities) Act 1976* gives a cause of action to one who was a foetus at the time of the accident and has suffered as a consequence. It is believed that a cause of action would be available under *NIA65* to a person not conceived at the time who had suffered as a consequence of their parents having been exposed to ionising radiations. However, the cases of *Hope* and *Reay* failed on the grounds that statistical associations were not causal nor was the causal relationship plausible.[32]

The property of persons on site is deemed to be the property of the licensee and therefore according to *NIA65* s7 (1) is not recoverable in the event of damage; therefore a person injured on site will be able to claim for his personal injuries but not for damage to his tools. Consequently if during the course of a contract on a licensed site the tools used by a contractor or property in the care of the contractor become contaminated with radioactive material and he is not allowed to take them off site or to use them on site, he is not able to claim compensation under the *NIA65*. It has been recommended by Contractors Associations and the Electrical Supply Industry that separate contractual arrangements be made to cover this eventuality. Similarly Contractors are warned to avoid the inadvertent assumption of liabilities by general conditions in contracts being deemed to be 'an agreement in writing' under s12 of the *NIA65* as amended by the 1969 Act.

The *NIA65*, under s12 (1)(a) and s16 (1), creates a right of action for damages when damage occurs due to more than one source of radiation, for example from two licensed sites, provided the plaintiff can prove a casual relationship: s17 (3) provides for a joint and several liability between the licensees. However, if one of the causes of damage is not from an occurrence on a licensed site but by some other source of radiation, for example from a radioactive source used in non-destructive testing (NDT) of a welded pipe, s12 (3) allows a cause of action separate from that under the *NIA65*. Under such circumstances double compensation cannot be obtained. The licensee is not liable for injury or damage that occurs due to hostile action s13 (4)(a) but is liable where injury or damage is caused by a natural disaster s13 (4)(b). Where the injury or damage is caused wholly or partly by the intentional or reckless behaviour of the plaintiff s13 (6) the licensee may be relieved of part or all liability but only if the act was committed with the intention of causing harm or with reckless disregard of the consequences of his act. Therefore, a contractor on the site would be vicariously liable for the

---

[31] See psychological damage p 230.
[32] *Reay v BNFL and Hope v BNFL*. [1994] Env. L.R. 320.

intentional non-nuclear damage from NDT equipment caused by his employee, under the ruling in *Photo Production Ltd v Securicor Transport Ltd*.[33]

Where injury or damage has been caused s12 (1) of the *NIA65* provides that any other person in respect of that injury or damage shall incur no other liability. Therefore a supplier of defective equipment, which has caused radiation injury or damage on a licensed site, will not be held liable. The plaintiff unable to claim under the *NIA65* for compensation of pecuniary loss or emotional disturbance might consider an action in tort or in contract against the supplier. Assuming that an actionable issue could be established the question would arise as to whether the *NIA65* with its exclusive and exhaustive liability regime would allow such an action. It is argued by Dr Leigh[34] that 'any occurrence' on the licensed nuclear site as applied to s7 (1)(a) of *NIA65* includes all activities on site, including normal operations that result in exposure to radiation, and is not confined to abnormal occurrences. The sole issue would be that of causation: has the radiation exposure in question caused or materially contributed to the condition. Where a nuclear site is operated without a licence by somebody other than the Authority or a Government department the provisions of s7 would not apply and all liability would be determined by the common law.

The problems of a relatively short limitation period of ten years as agreed under the *Paris Convention* are avoided in the NIA65 since under s15 (1) action may be taken up to thirty years after the occurrence, thus allowing a reasonable period in the context of the time taken for some cancers to develop. Any longer period is not allowed under the *Limitation Act 1963* even though the harm was undetectable. In the 'normal' situation claims after ten years and up to thirty years would be directed to the Secretary of State, as the licensee has no liability after ten years. In the event of nuclear matter being stolen, lost, jettisoned or abandoned s15 (2) allows claims to be brought up to twenty years from the loss etc in which an occurrence resulting in injury or damage may happen. Therefore it would appear to be possible for claims for compensation of injury or damage to be directed to the Secretary of State which may have occurred up to thirty years from an occurrence that happens up to twenty years after the radioactive material is lost etc.

As amended by s27 of the *Energy Act 1983*, s16 (1) of the *NIA65* which set a limit of liability of £20 million per occurrence[35] has been further amended by the *Nuclear Installations (Increase of Operator's Limits of Liability) Order 1994 No 909*, to increase the maximum payable as compensation by an operator to £140 million per incident. For prescribed installations posing a reduced risk the increase is from £5m to £10 million. Section 19(1) requires the licensee to be insured or otherwise covered. s16 (3) allows Parliament to satisfy claims where the limit of

---

[33] Photo Production Ltd v Securicor Transport Ltd [1978] 2 Lloyd's Rep.172.

[34] Leigh, Dr W.J. (1997), 'Liability and Regulation – Some Legal Challenges Faced by Operators of United Kingdom Nuclear Installations', [1997] Env. Liability 31-58, p 43.

[35] An interesting discussion of the financial advantages the owner of a nuclear installation has over the owner of a non-nuclear installation due to the limited liabilities provided by nuclear legislation may be found in the Nuclear Law Bulletin 63 Jun. 1999 by Marcus Radetzki.

amount or time is exceeded and there is no claim on foreign funds. A foreign operator is not expected to pay compensation other than as required by his own State laws or to the amount he is insured, S16 (2)(a) and (b). Recent changes regarding liability in the Paris and Brussels Conventions to increase compensation limits and to include environmental damage are discussed in chapter seven.[36] Powers to implement the changes are included Chapter Five of the *Energy Act 2004*.[37]

Property Damage[38] In the case of *Merlin v BNF plc*[39] it was held that the duty under the *NIA65* was restricted to physical damage to tangible property and not to economic loss. However, compensation for economic loss flowing from physical damage by radioactive overflow was allowed in *Blue Circle v Ministry of Defence*.[40] [41] Arising from contamination of the beach by radioactive particles near the Dounreay licensed site, operated by the UKAEA, in the *Margohand*[42] case the petitioners were seeking an order for specific performance of statutory duty under s7 of *NIA65*. In the Court of Session in Edinburgh Lady Paton was satisfied that the beach had suffered damage arising or resulting from the radioactive particles and that damage had occurred to fishing by the imposition of a food protection order, however s7 does not entitle petitioners to order for specific performance and she rejected to grant judicial review. However, she granted a declarator to the effect that UKAEA had failed, and continued to fail, to perform their statutory duty under s7 to secure that no occurrence involving nuclear matter causes damage to any property other than the UKAEA's.

Incident Reporting

The Nuclear Installations (Dangerous Occurrences) Regulations 1965, made under s22 of the *NIA65*, require the operator to report to HSE any dangerous occurrences of the kind specified in the regulations. These occurrences are the most serious ones that might occur on a nuclear site, involving the risk of death or serious injury from the effects of radiation and accidents involving fires and criticality. Under requirements imposed by the Secretary of State for Energy in 1977 and revised in 1982, other categories of incidents at the next level of significance need to be reported to the Secretary of State. The current criteria for reporting are as follows:

---

[36] See chapter seven p 250, The Future of Regulation in the UK.
[37] See also chapter seven ref. 117.
[38] See also chapter seven p 223, Legal Action.
[39] [1990] All ER 711.
[40] [1996] The Times 11 December 1996. [1997] Env L.R. 341. and C.A. [1999] Env. L. R., Part I , pp 22 - 61
[41] See also Tromans, (1999) Env Law Review, Vol 1, No. 1. and (1999) Journal of Environmental Law Vol 11, No 2.
[42] Unreported *Magnohard Limited and Others v UKAEA and the SEPA (Outer House, Court of Session – judgment 15 August 2003).*

- dangerous occurrences reportable under the Nuclear Installations (Dangerous Occurrences) Regulations 1965;
- exposures to radiation or contamination which have been confirmed as resulting in overexposures exceeding twice the maximum annual permissible limits as defined in the schedules attached to nuclear site licences or regulations; or
- examination, inspection, maintenance or test of any part of the plant revealing that the safe operations or condition of the plant may be significantly affected and abnormal occurrences leading to:
- a release or spread of radioactivity on the site outside a controlled area requiring special action or special investigation by the operator;
- a release or suspected release or spread of radioactivity off site that results in the need for special action.

The report to the Secretary of State is to be made within twenty-four hours of the incident. A Statement on each incident so reported is subsequently published by the HSE in its quarterly reports of incidents at nuclear installations. Under a condition attached to the nuclear site licence, the operator is required to make arrangements for notifying HSE of incidents that include some of lower significance than those discussed above. The arrangements also cover the investigation and the keeping of records of all incidents occurring on the site. There are also regulations made under the *HSWA74*, which require employers to notify HSE of radiological incidents and of conventional (i.e. non-radiological) accidents and dangerous occurrences.

On occasion there may be legitimate tensions between the main areas of regulation in the nuclear industry, these being, on the one hand, to ensure the safety of the nuclear plant and the protection of the public and the workforce and, on the other hand, to control discharges to the environment and the disposal of radioactive waste. An example of this conflict was manifest in the case where BNFL was prosecuted for releases into the North Sea;[43] the immediate alternative to the environmental consequences of a discharge was the storage on site with an increased risk to workers.

Regulation, Administration and Security of Radioactive Substances

While the control of work with radioactive substances is dealt with under the *HSWA74*, the definition of what constitutes a radioactive substance, its registration and authorisation of its disposal, is controlled by the *RSA 93*. There are many undertakings that use radioactive materials and generate or handle radioactive waste quite apart from the nuclear installations requiring nuclear site licences under the *NIA65*. These undertakings include commercial laboratories, hospitals, research facilities, engineering concerns and chemical plants. They, like nuclear installations are regulated by the system provided for in the *RSA93* (as amended by the *Environment Act 1995*). The use of radioactive material or of mobile

---

[43] *The Queen v BNF plc* [1985] Crown Court Carlisle.

radioactive apparatus is a criminal offence unless the premises where the radioactive material is to be used is registered with the Environment Agency under the *RSA93*, s6 and 7, or the mobile radioactive apparatus is itself registered, s9 and 10.

Radioactive Substances – Materials and Waste Radioactive material is defined in the *RSA93* as a substance which is not radioactive waste but which contains an amount of an element or elements that are defined in the *First Schedule to the Act*. The elements listed in the schedule are naturally occurring elements. In concentrations less than Stated in the schedule such elements do not fall under the *RSA93*; for example Uranium in solid form at 11.1 Bq per gm. The definition of radioactive material in s1 (2)(b) of the *RSA93* also includes a substance possessing radioactivity that is attributable to nuclear fission, bombardment neutrons, to ionising radiations, in the disposal of radioactive waste or by contamination in the course of a process. Radioactive waste is defined in s2 as any substance which constitutes scrap material, or an effluent or other unwanted surplus substance arising from the application of any process which, if it were not waste would be radioactive material, or a substance or article which has been contaminated in the course of the production, keeping or use of radioactive material, or by contact with, or proximity to, other radioactive waste. Contamination, according to s47 (5) is the absorption, admixture or adhesion of radioactive material or radioactive waste and the emission of neutrons or ionising radiations as to become radioactive or possess increased radioactivity.

A number of exemptions have been made for specific items with low radioactivity: these include testing instruments, under the *Radioactive Substances (Testing Instruments) Exemption Order 1985*;[44] gaseous titanium light devices;[45] luminous articles;[46] phosphatic substances;[47] lead;[48] uranium and thorium;[49] geological specimens;[50] closed sources used in schools[51] and exhibitions;[52] hospitals;[53] substances of low activity;[54] electronic valves[55] and smoke detectors.[56] In each case the level of radiation is specified; for example, smoke detectors containing Americium 241 in closed sources that do not exceed 40 kilo Bq.

Control of Materials Radioactive materials are controlled by registration of use and storage under s7 of the *RSA93* and by disposal only after authorisation under

---

[44] 1985 SI No 1049.
[45] 1985 SI No 1047.
[46] 1985 SI No 1048.
[47] SI 1962 No 2648.
[48] SI 1962 No 2649.
[49] SI 1962 No 2710 and 2711.
[50] SI 1963 No 1831.
[51] SI 1963 No 1832.
[52] SI 1962 No 2645.
[53] SI 1990 No 2512; (amendment) SI 1995 No 2395.
[54] SI 1986 No 1002; (amendment SI 1992 No 647).
[55] SI 1967 No 1797.
[56] SI 1980 No 953.

s13 of the Act. The power to ensure that all practices giving rise to radioactive wastes must be justified is given by the *RSA93* and the *NIA65*. Under the *RSA93* users of radioactive substances must be registered s7, such registration being granted by the Chief Inspector. An application for registration must contain, *inter alia*, the description and quantity of the material and the proposed manner in which the material will be used. Registration may be granted subject to conditions regarding the storage and disposal of radioactive materials. In deciding to grant an application the Chief Inspector must take into account the amount and character of the waste likely to arise. *The Radioactive Substances (Substances of Low Activity) Exemption Order 1986*[57] was made under s2 (6), s6 (5), s7 (4) and s20 (a) of the Act and came into operation on 14 July 1986. This exempted from registration under s1 of the *RSA93* persons keeping solid radioactive material of activity not greater than 0.4 Bq per gm (400 Bq per kg). The order also excluded from the requirement of s6 of the *RSA93* to obtain authorisation for disposal of radioactive waste, for a solid the activity of which does not exceed 0.4 Bq per gm, a liquid radioactive material because of the presence of carbon 14 or tritium or both the activity of which does not exceed 0.4 Bq per ml, or gas containing radionuclides, or the decay products of which, have a half life of greater than 100 seconds, i.e. the radioactivity level falls to half its value in 100 seconds.

Radioactive Waste The disposal s13 and the accumulation s14 of radioactive waste is prohibited except under an authorisation; however under s14 (3) authorisation of the accumulation of radioactive materials is not required for a site covered by a licence under the *NIA65*. It is the responsibility of the Environment Agency to ensure that operators in England and Wales comply with the requirements of the *RSA93*. Although no new radioactive waste disposal facilities have been provided in the UK for many years the environment agencies have issued guidance[58] which sets out regulatory requirements and principles. Relevant principles and requirements are:

- independence of safety from controls: following the disposal of radioactive waste, the closure of the disposal facility and the withdrawal of controls, the continued isolation of the waste from the accessible environment shall not depend on actions by future generations to maintain the integrity of the disposal system;
- facility design and construction: the facility shall be designed, constructed, operated and be capable of closure so as to avoid adverse effects on the performance of the containment system.

The guidance states that:

---

[57] The Radioactive Substances (Substances of Low Activity) Exemption Order SI 1986 No 1002.

[58] Disposal Facilities on Land for Low and Intermediate Level Wastes: Guidance on Requirements for Authorisation, EA, SEPA DoE for Northern Ireland (GRA).

disposal will not be regarded as complete until all the requirements of the safety case have been met, including sealing and closure of the facility. The developer should show that the design takes full account of these requirements and that suitable techniques are available.

Under the *RSA93*, an operator is not allowed to discharge on or from the site any radioactive matter except under the terms of an authorisation issued for that purpose. The limits on radioactive discharges are set on the basis of the 'justified needs' of the practice being conducted by the licensees, i.e. they must make a case that the proposed limits are necessary to allow safe and continued operation of the plant. In setting limits, the environment agencies use monitoring, discharge and plant performance data to ensure that the radiation exposure to the public as a consequence of the discharges would be less than the dose constraints and limits set by the UK Government. These constraints are a source constraint of 0.3 mSv per annum for an individual facility which can be optimised as an integral whole in terms of radioactive waste disposals; a site constraint of 0.5 mSv per annum for a site comprising more than one source, e.g. where 2 or more facilities are located together; and a dose limit of 1.0 mSv per annum from all sources of human-made radioactivity including the effects of past discharges but excluding medical exposure.

Where an authorisation is granted it is not sufficient just to satisfy the numerical limits given in the authorisation; the operator must reduce the discharges to as low as is reasonably achievable. The definition of material is 'consisting of matter'; therefore radioactive matter in the *RSA93* is synonymous with radioactive material in the *NIA65*. The *European Directive 96/29/EURATOM* is implemented by the *Radioactive Substances (Basic Safety Standards) (England and Wales) Direction 2000* and *European Directive 96/29/EURATOM* and the *Radioactive Substances (Basic Safety Standards) (Scotland) Direction 2000* which sets out the constraints.

Control of the Use, Storage and Disposal of Radioactive Substances The construction and operation of facilities for the use, storage and disposal of radioactive materials is the subject of legal control and political debate. A wealth of advice and information is therefore available to the Secretaries of State in considering the justification of a proposal to embark on a process that involves radioactivity. Formal application to build a Power Station must be made to the Secretary of State for Energy under s2 of the *Electric Lighting Act 1909* as amended by s33 and s34 of the *Electricity Act 1957*. Under s5 of the *Town and Country Planning Act 1990* the Secretary of State for the Environment is asked to give deemed planning permission. If the local planning authority objects to the proposals, or if it seeks to impose conditions which are unacceptable, then the Secretary of State is obliged by s34 of the *Electricity Act 1957* to ask for a public inquiry into the application. The Secretary of State may call for a public inquiry even if the local planning authority does not object. In 1986, the House of Commons Environment Committee investigated radioactive waste[59] and also in

---

[59] House of Commons (1986*), Radioactive Waste*, First Report from the Environment Committee, Jan. HMSO.

1986 the House of Lords Select Committee on the European Communities in its eighteenth report considered nuclear power in Europe. Radioactive Waste Management Policy was again reviewed in 1995[60] and at the time of writing, Spring 2003, DEFRA has launched a process to achieve a policy decision on the long term management of solid nuclear waste, backed by legislation if necessary, by 2007. In July 2002 the White Paper 'Managing the Nuclear Legacy'[61] proposed setting up a Liabilities Management Authority (LMA), now renamed the Decommissioning Management Authority (DMA), to be responsible to Government for developing and implementing an overall strategy for discharging the nuclear legacy. A draft *Nuclear Sites and Radioactive Substances Bill* has been issued for consultation.

The United Nations Scientific Committee on the Effects of Atomic Radiation (UNSCEAR) in producing risk estimates have taken into account the revised dosimetry of the survivors of the Japanese atomic bombings. On the basis of ICRP advice the NRPB has recommended that workers' doses do not exceed 0.015 Sv effective dose equivalent per year and that the dose to individual members of the public should not exceed 0.0005 Sv per year from effluent discharges from a single site. This arrangement satisfies the EEC EURATOM Directive 96/29 of an average dose of .02 Sv per year over 5 years (0.15v in 5 years) with no more than 0.05 Sv in a single year for radiation workers and 0.001 Sv per year for the general public.

Radioactive Substances and Planning Controls Under *EEC Directive 85/337* applications for the construction of a nuclear facility must include an Environmental Assessment Statement. The Royal Commission on Environmental Pollution in its fifth report[62] recommended that the concept of 'Best Practicable Environmental Options (BPEO)' be used in finding optimum solutions to environmental problems.[63] [64] Projects to construct, enlarge, modify or change the use of premises concerned with the handling of radioactive material or the accumulation or disposal of radioactive waste will invariably require development consents e.g. under the Town and Country Planning legislation. This will be in addition to a need to satisfy the specific authorisation requirements of the *RSA93* and, in the case of nuclear installations, the licensing and consent arrangements under the *NIA65*. In some instances, an application for planning permission may be 'called in' by the relevant Minister for ministerial decision. This usually reflects the fact that the development is seen as having national importance. The planning

---

[60] Cm 2919 (1995).

[61] Cm 5552 (2002).

[62] Royal Commission on Environmental Pollution (1976), *Air Pollution: An Integrated Approach*, Fifth Report, RCEP London.

[63] Guruswamy L.D. and Tromans S.R. (1986), 'Towards an Integrated Approach to Pollution Control. The Best Practicable Environmental Option and its Antecedents'. (1986) JPL Aug. pp 643-655.

[64] Farquhar, James T. (1986), 'Best Practicable Means (and the thought that Nanny may have known best after all)', *Chemistry and Industry*, Aug. 1986, pp 541-543.

authority may suggest the 'call in'. In England and Wales, the Secretaries of State for Wales, the Department for Environment, Food and Rural Affairs, and the Department of Health hold joint powers to call in applications for authorisations for their own determination, in which case a local inquiry may be held. The Secretaries of State can also issue Directions to the environment agencies. In Scotland, powers under *RSA93* are held and administered by the Scottish Ministers. These include powers to direct applications for authorisation to Scottish Ministers for their determination under s24 of *RSA93*. Also, the Scottish Ministers may cause a local inquiry to be held in relation to the application. Where an application for planning permission is 'called in', a local Public Inquiry is set up. In England and Wales the independent Planning Inspectorate arranges for one of its inspectors to hear and receive evidence for or against the proposal. The inspector then makes a report and a recommendation to the Office of the Deputy Prime Minister for England or the Welsh Assembly. In Scotland, the Scottish Executive Inquiries Reporter usually reviews written evidence and issues a decision letter. Some cases are considered by means of a Public Inquiry, with the decision taken by the Scottish Ministers. This decision is made public by letter issued by the staff of the Planning Division of the Scottish Executive Development Department. A large development is likely to become the subject of public or other statutory inquiries, as in the cases of Windscale in 1978 and Sizewell B in 1988. Following the local authority's refusal to grant planning permission to UK Nirex for an underground research laboratory to test a proposed site of a radioactive waste repository and a public inquiry in 1995/6, the Secretary of State for the Environment in 1997 rejected the application to construct at Sellafield.

The Environment Agency is charged with the specific responsibility for considering and authorising the use, accumulation and disposal of radioactive material and waste. It has a general duty in doing so to consider the public health and safety aspects of this proposed activity. However, the radiological and wider environmental effects of the development may also be matters requiring consideration in the planning process that, in most cases, will precede these other authorisation and consent processes. Of particular importance are: Article 6(i) of the Basic Safety Standards Directive, which provides that:

> The various types of activity resulting in an exposure to ionising radiation shall have been justified in advance by the advantages, which they produce.

The scope and nature of the issues to be considered under this 'prior justification' requirement of Community law are at present unclear. It is, however, unquestionable that one of the circumstances that in at least some cases the requirement will fail to be addressed is at the initial planning stage. Otton J goes further than this in *R v HMIP, ex p Greenpeace (No 2)*[65] and suggests that where a benefit and disbenefit analysis has been conducted at the planning stage of a plant from which radioactive discharges will be made, the relevant activity may be regarded as being 'justified in advance' and that a re-evaluation is not required, either by Article 6 of the Basic Safety Standards Directive or by the Radioactive

---

[65] [1994] 4 All ER 329.

Substances Act 1993, before the discharge authorisations themselves are granted. But see the later judgment of Potts J in *R v Secretary of State for the Environment, ex p Greenpeace*.[66]

Also to be considered prior to the planning process is the *Directive on the Assessment of the Effects of Certain Public and Private Projects on the Environment*[67] and the various regulations by which this Directive has been implemented in the United Kingdom. Of particular relevance to the nuclear industry are the *Town and Country Planning (Assessment of Environment Effects) Regulations*[68] and the *Electricity and Pipe-line Works (Assessment of Environmental Effects) Regulations*.[69] Pursuant to the Directive and these Regulations, environmental information has to be supplied to, and taken into account by the relevant planning authorities in forming the judgment as to whether certain developments should go ahead. The Regulations make the following specific provisions for 'nuclear' developments:

• applications to local planning authorities for development relating to the permanent storage or final disposal of radioactive waste are 'Schedule 1' applications i.e. applications for which, if not in respect of 'exempt development', environmental information and assessment is required.[70]

• 'Schedule 2' applications for which environmental information and assessment is required if the development in question is not an exempt development and is one which would be likely to have significant effects on the environment. These include applications to local planning authorities for developments relating to nuclear fuel production, enrichment and reprocessing plants and installations for the collection or processing of radioactive waste, other than installations which otherwise fall under Schedule 1.[71]

• environmental information must be submitted to the Secretary of State for Trade and Industry in connection with applications for the construction or extension of nuclear power stations, regardless of the level of likely effects, if any, of such developments on the environment.[72]

An emerging principle of planning law, supported by the adoption of the above-mentioned Directive and its implementation by the *Town and Country Planning (Assessment of Environmental Effects) Regulations 1988*, that the environmental

---

[66] [1994] 4 All ER 352, [1994] ENV L.R. 401.

[67] 85/337/EEC.

[68] SI 1988 No 1199.

[69] SI 1990 No 442.

[70] Paragraphs 2(1) and 4(1) and Schedule 1 to the Town and Country Planning (Assessment of Environmental Effects) Regulations 1988.

[71] Paragraphs 2(1) and 4(1) and Schedule 2 to the Town and Country Planning (Assessment of Environmental Effects) Regulations 1988.

[72] Paragraphs 1-3 and the Schedule to the Electricity and Pipe-line Works (Assessment of Environmental Effects) Regulations 1989.

effects in general, and the levels of emissions and pollution in particular, arising from a proposed industrial development may be relevant considerations for planning authorities to consider in relation to applications for such development.[73] In 2004 the *SEA Directive* will take effect requiring the assessment and reporting of plans and programmes while they are under preparation and before implementation.[74]

Security Wide powers to prevent the improper use of fissionable materials are conferred on the Secretary of State for Energy by the *Atomic Energy Act 1946*, the *RSA93* and the *NIA65* as amended and by the *Atomic Energy Authority Act 1971*. Under the Third Schedule of the *Atomic Energy Authority Act 1954*, for the purposes of the *Official Secrets Act 1911*, membership of or any office or employment under the Authority is deemed to be an office under Her Majesty and any contract with the Authority is deemed to be a contract with Her Majesty. The *Official Secrets Acts 1911-1920*, make provision for the security of certain Crown property by declaring certain activities in relation to such property to be criminal offences. Certain activities by Crown servants and those who have contact with the Crown are also offences. Under s6 (3) of the *Atomic Energy Authority Act 1954*, the Authority's premises come within the definition of places that may be declared to be 'prohibited places' under s3 of the *1911 Act*. The Secretary of State for Energy may, under s2 of the *NIA65* as amended by the *Atomic Energy Authority Act 1971*, make orders bringing any site, for which a permit to extract plutonium or uranium or to enrich uranium has been granted, into the definition of a place which may be declared a prohibited place.

Since 1955 the UKAEA has operated a force to police all Authority establishments under the powers given in the Third Schedule to the *Atomic Energy Act 1954*, which provided that the UKAEA could nominate persons to be sworn in as constables under s3 of the *Special Constables Act 1923*. The office for Civil Nuclear Security (OCNS) is responsible to the DTI and will report annually to the Minister for Energy. Under the Third Schedule the property of the UKAEA is deemed to be property of the Crown for the purposes of the *Metropolitan Police Act 1960*. For the purpose of s6 of the *Public Stores Act 1875* any person appointed to be a constable within the premises under the control of the Authority is deemed to be a constable deputed by a public department and property possessed by, or under the control of, the Authority is deemed to be Her Majesty's stores. Therefore, any Officer sworn in by the Authority under the *1923 Act* could exercise the powers of a constable with the same powers and privileges as a constable of the Metropolitan Police in England and Wales and as a constable in Scotland, in relation to premises possessed or controlled by the Authority and in relation to the Authority within a radium of fifteen miles of those premises.

---

[73] See the DoE Planning Policy Guidance (PPG23) on Planning and Pollution Controls (1994) and the case of *Gateshead Metropolitan Borough Council v Secretary of State for the Environment (1994)* 1 PLR 85, [1995] Env LR 37.
[74] See chapter five, *Environmental Impact Assessment*.

Under s19 of the *Atomic Energy Authority Act 1971* the UKAEA Constabulary police the establishments transferred to BNFL and by provisions in s2 and s4-6 of the schedule the Authority was also empowered to provide constables at the premises of other specified companies, e.g. URENCO. The Authority police are allowed to hold firearms without firearms certificates as they are deemed to be Crown Servants under s1 of the *Atomic Energy Authority (Special Constables) Act 1976* for the purposes of s54 of the *Firearms Act 1968*. Under s3 of the *1976 Act* the Authority police retain their powers as constables throughout the United Kingdom while escorting movements of special nuclear materials and when taking necessary action consequent upon any unlawful removal of nuclear matter.

Safeguards The *Nuclear Safeguards and Electricity (Finance) Act 1978* provides for giving effect to an international agreement for the application of safeguards in the United Kingdom related to the *Non-Proliferation Treaty*. The *Environmental Protection Act 1990* provides for the keeping of records by the Local Authority.[75]

Prosecution As a result of high levels of radiation being detected in parts of the beach at Seascale, BNF plc have been prosecuted and found guilty of being in breach of both the conditions attached to the nuclear site licence and the *Radioactive Substances Act 1960*.[76] The details of the charges for which they were fined were:

1. Contravention of a nuclear site licence contrary to s4(6) of the *Nuclear Installations Act 1965*.

a) In breach of a condition to keep adequate records of operations relating to Highly Active Washing Tank B of the reprocessing plant. Fined £1000.

b) In breach of a condition to take all reasonable steps to minimise exposure of persons to radiation by:

(i) discharging radioactive particulate matter and liquids to the sea and

(ii) failing to ensure that any person in the vicinity of the end of the discharge pipe or adjacent water or beaches was informed of the possible presence of radioactive particulate matter and liquids in the sea and the resultant increased risk of exposure. Fined £2,500.

2. Failure to comply with a limitation or condition of a certificate of authorisation for the disposal of radioactive waste contrary to s13 (1)(c) of RSA 60 by:

a) discharging highly radioactive particulate matter and liquids to sea to such amount and at such a rate that radioactive exposure from such discharge was not as low as was reasonably achievable. Fined £5,000.

b) failing to keep and retain for inspection records of disposal of radioactive material by discharge to sea. Fined £1,500.

---

[75] John, Edward (1995), 'Access to Environmental Information: Limitations of the UK Radioactive Substances Register', *JEL* vol 7 No 1.
[76] *Supra, The Queen v BNFL*.

BNFL was ordered to pay costs of the prosecution not in excess of £60,000. On summing up Mr Justice Rose said in the context of exposure not being as low as was reasonably achievable:

> Members of the jury; you decide what is reasonable. In doing so, you take into account all the circumstances both on and off site. You must weigh on the one hand the time, trouble, cost and other disadvantages of such alternative courses of action as may have been open to the Company, and on the other hand the nature and the extent of risk of higher exposure to people off site if these courses were not taken.

The jury was instructed that they must consider the amount and rate of discharge, the radiation exposure that resulted, and whether the discharges were as low as reasonably achievable. The judge explained:

> It is sufficient.... that off site people exposed to – that is in danger of coming into contact with – a level of radiation objectively measured which is above the minimum.

The basic objectives of the 1959 White Paper[77] have been enforced, the question of the interpretation of 'as low as is reasonably achievable' and the computing of the average effective dose are however still under debate. The discharge in the BNFL case was estimated as thirty three million Bequerels, i.e. less than the material contained in the Betalights that were being directly handled by the workers in the case of Tele-Trading.[78]

Transportation of Radioactive Substances

The *Transfrontier Shipment of Radioactive Waste Regulations 1993*[79] establish a general framework of authorisation and approvals, without which the shipment of radioactive waste (including recyclable waste) from, to or through the United Kingdom is prohibited under regulations 6 and 10. The Regulations are administered and enforced by the EA under the *RSA93*. They involve the prior notification of applications for shipments to the competent authorities in each other country to which the shipment relates. The approval for the shipment from these other authorities is also required under regulation 7(3). Regulation 5(1) imposes the duty of making an application for shipment on the person within the UK responsible for the proposed shipment. Failure to comply with the authorisation requirements and the making of false or misleading Statements in connection with applications are criminal offences punishable by a fine and imprisonment under regulation 18.

The export of nuclear materials, including spent fuel, is also regulated under *Council Regulation 1334/2000*,[80] *as amended*,[81] which sets up a European Community regime for the control of exports of dual use items and technology and

---

[77] Control of Radioactive Wastes. Cmnd 884 1959 HMSO.

[78] Supra, Radiation Protection Bulletin No 81.

[79] SI 1993 No 3031.

[80] Council Regulation (Euratom) No 1493/93 on shipments of radioactive substances between Member States. Official Journal of the European Communities (OJEC), 19 Jun. 1993, L 148, p 1–7.

[81] O.J. L 159, 30 Jun. 2000, p 1.

requires such exports to be authorised. The Regulation is implemented in the UK by the *Dual-Use Items (Export Control) Regulations 2000*.[82] In addition, the UK applies the IAEA Nuclear Supply Group (NSG) Guidelines.[83]

Road Transport Specific provision for carriage of radioactive materials by road is made by the *Radioactive Material (Road Transport) (Great Britain) Regulations 1996*[84] under the *Radioactive Material (Road Transport) Act 1991*. The regulations specify the circumstances in which radioactive material can be transported by road; lay down standards for the design and testing of transport packaging (certain types to be approved by the Secretary of State); provide for certain shipments to be approved by the Secretary of State; set maximum levels of radioactive contamination that are allowed on the surface; extend the use of quality assurance; introduce consignment documentation; specify requirements for labelling of packages and placarding of vehicles; introduce the requirement for vehicles to carry fire extinguishers; lay down the duties of a driver during transport and in the event of an accident; require the Secretary of State to be informed in the case of an undeliverable consignment; and to provide for the Secretary of State to be informed of the serial number of packages where their design requires the approval of the Secretary of State.

Rail Transport Specific provision for the transport of radioactive material is made by the *Packaging, Labelling and Carriage of Radioactive Material by Rail Regulations 1996*,[85] made under the HSWA74. These regulations implement EC Council Directive 96/49 on the approximation of Laws of member States with regard to transport of dangerous goods by rail in so far as it relates to radioactive material and makes provision for the carriage by rail of radioactive material. The regulations provide for the HSC to approve and publish requirements for the packaging, labelling and carriage of radioactive material by rail; provide for the approval of designs of packaging and the approval of shipments and shipments under special arrangements; provide for packaging requirements of quality assurance, testing, registration of serial numbers, inspection and notification of shipments; provide for prohibitions, loading and unloading, security measures, emergency arrangements and other displays of information during carriage.

Shipping The *Merchant Shipping (Dangerous Goods and Marine Pollutants) Regulations 1997*[86] implement *Council Directive 93/75/EEC* relating to vessels bound for or leaving Community ports and carrying dangerous or polluting goods. The Regulations made by the Secretary of State for Transport in exercise of powers confirmed the *European Communities Act 1972, the Merchant Shipping Act 1995, the HSWA74* and the *Merchant Shipping/Prevention and Control of Pollution*

---

[82] SI 2000/2620.
[83] IAEA Nuclear Supply Group Guidelines (see page 10, section 1.2).
[84] SI 1996/1350.
[85] SI 1996/2090.
[86] SI 1997 No 2367.

Order 1990,[87] which gives effect to Amex II of the *International Convention for the Prevention of Pollution from Ships 1973 (MARPOL)*, prohibit the transport of dangerous goods on any ship unless a written declaration is provided to the effect that the shipment is properly marked and labelled in accordance with the Regulations and is packaged so as to withstand the ordinary risks of handling and transport by sea. The classification and packaging of goods must be in accordance with the *International Maritime Dangerous Goods Code 1994* edition. *The Merchant Shipping (Reporting Requirements for Ships carrying Dangerous or Polluting Goods) Regulations 1995*[88] introduced requirements that masters of ships within UK waters carrying radioactive materials must keep a copy of the manifest on land and report any incidents which involve actual or probable discharge of the goods. The Regulations require the operator of a ship departing from a port to inform the Coast Guard Agency or other local competent authority about the nature, quantity and location of any dangerous goods aboard, the ship's destination and intended route. They also provide that prior notification of each shipment of radioactive goods must be made in accordance with the International Maritime Dangerous Goods Code, 1994 edition. *The Merchant Shipping (Prevention of Pollution: substances other than Oil) (Intervention) Order 1997*[89] lists in Schedule Part 3 radioactive material as a substance presented for the purposes of the *Merchant Shipping Act 1995* and allows, in the case of marine pollution, intervention on the high seas by the Secretary of State.

Comment

The law relating to radioactive waste can only be identified by extraction from the body of the laws relating to radioactive substances, health and safety and the licensing of nuclear facilities. The government is going through the consultation process to revise the law to isolate historic waste and sources of waste and to determine the future plans for the management of some of the types of radioactive waste. The approach is however fragmented and there remain many areas that require policy decisions as outlined in chapter seven.

Nuclear Law in the USA

Statute Law

The House of Representatives codifies Statute Law in the US;[90] [91] nuclear laws are collected under Title 42 – Public Health and Welfare which is in turn divided into chapters; chapter 23 deals with the development and control of atomic energy and chapter 108 with nuclear waste policy; chapter 108 is then divided into sub-chapters and parts as follows:

---

[87] SI 1990 No 2595.

[88] SI 1995 No 2498.

[89] SI 1997 No 1869.

[90] Nuclear Regulatory Legislation, 107th Congress; 1st Session, June 2002. NUREG-0980 Vol.1 No.6.

[91] [www.uscode.house.gov/].

Sub-chapter I – Disposal and storage of high level radioactive waste, spent nuclear fuel and low level radioactive waste; with parts including Part A – Repositories for disposal of high level radioactive waste and spent fuel; Part B – Interim storage programme; Part C – Monitored retrievable storage; Part D – Low level radioactive waste and Part H – Transportation.

Sub-chapter II – Research, development and demonstration regarding disposal of high level radioactive waste and spent nuclear fuel; Sub-chapter III – Other provisions relating to radioactive waste; Sub-chapter IV – Nuclear waste negotiator and Sub-chapter V – Nuclear waste technical review board.

A unique section number is given for each topic within a title, for example within Part B of Sub-chapter B Section 10155(c) relates to the environmental review of spent nuclear fuel; the reference 42 U.S.C. 10155c will, therefore, locate this topic within the US Code. Chapter 23 is divided into two divisions, A which deals with atomic energy and B with the US enrichment corporation and is also divided into sub-chapters that deal with, *inter alia*, the production of materials, military application of atomic energy, licensing, international activities and EURATOM cooperation.

Regulation and Environmental Protection The Nuclear Regulatory Commission (NRC) was established under the *Energy Reorganisation Act of 1974*[92] with the split of military and civilian use of nuclear materials such that the responsibility for the development and production of nuclear weapons, promotion of nuclear power and other energy related work were assigned to the Department of Energy (DOE) and the regulatory work, except the regulation of defence nuclear facilities, was assigned to the NRC.

The *Atomic Energy Act*[93] requires that civilian uses of nuclear facilities and materials be licensed and empowers the NRC to enforce such standards as they deem necessary to protect health and safety and to minimize danger to life and property. The NRC may enter into agreement with a State where its own regulatory programme is compatible with the NRC's for discontinuing the NRC's regulatory authority over some materials within the State. NRC's actions under the *Act* are subject to the *Act's* provision for the opportunity for hearings and federal review.

The Federal government's responsibility to provide a place for the permanent disposal of high level radioactive waste and spent nuclear fuel and the generators' responsibility to bear the costs of permanent disposal is established by the *Nuclear Waste Policy Act of 1982*.[94] The *Act* focuses on the possibility of a permanent repository being built at Yucca Mountain by the DOE, Congressional review of a recommendation to build and NRC authorization to construct a repository. The *Act* calls for tribal and public participation in the planning of permanent repositories. It supports the use of deep geologic repositories, establishes procedures to select and evaluate sites, the interaction of federal and State governments and a timetable of

---

[92] Pub. L. 93-438 (88 Stat. 1233) 11 Oct. 1974 42 U.S.C. 5801 et seq.
[93] Pub. L. 83-703 (68 Stat. 919) 30 August 1954.
[94] Pub. L. 97-425 (96 Stat. 2201) 42 U.S.C. 10101.

programme milestones. Responsibility is assigned to the DOE to build and operate, the EPA to develop standards of protection of the general environment, the NRC to license and the DOE to operate a repository. The *Nuclear Waste Policy Amendments Act*[95] directs the DOE to consider Yucca Mountain as the primary site for the first geologic repository and prohibits the DOE from conducting site-specific activities at a second site, unless authorized by Congress. It requires the Secretary of Energy to develop a report on the need for a second repository by 1 January 2010. The *Amendment Act* establishes a commission to study the need and feasibility of a monitored, retrievable storage facility.

The disposal of low level radioactive waste generated within the borders of a State is the State's responsibility under the *Low Level Radioactive Waste Policy Amendment Act of 1985*.[96] The *Act* allows the States to form compacts to locate facilities to serve a group of States. It provides that the facilities will be regulated by the NRC or by the States that have entered into agreements with the NRC.[97] The *Act* also requires the NRC to establish standards for determining when radionuclides are present in waste streams in sufficiently low concentrations or quantities as to be 'below regulatory concern'.

The NRC has regulatory authority over mill tailings from uranium and thorium processing at NRC licensed sites under the *Uranium Mill Tailings Radiation Control Act of 1978*[98] to prevent or minimize, *inter alia*, the diffusion of radon into the environment.

The *Nuclear Non-Proliferation Act of 1978*[99] seeks to limit the spread of nuclear weapons by, *inter alia*, establishing criteria governing US exports licensed by the NRC and taking steps to strengthen the international safeguards system.

Environmental Protection

The comprehensive law that regulates air emissions is the *Clean Air Act of 1963*[100] that provides the authority to identify hazardous air pollutants and to develop and enforce limits with an adequate margin of safety to protect the public.[101] The territorial waters of the US are protected under the *Marine Protection, Research and Sanctuary Act of 1972*[102] by EPA regulation, which permits the disposal of material only when it will not degrade or endanger human health, welfare, ecological systems, the marine environment or the economy. The ocean disposal of high level radioactive waste is specifically prohibited under the *Act*; low level radioactive waste disposal may be permitted but only with the approval of both houses of Congress. The long-term goal to achieve indoor air as free from radon as

---

[95] 42 U.S.C. 10101 et seq.
[96] Pub. L. 99-240 (99 Stat. 1842) 15 January 1986 42 U.S.C. 2021.
[97] *Atomic Energy Act* of 1954 section 274.
[98] Pub. L. 95-604 (92 Stat. 3021) 8 November 1978 42 U.S.C. 79 et seq.
[99] Pub. L. (99Stat. 1842) 15 January 1986 42 U.S.C. 2021.
[100] As amended in 1970, 1977 and 1990. 42 U.S.C. 7401 et seq.
[101] ibid section 112.
[102] As Amended in 1977, 32 U.S.C. 1401 et seq.

the ambient air outside the buildings is established by the *Indoor Radon Abatement Act of 1988*.[103] Primary standards for contaminants, including radionuclides, in public waste systems are set and enforced by the EPA under the *Safe Drinking Water Act of 1974*.[104]

Every proposal for a major federal action significantly affecting the quality of the human environment has, *inter alia*, an environmental impact assessment of the proposed action and alternatives as required by the *National Environmental Policy Act of 1969*.[105] The Act also establishes a council on environmental quality in the Executive Office of the President, which has issued regulations on the preparation of environmental impact Statements and on public participation in the preparation of the Statements. The regulation of radioactive materials from the production of nuclear energy and the establishment of related standards and guidance is the responsibility of the EPA.[106] The Environmental Protection Agency (EPA) was given a role in establishing generally applicable environmental standards for the protection of the general environment from radioactive material by *Reorganisation Plan No.3 of 1970*.[107] The Agency monitors environmental radiation levels and provides technical assistance to States and other federal agencies in planning for radiological emergencies[108] and regulates hazardous waste from cradle to grave.[109] Waste regulation includes waste minimization, generation, transportation, storage and disposal. Although special nuclear, source and by-product material are specifically not included, naturally occurring radioactive materials are. The EPA sets generally applicable public health and environmental standards to govern the stabilization, restoration, disposal and control of effluents and emissions at both active and inactive uranium and thorium mill tailing sites.[110] Titles I and II of the *Act* require the DOE to implement the standards and the NRC to review clean-ups and to license the sites; for active sites standards are in compliance with the *Solid Waste Disposal Act*[111] to be implemented by the NRC or Agreement States. Sites other than those licensed by the NRC and covered by the *Price Anderson Amendments to the Atomic Energy Act*,[112] which are governed by NRC rather than *CERCLA regulations*, are covered by '*Superfund*'[113] or *CERCLA* that imposes a tax on the petroleum and chemical industries and provides federal authority to the EPA

---

[103] Title 15 Chapter 53 Sub Chapter III.
[104] As amended in 1986 and 1996. 43 U.S.C. s/s300f et seq.
[105] As amended, Pub. L. 91-190 (83Stat. 852) I January 1970.
[106] *Atomic Energy Act* as amended in 1954 42 U.S.C. 2011 et seq.
[107] Prepared by the President and presented to Congress pursuant to the provisions of chapter 9 of title 5 of the US Code. 5U.S.C. App 1.
[108] *Public Health Services Act of 1944 as amended 1957, 1958, 1960 and 1976.* 42 U.S.C. 201 et seq.
[109] *The Resource Conservation and Recovery Act of 1976 as amended 1984 and 1986.* 42 U.S.C. 6901 et seq.
[110] *Uranium Mill Tailings Radiation Control Act* of 1978. 42 U.S.C. 2022 et seq.
[111] 42 U.S.C. 6901 et seq.
[112] *Atomic Energy Act* as amended section 170.
[113] The *Comprehensive Environmental Response, Compensation and Liability Act (CERCLA) as amended*, 1986 and 1990. 42 U.S.C. 9601 et seq.

to respond to releases or threatened releases of hazardous substances, pollutants and contaminants that may endanger public health or the environment, including radionuclides; the DOD and the DOE co-ordinate actions at their sites.

Each State is responsible for providing disposal capacity for commercial low level waste generated within its borders under the *Low Level Radioactive Waste Policy Act.*[114] The *Act* encourages States to form regional compacts to develop new disposal facilities. The *1985 amendment* was to extend the time to develop facilities and to provide incentives for volume reduction of waste.

The *Waste Isolation Pilot Plant Land Withdrawal Act of 1992*[115] sets aside land for developing and building a transuranic radioactive waste repository. It requires the EPA to set disposal standards, establish compliance criteria and a process to certify that the WIPP facility is technically able to meet the standards. The *Energy Policy Act of 1992*[116] requires the EPA by promulgating standards, to ensure public health from high level radioactive waste in a deep repository under Yucca Mountain in Nevada.

Public liability for damages arising out of nuclear waste activities is dealt with by the *Price Anderson Act*[117] that amends *Section 170 of the Atomic Energy Act of 1954;*[118] such activities are subject to an agreement for indemnification and are compensated from the nuclear waste fund to an aggregate limit of $500m. The Nuclear Waste Fund is collected and disbursed by the Secretary of State who is empowered by the *Nuclear Waste Policy Act of 1982*[119] to do so in connection with the generation of electricity by a civilian nuclear power reactor and management of spent fuel or solidified high level radioactive waste derived from spent fuel used to generate electricity in a civilian nuclear reactor. Title to the waste is taken by the Secretary of State at the start of operation of a repository in return for the payment of fees, a deadline of 31 June 1998 for commencement being given in *the Act*. This deadline was not achieved and as will be seen later in this chapter, the operators are taking legal action to recover damages.

Code of Federal Regulations

The *Code of Federal Regulations (CFR)* is a codification of the general and permanent rules published in the Federal Register by the Executive departments and agencies of the Federal Government. The *CFR* is divided into 50 titles that represent broad areas subject to Federal regulation. Each title is divided into chapters that usually bear the name of the issuing agency. Each chapter is further subdivided into parts covering specific regulatory areas. Large parts may be subdivided into subparts. All parts are organized in sections, and most citations to the CFR will be provided at the section level. The regulations concerning nuclear

---

[114] *Low level Radioactive Waste Policy Act* 42 U.S.C. 2021b et seq.
[115] *Waste Isolation Pilot Plant Land Withdrawal Act of 1992 As Amended in 1996.* Pub. L. 102-579.
[116] *Energy Policy Act of 1992* Pub. L. 102-186 42 U.S.C. 10141.
[117] *Price Anderson Act of 1988.* Pub. L. 97-425 (HR-3809).
[118] *Atomic Energy Act* Pub. L. 85-256 (72Stat576)(1957) 42 U.S.C. 2210.
[119] *Nuclear Waste Policy Act* Section 302 42 U.S.C. 10222.

waste are essentially included under Title 10 – Energy, for example, 10 CFR 60–Disposal of high level radioactive wastes in geologic repositories; 10 CFR 61–Licensing requirements for land disposal of radioactive waste and 10 CFR 62–Criteria and procedures for emergency access to non-Federal and regional low level waste disposal facilities.

The Law in Practice

Legal effects of objections to processing and storage facilities may be illustrated by two aspects of the waste situation; the processing of plutonium into a form that can be used for reactor fuel (the MOX programme) and progress of the deep repository project at Yucca Mountain. Legal effects of objections to and claims for alleged and actual damages from the wider field of nuclear activities and radiation exposure are extensive but beyond the scope of this work. The influence of public opinion on the law and regulatory practice may be illustrated by the 'saga' of the proposed policy of 'below regulatory concern' BRC.

Mixed Oxide (MOX) The MOX programme calls for converting the plutonium to a form that can be used by commercial nuclear reactors. Thirty-four metric tons of weapons-grade plutonium from the U.S. nuclear arsenal is now being shipped to the Savannah River Site from a closed weapons plant at Rocky Flats, Colorado. At SRS, the material will be converted into fuel for commercial nuclear reactors that produce electricity, or otherwise treated to be disposed of outside South Carolina. The program will require the construction of new secure factories at SRS to disassemble the plutonium bomb cores and to convert the weapons-grade material to reactor fuel. The factories are estimated to cost $4 billion. A provision that would award South Carolina up to $100 million a year if the federal government fails to remove surplus weapons-grade plutonium from the State on schedule was signed by President Bush in December 2002.[120] The amendment to the *Defence Authorization Act* requires that all plutonium leave the State at a certain date if the MOX program fails, and those requirements are backed by unprecedented financial penalties for non-compliance. The major elements of the plutonium provision are:

> The Secretary of Energy is to report to Congress on the progress of the MOX program. If the Secretary fails to certify the program is on schedule, provisions are in place to cease plutonium shipments. If the program is not producing MOX fuel on schedule by 2009, the Department of Energy must within two years produce one ton of MOX or remove one ton of plutonium from the State. A failure to meet this requirement results in a $1 million per day 'impact fee' of up to $100 million per year until the requirement is met. By 2017, the Energy Department must produce a total of three tons of MOX fuel. The production schedule must also produce one ton a year for two consecutive years. If the MOX program is not successfully operating by 2017, all plutonium remaining in the State shall be removed immediately. In addition, a $1 million per day impact fee, up to $100 million per year, will be assessed during the removal period to ensure expeditious removal.

---

[120] Hammond, James T. (2002), Capital News Tuesday, December 3.

Yucca Mountain The history and predicted future of the Yucca Mountain project may be illustrated by the following brief chronology of developments and forecasts:[121]

> 1978 – The first test hole was dug at Yucca Mountain in Nevada as part of a nationwide search for a nuclear waste site.
>
> 1982 – Congress ordered development of a permanent national disposal site for waste from commercial nuclear power reactors and the government's nuclear weapons program.
>
> 1986 – Government pledged to take responsibility for high level nuclear waste from commercial plants by 1989 and narrowed potential sites to Nevada, Texas and Washington State.
>
> 1987 – Congress designated Yucca Mountain as the only site to be studied.
>
> 1994-96 – Utilities sued the Energy Department for not taking wastes as promised. A Federal court sided with industry and said the government must pay damages if waste is not taken.
>
> 1998 – Energy Department failed to meet the deadline for taking waste.
>
> 2001 – Interim Energy Department report found no 'showstoppers' in the scientific review of Yucca Mountain site. Estimated cost for construction, operation and monitoring over 100 years was put at $58 billion.
>
> February 2002 – President Bush concluded that Yucca Mountain was scientifically sound and announced plans to seek a permit for the waste site.
>
> April 2002 – Nevada vetoed Bush's decision as allowed under federal nuclear waste law.
>
> May 2002 – The House voted 306-117 to override Nevada's veto.
>
> July 2002 – Senate approved that Yucca Mountain be considered as the nuclear depository.
>
> 2004 – Energy Department plans to apply for construction permit. The licensing process before the Nuclear Regulatory Commission is expected to take up to four years.
>
> 2010 – Construction is expected to be completed.
>
> 2010-2034 – Shipments of 3,200 tons of waste a year are expected to arrive at the Yucca site.

The Energy Department signed contracts with reactor owners in the early 1980s promising to accept their wastes for burial beginning in January 1998, in exchange for payments from them based on electricity production. The following extract from an article in the *New York Times*[122] illustrates the problem that has been caused by the delay from original expectations:

---

[121] Las Vegas Sun, 8 Jun. 2002.
[122] Wald, M. *New York Times*, 25 Sept. 2002.

To date, reactor owners have paid more than $10.5 billion. But now the department says it cannot take waste until 2010, and the operators of the reactors are suing because they have been forced to store the waste on site. Estimates of the damages run from $2 billion to $60 billion, and the decision, from the United States Court of Appeals for the 11th Circuit, in Atlanta, twice used the word 'nebulous' to describe them. At the National Association of Regulatory Utility Commissioners, which is made up of State officials, Brian J. O'Connell, the director of the Nuclear Waste Program office, said the number would run 'in the billions'. Asked if it would reach tens of billions, Mr. O'Connell, said, 'It gets fuzzy'.

He said that one utility, Northern States Power of Minnesota, put its costs at $1 billion because it might be forced to shut three reactors prematurely, for want of storage space for the radioactive waste.

The only settlement so far is much smaller. The department and the owners of the three-reactor Peach Bottom plant, in the Pennsylvania town of the same name, agreed on $80 million, to pay extra costs for storing the wastes on site, in giant steel and concrete casks. But 13 other reactor owners sued to block the deal, because the money would have to come from the Nuclear Waste Fund, money from power customers that they said was supposed to be used only to open a permanent repository.

In a decision dated Sept. 24 (2002), the appeals court ruled that money in the fund could only be used for permanent disposal. The court said that the *Nuclear Waste Policy Act*, the law that allowed the contracts, called for a quid pro quo 'in which each utility roughly pays the costs of disposing of its waste and no more'. The plan, the court said was for a system in which the burden of the government's breach of contract would 'fall on the government, not other utilities'.

Below Regulatory Concern (BRC) BRC is a waste classification proposed by the NRC such that waste with a radiation level below a level comparable with the natural radiation background would be excluded from regulatory control. Members of the public said that they did not want DOE to adopt the NRC's BRC policy because of potential occupational and public health risk from exposure to low level radioactive waste.[123] Examples of the range of public comments include:

NRC's BRC regulation should not be used by DOE because waste could go to ordinary landfills without traceability.

DOE should treat BRC waste because it can be hazardous.

Adopting BRC encourages the use of dilution to solve the low level radioactive waste disposal problems.

BRC would be contrary to CERCLA.

Exposure to BRC waste threatens workers and the public.

It was said that adopting a BRC waste policy would encourage the use of dilution to resolve low level radioactive waste disposal problems. The NRC instituted a moratorium on BRC policy implementation. DOE now treats BRC waste as low

---

[123] US Department of Energy, Office of Environmental Management [www.em.doe.gov/].

level radioactive waste and will continue to do so unless appropriate rule-making directs a change.

Comment

The systematic approach that is typical of the US has ensured that developments for the long-term storage/disposal of radioactive waste have proceeded within the law, albeit slowly.

French Nuclear Law

Classification of Nuclear Installations

From the regulatory standpoint, nuclear installations in France are classified in different categories corresponding to procedures that are more or less binding, depending on the degree of potential risk involved. The Nuclear Safety Authority is entrusted with definition and application of the regulations to the main permanent nuclear installations, known as 'Basic Nuclear Installations' (BNI), except for classified plants working on national security projects (CBNI), which report to the delegate for nuclear safety and radiation protection for activities and installations covered by national defence provisions (DSND). The relevant categories are stipulated by Decree:[124]

- nuclear reactors except for those equipping a means of transport;
- particle accelerators;
- plants for the separation, manufacture or transformation of radioactive substances, notably nuclear;
- fuel fabrication plants, spent fuel reprocessing plants or radioactive waste conditioning plants; and
- installations for the interim storage, disposal or use of radioactive substances, including waste.

However, the latter three types of installation are only required to comply with BNI regulations in cases where the total quantity or activity level of the radioactive substances exceeds an amount defined, according to the type of installation and the radioelement considered, by a joint ministerial order issued by the Ministers for the Environment, Industry and Health respectively. Nuclear installations that are not considered as Basic Nuclear Installations may be required to comply with the provisions of the law covering installations classified on environmental protection grounds (ICPE).[125]

---

[124] *Decree 63-1228* of *Dec. 11, 1963.*
[125] *Law 76-663 of July 19, 1976 amended*, concerning installations classified on environmental protection grounds (ICPE).

The Environmental Impact of Basic Nuclear Installations

Under normal operating conditions, nuclear installations release radioactive or non-radioactive liquid and gaseous effluents. The environmental and health impact of this release must be strictly limited. To this end, installations must be so designed, operated and maintained as to limit the production of these effluents, which must be so treated as to limit the corresponding release to a level as low as reasonably achievable. This release must not exceed the limits defined on a case by case basis by the public authorities, using the best available technology at an economically acceptable cost and taking into account the specific characteristics of the site considered. Finally, this release must be permanently metered and its effective impact regularly assessed, especially for all radioactive release constituting the specific hallmark of nuclear installations.

Licensing Procedures

In addition to the general regulations consistently applied, such as those pertaining to labour laws and environmental protection, basic nuclear installations (BNI) are subjected to licensing procedures and technical rules. Facilities concerned by regulations for installations classified on environmental protection grounds are required to comply with specific procedures when located within the perimeter of a BNI. French law and the relevant regulations prohibit the unlicensed operation of a nuclear installation. In this context, BNIs are currently regulated, pending a specific decree covering nuclear activities.[126] This decree provides for an authorization procedure followed by a series of licences issued at key points in plant lifetime: fuel loading or pre-commissioning stages, startup of normal operation, decommissioning and dismantling. It also enables the ministers in charge of nuclear safety to request the operator at any time to proceed to the safety review of an installation. BNIs must also comply with the authorization procedure for liquid and gaseous effluent release and water intake for Basic Nuclear Installations.[127] An operator who operates a plant either without having obtained the requisite licences or in a manner contradictory to specified licence conditions lays himself open to legal or administrative sanctions.[128] The application of these various procedures starts with site selection and plant design and terminates with the ultimate dismantling.

Procedures Applicable to Installations other than Power Reactors The authorization decrees for BNIs other than power reactors stipulate that their start-

---

[126] A draft of which was submitted to the National Assembly on July 4, 2001, by *Decree 63-1228 of December 11, 1963* amended for application of law 61-842 of August 2, 1961 amended concerning the abatement of atmospheric pollution and offensive odours.

[127] *Decree 95-540 of May 4, 1995*, for application of both the law of August 2, 1961 and law 92-3 of January 3, 1992 amended concerning water (articles L.210 to L.217-1 of the *Environment Code*).

[128] Articles 12 and 13 of *Decree 63-1228* of December 11, 1963 regarding the authorization decree and in articles 22 to 30 of the January 3, 1992 law on water (articles L.216-1 to L.216-13 of the *Environment Code*), concerning effluent release and water intake.

up is subject to authorization from the Ministers for the Environment and for Industry. This precommissioning authorization is accompanied by notification of technical requirements. It is granted after examination by the DSIN and its technical support organizations, especially the competent Advisory Committee, of the documents prepared by the operator, comprising the intermediate safety analysis report, the general operating rules and the onsite emergency plan. Furthermore, before an installation is definitely commissioned, which must take place within a time stipulated in the authorization decree, the operator must submit a final safety analysis report to the Ministers for the Environment and for Industry. Commissioning is subject to ministerial authorization involving, where necessary, the updating of technical requirements and general operating rules, according to a similar procedure to that adopted for power reactors. When an operator decides, for any reason, to close down his installation, he must inform the Director of the DSIN,[129] by sending him:

- a document justifying the selected configuration in which the installation will be left after final shutdown and indicating the various stages of subsequent dismantling;
- a safety analysis report covering the final shutdown procedures and indicating subsequent plant safety provisions;
- the general surveillance and servicing rules enabling maintenance of a satisfactory safety level; and
- an updated onsite emergency plan for the installation concerned.

In compliance with current environmental protection requirements, the operator must also submit an environmental impact analysis pertaining to the proposed provisions. The implementation of these various provisions is subject to their approval by decree, countersigned by the Ministers for the Environment and for Industry, after assent of the Minister for Health and prior consultation with the Interministerial Commission for Basic Nuclear Installations (CIINB). In some cases, operations such as the unloading and removal of nuclear material, the disposal of fluids, or decontamination and drainage operations can be performed under the provisions of the authorization decree for the plant considered, providing they involve no non-compliance with previously imposed requirements nor with the safety analysis report and general operating rules currently in force, subject to certain modifications if necessary. In all other cases, such operations come under the provisions of the decommissioning decree. From the regulatory standpoint, following these end of operation tasks, two successive sets of operations have to be carried out:

- final shutdown work, authorized by decree, as mentioned above, which mainly concerns the dismantling of equipment outside the nuclear island which is not

---

[129] As specified in article 6b of the *Decree of December 11, 1963*.

required for the latter's surveillance and safety, the preservation or reinforcement of the containment barriers, the assessment of a radioactivity inventory. In most cases, dismantling level 1 is then reached; and

- dismantling work on the nuclear part of the plant. This work can start as soon as the final shutdown operations are completed or can be delayed with a view to benefiting from radioactive decay in certain activated or contaminated materials. These operations can lead to dismantling level 2 or even 3, depending on the ultimate condition required.

As frequently occurs, as soon as the installation, although still a BNI, is affected in such a way by the dismantling operations that they alter its nature, it is considered as a new nuclear installation and consequently a new authorization decree is required, involving the procedure previously described including a public inquiry. In most cases, such plants become storage facilities for their own internal equipment. If dismantling work reaches the stage where the total radioactivity of remaining radioactive substances is below the minimum level necessitating classification as a Basic Nuclear Installation, the plant can be removed from the list of Basic Nuclear Installations, i.e. 'declassified'. Then, depending on the residual radioactivity level, it could come under the provisions of the law of July 19, 1976 concerning installations classified on environmental protection grounds,[130] in which case it would be subjected to registering or licensing procedures. The DSIN is preparing, in consultation with the nuclear operators, a directive concerning the various technical and administrative aspects of BNI decommissioning and dismantling. This document will notably take into account experience acquired on such operations since January 1990, when the previously mentioned decree of December 11, 1963 on nuclear installations was supplemented in this respect.

Liquid and Gaseous Effluent Release and Water Intake Licences The normal operation of nuclear plants produces radioactive effluents, release to the environment of which is subjected to stringent conditions stipulated in an administrative licence devised for the protection of staff, of the public and the environment. The licence concerns liquid and gaseous radioactive effluents, covering both their activity level and their chemical characteristics. The operation of most nuclear installations also involves, according to circumstances, intake of water from the site's immediate environment and release of non-radioactive liquid and gaseous effluents. For BNI liquid and gaseous effluent release and water intake, the same licence, issued at ministerial level, can cover where necessary both the radioactive and non-radioactive liquid and gaseous release and the water intake for a given BNI.[131] The procedures also apply to the installations classified on environmental protection grounds located within the perimeter of a BNI. This decree thus also enables assessment of the overall environmental impact of an installation's effluent release and water intake.

---

[130] Articles L.511-1 to L.517-2 of the *Environment Code.*
[131] *Decree 95-540* of May 4, 1995.

Submission of the Licence Application   The effluent release and water intake licence application covers all such operations for which authorization is required. It is sent to the Ministers for Industry and for the Environment. It comprises, in addition to various drawings, maps and information, a description of the operations or activities envisaged and an assessment of their environmental impact, comprising a list of proposed compensatory measures and the intended surveillance provisions.

Recommendations of the Ministers Concerned   The application is forwarded to the Ministers for Health and for Civil Defence and to the Directorate for the Prevention of Pollution and Risks at the Ministry for the Environment for their opinion.

Consultation of the Public and Local Authorities and Organizations   The Ministers for Industry and for the Environment, after having requested complementary data or modifications where necessary from the applicant, forward the application, together with the recommendations of the ministers consulted, to the Prefect of the department concerned.   The Prefect organizes an administrative conference between various decentralized State Departments that he feels should be consulted and subjects the application to a public inquiry under conditions similar to those described above for authorization decrees.   However, in the present procedure, the inquiry, lasting a maximum of two and a half months, is opened in the commune where the operations in question are to be carried out and also in other communes where the impact of these operations would probably be felt.   The Prefect consults the town councils concerned together with various organizations, such as the Departmental Health Council and, where necessary, the 'Mission déléguée de bassin' or the public agency administering the public domain. He also sends the application file, for information, to the Local Water Committee.

French Nuclear Industry Codes and Standards

French regulatory practice with respect to nuclear safety requires the plant operator to submit a document defining the rules, codes and standards he will implement for the design, construction, startup and operation of safety-related equipment.   This gave rise to formulation by the manufacturers of design and construction rules, known as the RCC codes concerning the different categories of equipment involved (civil engineering, mechanical and electrical equipment, fuel, etc.) at the design, construction and operation stages.   Some of these rules have been drawn up and published by the AFCEN (French association for NSSS equipment construction rules), of which EDF and Framatome are members.   The codes provide a means of both complying with general technical regulations and upholding good industrial practice. They are drawn up by the manufacturers and not by the Safety Authority, which nevertheless examines them in detail, both in their initial and revised versions.   In most cases, their contents are then integrated in a Basic Safety Rule.

Installations Classified on Environmental Protection Grounds

Installations liable to prove dangerous or harmful for the environment are governed by the law concerning installations classified on environmental protection grounds (ICPE).[132] This law is now included in the Environment Code.[133] The installations concerned are classified by type in a document regularly updated by the Ministry for the Environment and are the subject of special arrangements when they are located within the perimeter of a BNI. A distinction is made between BNI equipment and ICPEs:[134] BNI equipment is that constituting an element necessary to the operation of such installations and must comply with the procedure applicable to BNIs;[135] in particular, in all cases where new or modified equipment would be such as to substantially alter the initial capacity or purpose of a BNI or would increase the risks it entails, a public inquiry must be held; installations classified on environmental protection grounds located within the perimeter of a BNI are those which have no functional necessity for the latter. Effluent release from ICPEs located within the perimeter of a BNI is regulated by the decree of May 4, 1995 concerning BNIs. The DSIN is empowered to examine application files; the surveillance functions defined in the law of July 19, 1976 for installations falling within its scope are entrusted to the BNI inspectors.

Nuclear Safety Related Radiation Protection

The French Nuclear Safety Authority operates in cooperation with the DGS (Directorate-General for Health), the DRT (Directorate-General for employment relationships) and the OPRI (Office for Protection against Ionizing Radiation). Radiation protection is based on three basic principles.

- The principle of justification – A nuclear activity or action can only be engaged in or performed if it is justified by the advantages it procures, notably in the health, social, economic or scientific fields as compared with the risks inherent in the exposure of people to ionizing radiation liable to be thereby involved.
- The principle of optimization – The exposure of people to ionizing radiation resulting from a nuclear activity or action must be maintained at the lowest level reasonably achievable, given the current State of the art, economic and social factors and, where applicable, the required medical objective.
- The principle of limitation – The exposure of a person to ionizing radiation resulting from a nuclear activity shall not accumulate a total dose received exceeding limits set by the public authorities, except when the person concerned is subjected to exposure for medical reasons or in a biomedical research context.

---

[132] *Decree 76-663* of July 19, 1976 amended.
[133] Articles L.511-1 to L.517-2.
[134] *Decree 63-1228* of Dec. 11, 1963 amended and clarified by the recommendation of the Council of State of Oct. 4, 1983.
[135] This equipment is covered by articles 2 and 3 of the *1963 Decree*.

The legislative and regulatory framework of radiation protection results from texts elaborated in the course of the last forty years. For the most part, general provisions are defined by the Health Code and by *Decree 66-450 of June 20, 1966, amended in 1988, 1994 and 2001*, concerning the general principles of protection against ionizing radiation. This decree transposes the *European directive of July 15, 1980, amended on September 3, 1984*, prescribing basic radiation protection standards, being itself based on the recommendations of the ICRP (notably publication No. 26) and on certain elements of the *Euratom 96/29 directive of May 13, 1996*. Many special regulations concern the use of radiation sources for medical purposes. Others deal specifically with worker protection questions, making a distinction between the case of nuclear installations[136] and that of other workers.[137] The licensing or registration procedures framing practices involving ionizing radiation are placed under the supervision of different authorities. For example:

- the BNIs, authorized by decree, effluent release from which is authorized by Interministerial order, are supervised notably by the ASN (BNI inspectors), work and safety inspectors and the OPRI;
- installations classified on environmental protection grounds, using radioactive substances, authorized by prefectural order or requiring registration by the Prefect and supervised by the DRIRE (inspectors of classified installations) and by work and safety inspectors;
- radioactive sources containing artificial radioelements for non-medical use, authorized by the Chairman of the Interministerial Commission for Artificial Radioelements (CIREA); and
- ionizing radiation sources used in human biology, medicine and dentistry, requiring, according to circumstances, registration by the Departmental Health Directorate, prefectural approval, an authorization from the Minister for Health or from the French Agency for the sanitary security of health products (AFSSAPS).

Developments in the Renewal of the Legislative and Regulatory Framework

Work on radical modification of the system for protection of people against ionizing radiation has been undertaken in the framework of transposition into French law of the *European 96/29/Euratom directive of May 13, 1996* and of the *97/43/Euratom directive* concerning the protection of people exposed to ionizing radiation for medical purposes, known as the 'patients' directive. In France, work on transposition of *Directive 96/29* is being undertaken in the framework of an Interministerial committee, set up by the Prime Minister at the end of 1996 and

---

[136] Notably *Decree 75-306* of Apr. 28, 1975 amended.
[137] Notably *Decree 86-1103* of Oct. 2, 1986 amended.

directed jointly by the DGS and the DRT. The main innovations introduced by 2001[138] are as follows:

- updating the dose calculation method, notably by introducing the RBE dose concept; and
- reaffirming and updating the definition of the principles of dose justification, optimization and limitation; lowering the annual effective dose limit for the public to 1 mSv/yr[139] (corresponding to an overall dose to the organism) and the definition of dose limits for the skin, the extremities and the crystalline lens corresponding to one-tenth of the limits specified for workers.

Measures that, at the time of writing, have yet to be taken include:

- a reduction of the annual dose limits for workers, except for those concerning exposure of the skin, tissues, crystalline lens and extremities, which will remain unchanged;
- new provisions for emergency interventions or in the event of lasting exposure; and
- five decrees including protection of the population, protection of workers, protection of patients, quality control of medical devices and emergency interventions, certain of which will be covered in the framework of transposition of the 'patients' directive.[140]

This is the first stage in the setting up of a reformed system for the protection of people against ionizing radiation and will be supplemented by a large number of regulatory texts covering all activities comprising a risk of exposure of people to ionizing radiation, whether in the course of medical, industrial or research applications or of human interventions for the prevention or reduction of radiological hazards further to an accident due to environmental contamination. It inserts in the public health code the three radiation protection principles, on the basis of which it updates the ionizing radiation authorization and prohibition provisions and lays down by law the basis of rules for the management of artificial or natural radionuclides. One result of this updating is to oblige the CEA to comply with the requirements of the law, whereas it previously benefited from a permanent authorization procedure for the possession and utilization of radioactive sources. Another result is the abolition of the Interministerial Commission for Artificial Radioelements, whose permanent secretariat was entrusted to the CEA. The ruling extends existing rules for the management of artificial radioactive sources to

---

[138] Ruling 2001-270 and *Decree 2001-215* of Mar. 8, 2001, amending *Decree 66-450*.

[139] Enacted by *Decree 2001-215* of Mar. 8, 2001, amending Decree 66-450.

[140] Ruling 2001-270 of Mar. 28, 2001 concerning transposition of EC directives in the field of protection against ionizing radiation modifies the public health and labour codes with a view to introducing modifications concerning respectively population and worker protection.

natural radioactive sources. In addition, it necessitates the introduction of new provisions for the assessment and reduction of exposure to natural radiation, in particular radon, in all cases where human activities contribute to its reinforcement. In application of *Directive 97/43,* it introduces an overall obligation to provide members of the medical professions with training in questions related to patient protection. Finally, it provides a new system of penal sanctions for infringements of authorization and prohibition provisions concerning the possession and utilization of ionizing radiation sources. The ruling extends the scope of worker protection to non-salaried workers. It also reinforces the protection of precarious workers, whether external or not, with a view to ensuring their medical surveillance and preventing on-the-job high level exposure from reducing their future possibilities of employment. It also provides for the setting up, mainly by regulatory channels, of an overall, innovatory worker protection system.

Basic Nuclear Installations (BNIs) The BNIs are included in the 'practices', in the meaning of the 'basic safety standards' directive, specifically regulated and supervised owing to the risks of severe exposure to ionizing radiation. In particular, pursuance of such practices is subjected to prior authorization on radiation protection grounds.[141] Within the framework of these procedures, the BNI operator provides the necessary justifications evidencing compliance with the general radiation protection principles and specific rules applying to this field. Worker protection against ionizing radiation hazards in BNIs is regulated by decree imposing the same general rules as those applying to all workers exposed to ionizing radiation[142] (annual dose limits, categories of workers exposed, definition of monitored zones, limited access zones...), together with specific BNI provisions, both technical and administrative (work organization, accident prevention, keeping of records, workers from outside companies, etc.). In order to obtain a radioactive effluent release permit, a BNI operator must show that the effluents produced are collected and processed, so that release is kept as low as reasonably possible, and must assess the foreseeable radiological impact on the most exposed populations (known as a 'reference group') in order to ensure that annual exposure limits are respected. Finally, in the event of a radiological accident, the regulations stipulate that emergency plans must be prepared (an onsite emergency plan set up by the operator, an offsite emergency plan set up by the Prefect), defining the structures and resources provided to bring the accident under control, mitigate its consequences and take appropriate measures to protect people against its effects.

The Transportation of Radioactive and Fissile Materials for Civil Use

The main risks incurred during transportation of radioactive or fissile materials involve internal or external exposure, criticality or chemical hazards. The safe

---

[141] Covered by procedures defined by *Decree 63-1228* of Dec. 11, 1963 modified, concerning Basic Nuclear Installations and *Decree 95-540 of May 4, 1995* concerning BNI liquid and gaseous effluent release and water intake.
[142] *Decree 75-306* of April 28, 1975 amended, together with several ministerial orders enforcing its application.

transportation of radioactive materials is based on defence in depth strategy: the package, comprising container and contents, is the first line of defence. Its function is essential and it must withstand all conceivable transport conditions. The transport medium and its reliability form the second line of defence. Finally, should the need arise, the means provided to contend with an incident or accident would form a third line of defence.

The shipper is, in the first instance, responsible for implementation of these lines of defence. Since June 1997, the Safety Authority has been in charge of supervision of the transportation of radioactive and fissile materials for civil use. As regards the transportation of radioactive or fissile materials for national security purposes, these operations are the responsibility of the delegate for nuclear safety and radiation protection for activities and installations covered by national defence provisions (DSND).

The radiological protection of workers and population is ensured by respecting:[143]

- the radiation level in all places normally occupied in a vehicle, in cases where individual dose monitoring devices are not used, the dose rate must not exceed 0.02 mSv/h;
- distances between packages, over-packing, containers and tanks and regularly occupied rest areas and work stations, calculated for an exposure time not exceeding 250 hours per year and are currently based on a 5 mSv dose limit for each 12-month period; and
- certain limits, such as the dose equivalent rates at the surface or in the immediate vicinity of the packages, the limits of contamination fixed or non-fixed to surfaces, etc.

Various specific transport regulations provide for the setting up of a radiation protection programme integrating: training with respect to radiological hazards; provisions made, depending on the annual professional exposure level (below 1 mSv, between 1 and 6 mSv, exceeding 6 mSv) to ensure appropriate surveillance for workers and places of work.

Radioactive Waste Management

Stringent waste management provisions are based on three basic principles: the responsibility of the waste producer, waste traceability and the information of the public. In the case of very low level radioactive waste, the effectiveness of a management system based on these principles would be impaired by definition of an all-purpose clearance threshold for regulatory supervision. Suitable technical management provisions must be commensurate with the risk involved, which is gauged for the two main parameters, the activity level, reflecting the toxicity of the waste, and the half-life (period during which the activity of the waste is halved). Finally, the radioactive waste management system shall be determined prior to any

---

[143] Ministerial order of Jun. 1, 2001 (and its annexes), known as the ADR order.

development of fresh activities or any modification to those existing, with a view
to:

- optimizing waste management systems; and
- ensuring complete mastery of the treatment channels for the different
  categories of waste liable to be produced, from front-end (waste production
  and packaging) to back-end (storage, transport, disposal).

Radioactive waste management falls within the general scope of the law
concerning waste disposal[144] and the recovery of materials. The basic principles of
this law are the prevention of waste production, the responsibility of the waste
producers, the traceability of this waste and the necessity to inform the general
public. Management of radioactive waste from Basic Nuclear Installations is
structured on a strict regulatory framework stipulating the general technical
regulations[145] intended to prevent and limit the detrimental effects and external
hazards resulting from the operation of BNIs. It entails:

- drafting 'waste surveys' for each nuclear site, adopting an approach already
  used for certain installations classified on environmental protection grounds
  (ICPE). The waste survey will involve drawing up an inventory of waste
  management provisions on a site, comprising notably a definition of 'waste
  zones', with a view to identifying areas of the installation where waste could
  have been contaminated by radioactive substances or activated by radiation
  and those where waste produced contain no added radioactivity. The waste
  surveys must be approved by the ASN;
- definition for each type of radioactive waste of authorized and well-adapted
  disposal channels, based on impact studies and on which the general public
  has been informed or consulted; and
- setting up of waste monitoring systems, ensuring traceability.

Wastes from areas in a nuclear installation where they may have been
contaminated by radioactive substances or activated by radiation are considered, as
a safeguard, at least as 'very low level' waste in the management channels
provided in this respect. As regards waste traceability, whether the waste be
radioactive or not, a draft decree concerning the monitoring of waste treatment
channels is in preparation at the Directorate for the Prevention of Pollution and
risks. The purpose of this decree is to improve waste supervision and follow-up
provisions throughout the treatment and disposal stages, by imposing traceability
systems (registers, periodic administrative reports and waste follow-up dispatch
notes).

---

[144] *Decree 75-633* of July 15, 1975 (article L.541 of the Environment Code) and its
implementation decrees.
[145] Ministerial order of December 31, 1999.

Long-lived High Level Waste   The main research paths for radioactive waste management have been set down in law:[146] long-lived high level waste must be managed with due regard for the protection of nature, the environment and health and for the rights of future generations. Research is proceeding on separation and transmutation of the long-lived radioactive elements in these wastes, reversible or irreversible storage in deep geological formations, the feasibility of which would be assessed by the construction of underground laboratories and processes permitting the packaging and long-term surface storage of these wastes. Parliament is required to report progress in 2006.

Comment

Belatedly French law has taken on the regulation of radioactive waste, prompted by European Union directives; nevertheless, the systematic approach that is moulding those laws could well be emulated elsewhere as pressures to update mount.

Nuclear Waste Law in Finland

Nuclear regulation in Finland comprises the *Nuclear Energy Act (The Act)*,[147] the *Nuclear Energy Decree*,[148] *Decisions of the Council of State* and *Regulatory Guides*. The purpose of *the Act* is to keep the use of nuclear energy in line with the overall good of society, and in particular to ensure that the use of nuclear energy is safe for man and the environment and does not promote the proliferation of nuclear weapons. *The Act* prescribes general principles for the use of nuclear energy, the implementation of nuclear waste management, the licensing and control of the use of nuclear energy and the competent authorities.[149] *The Act* applies, *inter alia*, to: the construction and operation of nuclear facilities; the possession, fabrication, production, transfer, handling, use, storage, transport, export and import of nuclear materials and nuclear wastes as well as the export and import of ores and ore concentrates containing uranium or thorium.[150] Nuclear waste refers to: radioactive waste in the form of spent nuclear fuel or in some other form, generated in connection with or as a result of the use of nuclear energy; and materials, objects and structures which, having become radioactive in connection with or as a result of the use of nuclear energy and having been removed from use, require special measures because of the danger arising from their radioactivity.[151]   Nuclear waste

---

[146] Article L.542 of the *Environment Code* (derived from Law 91-1381 of Dec. 30, 1991).

[147] *Nuclear Energy Act* Issued on 11 Dec. 1987 (990) as amended by the Acts of 29 Dec. 1994 (1420), 21 Apr. 1995 (593), and 12 Dec. 1996 (1078).

[148] *Nuclear Energy Decree* Issued on 12 Feb. 1988 as amended by the Decrees of 26 March 1993 (278), 25 Aug. 1994 (794), 16 Jun. 1995 (881), 20 Jun. 1996 (473) and 20 Dec. 1996. On the submission of the Ministry of Trade and Industry and in accordance with the *Nuclear Energy Act* (990/87) issued on Dec. 11, 1987.

[149] *Nuclear Energy Act*, Section 1.

[150] ibid Section 2.

[151] ibid amendment of 29 Dec. 1994/1420.

management refers to all measures necessary to collect, store and handle nuclear wastes and permanently dispose of them (disposal). Nuclear facilities refer to facilities necessary for obtaining nuclear energy, including research reactors, facilities performing extensive disposal of nuclear wastes, and facilities used for extensive fabrication, production, use, handling or storage of nuclear materials or nuclear wastes.

Except for small amounts of nuclear waste delivered abroad for research purposes, or nuclear waste which has been generated in connection with or as a result of the operation of a research reactor in Finland, nuclear waste generated in connection with or as a result of the use of nuclear energy in Finland is handled, stored and permanently disposed of in Finland.[152] Other than small amounts of nuclear waste delivered to Finland for research purposes or nuclear waste of unknown origin, nuclear waste generated in connection with or as a result of the use of nuclear energy elsewhere than in Finland, is prohibited from being handled, stored or permanently disposed of in Finland.[153]

The use of nuclear energy without the licence prescribed by *the Act* is prohibited.[154] It is the licence-holder's obligation to assure the safe use of nuclear energy and to assure such physical protection and emergency planning and other arrangements, necessary to ensure limitation of nuclear damage, which do not rest with the authorities. A licence-holder whose operations generate or has generated nuclear waste (a licence-holder with a waste management obligation (LWMO)) shall be responsible for all nuclear waste management measures and their appropriate preparation, and is responsible for their costs.[155] The licence to operate a nuclear facility may be issued as soon as a licence has been granted to construct it and if: the operation of the nuclear facility has been arranged so that the protection of workers, the population's safety and environmental protection have been taken into account appropriately; the methods available to the applicant for arranging nuclear waste management, including the disposal of nuclear wastes and the decommissioning of the facility, are sufficient and appropriate; the applicant has sufficient expertise available and, in particular, the competence of the operational staff and the operational organisation of the nuclear facility are appropriate; the applicant is otherwise considered to have the prerequisites to engage in operations safely and in accordance with the obligations under Finland's international treaties.[156] Operation of the nuclear facility shall not be started on the basis of a licence which has been granted: until the Radiation and Nuclear Safety Authority (STUK) has ascertained that the nuclear facility meets the prescribed safety requirements, that the physical protection and emergency planning are sufficient, that the necessary control to prevent the proliferation of nuclear weapons has been arranged appropriately, and that the licence-holder of the nuclear facility has, as prescribed, arranged indemnification regarding liability in case of nuclear damage;

---

[152] ibid Section 6, amendment 29 Dec. 1994/1420.
[153] ibid Section 6 b, amendment 29 Dec. 1994/1420.
[154] ibid Section 8.
[155] ibid Section 9.
[156] ibid Section 20.

and until the Ministry of Trade and Industry has ascertained that provision for the cost of nuclear waste management has been arranged.

Nuclear Waste Management

Having granted a licence for operations generating nuclear wastes, STUK decides, having consulted, if necessary, the Ministry of the Environment, the principles on which the waste management obligation is to be implemented. For this purpose the Ministry of Trade and Industry or STUK may require the LWMO to present a plan for carrying out nuclear waste management.[157] The Ministry of Trade and Industry may order various LWMOs to undertake waste management measures jointly, if by doing so safety can be increased or costs can be substantially reduced or for other good reason. At the same time, an order shall be given, if necessary, on the distribution of the costs incurred due to the measures to be carried out jointly.[158] When the possession of a nuclear facility, a mine or an enrichment plant intended for the production of uranium or thorium, or nuclear waste is transferred, the Ministry of Trade and Industry may, on request, completely or partially transfer the waste management obligation from the transferor to the transferee, if the transfer of the obligation does not endanger the carrying out of nuclear waste management.[159] If the Ministry of Trade and Industry considers that a LWMO has substantially failed to observe the confirmed time-schedules for nuclear waste management of the nuclear wastes he has generated or has otherwise violated the authorities' orders for the implementation of nuclear waste management, the Ministry brings the matter to the Council of State to decide whether the LWMO's actions mentioned above, judged on the whole, give good reason to confirm that nuclear waste management completely or in part cannot be carried out by the LWMO. If the Council of State finds that nuclear waste management completely or in part cannot be carried out by the LWMO, the Council of State orders that such nuclear wastes be transferred to the State, or to a domestic corporation under the control of the State, for the implementation of the nuclear waste management measures still required.[160] Notwithstanding these provisions the Council of State may not order the transfer of the nuclear wastes insofar as making such an order would place the State in a disadvantageous financial position with respect to implementation of the final outcome of measures for financial provision.

The Ministry of Trade and Industry and STUK, having granted a licence for operations that generate nuclear wastes, determines that the waste management obligation has expired when: it has been transferred to another party or the nuclear wastes have been transferred outside Finland's jurisdiction, in an approved permanent manner;[161] and the LWMO has paid a lump sum to the State for the control of the nuclear wastes. Should the Council of State issue an order as referred to in section 31, the State shall be responsible thereafter for the nuclear

---

[157] ibid Chapter 6 Nuclear waste management Section 28.
[158] ibid Section 29 Mandatory waste management co-operation.
[159] ibid Section 30 Transfer of waste management obligation.
[160] ibid Section 31 Transfer of nuclear wastes to the State.
[161] ibid Section 32 Expiry of waste management.

waste management measures not yet carried out for the wastes referred to in the order, and for the costs to be incurred in carrying out these measures by the LWMO. Disposal shall be considered implemented when STUK has confirmed the nuclear wastes to be permanently disposed of in an approved manner.[162] When the LWMO's waste management obligation has ceased, the rights of ownership to the nuclear wastes are transferred to the State, which shall be responsible thereafter for the nuclear wastes. Should it become necessary after disposal, the State has the right, at the disposal site, to take all measures required for the control of the nuclear wastes and for ensuring the safety of the repository.

Financial Provision for the Cost of Nuclear Waste Management

The LWMO makes financial provision for the costs of nuclear wastes including materials, objects and structures and the costs of nuclear waste management.[163] The LWMO fulfils the financial provision obligation by payment for each calendar year of the charges referred to below into the State nuclear waste management fund, and furnishes to the State the securities prescribed below as a precaution against insolvency.[164] The liability for costs referred to include the assessed amount of costs incurred in the future managing the nuclear wastes generated by the LWMO.

For purposes of implementing the financial provision, there is a State Nuclear Waste Management Fund, independent of the State budget but controlled and administered by the Ministry of Trade and Industry. The State Nuclear Waste Management Fund has a Board of Directors, appointed by the Council of State for three calendar years at a time. The tasks and administration of the State Nuclear Waste Management Fund are prescribed by decree.[165] The assessed liability is estimated on the basis of the price and cost levels prevailing at the time for which the assessed liability is confirmed. The Fund target for each calendar year shall be equal to the assessed liability at the end of the previous calendar year[166] with arrangements to distribute the costs of nuclear waste management evenly among the operating years of a nuclear facility.

The provision by the LWMO[167] is to be founded on a waste management scheme and on the calculations of waste management costs that are based on that scheme. The LWMO is to draw up a proposal for the waste management scheme and for the calculation based on it presenting all the measures that are called for by waste management and describe them in sufficient detail for the calculation of the assessed liability and to revise them in line with technological and other developments. The scheme is to be submitted to the Ministry of Trade and Industry for approval, initially prior to commencing operations that produce nuclear waste and finally at the licence application for operations with an annually updated supplement and the associated calculations. The LWMO must submit his proposal

---

[162] ibid Section 33 Disposal of nuclear wastes.
[163] ibid Chapter 7 Section 35, Financial provision obligation.
[164] ibid Section 36 Financial provision measures.
[165] ibid Section 38 The State Nuclear Waste Management Fund.
[166] ibid Section 40 Amount of the Fund target.
[167] Chapter 13 Section 86.

for the securities to be supplied and make an application to the Council of State for their approval and supply them to the Finnish State Treasury. The Ministry of Trade and Industry annually examines the securities and decides whether their security value can still be considered sufficient. If necessary, the Ministry takes the matter to the Council of State for decision. If the security can no longer be considered sufficient, the Ministry of Trade and Industry has the right to demand a supplementary security or a new security and to set a deadline by which such security is to be supplied. The regulations in chapter 7 of the *Nuclear Energy Act* are not applied to an LWMO if the Ministry of Trade and Industry estimates that the future costs incurred by the management of the nuclear waste, that is or will be produced as a result of his operation, will be no more than FIM 200,000.

Protection of Workers

Those licensed to use nuclear energy assure the employees' safety at work by observing the provisions of the *Safety at Work Act*,[168] and those of the *Radiation Protection Act*[169] and the *Mining Act*[170] to the extent applicable as well as *the Act*. When ensuring safety at work requires consideration of the special requirements concerning the safe use of nuclear energy, provisions to this effect shall be issued, and supervision of the observance of such provisions shall be the responsibility of STUK.[171] In addition to the provisions of *the Act*, separate laws and regulations have been enacted on radiation protection and transport of nuclear material and *nuclear waste*.[172] A special law and regulations have been enacted on liability for nuclear damage.

Nuclear Energy Decree[173]

The provisions given in the *Nuclear Energy Act* and in the decree on both nuclear material and nuclear waste are applied to spent nuclear fuel.[174] Nuclear waste does not include: radioactive materials that have spread into the environment along with emissions that result from the use of nuclear energy and that do not exceed the limits set for emissions; a radioactive material or product which has been manufactured or used for commercial, industrial, agricultural, medical, scientific or educational operations or for other comparable operations which are not part of

---

[168] *Safety at Work Act (299/58).*

[169] *Radiation Protection Act (174/57).*

[170] *Mining Act (503/65).*

[171] The division of executive power between the authorities in cases referred to in this subsection shall be prescribed by decree if necessary.

[172] Section 61, Radiation protection, transport of nuclear material and liability for nuclear damage.

[173] *Nuclear Energy Decree*, Issued on 12 Feb. 1988 as amended by the Decrees of 26 Mar. 1993 (278), 25 Aug. 1994 (794), 16 Jun. 1995 (881), 20 Jun. 1996 (473) and 20 Dec. 1996. On the submission of the Ministry of Trade and Industry and in accordance with the *Nuclear Energy Act* (990/87) issued on Dec. 11, 1987.

[174] ibid Section 4.

nuclear waste management; or samples taken at a nuclear facility in Finland or from nuclear waste generated in Finland for research purposes in Finland.[175]

Extensive disposal of nuclear wastes is considered to be disposal in a facility to contain an amount of nuclear waste in which the total activity of radioactive materials, excluding natural uranium, thorium and depleted uranium, is higher than 1 TBq or the alpha activity is higher than 10 GBq.[176] A nuclear facility of considerable general significance is a nuclear facility in which nuclear materials or waste are fabricated, produced, used, handled or stored to the extent that the amount of nuclear materials at a given moment is more than 50 effective kilograms or the amount of nuclear waste is such that its total activity is higher than 100,000 TBq or the alpha activity higher than 1000 TBq.[177] A vehicle or a temporary storage directly associated with transport is, however, not considered a nuclear facility. A licence for the transportation of nuclear materials and nuclear waste in Finland or through Finnish territory is granted by STUK.[178]

Nuclear Waste Management Plan[179]

To fulfil the intent of *the Act* a LWMO is required each calendar year, by the end of September, to submit to the authority:[180] a plan on how he has planned to carry out the nuclear waste management measures and their preparation; the plan shall include at least the following parts: an overall plan for carrying out the LWMO's entire nuclear waste management obligation, with the relevant timetables and specifications, including the necessary preparations and research and the administrative arrangements and other duties required by the waste management obligation; a detailed plan on the measures that the LWMO intends to undertake during the next calendar year; and an outline plan for the measures that the LWMO plans to undertake in the course of the next five years; a description of the agreements and other arrangements that the LWMO has made to arrange nuclear waste management; and any other information considered necessary by the authorities. When the nuclear waste management obligation includes the decommissioning of a nuclear facility or the cessation of mining or enrichment operations, the nuclear waste management plan submitted by the LWMO is to contain: the method and timetable of the decommissioning or cessation of operations; storage of the nuclear waste resulting from the decommissioning or cessation of operations before disposal, and a description of the disposal; and any other information considered necessary by the authorities. The authority can exempt an LWMO from submitting the plans and reports referred to above if they

---

[175] Section 5 (26 Mar. 1993/278) Nuclear waste as referred to in point 3 of section 3 of the *Nuclear Energy Act*.

[176] Section 6 Extensive disposal of nuclear wastes, as referred to in point 5 of section 3 of the *Nuclear Energy Act*.

[177] As referred to in subsection 2, point 3 of section 11 of the *Nuclear Energy Act*.

[178] Chapter 8 Transport licences Section 56 20 Jun. 1996/473.

[179] Chapter 12 Section 74.

[180] Mentioned in section 28 of the *Nuclear Energy Act*.

are not necessary from the point of view of the control of nuclear waste management.[181]

The Council of State Decisions

By the Decision of the Council of State a LWMO is responsible for ensuring the safety of a disposal facility for reactor waste located in the bedrock of a nuclear power plant site,[182] for physical protection[183] and for emergency planning.[184]

Radiation Protection[185] The radiation exposure arising from the disposed waste is to be kept as low as reasonably achievable (ALARA). The upper level for the expectation value of the annual dose to any member of the public is 0.1mSv. The upper level for the annual dose to any member of the public, arising from accident conditions which are caused by natural events or human action and which are considered possible, is 5mSv. The increase in the total activity concentration of radioactive substances in the biosphere, arising from the disposed waste, shall remain insignificant in any part of the biosphere.

Disposal is based on multiple natural and engineered barriers. Engineered barriers effectively limit the migration of radioactive substances from the waste emplacement rooms for at least 500 years. Thereafter, natural barriers limit the migration of radioactive substances to the biosphere at a level that is in compliance with the requirements for radiation protection. The disposal facility is to be so designed that interactions that might, within a short period of time, substantially impair the performance of any barrier, are excluded.

Compliance with the regulations for radiation protection and the performance of barriers is to be demonstrated by safety analyses covering expected conditions and events as well as disturbances and accidents significant to radiation protection. Possible technical post-closure surveillance measures are not taken into account in the safety analyses. The safety analyses are to be based on reliable calculation models and on such data and assumptions that the analysed radiation exposure, with a high certainty overestimates the exposure likely to occur. Comparisons of alternative disposal concepts may be based on best estimate data and assumptions. To ensure the suitability of the disposal site and the waste emplacement rooms and to acquire the data needed for the safety analyses, bedrock characteristics at the disposal site are to be experimentally investigated.

Implementation The siting, excavation and construction of the disposal facility is to be so designed and implemented that the performance of the bedrock as a barrier

---

[181] Section 79.

[182] Council of State Decision on the submission of the Ministry of Trade and Industry and by virtue of Section 81of the *Nuclear Energy Act (990/87)* given on 11 Dec. 1987.

[183] Sections 3-5, 7-10 and 25-27 of the Decision of the Council of State on the *General Regulations for the Safety of Nuclear Power Plants (395/91)*.

[184] Decision of the Council of State on the *General Regulations for Emergency Planning at Nuclear Power Plants (379/91)*.

[185] Decision of the Council of State (1991/398) Chapter 2 Section 3.

is not significantly impaired and that the safety of other nuclear facilities on the site is not endangered. The disposal facility is to be equipped with reliable safety systems to provide against disturbances and accidents causing radiation danger during the operational period. The underground spaces of the disposal facility are to be closed so that intrusion into the waste emplacement rooms is difficult and that there will be no adverse effects on groundwater flow rates or flow paths in the rock surrounding the waste emplacement rooms due to the excavations. Closure may commence after the Finnish Centre for Radiation and Nuclear Safety has approved the closure plan for the disposal facility in question.

Post-closure Surveillance Provisions are to be made for reliable technical post-closure surveillance measures. A record is to be kept of the emplaced wastes in which waste package specific information on waste type, radioactive substances, location in the waste emplacement rooms and other necessary data is included. This record is to be sent to the Finnish Centre for Radiation and Nuclear Safety who arrange for its long-term deposit. An adequate protection zone is to be reserved around the disposal facility.

Regulatory Guide

General radioactive waste is defined by a regulatory guide[186] and comprises radioactive substances, and equipment, goods and materials contaminated by radioactive substances that have no use and must be rendered harmless owing to their radioactivity. The method used for rendering the waste harmless depends on the type and activity of the waste, as well as on the characteristics of the radionuclides in the waste, such as half-life and type of radiation. The leading principle in planning and implementing waste management is to effectively prevent the radioactive substances from spreading into the environment or passing into the hands of unauthorised persons. Arrangements are to be made for the storage or final disposal of the sealed sources used in industry, research and medicine at sites specifically intended for radioactive waste. The waste from radionuclide laboratories is often low-activity, and it is therefore not necessary to arrange the storage or final disposal of such waste in the same way as for radioactive waste. STUK lays down the principles and limits applying to concentration and activity needed for determining whether a given waste is defined as a radioactive waste or not.[187] The radiation safety requirements and limits for the treatment of radioactive waste are to be observed when discharging radioactive substances into the atmosphere or sewer system, or when delivering solid, low-activity waste to a landfill site without a separate waste treatment plan but not to the radioactive waste resulting from the utilisation of nuclear energy or natural resources.

Radioactive Discharges

If the nature of the practice results in unavoidable minor discharges of radioactive substances into the air, sewage system or otherwise into the environment, special

---

[186] Guide ST 6.2 S T U K 3.
[187] According to section 24 of the *Radiation Decree* (1512/1991).

care is taken to ensure that the quantities of substances discharged remain as low as reasonably possible, and in all cases below the limits specified by STUK.[188] When treating radioactive waste, the general radiation safety requirements are: the effective dose for an individual in the so-called critical group, a group of members of the public whose exposure may be assumed to be highest because of its place of residence or way of life,[189] is not to exceed 10 mSv in a year; and the collective effective dose commitment resulting from one year's operation is not to exceed 1 manSv. These limits are applied separately to gaseous and liquid discharges and to solid radioactive waste. The undertaking that intends to release radioactive substances into the sewer system or atmosphere, or deliver solid radioactive waste to a landfill site or to an incineration plant, is obliged to prepare a waste treatment plan. The plan is to be submitted to STUK for approval and the conditions and special regulations to be followed when disposing of waste are specified in the approval decision. These special regulations may apply, for example, to the measurement of discharges, the control of radioactivity in the environment and external dose rate, the time intervals between the control measurements and reporting the results to STUK for estimation of the radiation dose of the population and reference groups of the population and for recording. For dose estimation, the results of control measurements, radionuclides released into the environment, and their physical and chemical form and activities, are declared in the report. The waste referred to above can be treated as ordinary laboratory waste in which case markings on the waste indicating a danger of radiation are removed or cancelled prior to disposal, and the waste packed in such a way that there is no danger of contamination when handling it. Liquid scintillation solutions or similar waste containing organic solvents are not considered radioactive waste if: the activity concentration of the waste does not exceed 10 Bq/ml, and there are no alpha active radionuclides and the activity concentration of the waste does not exceed 100 Bq/ml, and there are no radionuclides other than H-3 or C-14.

Comment

The law relating to radioactive waste in Finland is unencumbered by uncertainties relating to the definition of radioactive waste; all material discharged from or contaminated by radiation from a nuclear facility is waste. Used fuel is waste. There is a clear difference between storage and disposal. Such clarity comes from the creation of laws and regulations following separation from the Soviet hegemony. The law is clear and straightforward for the ordinary citizen, which has contributed in no small way to the success in conveying to the public the importance of the continuation of the nuclear programme and the waste management strategy. Much can be learned from the Finnish paradigm.

---

[188] Section 23, *Radiation Decree.*
[189] S T U K Guide ST 6.2.

Nuclear Law in Korea

The division of the Korean peninsula under the extremes of totalitarian and liberal ideologies is exemplified in the nuclear regulation in the two nations; in the North is the Russian technology with the scientific-led and essentially secret system and in the South a mirror image of the systems that are in operation in the US, UK and France. Curiously the situation in Korea also reflects the changing scene of East – West rapprochement and until recent months an example of the intent of the Non-proliferation regime; the economic support of the North in the form of economic aid in oil and food, the technological aid in western nuclear technology, design, supply and construction of two pressurised water power units in exchange for the mothballing of the manufacture of fissile material in Russian supplied facilities.

The Democratic Peoples' Republic of Korea (DPRK)

In the absence of a recognisable regime of nuclear legislation in the DPRK and in order to establish a system to enable the construction of light-water reactors in the country, the Korean Peninsula Energy Development Organisation (KEDO) was mandated through international agreements. While the arrangements between the US and the DPRK are in suspense at the time of writing it is, nevertheless, instructive to consider them. The objectives and structure of the organisation are outlined in the *KEDO Establishment Agreement*[190] between the DPRK and the U.S. A *Supply Agreement*[191] between KEDO and DPRK sets down provisions for the construction of light-water reactors. Supplementary agreements between EURATOM and KEDO,[192] a Supply Agreement[193] an Agreed Framework: U.S. – DPRK[194] and the Kuala Lumpur Statement U.S.-DPRK[195] are also supported by protocols covering quality assurance and warranties; training; site takeover, access and use of the site; labour, goods and facilities, juridical status, privileges and immunities and Consular protection in the DPRK; and communications and transport. A Nuclear Safety Confirmation System was set in place in 1998 to confirm the safety and reliability of the reactors while KEDO oversees all nuclear safety aspects of the project. *The Supply Agreement*[196] specifies that the project shall conform to a set of codes and standards equivalent to those of the IAEA and U.S. that apply to the design, manufacture, construction, testing, commissioning and maintenance of the plants, including safety, physical protection, environmental protection and storage and disposal of radioactive waste. Additionally KEDO initiated a process to provide oversight of nuclear safety related activities 'the

---

[190] KEDO Charter Agreement on the Establishment of the Korean Peninsular Energy Development Organisation 1995.
[191] Supply Agreement KEDO-DPRK 1995.
[192] KDEO – European Atomic Energy Community (EAEC) Accession Agreement 1997.
[193] Supply Agreement KEDO – DPRK 1995.
[194] Agreed Framework: U.S. – DPRK, Geneva 1994.
[195] Kuala Lumpur Statement U.S. – DPRK 1995.
[196] Article 1 paragraph 3.

Nuclear Safety Confirmation System (NSCS)' using multinational advisors. KEDO's Nuclear Safety Policy follows five principles: Safety Assessment Verification, Safety Regulation (according to the *Supply Agreement* the DPRK must have a regulatory infrastructure with a competent independent regulatory body consistent with international standards and Safety Confirmation.[197] There are three components to the NSCS; policy development; safety reviews and oversight. The reference plant is the Korean Standard Nuclear Power Plant (KSNP) licensed in the Republic of Korea. To perform design and safety reviews, KEDO has entered into a co-operation agreement with the Korea Institute of Nuclear Safety (KINS) that performs regulatory functions for the Ministry of Science and Technology in the ROK, the regulating authority in the ROK in connection with the KSNP.

The regulating authority in the DPRK responsible for nuclear safety and radiation protection is the State Nuclear Safety Regulatory Commission (SNSRC). KEDO is focusing its attention on strengthening the regulating infrastructure by training provided by KINS and the provision of codes and standards and the attendance of meetings of the Nuclear Safety Advisory Group.

The DPRK became a party to the Treaty on the Non-proliferation of Nuclear Weapons (NPT) in December 1985. An NPT Safeguards Agreement entered into force in April 1992. The IAEA has reported[198] that it has never been able to verify the completeness and correctness of the initial report of the DPRK under the NPT Safeguards Agreement. Effective as of 11 January 2003 the DPRK announced its withdrawal from the NPT. In the uncertain situation created by the threats on the part of the North and the suspension of aid, but interestingly not of the construction project, an agreed Statement has not been issued by the NPT States Parties, nor by the NPT depository States (Russia, UK and the USA), nor by the UN Security Council. Article X.1 of the NPT allows a State Party to withdraw having given three months notice to all other Parties and to the UN Security Council and includes a Statement of the extraordinary events it regards as having jeopardised its supreme interests. An end to a promising example of nuclear technology transfer in exchange for a retreat from nuclear confrontation is threatened that conceivably could lead to nuclear waste on an enormous scale.

Republic of Korea

Atomic Energy Laws

The *Atomic Energy Act (The AEA)* for the peaceful development of nuclear energy was established in 1958 to enable the supply by the US of two zero-energy research reactors. It is part of a system of *Atomic Energy Laws* that includes the *Enforcement Decree of the Act* (Presidential Decree) describing the principles and technical standards embodied in *the Act*; the *Enforcement Regulations of the Act*

---

[197] The principles are as outlined in the Basic Safety Principles for Nuclear Power Plants (Safety Series No 75–INSAG–3).
[198] IAEA Fact Sheet on DPRK Nuclear Safeguards (8 Jan. 2003).

(Ordinance of the Minister of Science and Technology) that guides the procedures and documents entrusted by *the AEA* and the *Decree* and the *Notice of the Minister of Science and Technology* that prescribes details and particulars for technical standards and guidelines. The Korea Institute of Nuclear Safety (KINS) is the body responsible for developing the guidelines for safety reviews and regulatory inspections. *The AEA* establishes functions and composition of the Atomic Energy Commission and the Nuclear Safety Commission.[199] It establishes and enforces the plan for comprehensive promotion of atomic energy, research and development, and the collection of costs and funding for the work.[200] *The AEA* sets down criteria for licensing, regulatory procedures, operation and decommissioning of nuclear power reactors, related facilities,[201] the nuclear fuel cycle,[202] and the use of nuclear material, radioisotopes and radiation generating devices.[203] *The Act* sets down criteria for the permits for construction, operation and regulatory inspections of disposal facilities.[204] The establishment of exclusive areas and preventative measures against radiation hazards[205] and the personnel dosimetry service[206] are regulated. Penal provisions and fines for negligence are included.[207]

Long-term Atomic Energy Policy

The Atomic Energy Commission has determined a long-term policy towards 2030 and a legal basis to formulate a Comprehensive Nuclear Energy Promotion Plan (CNEPP) every five years through amendment of *The AEA in* 1995. *The AEA* stipulates that the Minister of Science and Technology and the heads of the concerned Ministries shall formulate sector-by-sector implementation plans in accordance with the CNEEP and annual action plans. The long-term policy emphasises the safe and peaceful use of atomic energy under a spirit of pursuing a better life in harmony with nature and describes four primary objectives: to enhance the stability in energy supply by promoting atomic energy as a major source of domestic generation; to achieve self reliance in a nuclear reactor and proliferation-resistant nuclear fuel cycle technology through comprehensive and systematic nuclear energy research and development; to foster atomic energy as a strategic export industry by securing international competitiveness through the advancement of atomic energy technology, on the basis of active participation and initiatives of the civil sector and to play a leading role in the improvement of human welfare and the advancement of science and technology by expanding the use of atomic energy technology in agriculture, engineering, medicine and industry and by enacting basic research of nuclear technology. To achieve these

---

[199] The *Atomic Energy Act 1958*, Chapter 2.
[200] ibid Chapter 3.
[201] ibid Chapter 4.
[202] ibid Chapter 6.
[203] ibid Chapter 7.
[204] ibid Chapter 8.
[205] ibid Chapter 11.
[206] ibid Chapter 9.
[207] ibid Chapter 13.

objectives ten basic directions are established. It is noteworthy that the first direction is to continue to expand the development and utilisation of atomic energy but significantly this aim leaves the way open for alternative energy processes being qualified by the Statement 'unless an epoch-making alternative energy source becomes available in the foreseeable future'. The remaining directions include a policy of peaceful use, strengthening of nuclear safety, improving the economy, increasing public understanding (while respecting the right to know under the ideals of democracy and openness), to implement a balanced development, to promote creative research and development, to collaborate with industries, universities and research institutes to keep up with international harmonisation and to implant the atomic energy policy on the basis of long-term perspectives on the techno-economic and socio-political environment.

Nuclear Fuel Supply

The major nuclear fuel consumer in Korea is the Korea Hydro and Nuclear Power Company (KHNP) that pursues economic efficiency through international open bidding for uranium concentrates by long-term contacts and spot market purchase from Australia, Canada, UK, France, Russia, the USA and South Africa. From 2001 Korea expects to account for more than five percent of the world's demand. Conversion and enrichment services come from the US, UK, France, Canada and Russia by long-term contracts. Fuel fabrication services are local to meet domestic needs.

Radioactive Waste Management

The Ministry of Commerce Industry and Energy (OCIE) is responsible for radioactive waste management and according to a plan approved by the Atomic Energy Commission in 1998 a low and intermediate level waste (LILW) repository will be constructed by 2008 and spent fuel will be stored at each nuclear power plant until interim storage facilities are constructed in 2016. Site selection is currently in process at 2003.

Nuclear Safety Regulation

The Minister of Science and Technology bases the regulation and licensing of nuclear facilities on the provisions of *The AEA*, it's Enforcement Decree and the Notice. The Nuclear Safety Commission (NSC) is the decision making body within MOST; it is independent of the Atomic Energy Commission and is aided by the technical expert body, the Korea Institute of Nuclear Safety (KINS). Licensing proceeds in the first instance by the issue of a construction permit followed by an operating licence under *The AEA*. Early site approval can be granted for a construction site prior to the construction permit. Regulatory inspections of nuclear installations are conducted prior to operation; periodically during operations; quality audits and daily inspection by resident inspectors. In 2000 *The AEA* was amended to introduce the recommendations of ICRP Pub 60 on a staged basis from January 2003. A Periodic Safety Review (PSR) was introduced and a Standard Design Certificate to streamline the licensing process for the construction of nuclear power plants with the same design. The PSR was introduced to satisfy the requirement of the *Convention on Nuclear Safety* that the safety of the older nuclear power plants is maintained at current safety standards and practices. The implementation of the PSR is planned in accordance with the requirements of the NSC; a pilot application for KoRi Unit 1 was started in 2000.

Nuclear Liability

Liability and compensation for nuclear damage are covered by the Act on Compensation for Nuclear Damage (Compensation Act)[208] and the Act on Indemnification Agreement for Nuclear Liability (Indemnity Agreement Act).[209] The Compensation Act was amended and entered into force on 1 January 2002 to reflect developments in the international conventions to:[210] include nuclear incidents in the Exclusive Economic Zone; to increase compulsory insurance to 300 million SDRs; to extend and clarify the definition of 'nuclear damage' according to the 1997 Protocol to Amend the Vienna Convention; to exclude a grave natural disaster from the exonerations and to extend the prescription period for personal injury to 30 years.

Radiological Emergency Exercises

The criteria for establishing and implementing the radiological emergency plan are specified by MOST.[211] All on-site and off-site emergency organisations are required to participate in an exercise at each installation at least every three years; a small scale on-site emergency exercise is to be held at least once every year.

Radiation Protection

The *AEA* prescribes; provisions on protective measures against radiation hazards to keep the release of radioactive material and the exposure to occupational radiation as low as reasonably achievable (ALARA); provisions on safety measures relating to operations of nuclear installations; performance criteria for the personnel dosimetry service for radiation workers or persons having access to nuclear installations and training requirements for nuclear workers. The *Enforcement Decree* and the *Regulation of the Atomic Energy Act* specifies the details necessary for implementation of *The AEA*. *Radiation Protection Standards* specified under the *MOST NOTICE* prescribes technical requirements on radiation protection and conditions for radioactive effluent release and dose limits. Safety regulating

---

[208] *Act on Compensation for Nuclear Damage (Compensation Act)* Act No. 2094 of 24 January 1969, as amended by : Act No. 2765 of 7 April 1975, Act No. 3549 of 1 Apr. 1982 (the *Atomic Energy Act*), Act No. 3849 of 12 May 1986, Act No. 4940 of 1 Jan. 1995 (the *Atomic Energy Act*), and *Act No. 6350 of 16 Jan. 2001*. More detailed provisions were introduced by Presidential Decree (No. 6701, May 25, 1973).
[209] *Act on Indemnification Agreement for Nuclear Liability (Indemnity Agreement Act)* Act No. 2764, Apr. 7 1975.
[210] Kim Sangwon and Kim Hhojung, 'Improvement of Nuclear Liability System of the Republic of Korea and Remaining Issues Thereof,' Nuclear Inter Jura, Cape Town, April 2003.
[211] MOST Notice No. 98-13.

activities include safety reviews, regulatory inspections and the development of technical standards. An Information System on Integrated Radiation Safety (ISIRS) is being developed to monitor all processes related to the use of radioactive sources from production and importation to final disposal through the internet on a real time basis to the general public and all other related organisations.

National Environmental Radiation Monitoring

A nationwide monitoring network is operated by KINS for MOST to measure radioactivity in airborne dust, fallout, rainwater, livestock products, farm products, soil, and drinking water and background radiation. Local monitoring stations are situated at ten cities and nuclear installation sites with a monitoring centre in KINS. Interestingly, on the map of the Monitoring Network the nuclear station under construction by KEDO in the DPRK at Shinpo is included on a Korea-wide geographical layout.

IAEA Safeguards

The NPT was ratified by the ROK on 23 April 1975 and a Safeguards Agreement with the IAEA has been in force since 14 November 1975. At present 33 facilities are under the IAEA Safeguards. A national inspection system responds to all international obligations and ensures international transparency and credibility of atomic energy activities in ROK. The Centre for Nuclear Control (TCNC) was authorised by MOST in 1996 to develop safeguard's technology and to provide technical assistance to the Government. Each nuclear facility has a designated person in charge of safeguards to strengthen the States System of Accountability for and Control of Nuclear Material (SSAC).

Comment

The law relating to nuclear activities in the Republic of Korea has followed the ICRP recommendations guided by the IAEA and the requirements of the export control regulations of the western supplier States, thus enabling a nuclear programme to commence with the construction by US and UK contractors of the first 594 MWe PWR in 1970. Flexibly this regulatory system is expected to extend to the supply of equipment and technology for the two PWRs under construction in the DPRK. The civil works has already started in advance of the permissions from exporting States.

Summary

The review of the laws that apply to nuclear waste bear out to a large extent the three perspectives in relation to the siting of an installation for the storage or disposal of radioactive waste identified in the INLA nuclear waste working group report[212] namely:

---

[212] INLA Working Group 5 Report, Nuclear Inter Jura 03, Cape Town, Apr. 2003.

The technical perspective, which attempts to achieve sites providing the most adequate safety conditions, especially regarding the possible occurrence in the future of adverse natural phenomena (risk of earthquakes, floods or the undesired ingress of water, etc.). Such demands are especially important when radioactive waste is to be disposed of, since the geology is usually the main confining barrier.

The environmental perspective, which requires safety of the medium and of living populations with respect to the disturbance generated by the new installations. There is also the consideration of other natural resources existing in the area surrounding the site, whose use might be compromised in the future.

The social perspective, which requires guarantees that there will be no affect for the health of persons or their property and, in general, for their present or future rights, the latter including the right to an equitable decision among all the communities involved and the application of the principle of responsibility and justice with respect to future generations.

The INLA Waste Management Group members in responding to questionnaires also reflected the situation of the five specific States described in this chapter with their report that:

None of the analysed countries have set up a legal procedure for site screening, neither have they legal or regulatory provisions regulating site selection. The most frequently adopted practice is to consider waste management facilities under the general rules governing the authorisation of nuclear installations, the provisions under Environmental Law and Town Planning Law also being applicable. In most of the countries the future operator reports to the Administration and to the local authorities on the locations considered prior to applying for a licence.

Specialised agencies operate in many of the countries to provide an overall management of radioactive waste. Main functions of these bodies are to establish guidelines for the choice of a site and to co-ordinate the construction and operation of repositories. Agencies are mainly those that apply for licences and, when issued, the ones that take title of the authorisation. A preferred option is these Bodies to be administrations accountable to the central power, with a clear strategic link with the corresponding central executive office. This scheme has proved to be very efficient, taking account of the high safety standards recorded to date. Nevertheless, most of the rapporteurs feel that the role of the Agencies in the whole management process should be encouraged by developing additional provisions to allow deeper insertion in field research activities. If so, better understanding of the scientific and technical processes involved in long-term disposal technologies could be achieved.

Licensing according to the requirements of nuclear safety and radiological protection is usually a competence of the Central Administration while the scrutiny of environmental and territorial requisites is more often the responsibility of local or regional Administrations. The latter can also be applied to other kind of licences regarding water permits, underground rights, etc. On several occasions, this scheme brings along a conflict of laws, largely responsible for past failures to site disposal facilities. The issue is a crucial one specially in the field of high level waste disposal, where no solution could be envisaged and conveniently implemented while not having developed an adequate 'in situ' R&D programme and a further characterisation plan. On the other hand, most of the rapporteurs are insisting on the consideration of a co-ordinated procedure facing this problem. Whether it could be an integrated one or should be achieved under co-operative agreements between the different Administrations involved is a question concerning the territorial organisation of each of the countries. Experience and rapporteurs' understanding suggest the first to fit more properly in countries with a unitary structure, the second being more advisable for federal structures.

It has been verified that the current trend is Parliaments to ratify general licences for waste disposal facilities, specifically those concerning high level waste repositories. Although it is not the function of Parliament to intervene throughout the process, its backing for different initiatives or the ratification of governmental authorisations might provide stronger guarantees of robustness, continuity and legitimacy that this type of solution requires. Moreover, it is advisable to discuss the implications of the whole compound of managing options at the highest political level. Public participation under well-defined procedures is an adequate means to gain acceptance of the chosen options and the designated sites as well. Experience shows that approaching public concerns at the very early stages of waste management promotes better understanding and wider agreement between the population and those responsible for radioactive waste management. Legislation should include appropriate provisions for public involvement to be encouraged and expanded. Societal co-responsibility should be a goal avoiding simple releasing of information to be the only way to public participation.

Further Reading

Farquhar, James T. (1986), 'Best Practicable Means (and the thought that Nanny may have known best after all)' (1986) *Chemistry and Industry*, pp 541-543.

Guruswamy L.D. and Tromans S.R.(1986), 'Towards an Integrated Approach to Pollution Control. The Best Practicable Environmental Option and its Antecedents', *JPL* pp 643-55.

HSE (1992), Safety Assessment Principles for Nuclear Plants, HMSO London.

HSE on behalf of DEFRA (2003), *National Report on conformance with the obligations of the Joint Convention on the Safety of Spent Fuel Management and on the Safety of Radioactive Waste Management*, HMSO London.

John, Edward (1995), 'Access to Environmental Information: Limitations of the UK Radioactive Substances Register', *Journal of Environmental Law* Vol 7 No 1.

Kim Sangwon and Kim Hhojung (2003), *Improvement of Nuclear Liability System of the Republic of Korea and Remaining Issues Thereof*, Nuclear Inter Jura, Cape Town.

Lee, Maria (2000), 'Civil Liability of the Nuclear Industry', *Journal of Environmental Law* Vol 12 No 3.

Tromans S. (1997), *The Law of Nuclear Installations and Radioactive Substances*, Sweet & Maxwell.

Chapter Seven
Practice, Pragmatism and the Way Ahead

In his analysis of reflexive modernism Ulrich Beck uses the example of the development of nuclear energy to demonstrate the reflexive nature of scientists and the critical application of science to the risks of radiation.[1] He appears to conclude that the result of this critical application is the closure of the nuclear option. However, his work fails to appreciate that critical review also leads to change and improvement.[2] As may be seen from the foregoing chapters the management of radioactive waste has benefited from the reflexive process and from the pragmatic[3] application of laws and regulations. Lessons have been learned and the application of the law is continuing to develop; international shepherding has allowed a degree of consistency in the application of risk while allowing more diverse interpretation of the definitions of waste and consequent range of technological waste management solutions. Public participation in possible management solutions allows non-scientific restraints to those solutions to be taken into account but risks the distortion of the solution due to lack of understanding of the technological and practical restraints.

The Law in Practice

In the UK the law relating to radioactive waste is indistinguishable from the laws relating to the control of radioactive materials, the laws relating to the protection of the public and the workforce and the laws relating to the licensing of nuclear facilities.

The Hazards of Radiation

The hazards of radioactive waste are those that apply to radiation in general. While all substances are poisonous to any organism in high enough doses toxic substances are generally considered to be those that even in small doses have the potential to damage the natural environment and/or adversely affect human health.[4]

---

[1] Beck, Ulrich (1992), *Risk Society: towards a new modernity*, Sage Publications, London.
[2] Duncan, I. J. (2003), 'What to do with nuclear waste', *Nuclear Energy*, 42 No.3. Jun. pp 145-148.
[3] Pragmatism – action or policy dictated by consideration of the immediate practical consequences rather than by theory or dogma, Collins English Dictionary, Third Edition 1994, HarperCollins Publishers.
[4] Williamson Richard L., Burton Dennis T., Clarke James H., and Fleming Lora E. (1993), 'Gathering Danger: The Urgent Need to Regulate Toxic Substances That Can Bioaccumulate'. *Ecology Law Quarterly*, Vol 20 p 604.

Risks to human health and the natural environment are seen to be severe when toxic substances bioaccumulate, persist in the environment and are capable of building up in living tissue. Radioactive substances are unique since they have both the characteristics of toxic substances and high doses are capable of causing harm to living tissue from a distance by ionising radiation. For various reasons, in particular the association with nuclear weapons, they have the capacity for inducing psychological fears. Everything is radioactive; life exists in a sea of terrestrial and cosmic radiation. According to the Supreme Court of the USA; '(We) live in a world of low level radioactive waste'. The contribution of man-made radiation to the environment is small compared to the natural background. Man-made radiation arises from the diagnostic use and treatment in medicine, the testing of nuclear weapons, the nuclear power industry, research activities and excavated material. The contribution from medical sources is over 90 percent of the total manmade dose. Radiation causes damage to the cell; the damage will depend upon the energy of the radiation source, the energy absorbed by the tissue and the sensitivity of the tissue to radiation. A quantity called the effective dose (commonly called the dose), measured in Sieverts, takes these factors into account. In the case of late radiation injury the effective dose equivalent addresses the non-uniform nature of the whole body exposure.

The relationship between radiation and damage to life is immensely complex.[5] Following an alleged quote from Einstein that, '(t)he whole of science is nothing more than a refinement of everyday thinking' and while not an everyday occurrence in normal circumstances, the nature of radiation damage can be explained by analogy to that which might be caused by handguns. The damage caused to the cell in the case of exposure to high levels of radiation may be likened to the damage caused by a spray of bullets from high velocity automatic weapons; a massive, immediate destruction that results in total loss of function of the cells, the organs and the body. Low level radiation may be compared to a single shot fired randomly; the ray or particle may or may not strike a cell causing ionisation and subtle damage to the messages contained therein. The damaged message may or may not affect the development of the cell and if it does cause damage that cell may or may not be repaired or rejected by the body's protective mechanisms. The damaged cell may contain changed genetic messages. This series of events having persisted the effect may appear many years later as cancer. The higher the energy level of the radiation the faster and more damaging are the bullets. The larger the amounts of radioactive material the more 'equivalent bullets' there are thus increasing the probability of hitting a target. One could compare radiation with fire[6] but unlike fire radiation is poorly understood by the public and also subject to unreasonable fear.[7] Like fire, radiation can cause injury very soon after the

---

[5] Clarke, Roger (1996), 'Implications of new data on cancer risk', *NRPB Bulletin* No 179 July, Chilton.

[6] Gooden, David, S. (1985*), Radiation Injuries - ionizing radiation*. 14Am Jur Proof of Facts 3d.

[7] Cohen, (1983), *Clinical Oncology for Medical Students and Physicians: A Multidisciplinary Approach.* American Cancer Society (6th Ed. 1983).

exposure. Such injuries are termed early effects, but unlike fire, injury may be delayed, these injuries being termed late effects. Early effects may include reddening of the skin, hair loss, nausea, diarrhoea, sterility, organ atrophy and death depending on the amount of radiation dose received. Late effects are related to cell damage and include genetic effects which although not yet seen in human victims are predicted to occur following animal experiments, and cancers the type and severity not being related to the radiation dose experienced.[8]

Regulation of the Nuclear Facility Operator/User[9]

Regulation of the user of radiation, either as a 'user' or a 'nuclear facility operator' (operator), is concerned with the management of radioactive materials and with limiting the exposure to radiation of workers and the general public. Radioactive substances and the nuclear industry are regulated by statute as described in chapter six. Breach of regulations and of conditions imposed under statute may lead to liability under the criminal law where the standard of proof is that the facts of the instance must be beyond reasonable doubt. In the event that there are claims for compensation other than determined by statute, for example for injury caused by industrial radiography, such claims may be decided by the common law where the standard of proof is that the facts must be established on the balance of probabilities.

In the US the *Price Anderson Act* provides a mechanism for compensating persons who are injured from a nuclear accident. According to Donald E. Jose[10] such accidents are rare and almost all the case law relates to simple occupational exposure. Experience shows that unusual radiological events coupled with the natural incidence of cancer cause lawsuits. The natural incidence of cancer in an ageing population near a nuclear plant, unexpected exposure causing emotional distress and any cancer in a person who worked at or lived near a nuclear plant can result in a lawsuit.

Where injury is caused by a nuclear incident on a licensed site the operator is strictly liable, however, where injury caused by radiation is not a liability under the *Nuclear Installations Act*, a claim could be made in the UK courts for damages in negligence or for breach of statutory duty. In the latter case the relevant statute would be the *Radioactive Substances Act* or *the Health and Safety at Work Act*. In a case of breach of regulations against BNFL involving the release of radioactive material to the environment the jury was instructed that they must consider the rate of discharge, the radiation exposure that resulted and whether the discharges were ALARA.[11] In order to make a case for negligence, however, a breach of the duty owed must be established. Numerical dose limits are a statement of the balance between hypothetical risks from small doses and a safe environment for radiation

---

[8] *La Porte v United States Radium Corp.* (135,DCNJ) 13F Supp263.
[9] Riley, Peter (1997), *The regulation of the user of ionising radiation and the relevance of nuclear facility operators in litigation*, Nuclear Inter Jura '97, Tours, France.
[10] Jose, Donald, E. (2001), *Recent Litigation Involving Exposure to Radiation*, Nuclear Inter Jura 2001, Jun. Budapest.
[11] *The Queen v BNF plc (1985)*, Crown Court, Carlisle.

workers. The ALARA principle keeps doses even lower than regulatory limits but in the US it cannot serve as a minimum standard of care. In the cases of *O'Connor*[12] and *In re TMI*,[13] it was established that a radiation dose within the permissible dose limits cannot result in liability to a person who received that dose and the jury cannot set their own dose limits under the guise of applying ALARA.

Operator The operator is involved with nuclear research, the manufacture and processing of radioactive materials, the generation of electricity, the storage of radioactive material and the disposal of radioactive waste. The characteristic that distinguishes the operator from the user is that the operator operates nuclear reactors and plant with the potential for a nuclear incident causing radiation levels off the site that may result in damage to persons or property. This potential for damage has encouraged the creation of international conventions and national legislation to create a strict liability regime with limited liability. The user is not necessarily subject to such arrangements[14] and is primarily involved in the use of radioactive sources in industrial, medical (including dental) and agricultural applications. The operator on the licensed site also carries many of the activities carried out by the user and the user carries out his activities under the operator's supervision on the licensed site. The term 'user' is used here to describe all users other than the licensed operator and the military. The implication that the user is small in comparison to the operator however, is misleading as to the extent to which radiation is used outside the ambit of the nuclear facility operator. While individual users may be small the use of radiation is in fact much greater outside the licensed site than on it and the potential for serious radiation incidents is evident as will be seen later.

> Much of the world relies to a far greater extent than most people realise on the medical, industrial and agricultural applications of radioisotope technology...in the United States the industries which rely on those technologies are about four and a half times as large as the power based industry[15]

According to the US Nuclear Regulatory Commission[16] there are 110 nuclear power plants holding operating licences in the US and there are about 22,000

---

[12] *O'Connor v Commonwealth Edison Company*, 748 F.Supp. 672, 687 (C.D.Ill. 1990), aff'd, 13F.3d 1090 (7thCir), cert.denied, 512 U.S. 1222 (1994).
[13] *In re TMI* 67 F.3d 1103 (3rd Cir. 1995).
[14] In the UK the control of radioactive materials is by the *Radioactive Substances Act 1993*; in the US the standards are set down in the *Code of Federal Regulations, 10CFR* paras 1-171.25 (1989).
[15] Clark, Gerald (1996), International Safeguards: An Industry Perspective, *IAEA Bulletin* 4/1996.
[16] Dicus, Greta Joy (1997), Commissioner of the US NRC, Materials Safety and Regulation at the Regulatory Information Conference, Capital Hilton Hotel, Washington, DC, 2 April 1997.

radioactive materials users holding specific licences. According to the ICRP the smaller sources are responsible for a number of deaths from misuse each year.[17]

Small Users Significant damage has been caused by accidents involving small users that are comparable in their effects on people and property to the damage that might be caused by the escape of radiation from a licensed site. The following brief descriptions are only a selection of such accidents and their effects.

- In 1979 in California an industrial radiographer failed to secure the mechanism of a radiographic camera and an Ir-192 source fell out of the camera and was handled by other workers who were unaware that it was radioactive and suffered localised radiation injuries as a result.[18]
- In 1983, a Co-60 source, used in medical radiation therapy, was accidentally included in a shipment of scrap steel from Ciudad Juarez, Mexico. This source subsequently found its way into processed steel in the US. Approximately ten people in Mexico were exposed to radiation levels high enough to cause acute injury.[19]
- In 1984, an industrial radiation source Ir-192 was lost in Mohammedia, Morocco. An individual discovered this source and took it home; many people were exposed to high levels of radiation, and eight died.[20]
- In September 1987 in Goiania, Brazil, the head of a stolen teletherapy device was broken open causing the contamination of a wide area by Cs-137; 129 people had been contaminated.[21] Fifty people showed symptoms of whole body irradiation, fourteen of those fifty developed moderate to severe bone marrow injury; ultimately four of these died.[22]
- In 1990, there was an accident in Tel Aviv, Israel, involving a Co-60 facility used to sterilise medical instruments. A worker who tried to fix a jammed source received in excess of 1000 rads to the whole body, equivalent to 1000 times the regulatory limit. The worker died thirty-four days after the accident.[23]
- In October 1994, a stolen Cs-137 source was taken to a house in Estonia and kept there for four weeks where it irradiated 19 people. One person died before irradiation was identified. Five others received protracted exposures ranging from 0.5 - 2.7 Gy and the remainder received lesser doses. Four of the

---

[17] Clarke, Roger (1996), reporting the ICRP meeting in Paris Nov 1996, NRPB Bulletin No 184.
[18] Supra Dicus.
[19] Supra Gooden.
[20] ibid p 97.
[21] Caubit, Ayrton (1993), *Radiological Accident in Goiania - Six Years Later*, Nuclear Inter Jura '93, Rio de Janeiro.
[22] Brandao-Mello, Carlos Eduardo MD et al (1992), *A Medical Follow-up of Cs-137 Goiania Radiation Accident - An Update (1990-1992)*.
[23] Supra Gooden.

more seriously irradiated survivors showed deterministic effects, skin lesions and depressed blood cell counts.[24]

- Materials safety problems can have trans-boundary implications: in 1990 a company in Bristol, UK, who operate a metal smelter undertook a precautionary survey for radioactivity and found Cs-137 in steel pellets which had been imported from Ireland. Subsequent investigation by the HMIP (now the Environment Agency) traced the contamination to a missing nucleonic gauge from a coal conveyor lost during dismantling of the plant and passed through various shippers to the Irish steel plant. The investigation and the segregation for disposal took three years and is estimated to have cost in excess of £1 million.[25]
- In 1992 a waste company reported finding a radiation source in waste. The NRC investigation revealed that in November 1992 a Co-60 source accidentally left in a patient in Indiana was removed by the nursing home and disposed of as biohazardous waste. As many as 94 persons were exposed to doses from 0.034 to 2.57 rem.[26]
- In 1996 industrial radiography devices in storage in Texas were stolen and sold as scrap metal and a 35 Curie Co-60 source irradiated workers, officials and relatives of the scrap yard owner to doses up to 10 rem.[27]
- In the UK it was reported in May 1996 that a nuclear density meter, which often incorporates a neutron source (typically Am-241/Be) and a gamma source (typically Cs-137), was crushed by a road roller and was driven 100 meters over hot sticky tarmac and rough ground and about half a tonne of limestone chippings poured over the remaining wreckage.[28]

In recent years US metal manufacturing mills have accidentally smelted radioactive sources resulting in costs for decontamination and losses resulting from the shutdown of the mills. In one case these costs totalled $23 million. Each year about 200 reports are received of radioactive sources lost or stolen.[29] Moves are in process to tighten international legislation in relation to sealed sources[30] and as noted in chapter six a European Council Directive is in preparation.[31]

Risk and Near Misses Experience shows that radiation accidents may be avoided by following proven procedures when carrying out operations involving use and

---

[24] Radiological Protection Bulletin No: 187 Mar. 1997.

[25] McHugh, J. O. and Marshall, B. P. (1997), 'Radioactive Waste and Small Users: The 3Rs-Responsibilities, Rights and Regulation', *[1997] Env.Liability 38.*

[26] Supra Dicus.

[27] Supra Dicus.

[28] The Radiation Protection Adviser, Issue 9, May 1996, Health and Safety Executive.

[29] Supra Dicus.

[30] Boustany, Katia (2000), 'A Code of Conduct on the Safety of Radiation Sources and the Security of Radioactive Materials. A New Approach to the Normative Control of a Nuclear Risk?', *Nuclear Law Bulletin* 65, Jun. OECD – NEA.

[31] Proposal for a Council Directive on the control of high activity sealed radioactive sources. COM(2003) final. Brussels 24 Jan. 2003.

maintenance of systems and equipment. Failure to follow procedures risks an accident and when this happens but an accident does not occur it may be termed a 'near miss'. ICRP 1990 Recommendations[32] include in the system of protection for practices the restriction on risks to individuals from potential exposure to radiation. It is axiomatic that activities, which may lead to situations such as near misses, which risk exposure to radiation, are also constrained. That the regulatory bodies take this approach is demonstrated by the following examples.

- Nuclear Electric was prosecuted at the Mold Crown Court following an incident in July 1993 at Wylfa Power Station,[33] which involved the failure of a grab used in the on-load refuelling of the reactors. The flow of coolant gas through the fuel channel was reduced and there was the risk of the fuel in the channel overheating with the possibility of release of fission products to the atmosphere. Nuclear Electric pleaded guilty to contravention of the health and safety legislation in that it failed to conduct its undertaking so as to ensure the health and safety of all its employees and were fined £250,000 with £138,000 costs.
- The NRC staff has proposed to fine the Public Service Electric and Gas Company (PSE&G) $150,000 for alleged violations of NRC requirements at its Hope Creek Nuclear Generating Station.[34] The violations were failure to plan surveillance testing following maintenance testing of control rod drive systems; failure to correct isolation dampers incorrectly installed; failure to correct excessive control rod drive speeds and failure to obtain NRC approval of design changes to service water valves.
- The NRC proposed a $100,000 fine against Commonwealth Edison Company for engineering violations at the Zion Nuclear Power Station.[35] Three examples cited by NRC were the failure of the utility to evaluate the effect of temporary scaffolding coming into contact with safety related plant during station operation; the failure to issue formal documentation for deficient plant items and the failure to set tank instrumentation correctly.
- NRC on Northeast Utilities proposed a civil penalty of $650,000 for alleged violations at Haddam Neck nuclear plant. The penalty is made up from a $350,000 fine for long-standing deficiencies in engineering programs and practices and a $300,000 fine for errors relating to a nitrogen build up in the reactor vessel.[36]

While the examples given all apply to instances on licensed sites, there have been many which occurred outside the licensed site involving small users where the

---

[32] ICRP Publication 60. Ann. ICRP, 21 Nos. 1-3(1991).

[33] Nuclear Safety, Feb 1996, Health and Safety Executive.

[34] NRC Announcement 1-96-70 October 24, 1996.

[35] NRC News Announcement: R111-97-28, Mar. 12, 1997.

[36] NRC Announcement 1-97-52 May 12 1997.

penalties have been much less.[37]   The contamination caused by the incident at Goiania, for example, was many times that caused by the overspill in the Blue Circle case. It follows that in future failure to take precautions, failure to follow procedures etc., which risk an incident involving a device containing a radioactive source will risk penalties equivalent to those given in the examples above. It is clear from the evidence of reported incidents, samples of which are given above, that damage caused by radiation incidents involving users is often of the same order as that caused by incidents on licensed nuclear sites. In the US, except in the case of an extraordinary nuclear occurrence, the user has no limit to his liability but the claimant must establish proof of fault. In the UK the user outside the licensed site is in a similar position, however, on the licensed site he is absolved from liability, the operator being strictly liable for any occurrence.

The principle of optimisation requires the user and the operator to adhere to the ALARA principle; it is the case that in the UK and in some states of the US that failure to do so would be the basis of a claim in negligence even though the release or dose levels permitted by regulations or authorisations were not exceeded. The question of failure to show justification and exceeding risk limits are open to being tested. The user is liable to prosecution in the event of a breach of regulations, including operational procedures, and the evidence of prosecution of licensed operators points to the possibility of heavy penalties even though damage to persons or property is only risked by a near miss.

Extending these observations to the international context leads to the conjecture that if the example of the common law experience is anything to go by, since the definition of limits and the nature of the liability in the event of a nuclear incident in different legal regimes is open to interpretation, the peripatetic user risks heavy fines for incidents which involve the actual release of radiation, the risk of release of radiation, failure to follow ALARA principles, failure to show justification and he may not be protected from a claim for damages including punitive damages in the event of an incident caused by him at a licensed facility. There is a clear need for radioactive materials and radiation to continue to be closely regulated. The paradox is that on the one hand we live in an environment of low level radiation and that regulatory levels reflect this but on the other hand we work to the assumption that there is no threshold below which harm will not occur. This adds to an understandable public fear of radiation *per se* and leads to distrust of the rule makers. The courts have taken a cautious view; compensation claims by the public for alleged damage caused by low level radiation have been rejected in the UK. The US courts in claims for personal injury and loss of tourist business arising from the accident at Three Mile Island which released amounts of radiation below regulatory limits have determined that while the standard of care set by federal regulation prescribing maximum permissible radiation exposure levels and requiring radiation releases to be ALARA[38] it was not to be construed as a radiation standard for the purpose of personal injury claims; each plaintiff had to prove individual exposure to radiation to establish causation. Where the substance

---

[37] Supra McHugh, p 39.
[38]*In re TMI,* 67 F.3d 1103 (3rd Cir. 1995).

that allegedly injured the plaintiff also occurs naturally in the environment this exposure requires that the plaintiff demonstrates that they have been exposed to a greater extent than anyone else; that their exposure exceeds the normal background level.

In an attempt to remove large quantities of material from regulatory control, such waste being no more radioactive than the natural background, the Nuclear Regulatory Commission in the USA has promulgated a policy of Below Regulatory Concern (BRC).[39] This policy which still awaits government approval would remove from regulatory control buildings and land contaminated by small but detectable levels of radioactivity, consumer products containing small quantities of radioactive material, disposal of low level radioactive waste at disposal sites that are not licensed and recycling of slightly contaminated materials (e.g. chemicals used in manufacture of nuclear fuel). The policy specifies individual and collective doses that are not to be exceeded which are small in comparison with the average personal doses that result from natural background.

Legal Action

It can be seen from the foregoing that the user risks radiation accidents with consequences not unlike those anticipated from a nuclear facility. Nuclear facilities have been pursued for damages, prosecuted and fined heavily for the effects of radioactive contamination causing damage to property, notably the *Three Mile Island* cases in the USA[40] and The *Blue Circle* case in the UK (see below). A large number of prosecutions have been levelled against nuclear operators and users for breach of regulations which include a number of incidents which would be classed as 'near misses' and hence as a risk of causing damage. A limited number of personal injury claims have been settled in the US Courts; the TMI cases are still ongoing. Employees of nuclear operators have settled personal injury claims in the UK out of court for claims and claims by the general public have been rejected.

Damages have been awarded against an operator in the UK. In 1996 in the High Court in the case of *Blue Circle v MoD*,[41] Mr Justice Carnwath held that landowners whose soil was contaminated by radioactive material from an adjoining nuclear establishment because of the overflow of a pond during a storm and required extensive decontamination, had suffered physical damage to property which entitled them to compensation under the Nuclear Installations Act for, inter alia, the resulting diminution in the value and saleability of their property. Damages in excess of £5 million were awarded. The claim was distinguished from an earlier case[42] where contamination of the airspace within the building that did not require decontamination was determined not to be damage to property. The

[39] US Congress Subcommittee on Energy and the Environment(1990), Hearing on the Nuclear Regulatory Commission's Below Regulatory Concern (BRC) Policy. 26 July.
[40] *Stibitz v General Pub. Util. Corp.*, 746 F 2d 993 and In re TMI Litig. Cases Consol. II, 940 F 2d 832 (3rd cir. 1991), 503 U.S. 906,112 S.Ct. 1262, 117 L.Ed.2d 491 (1992).
[41] *Blue Circle Industries plc v Ministry of Defence*, The Times 11 Dec 1996,[1997] Env.L.R.341, and C.A.[1999]Env.L.R. Part1, pp 22-61.
[42] *Merlin v British Nuclear Fuels* [1990]2 QB 557.

nature of the damage caused in the *Blue Circle* case was similar to that in a number
of the incidents involving users outlined above. Its main distinguishing feature is
that it was a claim against the licensed operator of a nuclear facility subject to strict
liability provisions. The claimant in an action against a user other than an operator
would be constrained to follow an action in negligence, to show that the user owed
a duty of care, that he had breached that duty and the damage caused was a direct
result of the breach.

In the US even in the event of an incident at a licensed facility, other than in the
event of an extraordinary nuclear occurrence[43] the claimant, either as an employee
of the operator or of a user, would be constrained to resort to an action in
negligence.[44] [45] To prove fault the plaintiff would have to show that he had been
exposed to radiation outside the regulatory limit. The possibility of waiving the
requirement to prove negligence in the absence of an extraordinary nuclear
occurrence was denied in the case of *O'Connor*[46] where the employee claimed that
the defendant was strictly liable for radiation injury caused by radiation exposure
in the course of his employment. The District Court ruled that the *Price-Anderson
Act* waives the requirement to prove negligence only in the case of an
'extraordinary nuclear incident'. Such an event involves the discharge of nuclear
material off site or causes radiation levels off site resulting in substantial damage to
persons or property off site.

In the UK in the event of any activity on the licensed site which leads to an
exposure to radiation above regulatory limits the operator would be strictly liable
and the plaintiff, either an employee of the operator or a user, would not be
required to show proof of fault. There is no apparent restriction in the UK *Nuclear
Installations Act* on the cause of the exposure to radiation such as provided by the
definition of an extraordinary nuclear occurrence in US law. The meaning of the
term 'occurrence' in the *Nuclear Installations Act* has not been examined in the
UK courts as litigation has been avoided since radiation workers on nuclear
installations in the UK in the employment of the operator benefit from an
agreement between their trade unions and the major nuclear operators to a
compensation scheme for radiation linked diseases.[47] The scheme pioneered by
BNFL has met with considerable success by using a formula which:

---

[43] An 'extraordinary nuclear occurrence' is defined at 42 U.S.C. para 2014(j) to mean 'any
nuclear event causing a discharge or disbursal of source, special nuclear, or by-product
material from its intended place of confinement in amounts off site, or causing radiation
levels off site, which the Nuclear Regulatory Commission or Secretary of Energy, as
appropriate, determines has resulted or will probably result in substantial damages to
persons or property off site'.
[44] Supra Gooden.
[45] Sarno, Gregory, G. J.D., Tort Liability for Nonmedical Radiological Harm, 73ALR 4th
582.
[46] *O'Connor v Commonwealth Edison Company*, 748 F. Supp. 672 (C.D. Ill 1990).
[47] Leigh, Dr. W. J. (1997), 'Liability and Regulation - Some Legal Challenges Faced by the
Operators of United Kingdom Nuclear Installations'. *[1997] Env. Liability 44.*

utilises published risk factors from epidemiological studies to which negotiated generosity factors have been applied, whereby the probability of occupational radiation exposure having caused a particular cancer in a particular individual can be determined by reference to agreed technical criteria, rather than by means of litigation.

It is reported that since its introduction in 1982 over 650 cases have been dealt with under the scheme. Around 73 cases have been awarded a payment and in total about £3.25 million has been paid in compensation. None of the cases, which have been determined as not qualifying for a payment, have subsequently been pursued at law.[48]

Off-site damage caused by radioactive waste from a licensed site has been tested in the Scottish Court of Session where 'hot particles', particles accepted by UKAEA as being 'nuclear matter' and 'radioactive waste' from Dounreay licensed site, have been found on the Sandside Beach since 1984, totalling 38 at the time of writing. The radioactivity level of the particles are 300,000 Bq, where a level of 400,000 Bq has no observable affect on human health, and the probability of bait diggers, the most frequent users of the beach, coming into contact with a particle is 1 in 200,000. SEPA view was that the risks to the public encountering particles are sufficiently low and insignificant that no action other than continued monitoring was warranted.[49] Nevertheless the *Food Protection (Emergency Prohibitions) (Dounreay Nuclear Establishment) Order 1977*[50] imposed a ban on fishing within two kilometres radius from the Dounreay site outlet pipe. Although, as reported in the House of Lords[51] no fragments of irradiated nuclear fuel had been found in any fish or shellfish during aquatic monitoring by SEPA, fixed nets were removed from the foreshore of the Sandside estate.

In the Outer House, Court of Session, *Margohand Limited and others* petitioned for judicial review. They claimed that their land had been materially damaged by the particles and that three of the petitioners had suffered injury, stress and anxiety by the continuing uncertainty caused by the presence of the particles. They sought specific performance of a statutory duty imposed on UKAEA by s7 of *NEA65*; a declarator that the UKAEA were in breach of their duty under s7 of the *NIA65*; and for the UKAEA to restore the beach to a clean, pristine condition. In future they may seek specific performance of a statutory duty imposed by the human rights legislation and presented petition for judicial review under s45(b) of the *Court of Session Act 1988*.

In the Opinion of Lady Paton in *Margohand*, the arrival of a particle at Sandside Beach was considered to be an 'occurrence' within s7(2)(c) of *NIA65* and the remaining of a particle on the beach was also an 'occurrence', but she was not persuaded that a breach of s7 had caused injury to any person. She said:

[149] In the present petition, there are no averments of physical injury suffered by anyone. In relation to the petitioners' averments about stress and anxiety, it is a well-

[48] ibid p 45.
[49] *Margohand Limited and others v UKAEA and SEPA* (Outer Court House, Court of Session) 15 August 2003, paras 26 to 28.
[50] S.I.1997 No. 2622.
[51] 24 November 1997.

established principle in the law of damages for personal injuries that damages are awarded *ex delicto* only where a pursuer is able to prove that he has, or had, an identifiable psychiatric or possibly psychological illness or condition caused by the wrongful act: cf. Lord Bridge of Harwich in *McLoughlin* v *O'Brian* [1983] 1 A.C. 410, at page 431H; Lord Ackner in *Alcock* v *Chief Constable of South Yorkshire Police* [1992] 1 A.C. 310 at page 401C; Lord Goff of Chievely in *White* v *Chief Constable of South Yorkshire Police* [1999] 2 A.C. 455; Lord Reed in *Rorrison* v *West Lothian College*, 2000 S.C.L.R. 245, at page 254D-F. While a pursuer who has suffered physical injury is usually able to recover damages reflecting any related shock, stress, anxiety or upset, a claim in respect of damage to mental health alone, without any physical injury, is governed *inter alia* by the principle set out above. The courts' restriction of a stateable common law claim to one involving an identifiable psychiatric or psychological illness or condition is a reflection of policy considerations. As Lord Wilberforce observed in *McLoughlin* v *O'Brian* [1983] 1 A.C. 410:

'... at the margin, the boundaries of a man's responsibility for acts of negligence have to be fixed as a matter of policy ... there remains, in my opinion, just because "shock" in its nature is capable of affecting so wide a range of people, a real need for the law to place some limitation upon the extent of admissible claims'.

Similar observations were made by Lord Ackner and Lord Oliver of Aylmerton in *Alcock* v *Chief Constable of South Yorkshire Police* [1992] 2 A.C. 310, at pages 400E *et seq.*, and page 418C-D; and Lord Steyn and Lord Hoffmann in *White* v *Chief Constable of South Yorkshire Police* [1999] 2 A.C. 455, at pages 494C-G, 497B-C, and 511B.

[150] It seems to me that such policy considerations apply *a fortiori* in relation to the 1965 Act. Countless people may suffer stress and anxiety as a consequence of the operation of, or a breach of, the 1965 Act - particularly those living in the vicinity of nuclear installations. To adopt the words of Lord Wilberforce, there is 'a real need for the law to place some limitation upon the extent of admissible claims'. In the present case, the averments relating to stress and anxiety do not satisfy the policy-guided requirements for injury set down by the House of Lords in the field of injury to mental health.

However, relating to stress and anxiety there may be relevance in the context of human rights, for example in the extent and effect of interference with the petitioners' human rights.

In relation to damage Lady Paton was satisfied that Sandside Beach had suffered damage arising or resulting from the radioactive particles deposited on the beach and she was of the view that the food protection order had caused damage to fishing rights as fishing licences had to be terminated and fixed nets removed. However s7 does not entitle the petitioners to order for specific performance, it was observed that:

[162] Section 7 does not impose any clear statutory duty to monitor, or to attempt to cure or to clean up, any damage to or contamination of property caused by an occurrence involving nuclear matter. It is impossible in my view to 'read in' such a duty, far less to construe the section as imposing the detailed duties set out in Schedule A to the petition. If the petitioners' approach to section 7 were to be adopted, one could envisage a multiplicity of acts which members of the public might petition the court to direct the UKAEA to perform, all said to be implied in the general duty set out in section 7. But authorities such as *Carlton Hotel Co.* v *The Lord Advocate*, 1921 S.C.

237; *Annan* v *Leith Licensing Authority* (1901) 9 S.L.T. 63; *T. Docherty Ltd.* v *Monifieth Town Council,* 1970 S.C. 200, and *Davidson* v *Scottish Ministers,* 2002 S.C. 205, have repeatedly emphasised that it is appropriate for a court to order specific performance of a statutory duty only where a duty is clearly set out in the statute. Even the case of *Walker* v *Strathclyde Regional Council,* 1986 S.C. 1, cited by counsel for the petitioners, does not go so far as the petitioners might wish. In that case, the petitioners sought an order compelling the education authority to comply with their duty under section 1 of the Education (Scotland) Act 1980 in respect of adequate and efficient provision of school education for the petitioners' children. The court was not asked to grant an detailed order ordaining the authority precisely how to fulfil that duty, and it is far from clear that the Lord Ordinary would have agreed to grant such an order. The court merely repelled the respondents' plea to competency, declined to determine the application, and ordered a second hearing.

[163] I am not therefore persuaded that an order for specific performance in the terms sought by the petitioners should be granted.

A declarator was granted to the effect that UKAEA have failed, and continue to fail, to perform their statutory duty under s7 of *NIA65* to secure that no occurrence involving nuclear matter causes damage to any property other than the UKAEA. Since the hearing SEPA appears to have inserted conditions in the relevant *RSA 93* authorisations it granted to the UKAEA so as to require the UKAEA to monitor the beach and remove any radioactive particles found.

Compensation for Injury[52]

The study of the effect of radiation on man and animals under varying conditions has led to an understanding of the effects at high radiation dose levels and allows predictions of the effect of low radiation levels. Studies have been made of the consequences of the atom bombs at Hiroshima and Nagasaki; evidence is available from observations of the use of radiation therapy in medicine and medical treatment; the effects on early research workers are known;[53][54] studies have been made of the health of workers in nuclear facilities and the effects have been seen on workers and firemen after the Chernobyl accident. The validity of estimation of the effects on man of low level radiation by extrapolation from the death rate caused by high radiation levels is a source of some debate. It is argued that precaution[55] dictates that any increase above the natural background must be avoided because of unknown factors; the occurrence of leukaemia clusters is seen by some to be an indicator of these unknown factors,[56][57] however, research by

[52] Riley, Peter, 'Radiation risk in the context of liability for injury', *Journal of Radiological Protection*, Vol.23, Issue 3, Sept. 2003, pp 305-315.
[53] Bertell Rosalie (1985), *No Immediate Danger*. The Woman's Press, p 50.
[54] Beral, V. et al (1985), 'Mortality of Employees of the United Kingdom Atomic Energy Authority 1946-1979' Brit. Med. J. 291 (6493), pp 440-447.
[55] Riley, Peter (2000), 'The precautionary principle and its practice', *Engineering Management Journal*, Vol.10 No.6, Dec.
[56] The Evidence of A. Stewart to the EDRP Inquiry at Thurso, 1986.
[57] European Committee on Radiation Risk (2003), *2003 Recommendations of the ECRR. Health Effects of Ionising Radiation Exposure at Low Doses and Low Dose Rates for*

Prof. Leo Kinlen confirms that population mixing is likely to be responsible.[58] On the other hand it is thought that the rate at which the dose is administered may affect the carcinogenic risk[59] and that these linear extrapolations of the effect of high doses may lead to undue pessimism about the effects of low doses. The present assumption regarding delayed effects of radiation and the development of cancer is that there is no lower threshold below which harm will not occur.[60] [61] There may always be a risk from radiation in the environment but this risk is very difficult to quantify and would involve a study incurring several million person-years to expect any hope of a significant result.[62] The policy of dose limitation practised internationally is to assume a linear relationship until the alternative theory is proved or rejected by continued observation of the effects of low doses. Concern about radiation and cancer must be considered against a background of cancer as the cause of one in five of all deaths.

Progress has been made to determine scientifically the probability that specific cancers are caused by exposure to radiation. Tables have been produced showing relationships between various forms of cancer and levels of radiation exposure.[63] However, before these tables can be used confidently, uncertainties must be resolved concerning the sorts of cancer, cell types, source tables of cancer in the population, minimal latent periods, dose response function, influence of age at the time of exposure, sex, dosimetry, coefficients describing the dependence of risk on dose, dose rate, time response models and interaction with other carcinogens. From the study of animal populations radiation, as well as having late effects, is known to have hereditary effects. The estimates of possible hereditary effects on man are based on extrapolations from results in other species, in particular mice, even though no unequivocal evidence of similar effects in humans is evident at any dose level. However, radiation of the foetus in pregnant women is known to cause leukaemia in the child[64] and the practice of X-ray examination of pregnant women has ceased.[65]

The question of psychological damage or nervous shock from the fear of the consequence of a release of radiation from, for example, low level radioactive waste must also be considered. This type of damage in the context of radiation has been termed nuclear phobia which is a recognised clinical condition characterised

---

Radiation Protection Purposes, Green Audit, Avenue de La Fanconnerie 73, B-1170, Brussels.

[58] British Journal of Cancer Vol. 81, issue 1, Sept. 1999.

[59] Barry, S.F. 'Person years at risk in radiation epidemiology'. *Radiation Protection Bulletin* No 81. NRPB.

[60] Pochin, Sir Edward E. (1986), 'The Evolution of Radiation Protection Criteria'. *Nucl.Energy* 25 NO. 1, Feb., pp 19-27.

[61] Pochin, 'The 1984 Sievert Lecture, Sieverts and Safety'. *Health Physics*, vol. 46.

[62] United Nations (1985), *Radiation, Doses, Effects, Risks.* United Nations Environment Programme, p 57.

[63] Op. cit. Beral, V.

[64] Stewart A, et al (1956), 'Malignant Diseases in Childhood and Diagnostic Irradiation in Utero' *Lancet*, (ii) 447.g.

[65] Sir Frank Layfield, Sizewell B. Inquiry, Ch. 11, Para. 73-76.

by severe anxiety in relation to nuclear stimuli.[66] In the case of Chernobyl, according to Professor V. Knizhnikof of the Soviet Health Ministry's national commission on radiological defence,[67] a new form of 'radiation phobia' has developed since the explosion. This is described as '...a fear which is first and foremost the result of lack of objective information and poor training of doctors in radiation medicine'. He is reported as having said:

> But this has meant that, in some places, women had dangerous abortions late on in their pregnancy. Parents were afraid of giving their children milk, believing it was contaminated, as a result of which cases of rickets among children have been registered.

It is clear from this brief summary that the man in the street believes that all radiation is dangerous and that even the fear of radiation may cause harm.

Compensation   There is no European Community regime or system for compensation of workers in the case of damage caused by exposure to ionising radiation; the European Commission view is that it is governed by national legislation.[68]   In the UK industrial injuries benefits are payable to a worker under the *Social Security (Consequential Provisions) Act 1992*.   In the US a worker would claim under workers compensation legislation when he contracts a disease as the result of ionising radiations in the course of employment. The claimant in the UK must satisfy the insurance officer or, on appeal, a medical board, that he is suffering from a prescribed disease, i.e., inflammation, ulceration, or malignant disease of the skin or subcutaneous tissues or of the bones, or blood dyscresia, or cataract due to electromagnetic radiations (other than radiant heat) or to ionising particles.[69]   There is a presumption that the disease is caused by the nature of the relevant employment which is rebutted if the insurance officer, or on appeal a tribunal, is satisfied in the light of evidence advanced that on the balance of probabilities the disease was not so caused.

Psychological Damage Claims for psychological damage alleged to be caused by an occurrence involving nuclear matter or ionising radiations emitted on or from a nuclear licensed site might be made under *NIA 65*,[70] and such damage could be considered as injury for the purposes of the Act. Death or disablement caused by experiencing fear for his own safety, for example by suffering a heart attack or mental breakdown, is compensable according to *Dulieu v White*;[71] nervous shock to a mother of a victim of an accident who was two miles away and learned of the

---

[66] Brown, J., Henderson. J. and Fielding, J. (1983), *Differing Perspectives on Nuclear Related Risks. Department of Psychology,* University of Surrey.

[67] Walker, Christopher (1987), *Russia comes clean on extent of Chernobyl panic*, The Times, Jun. London.

[68] OECD–NEA (2000), 'Compensation regimes applicable to radiation workers in OECD countries'. *Nuclear Law Bulletin* 66/December, OECD.

[69] National Insurance (Industrial Diseases) (Prescribed Diseases) Regulations 1980: SI 1980, No. 377, item 25 of Part 1, sch. 1.

[70] *NIA 65 s7.*

[71] [1901] 2 KB 669.

death in the hospital was not too remote to be owed a duty by the defendant, *McLoughlin v O'Brien*;[72] compensation may be obtained where shock is experienced directly by the plaintiff's own senses from fear for the safety of another. In *Hambrook v Stokes*[73] the shock was experienced from fear for the safety of a child relative; in *Dooley v Cammell Laird & Co.*[74] it was a workmate. In *Attia v British Gas plc*,[75] the Court of Appeal decided that a plaintiff who suffered psychiatric illness from witnessing the destruction of her home could claim damages notwithstanding the absence of any physical injury. In the case of a nuclear incident at a nuclear installation which endangered an individual or someone close to him so that he experienced the harm with his own senses and as a consequence he suffered nervous shock that individual would be entitled to damages for that nervous shock and the operator would be strictly liable under the *NIA 65*. Therefore, compensation may be claimed for psychological damage. Nuclear phobia may be considered as psychological damage, however, it could be considered as distress or fear and as a matter of policy not compensable,[76] [77] [78] however, human rights legislation may offer alternative analysis. Some help may be obtained in understanding the court's attitude to the consequences of the fear of nuclear energy by reference to the US cases *Metropolitan Edison v People against Nuclear Energy et al.*[79] The US Supreme Court reversed a ruling of the Court of Appeals for the District of Columbia that the Nuclear Regulatory Commission (NRC) was required to consider whether the risk of an accident after the restart of the Three Mile Island nuclear plant might cause harm to the psychological health and community well being of the residents of the area.[80] The court reasoned the risk of an accident was not an effect on the physical environment, and the causal chain from renewed operation of TMI-1 to psychological health damage was too attenuated. The question of psychological damage caused by the risk of accident was avoided and that it might be caused by normal operation was considered too remote. The implication is that in the USA nuclear phobia would not be considered as damage arising from a nuclear accident.

Establishing Cause

Compensation for personal injury would be due only where it could be shown that the injury was caused by radiation resulting from the incident for which the defendant was liable. Where the radiation dose experienced by the individual was low or where the alleged injury is not one recognised as resulting from radiation

---

[72] [1983] 1 AC 410.
[73] [1925] 1 KB 141.
[74] [1951] Lloyd's Rep. 271.
[75] [1987] 3 All E.R. 455
[76] Winfield & Jolowicz on Tort. 16th ed., p 90, Sweet & Maxwell.
[77] Trindale, F.A. (1986), 'The Principles Governing the Recovery of Damages for Negligently Caused Nervous Shock', *Cambridge Law Journal*, 45(3). November, pp 498-500.
[78] See also the judgement of Lady Paton in *Margohand* note 49 above.
[79] U.S.C. 75L Ed 2d 535.
[80] Nuclear Law Bulletin. 32 NLB 19.

exposure there should be no right to compensation. However, it is for the court to decide and case law in the UK and the US demonstrates the inconsistency with scientific understanding of such decisions.[81] The social security laws provide a presumption that a prescribed disease is caused by radiation unless the insurance officer or tribunal is satisfied otherwise. Those laws have also been applied in the context of inquests. In an article in *The Lancet*, details are given of six inquests into deaths from cancer of workers at Sellafield.[82] The coroner explained to the juries that 'industrial disease' meant a 'prescribed disease' under the *Social Security Act 1975*. He explained that if the disease was not one prescribed, a verdict of death by industrial disease was not available; if the exposure caused a cancer that was not prescribed, an open verdict would be appropriate; if it did not then death was by natural causes. An open verdict in such cases suggests that the jury did not accept the medical/scientific evidence that the deceased's cancer was or was not caused by radiation. The juries brought in two verdicts of death caused by an industrial disease, three open verdicts and one of natural causes.[83] The one verdict of natural causes was given where the evidence was that there was no known connection of radiation with the disease. The coroner's explanation is not now good law; Halsbury's[84] states that in the case of death from an industrial disease it is not necessary that the disease be prescribed in any legislation but there must be evidence that the deceased had been engaged in employment where he had been exposed to the agent concerned and that this had led to the disease causing death, or had contributed to it. In the case of *R v HM Coroner for South Glamorgan, ex p BP Chemicals Ltd*[85] it was ruled that a verdict of 'industrial disease' is acceptable where there is evidence to support it. Therefore, for example, if a radiation worker develops a fatal cancer which is not prescribed under the social security legislation but which is found by the coroner to have been induced by exposure to occupational radiation, then a verdict that he died from the industrial disease of (name of cancer) would be appropriate.

Where a person suffers radiation injury from a licensed site the licensee is liable for compensation without the claimant having to show negligence. It is understandable therefore that the level of radiation that might cause damage will be strongly contested. In determining cause, however, jury verdicts are notoriously inconsistent. In September 1987 a verdict of death from an industrial disease caused by radiation was returned by a coroner's jury at an inquest at Whitehaven, Cumbria, on a Mr. John Adair aged 67 who had contacted myeloid leukaemia from radioactive contamination received while working at the Sellafield plant of BNFL. The decision was given in spite of evidence that the amount of radioactivity in the body was only five per cent of that which would accrue from normal background. However, the family of a Cornish tin worker failed to convince a jury that his death

---

[81] The examples that follow are taken from; Peter Riley, 'Radiation as the Cause of Personal Injury', Anglo-American Law Review, Vol. 18, No. 1 1989, pp 75-89.

[82] Brahams, Diana (1988), 'Occupational Cancer and Radiation', *The Lancet* pp 174-5, July.

[83] ibid, p 174.

[84] Halsbury's Laws of England (4th Edition) Vol.9 (2) at para. 930.

[85] 151 JP 799 Divisional Court (1987).

at 66 from lung cancer was the result of inhaling radon gas over a period of 20 years while working in the South Crofty tin mine at Camborne.

British Nuclear Fuels Limited (BNFL) has paid compensation after settlement following the procedures in a voluntary agreement between BNFL and the staff unions. In three reported cases[86] where settlement was made the radiation doses were in the region of the ICRP limit for radiation workers. In two of those cases, *Traughton* and *Pattison*,[87] there was evidence of radiation dose in excess of the ICRP limit and the cancer was of a type known to be caused by radiation; the liability was not questioned. In the third case, *King*;[88] the radiation dose was less than the ICRP limit, and liability was not admitted and there was divergence of expert opinion. Although details are not available it is understood that the use of the voluntary procedures has resulted in compensation in about ten percent of the cases processed. It should be noted that the compensation scheme does not apply to non-radiation workers or to members of the public. Background to the Radiation Worker Scheme operated by BNFL may be obtained from two articles in the Health Physics Journal.[89] [90]

In cases where juries are not involved the outcome has been consistent with scientific understanding. The question of cancer death and exposure to radiation came before Mr. Justice Macpherson at Liverpool in July 1987 and was abandoned after cross-examination of the evidence.[91] The claim that Hodgkin's disease had been caused by radiation while at work at Sellafield was refuted by medical opinion that there was no case where the disease had ever been caused by radiation. In the second case a worker at Dounreay had received 0.19 Sv over seven years. The plaintiff's experts, including Dr. Alice Stewart and Professor E. Radford, rated the likelihood of radiation as the cause at 30-50 per cent; the defendants' experts rated it at 3-6 per cent. Two cases[92] followed the epidemiological study, 'the Gardner Report', published in 1990, that found strong statistical association between paternal irradiation and an excess of childhood leukaemia and non-Hodgkin's lymphoma (NHL) occurring in the village of Seascale near to BNFL's Sellafield plant. After hearing evidence in an eight month trial the judge held that the statistical associations were not causal; the causal relationship was not plausible.

In the US compensation to individuals affected by radiation from military activity is further advanced than is the case in the UK. *The Radiation Exposure*

---

[86] Nuclear Law Bulletin 25, NLB 30.

[87] ibid. pp 30-31.

[88] ibid. p 30.

[89] Leigh, Dr W. J. and Wakeford, Dr Richard (2001), 'Radiation Litigation and the Nuclear Industry – the Experience in the United Kingdom', *Health Physics* 81 (6), pp 645-646.

[90] Wakeford, Antell, Leigh (1998), 'Review of Probability of Causation and its use in a Compensation Scheme for Nuclear Industry Workers in the United Kingdom', *Health Physics* 74 (1), pp 1-9.

[91] Hainan, Keith E. (1988), 'Failure to Substantiate Two Cases of Alleged Occupational Radiation Carcinogenesis', *The Lancet*, Mar. 19, p 639.

[92] *Reay v BNFL and Hope v BNFL.* [1994] Env. L.R. 320.

Compensation Act (2000) (RECA 2000)[93] provides for payment of compensation to individuals who contracted certain diseases due to unintended exposure to radiation resulting from the US nuclear weapons testing programme. Indemnification is to be paid on the following bases:[94]

> USD 50,000 to an individual who was physically present in an affected area for a period of at least one year between 21 January 1951 and 31 October 1958 or for the month of July 1962 and contracted one of the specified cancers;

> USD 75,000 to an individual who participated onsite in a test involving the atmospheric detonation of a nuclear device and developed leukaemia; and

> USD 100,000 to an employee of a uranium mine or mill in a designated State between 1942 and 1971 who was exposed to a defined dose of radiation and developed lung cancer or another respiratory disease associated with radiation.

Nevertheless, the repeal of the *Crown Proceedings Act* in 1987 opened the gates for claims by UK servicemen; 15 generic cases from over 2,000 claimants are yet to be heard.[95]

In the US the *Price Anderson Act* provides a mechanism for compensating persons who are injured from a nuclear accident. According to Donald E. Jose[96] such accidents are rare and almost all the case law relates to simple occupational exposure. Experience shows that unusual radiological events coupled with the natural incidence of cancer cause lawsuits. The natural incidence of cancer in an ageing population near a nuclear plant, unexpected exposure causing emotional distress and any cancer in a person who worked at or lived near a nuclear plant can result in a lawsuit.

In a paper delivered to the OECD - NEA Symposium on nuclear liability in September 1984,[97] N.G. Schaffer cites four cases where he alleges the courts have distorted fact, science and well established precedent to award compensation. The fourth case considered by Schaffer is *Irene H. Allen et al v the USA*[98] which involves over one thousand claimants who were exposed to varying amounts of radiation downstream of the Nevada atom bomb test site during atmospheric nuclear weapon tests. The court recognized that direct proof of causation was impossible and set down the following rule:[99]

> Where a defendant who negligently creates a radiation hazard which puts an identifiable population group at increased risk, and a member of that group develops a biological condition which is consistent with having been caused by the hazard to which he has been negligently subjected, such consistency having been demonstrated by substantial

---

[93] Amended by the *Public Law No. 106-245*, approved by the President on 10 July 2000.

[94] Nuclear Law Bulletin 67 Volume 2000/1.

[95] Liability and Risk Insurance, issue 141, April 2002, Informa UK Ltd.

[96] Jose, Donald E. (2001), *Recent Litigation Involving Exposure to Radiation*, Nuclear Inter Jura 2001, Jun. Budapest.

[97] Shatter, W.G. (1985), *Claims for Injuries from occupational radiation exposures in the US: recent developments*, OECD Paris, pp 262-276.

[98] Civil Action No. C79-0515.588 F Supp 247105 84.

[99] Op. cit., Shaffer, p 273.

appropriate, persuasive and connecting factors, a fact finder may reasonably conclude that the hazard caused the condition absent persuasive proof to the contrary offered by the defendant.

Schaffer argues that the court has thereby eliminated the requirement of proving causation in fact and has substituted the requirement of demonstrating a 'consistency' between the risk created by the defendant's conduct and the injury suffered by the plaintiff. The burden of proof is thus shifted to the defendant who is required to rebut the inference of causation. This would appear to contradict the *Price Anderson Act* that requires that the claimant demonstrate that the injury resulted from the accident in question. The decision in Allen is consistent with that in *Summers v Tice*[100] where the plaintiff suffered injury from a gunshot by one of two hunters, both having fired negligently in his direction. The court shifted the burden of proof on to each hunter to show he was not responsible for the plaintiff's single injury. The principle was extended to a claim against nine defendants in *Sindell v Abbott Laboratories*[101] where the plaintiff, a cancer victim, had ingested DES when pregnant but was unable to present evidence linking her injury to a particular drug manufacturer. Each manufacturer was sued and the court upheld the plaintiff's claim as an extension to *Summers*. Manufacturers unable to absolve themselves were held liable each in proportion to its share of the DES market. The Supreme Court of Canada in *Cook v Lewis*,[102] a case similar to *Summers*, expressed the view that the plaintiff could recover from both hunters in such a case.

For a short interlude it appeared that, following *McGhee v National Coal Board*,[103] the law in England was moving towards the position in the USA, leaving the defendant to rebut the inference of causation. The House of Lords in *Wilsher v Essex Area Health Authority*[104] however, reasserted that both policy and principle required that the plaintiff should, in most cases, continue to shoulder the burden of proof and suffer the consequences of evidential gaps.[105] The recent decision of the House of Lords in *Fairchild v Glenhaven Funeral Services and others and conjoined appeals*[106] has again brought the UK courts closer to the US position and has significance in radiation related cases where there is more than one possible cause of damage.[107] *Fairchild* was a case of mesothelioma where the initial cause may be a single unidentifiable fibre of asbestos inhaled at any stage in the overall exposure and is not necessarily related to the totality of the exposure. The House of Lords ruled that claimants who have worked for a variety of employers in circumstances where on each occasion they were exposed to asbestos fibres do not

---

[100] 33 Cal 2d 80,199 P 2d 1 (1948).
[101] 449 US 912 (1980).
[102] [1952] 1 DLR 1.
[103] [1973] 1 WLR 1.
[104] [1988] IAIIER 872.
[105] Boon, Andrew (1988), 'Causation and the Increase of Risk', 51 MLR 508.
[106] [2002] UKHL 22, [2003] 1 A.C. 32.
[107] Morgan, Jonathan (2003), *Lost Causes in the House of Lords*: Fairchild v Glenhaven *Funeral Services*. March, 66 M.L.R. 2, pp 277-284.

need to be able to prove which employer was responsible for them having contracted mesothelioma before they can claim compensation.

The Way Ahead

Although much argument will be removed from the US courts by the *RECA 2000* arrangements, the situation is still open in the UK. In both UK and US legal regimes allegations of damage caused by radiation in non-military circumstances will continue to be strongly contested. The 'man in the street' test of causation is a pillar of jurisprudence and according to Hart and Honore[108] it is the plain man's notion of causation, not the philosopher's or the scientist's, with which the law is concerned. This follows Lord Wright in *Yorkshire Dale Steamship Co. Ltd v Minister of War Transport*, where he said,[109] 'Causation is to be understood as the man in the street; and not as either the scientist or the metaphysician would understand it'.

The media influences the views of the man in the street; radiation for many reasons evokes a feeling of dread and is difficult to understand without technical knowledge. This would lead to the conclusion that a claimant suffering injury of a type known to be caused by radiation who had received a radiation dose, no matter how small, which could be shown to come from a nuclear installation would be awarded damages against the licensee of the site of the installation unless it could be shown that the injury was predominantly caused by another source (radioactive or otherwise). It seems that since about a fifth of the population will suffer cancer and that a large proportion of those who have worked on licensed sites will have experienced some radiation exposure, a large number of potential claimants exist. However, the small number of valid non-military associated claims so far, demonstrates the soundness of the safety standards and the ALARA principle. It is essential that the legal systems reflect this by continuing to compensate only genuine cases of damage by radiation. A helpful analysis by Donald E. Jose may assist the court and may be summarised firstly by distinguishing general and specific causes of cancer.[110] The general cause is established by the fact that although high doses and dose rates cause cancer there is no epidemiological evidence to show that there is an excess of cancer in the workforce exposed to no more than the occupational limits. Where there is evidence of exposure to greater than the occupational limits it is necessary to show that the specific cancer, on the balance of probabilities, was caused by radiation exposure. In coming to a decision it is suggested that, *inter alia*, the court address the following points:

- that the diagnosis of cancer is valid;
- that the cancer is one of the type caused by radiation;

---

[108] Hart, H.LA. and Honore Tony (1985), *Causation in the Law*, p 1, 2nd ed., Clarendon Press.
[109] [1942] 1 QB 641.
[110] Supra Jose.

- that the latency period (the time between the specific exposure to radiation and appearance of the cancer) is consistent with the latency period of a radiation induced cancer;
- that the time of appearance of the cancer is inconsistent with those naturally occurring;
- that no other risk factors are present in the persons lifestyle;
- a need to determine the actual radiation dose experienced by the person; and
- a need to be satisfied that the radiation dose is not consistent with the risk of occurrence of that cancer.

To educate the man in the street to achieve a level of competency to implement such a decision-making process will require an enormous effort on the part of the radiological community. Clear facts and straightforward presentation will be necessary!

Some Problems in Implementing the Legal Control of Nuclear Energy in the UK

Throughout the previous chapters many problems have been identified or implied. The RWMAC report of 2001[111] identifies and addresses the most pressing problems and further work of RWMAC and NuSAC[112] have focused on some of them. It is beyond the scope of this work to fully identify those problems other than to outline them with references so that a deeper understanding may be pursued.

- The policy for the control and remediation of radioactively contaminated land was the subject of a Government consultation paper in 1984[113] where draft guidance on the management of contaminated land was promised but still awaited in mid 2003.
- The principle of segregating waste by half-lives[114] while being actively pursued in France and the US is the subject of procrastination in the UK.
- Policy on separated plutonium and uranium including whether some of these should be considered waste[115] is not limited to the UK but requires open decision-making.
- Regulatory body initiatives including agreements in relation to licensed sites.[116]
- Conditioning, packaging and storing ILW on an interim basis prior to a long-term management solution appears to be decided on an *ad hoc* basis.[117]

---

[111] RWMAC (2002), Twenty Second Annual Report of The Radioactive Waste Management Advisory Committee, October, HMSO London.

[112] Nuclear Safety Advisory Committee (NuSAC)/Radioactive Waste Management Advisory Committee (RWMAC) joint regulatory review (2003), Structures and principles of the regulation of the nuclear licensed sites, March, HSE, HMSO London.

[113] RWMAC 22nd Report paras. 2.5 and 6.10 to 6.15.

[114] ibid para. 2.12(ii).

[115] ibid para. 2.12(vi).

[116] ibid para. 3.1 to 3.7.

- Clarification of those issues not covered by the 'Managing Radioactive Waste Safely' consultation leaves areas of policy currently covered by Cm 2919 uncertain.[118]

- A fundamental review of the letter of comfort system between NIREX and the waste producers is required[119] together with the interim packaging arrangements for ILW.[120] These arrangements have been in place to allow sensible standard measures to be practised by waste producers in the hiatus created by the suspension of long term waste management activities following the Minister's intervention in 1997.[121]

- The relationship between the classification of exemption orders in relation to radiation as a result of the extraction of natural gas and the exposure to radiation that is so low to be not of regulatory concern in connection with the de-licensing of nuclear sites.[122] The current arrangements imply incorrectly that radiation emanating from decommissioned nuclear sites at levels below regulatory limits is of a different nature than radiation from the ground as part of an oil or mineral extraction activity.

- NuSAC/RWMAC conclusions[123] that nuclear safety and environmental regulations are working to essentially different sets of basic principles and standards, for example, in terms of risk management the relationship between the tolerability of risk, followed by the HSE, and the application of BPM/ALARA, followed by the EA.[124] In basic terms this contradiction is that the tolerability of risk is based on the fact that below a certain level of exposure to radiation the risk of harm is so low that further reductions in the release or exposure to radiation should not be pursued, whereas the application of BPM/ALARA will require continuing reductions leading inevitably to near zero exposure from controllable sources of radiation in a background of existing natural radiation. The ongoing debate about the release of Technetium −99 to the Irish Sea illustrated this dichotomy.[125] [126]

---

[117] ibid para. 4.1 to 4.6.

[118] ibid para. 4.7 to 4.14.

[119] ibid para. 4.15 to 4.20.

[120] ibid para. 4.21 to 4.23.

[121] Chapter Three, UK Government Policy.

[122] RWMAC 22nd Report Para. 6.5 to 6.9.

[123] Supra, Nuclear Advisory Committee.

[124] ibid Para. 59 p17.

[125] Food Standards Agency, Press release. 23 June 2003. The FSA response to a Greenpeace survey [www.greenpeace.org.uk − nuclear waste found in supermarket salmon 23 June 2003] where radioactive traces of Technetium in farmed salmon sold in leading supermarkets are at such a low level that a person would have to eat 700 portions a day for a year to reach the annual permitted EU radiation dose. [www.food.gov.uk/news/newsarchive/farmedsalmonsurvey]

[126] The HSE has nevertheless agreed on the modification of processes at Sellafield to satisfy the EA decision on future discharges to reduce them to near zero, by retaining Technetium-99 on site.

This last point gives credence to public anxiety about the control of radioactive releases and will continue to be an obstacle to public acceptance of any policy of radioactive waste management. The interpretation of the philosophies of the control of radiation is fraught with difficulties such as:

- the regulatory body's inspector may challenge detailed advice given by the individual operators;
- practical implementation means interpretation and as regulatory authorities are reluctant to give advice the interpretation of 'reasonably practicable' is different in different circumstances, the balance can be altered by public opinion; and
- for political reasons there is a tendency in the nuclear industry to take measures that result in radioactive releases to the environment, which are as low as technically achievable (ALATA). This may squander valuable resources.

In deciding whether the requirements of regulations or conditions in a licence have been properly carried out, an assessor must consider whether the design and implementation of a system of control has been carried out to ensure that the dose rates have not been exceeded. He must also consider whether the BPM/ALARA/ALARP principle has been properly applied. This would involve examination of the cost/benefit analysis that in turn would pose questions that are as yet unanswered, for example:

- What is the cost of a life probably lost in twenty years time?
- Is the value of a life in twenty years time to be based on today's values or on a discounted value?
- Is the availability and cost of medical treatment in twenty years' time to be taken to account and if so, what is it?
- What has to be sacrificed today to allow preventative measures and would this loss cause a greater harm?

A major problem in the operation of ALARA/ALARP in connection with the disposal of radioactive waste is the balance between the collective doses to the public when the waste is released to the environment against the collective dose to the workforce when the waste is retained on the site. Evidence currently available is that release to the environment at levels less than the authorised limits will not significantly add to the background radiation and will not cause harm to critical groups. Retention on the site may increase the worker dose and an incident, for example terrorist action, may expose the public to higher than background doses. This dilemma was presented to the operator at BNFL; his decision to release the waste even though it was within the authorised limit lead to BNFL being found to be in breach of a condition of their licence because the release was not ALARA.[127]

---

[127] Times 13 May 1991.

There are views that in addressing an ever-increasing number of diverse radiological problems the complexity of the system of radiation protection has resulted in incoherence. The OECD-NEA Committee on Radioactive Protection and Public Health (CRPPH)[128] has reviewed the current system and feels that clarification and improvement of the system can be achieved.[129] [130]

International Ingredients

Shepherding

Both the IAEA and OECD-NEA monitor nuclear activities around the world, for example in June 2003 the OECD-NEA published the 2003 Edition of Nuclear Energy Data that gives an overview of the status of and trends in nuclear electricity generation and the fuel cycle up to 2020 in OECD member countries. This shows that at the end of 2002, 362 nuclear units, representing 309 gigawatts electrical (GWe), were connected to the grid and seven units were in construction; the worldwide equivalent was 441 units, 359 GWe and 32 under construction. The total world operating experience to the end of 2002 was 10,696 years. The IAEA in an endeavour to assess the worldwide quantities of radioactive waste compiled a report in 2002, 'Radioactive Waste Management and Trends' that indicated that the Agency had implemented a system, the Net Enabled Waste Management Data Base (NENMDB). The database allows Member States to report their waste inventories according to the waste classification schemes used in their own countries. The NEWMDB, however, requires Member States to describe how their waste classification schemes compare with the common classification scheme proposed by the Agency. A comprehensive database is however a 'vain hope' because of the differences in nationally based information making a common information system difficult. Limited participation by Member States and the scope of the NEWHDB's data collection has hindered the collection process. The scope of data collection is complicated, for example, by interim storage of materials waiting processing and by the reality that spent fuel is not considered as waste in some Member States. Also, not stated by the Agency but suspected by the Author, some Member States do not wish to declare their detailed stocks of radioactive material, the example of DPRK proving this point.

Sovereignty

The threat of nuclear arms being held by a dissident regime and since 9/11 the implied threat of a dirty bomb from terrorists sources means that all states, to protect nuclear material adequately, need to consider the boundaries between the state and the international system; in particular the demands of sovereignty are also

---

[128] OECD-NEA (2002), *A Critical Review of the System of Radiation Protection*, OECD Paris.

[129] See also *Clarke, R.* (1999), 'Control of low level radiation exposure: time for a change?', *J Radiol Prot* vol. 19 No.2 pp 107-115.

[130] Pentreath R.J. (2003), 'A system for radiological protection of the environment: some initial thoughts and ideas', *J Radiol Prot* vol. 12 No.2 pp 117-128.

the legitimate demands of the international community. In regard to the physical protection of nuclear material, including radioactive waste, global adherence to the *Convention on the Physical Protection of Nuclear Material* is required; the Convention should be modified to reach more comprehensively into domestic state practice, law and regulation; and with respect to all international nuclear transactions and internal movement of nuclear materials all states should treat the recommendations of INFCIRC/225/Rev4, on the physical protection of nuclear facilities and materials, as binding obligations.

The nuclear Conventions are listed in chapter five, under 'International Law', and while the positive features of the five that deal with civil liability, Paris, Vienna, Brussels, Nuclear Ships and the Carriage of Nuclear Material, only Western European States that are parties to the Paris Convention accept international agreement on civil liability.[131] This means that with the exception of parties to the Paris Convention, in the event of an accident causing nuclear damage, claimants in most countries will be forced to resort to civil proceedings or invoke State responsibility.

The liability agreements have distinctive features that are a model for other areas of environmental interest:[132] a strict, not conditional or fault liability; the liability is channelled to the operator; no other subject can be liable; and a maximum amount of liability is expressly stipulated. This latter characteristic that is interpreted in national legislation may be considered to transfer the risk to governments or the damaged third parties for damages above the limit. The risk transfer may be regarded as a subsidy to the nuclear industry and thereby distort competition and for economic reasons to reduce the precautionary measures. In respect of nuclear waste management being allocated to private industry either the imposition of a government tax on the industry to represent the external cost of potential catastrophes or shifting the risk to the industry itself would remove both the subsidy and the suspicion that full precautionary measures are being avoided.

Radioactive Waste and Terrorist Threats

Apart from speculation about terrorist organisations and rogue nations obtaining nuclear weapons[133] there is a risk that radioactive waste may be the focus of terrorist action or it may be used in a so called 'dirty bomb'. Radioactive waste, stored, as indicated in chapter two, is a credible target for terrorist attack. In particular in the case of the storage of highly radioactive liquid waste the loss of containment represents a hazard with potential catastrophic consequences. Studies of such accidents, or deliberate destruction to the containment of liquid radioactive waste have been performed in the US,[134] in Germany[135] and in the UK.[136] The latter

---

[131] Birnie, P. and Boyle, A.E. (1992), *International Law and the Environment*, Clarendon Press, Oxford. pp 283 – 285.

[132] Radetzki, M. (1999), 'Limitation of Third Party Nuclear Liability: Causes, Implications and Future Possibilities', *Nuclear Law Bulletin* 63 June, OCED-NEA.

[133] Doyle, N. (2002), *Al Quaeda nukes are reality, intelligence says*, The Washington Times 28 October [www washtimes.com].

[134] Details of the Oak Ridge Studies were discussed at the Windscale Inquiry.

study concludes[137] that countermeasures would be necessary to avoid the high levels of health damage that would otherwise occur. The countermeasures would include sheltering indoors followed by evacuation and relocation, and food bans in contaminated areas. Clearly such actions would create panic and psychological damage to residents over a wide area. It is postulated that a radiological dispersal device (RDD)[138] a 'dirty bomb'[139] could be manufactured using radioactive materials combined with conventional explosives. Radioactive waste could be used such as that removed by looters from Iraq's largest nuclear facility[140] prior to the facility being secured by US troops on 7 April 2003. That waste included radiated sealed barrels and plastic bags containing uranium. As well as such material, more accessible sources, for example, radioactive materials used in hospitals and in domestic use such as smoke detectors might be used. While the radiation released in a dirty bomb explosion would be low and unlikely to cause immediate radiation damage and with a low probability of future damage the panic caused, and voluntary evacuation from the area by concerned individuals would be significant.

The Office for Nuclear Security in the UK concludes[141] that strict security precautions are being taken to protect nuclear material and radioactive materials on licensed and nuclear sites against terrorist attacks, however OCNS is not responsible for the security of radioactive material held outside licensed sites such as hospitals, research facilities and industry or when sources are being transported. Nevertheless, in October 2002, 103 Greenpeace demonstrators were able to gain access to Sizewell B and again in January 2003, 34 demonstrators were able to gain access. On both occasions some of them gained access to inner security areas. The Greenpeace action was not intended to cause damage to the plant, but to draw attention to lax security.

While on an international scale the IAEA Safeguard arrangements and activities in the security of nuclear materials, including measures to help States combat illicit trafficking[142] the unfolding scenes in Iraq, Iran and DPRK show that even when closely monitored, it is possible for States to practice nuclear activities or to go through the motions of having clandestine nuclear programmes. The International

---

[135] Bachmer et al (1976), Report No 290, Institut for Peaktorsicherheit, Koln.

[136] Taylor, P. *Consequence Analysis of a Catastrophic Failure of Highly Active Waste Tanks Serving the Thorpe and Magnox Nuclear Fuel Reprocessing Plants at Sellafield*, Nuclear Policy and Information Unit, Town Hall, Manchester, M60 2LA.

[137] ibid para. 505 p 18.

[138] Ferguson, Charles, C. (2003), 'Reducing the Threats of RDDs', *IAEA Bulletin*, Vol. 45, No. 1, June, IAEA, Vienna.

[139] Supra Doyle.

[140] The Olympian Washington (2003), Iraq clinics suspect radiation exposure, 22 July 2003.

[141] A Report to the Security of State for Trade and Industry by the Director of Civil Nuclear Security (2003), *The State of Security in the Civil Nuclear Industry and Effectiveness of Security Regulation*. Apr. 2002 – Mar. 2003. Office for Civil Nuclear Security, DTI.

[142] IAEA (2001), *Nuclear Security and Safeguards*, IAEA Bulletin Vol. 43, No. 4, Vienna, Austria.

Nuclear Law Association concludes[143] that the current legal measures are insufficient in the context of the large number of power reactors, 651 research reactors and 250 factories involved in the fuel cycle, as well as the tens of thousands of radioactive sources in circulation around the world. Nuclear export contracts could be reinforced by the improvement in the efficiency of customs controls; suspect operators could be subject to financial investigation and the transporting of commercial operations could be improved. The principle of precaution indicates the need for special protective measures; effective systems must be implemented to protect nuclear material and installations from theft, sabotage and other uncontrolled events.

Assessment of Risks Associated with Radioactive Waste

In the context of the risk of damage from nuclear waste whether by deliberate discharge from nuclear activities, by the leaching of radioactive materials from storage or by the deliberate spreading of radioactive materials by terrorist activities, it is the long-term effects that are of public concern. Radiation releases sufficiently high to cause deterministic effects have a low probability in the context of radioactive waste and so it is the stochastic damage to the cell by low level radiation causing cancer many years later than the exposure that draws attention.

All predictions of damage by low level radiation use the thin spread of radiation over large populations to predict large numbers of 'late effects' in the form of death from cancer. Low dose studies are considered to be those in which the majority of subjects have doses less than 50 mSv. Etymological studies[144] are performed to determine whether a statistical association exists between exposure and disease; to quantify any such association; to assess the potential causality of any observed association and to demonstrate the lack of a measurable association between exposure and disease. There are generally three types of study that involve low doses: those of the general population exposed to radiation, e.g. studies of high background areas; studies of individuals exposed for medical reasons, where high doses may be given to a specific organ and lead, consequently, to low doses to other organs; and of workers in the nuclear industry. In general, low dose studies possess both strengths and limitations. The strengths include: as the studies are conducted in humans they do not require extrapolation; the exposure circumstances are generally close to those of public health interest; and since the studies come from direct monitoring the quality of dose estimation in occupational studies is generally high. However there are limitations that include: because they are low-dose studies they have low power to measure radiation effects; because of the low-doses and low risks the studies are prone to the effect of confounding; data on potential confounders are often lacking; many of the workers' studies depend on mortality, which is generally adequate for diseases with a high mortality rate but is

---

[143] Report from Working Group 3 (2003), *The Risk of Terrorism in International Trade*, Nuclear Inter Jura 2003, Apr., Cape Town. Para 222 p 21.

[144] The following paragraphs are extracted from; Howe, G, Epidemiology: strengths, limitations and interpretation application to studies of low-dose radiation. 4th International Conference on Health Effects of Low level Radiation, Oxford, Sept. 2002.

much less satisfactory for other diseases; and although dosimetry may be good, there are still problems of measurement error.

Following from the radiation epidemiological studies the nuclear industry has compared risks from radiation sources by the use of 'collective dose', the radiation dose a group of people receive from a source over a period of time. However, the use of collective dose techniques is open to misinterpretation since there are considerable uncertainties in its calculation and application and it is not considered reliable in predicting the actual effect of the dose on health.

Protection of the Environment

The ICRP has stated[145] that it believes that '... if man is adequately protected then other living things are also likely to be protected'. In later recommendations[146] this has been qualified by '... individual members of non-human species might be harmed but not to the extent of endangering whole species or creating imbalance between species'. In response to criticism of this position, not least what is meant by environmental protection, the ICRP has set up a task group on the subject, the IAEA is developing guidance,[147] the OECD-NEA held a forum in Sicily in February 2002[148] and the EU has funded R&D programmes.[149]

Centralised Waste Disposal

A central repository for radioactive waste would have an advantage of scale and running costs. This may be inferred from the information about investigations of waste containment methods and practicalities described in chapter two. Geological investigations, in particular, could be co-ordinated to select a best environmental option for a group of states. The widespread of waste storage sites could lead to greater exposure to the risk of terrorist action, however this might be countered by the risk due to the greater vulnerability of transport from the originating sources of waste to the central location. A practicable institutional framework has been prepared for a multinational waste disposal system,[150] which with the imminent enlargement of the EU could be a basis for further investigation.

Sustainable Development

A sustainable solution to the question of nuclear waste requires that at each stage the nuclear processes are safe, economic and do not leave unresolved problems for

---

[145] ICRP Publication 26, 1977.

[146] ICRP Publication 60, 1991.

[147] IAEA (2002), *Ethical considerations in protecting the environment from the effects of ionising radiation*, IAEA TECHDOC-1270, IAEA, Vienna.

[148] OECD-NEA (2003), *Radiological protection of the environment. Summary Report of the Issues*, OECD Paris.

[149] Strand, P. and Larsson, C. M. (2001), *Delivering a framework for the protection of the environment from ionising radiation, Radioactive Pollutants, Impact on the Environment*, (Brechignac and Howard eds), EDP Sciences, Les Ulis, France.

[150] Bredell, P. J. (2003), *The Institutional Framework for Establishing a Multinational Radioactive Waste Disposal System*, Nuclear Inter Jura, Apr. Cape Town.

the future. A number of outstanding issues have been identified in earlier chapters and may be considered under the heads considered in the first chapter: technological, practical, institutional and social.

Technological

The term radioactive material includes both useful materials and waste and where the question of re-usability of radioactive waste does not occur that is an adequate classification. Used fuel can be reprocessed to extract useful materials in which case it is useful material or it may be stored pending final disposal in which case it is waste. New, unused, nuclear fuel is not highly radioactive comprising mostly natural uranium with a small amount of enrichment by uranium or plutonium, the enriching material being evenly distributed through the fuel element, the mixing providing both shielding and physical security i.e. it would be difficult and expensive for a 'would be' thief to extract the enriching material to make a weapon. Care must be taken in storing new fuel to avoid accumulating a critical mass that would cause heating and release radiation. For a user of nuclear fuel sustainable solutions are: prior to use to store avoiding a critical mass; to use in the nuclear system and then to unload, store and dispose. This is termed a once through process. In the case of Finland, described in chapter two, the once through process is nearing a complete solution. Other sources of radioactive or radioactive contaminated such as isotopes used in industrial medical applications, or materials used in research or in handling the used, irradiated nuclear fuel, may be treated as low/intermediate level waste and stored/disposed of accordingly.

In the UK, France and US, and countries involved in making nuclear weapons, high level waste from the development and weapons programmes exist that must be treated to render it stable and suitable for future use, storage or disposal. In France and the UK the fuel cycle is closed, i.e. after use the irradiated fuel is reprocessed to take out useable materials to make new fuel. The process of making new fuel may introduce materials from other sources; in particular plutonium from the weapons programme is introduced into new fuel to provide the enrichment. A significant stockpile of separated civil plutonium is stored in the UK (54 tonnes).[151] The option is available in the UK to use mixed oxide fuel (MOX), fuel enriched with uranium and plutonium, and burn the plutonium or to store against future use or to dispose of the plutonium as high level waste.[152] In reprocessing used nuclear fuel, radioactive materials are separated from the usable uranium and plutonium that have no further use and are initially stored as high and intermediate level liquid radioactive waste. Storage in liquid form is not satisfactory as a long-term solution as there is always a risk of spillage.[153] For waste that contains decaying materials, the heat generated in the decay has to be dispersed and so there is also a

---

[151] The Royal Society (1988), *Management of Separated Plutonium*, Feb, The Royal Society.
[152] Duncan, I.U. (2003), 'What to do with nuclear waste', *Nuclear Energy*, 42, No. 3, June, 145-148.
[153] Taylor, Peter, *Consequence Analysis of a catastrophic failure of highly active liquid waste tanks serving the Thorpe and Magnox nuclear fuel reprocessing plants at Sellafield*, Nuclear Policy and Information Unit, Town Hall, Manchester.

risk of failure of the cooling system. For these reasons it is desirable to store the waste in a more stable, passive, form. Decisions have to be made about the point at which the conversion to a passive state should be initiated. The current processes that are available include, for low and intermediate level liquid, mixing with cement or resin after the liquid has been rendered chemically inert and, for high level liquid, a storage period for the release of decay heat then to vitrify into a glass or sinter into a rock form.[154]

Throughout the chemical processing of nuclear fuel it has been the practice to release small amounts of radioactive liquids and gases to the environment under suitably controlled conditions under the control of the regulatory authority, in the UK with the authorisation of the Environment Agency. This practice has lead to criticism and legal action on the part of the Irish and Norwegian governments. It is planned to stop the process by 2020 as a commitment under the OSPAR Convention. In the meantime BNFL and NIREX have been persuaded to seek means to cease the release of Technetium in the Irish Sea and to store on site at Sellafield eventually to solidify with other intermediate level waste.[155] By chemical treatment and or irradiation the radioactive waste may be changed so that it may be reclassified and less costly storage or disposal methods employed. However, such action is fraught with difficulties and must proceed with full authorisation. Failure to do so resulted in technically acceptable plans being halted by US District Judge Winmill deciding that the US DoE violated the law when it granted itself the authority to reclassify radioactive wastes stored in Washington, Idaho and South Carolina.[156]

Materials used in the construction of the facilities used for nuclear power, research, reprocessing and storage become radioactive or contaminated to varying degrees during their lifetime. Decisions have to be made as to the best predictable option when faced with complete removal or staged removal over periods up to hundreds of years. A process of staged removal allows radioactive decay of the materials to be handled and increased accessibility under low radiation fields. The disadvantage is that local residents may consider remaining structures an eyesore and a source of concern. In the case of Trawsfynydd Power Station in Snowdonia in Wales it is hoped by BNFL to cover the reactor block with an earth mound, leaving a hillock of about 100m high in an already mountainous area. Occasional inspection and remote monitoring would be necessary for a few decades. Future developments may find valuable use for radioactive materials currently classed as waste. The use of decay heat from high level waste could be used for low temperature process heat or even for district heating.

---

[154] Butler, G and Curtis C. (2003), 'Passive storage of radioactive waste', *Nuclear Energy*, 42, O. 3, Jun. pp 157-162.
[155] HSE press release: E100:03 - 17 June 2003 – 'HSE Agrees move to reduce Sellafield discharges'.
[156] Wiley, John, K. (2003), *Nuclear Waste ruling could prove costly, warns Energy Department*, 8 July, Seattle Times.

As discussed below it is important to keep the public well informed and the use of the internet and global information (GIS) may give the nuclear industry and regulatory bodies facilities for consultation and information interfaces to:[157]

- allow the public to explore and experiment with available data and information sources;
- be understandable by all sectors of the community;
- provide information that is explicit and bipartisan; and
- foster a high degree of trust and transparency.

Practical

The words 'storage' and 'disposal' are used interchangeably in this context; the practical measures for each being of similar nature with the exception of the length of time the facility is expected to operate and possibly accessibility. In moving towards a practical solution the ethical basis for geological disposal, the question of reversibility and retrievability and the role of underground laboratories in nuclear waste disposal/ storage programmes are considered. The practical solution is then translated into an environmental impact assessment and formally accepted through planning procedures, usually following a public enquiry.

Ethical Considerations The OECD Radioactive Waste Management Committee reviewed the ethical issues of geological disposal of long-lived radioactive waste at a workshop in 1995[158] and arrived at collective opinions that:

> confirm that the geological disposal strategy can be designed and implemented in a manner that is sensitive and responsive to fundamental ethical and environmental considerations;

> conclude that it is justified, both environmentally and ethically, to continue development of geological repositories for those long-lived radioactive wastes which should be isolated from the biosphere for more than a few hundred years; and

> conclude that stepwise implementation of plans for geological disposal leaves open the possibility of adaptation, in the light of scientific progress and social acceptability, over several decades, and does not exclude the possibility that other options could be developed at a later stage.

In coming to this view the committee considered that the ethical principles of inter-generational and intra-generational equity must be taken into account; that responsibilities to future generations are better discharged by a strategy of final disposal than by reliance on storage; that geological disposal is the most favoured strategy; that geological disposal does take into account inter- and intra-generational equity; and that the geological disposal does not require deliberate provision for the retrieval of waste from the repository. They cautioned that in

---

[157] OECD-NEA (2002), *Society and Nuclear Energy: Towards a better understanding*, OECD Paris.
[158] OECD-NEA(1995), *The Environmental and Ethical Basis of Geological Disposal. A Collective Opinion of the NEA Radioactive Waste Management Committee*, OECD Paris.

pursuing the reduction of risk from a geological disposal strategy the resource deployment should be kept in perspective in relation to the potential for more effective use elsewhere in reducing risks to humans and the environment.

The question of reversibility and retrievability has been considered more fully by the NEA[159] who concluded, *inter alia*, that the decision whether or not to include provisions for retrievability in a repository design could only be made in the context of a specific repository programme and not for all repositories in general.

Before deciding the location of a geologic disposal facility the suitability of the area has to be determined. The information gained from underground research laboratories on the proposed site builds confidence and can be beneficial to regulators by developing methods and equipment and determining the reliability of surface-based methods of site characteristics. However, as experience is gained in different locations the extent of the research can be curtailed and international co-operation can promote confidence in specific projects.[160] Those opposing the construction of geologic disposal facilities fearing the inevitable extension of the laboratory, oppose such research in principle. The NIREX proposals for the laboratory on the Sellafield site was opposed by NGO's and due to ill-prepared argument to support the project they were unable to convince the Minister to agree that the project should proceed.

Institutional

Legal aspects, regulatory control and public acceptance override the technological and practical considerations. While the situation in the UK may not be typical it serves to identify outstanding problem areas. At the root of the question of management of radioactive waste is the definition of the waste and to determine who is responsible, who owns the waste. The laws and regulations that apply, the advisers and regulators and implementation of the management solution can then be finalised and the technological and practical solutions implemented by obtaining public acceptance, planning permission and deciding a firm programme.

What is the Waste? The various types of waste have been identified. The outstanding question is whether the system continues to treat the management of the various forms separately or in a comprehensive way with an overarching policy. Should used fuel, the various levels of waste, disused and spent radioactive sources and waste discharges be treated, using current jargon, in a 'joined up way'?

Who is Responsible and Who owns the Waste? In the UK the government is responsible and while it has attempted to 'privatise' the problem of waste management it is now in the process of setting down arrangements for government action. The *Energy Act 2004*[161] contains provisos implementing proposals in the

---

[159] OECD-NEA (2001), *Reversibility and Retrievability in Geologic Disposal of Radioactive Waste. Reflections at an International level*, OECD Paris.
[160] OECD-NEA (2001), *The role of underground laboratories in nuclear waste disposal programmes*, OECD Paris.
[161] The *Energy Act 2004, Chapter 20*.

White Paper 'Managing the Nuclear Legacy – A strategy for Action' (Cm 5552) published in July 2002 for new arrangements for managing the decommissioning and clean up of public sector civil nuclear liabilities. The *Act* deals with the establishment of a Nuclear Decommissioning Authority (NDA); it give powers to the Secretary of State to restructure BNFL and enable the NDA to improve arrangements for the management of the nuclear sites for which it is given responsibility; it amends the *RSA 93* to allow the EA and SEPA to use streamlined and simplified process in dealing with applications for the transfer of radioactive discharge authorisations where there is a change of nuclear site operator; and it provides the Secretary of State with a power to make an order amending UK legislation to give effect to international obligations governing third party liability in the event of nuclear accidents. The *Act* in chapter three creates a Civil Nuclear Police Authority and a Civil Nuclear Constabulary to protect licenced sites and to safeguard nuclear material in Great Britain and elsewhere. The process of the legislation through Parliament coincided with the consultation processes concerning solid radioactive waste[162] [163] and the UK strategy for radioactive discharges to 2020.[164] RWMAC has also put forward its own recommendations to the Government on the process of deciding how radioactive waste itself should be managed.[165] Government has also launched a new Committee on Radioactive Waste Management (CoRWM)[166] to oversee the consultation. The operation of RWMAC has been suspended for the period while CoRWM makes its recommendations. In what could be one of its final pieces of advice to Government[167] the RWMAC has drawn attention to an area previously low on the list of concerns in the area of low activity solid radioactive waste; that waste lying below the defined low level waste (LLW) category upper limit but above either the levels specified for exclusion from the provisions of the *RSA 93* or for exception from specific regulatory action under the *Act*.[168] The Committee has termed this, 'low activity solid radioactive waste', which includes Very Low Level Waste (VLLW) and a new category, provisionally called, Very Low Radioactive Material (VLRM). RWMAC review was carried out at the same time as its study on the Radioactive Waste Inventory (RWI) and concluded that the problem of managing low activity wastes in the future is likely to be greater than previously realised. The values could be substantially larger than previously anticipated, consequently

---

[162] DEFRA (2001), *Managing Radioactive Waste Safety*, see chapter three, National Policies UK, Policy Ref 57.

[163] DEFRA (2002), *Managing Radioactive Waste Safely*, Summary of Responses to the Consultation, September 2001 – March 2002, July, DEFRA Publications.

[164] DEFRA (2000), *UK Strategy for radioactive discharges 2002-2080*, see chapter three.

[165] RWMAC (2001), *Advice to Ministers on the Process for Formulation of Future Policy for the Long Term Management of UK Solid Radioactive Waste*, September, DEFRA Publications.

[166] DEFRA News Release, 26 March 2003.

[167] RWMAC (2003), *Advice to Ministers on Management of low activity solid radioactive waste within the UK*, March, DEFRA publications.

[168] Under the *Substances of Low Activity Exemption Order (SoLA)*.

reducing the working life of the current facilities at Drigg and Dounreay. A number of recommendations are made including:

- an open review of the policy of disposal of LLW and VLLW;
- consideration of a fuller category of waste above VLLW (VLRM) arising from decommissioning and nuclear site clean up operations; and
- consideration to on-site burial of LLW particularly VLRM.

RWMAC has drawn attention to the possible implications of new or emerging EU Directives that could potentially affect the availability of disposal routes such as the EU Landfill Directive 1999/31/EC, the EU Water Framework Directive 2000/60/EC in respect of land fill sites and the EU Waste Incineration Directive 2000/EC/EC, since they may impact on the availability of existing disposal routes.

RWMAC also recommend that the UK Radioactive Waste Inventory should include low activity wastes and reflect all its management implications.

Arising from mutual interests the RWMAC and the Nuclear Safety Advisory Committee (NuSAC) undertook a joint study in 2001 of the requirements for conditioning, packaging and storage of intermediate level radioactive waste (ILW) and reported to Government Ministers and the HSE in April 2002.[169] The Committees drew attention to what they saw as a policy deficit in relation to the management of ILW while a long-term management solution is being decided and implemented.[170] They recommended that the Government update the White Paper policy of July 1995 expressed in Cm 2919 to carry forward more vigorously the treatment of some of the older legacy wastes held on nuclear sites and to balance treatment of the wastes to make safe in the shorter term with the need to ensure that it can be appropriately managed in the long term. The committees also drew attention to the need for clarity of policies and approaches in the context of introducing a further body, the NDA, to manage the public sector nuclear liabilities.

The RWMAC is currently revising the following issues:

- the interpretation and application of Best Practicable Means (BPM) and Best Practical Environmental Option (BPEO) in current regulatory arrangements;
- the joint review with NuSAC of UK regulatory arrangements; and
- a review of partitioning and transmutation.

The Chairman of RWMAC has written to the Minister for the Environment to express the concerns of the Committee on their perceived threats to its future and in particular pointing out that CoRWM and the NDA cannot replace RWMAC.

---

[169] RWMAC (2002), NuSAC, *Current Arrangements and Requirements for the Conditioning, Packaging and Stor age of Intermediate level Radioactive waste*, A DEFRA Publication.

[170] They are concerned that national policy regarding conditioning, packaging and storage of ILW, 'is effectively being set by default and in a potentially fragmented fashion by the waste producers, the regulators and NIREX'.

The Future of Regulation in the UK

In the context of the changes identified above the White Paper Cm 5552 explains the basis of the UK nuclear regulatory framework and the Government's plans for improving its effectiveness.[171] In particular the paper indicates that more needs to be done to ensure that:

- there is greater consistency in the treatment and management of risk and hazard;
- proportional and cost effective delivery of public, worker and environmental protection; and
- an open and transparently applied regulatory system.

The White Paper draws attention to EU Directives, International Conventions and IAEA guidelines on nuclear security and it identifies changes necessary to implement the recent changes regarding liability in the Paris and Brussels Conventions as follows:

- Increased liability for operators in the event of an accident [not specifically indicated but presumably due to nuclear damage] at a UK nuclear installation from £140 million to £430 million with further compensation where damage is in excess of that of £930 million from public funds.
- Obligations on Government to cover liability if there is insufficient commercial insurance cover for any reason.
- A wider definition of 'nuclear damage' to include environmental damage which includes making good damage to the environment; loss of income deriving from such damage and the cost of measures to prevent an accident occurring again.
- An extension to the geographic scope of the Conventions to include the automatic right of compensation for victims in countries with no nuclear installations.
- An extended jurisdiction to enable victims to sue for compensation in their domestic courts where a nuclear accident occurs in the exclusive economic zones of their countries.
- UK participation in a global compensation regime through ratification of the Joint Protocol providing for reciprocal benefits between the largely Western European parties to the Paris Convention and the parties to the Vienna Convention on nuclear liability which include the FSU and Eastern European states.

The powers to implement these are included in the *Energy Act 2004* at chapter five and go some way towards easing some of the anomalies of the Conventions that have been identified.[172] The White Paper refers to the RWMAC/NuSAC joint

---

[171] *Managing the Nuclear Legacy*, Chapter 7. p 62.
[172] Leigh Dr W. J. *The Nuclear Liability Conventions – the only word on Liability?* New Developments in Nuclear Energy Law – EEC/NIS.

review of nuclear regulation particularly on the interactions between the safety and environmental regulatory systems.[173] The interrelationship between environmental regulation and health and safety is not one that could be characterised simply as interdepartmental rivalries between the two regulators, the EA and the HSC. The dichotomy is one between basic physical principles;[174] environmental regulation is based on the measurement of radiation in Becquerels, the rate of release of particles, and health and safety regulation is based on the potential incidence of radiation and its effect on tissue. A measurement of the rate of release of particles takes no account of the harm that may be caused by the radiation; it may be a measure of the issue of low energy particles or high-energy particles. Using the analogy of the bullet, used at the beginning of this chapter, a low energy particle may be likened to a bullet at the end of its trajectory, falling under gravity, a high energy particle one at the muzzle of the gun; one is almost harmless the other lethal. Therefore a measurement of the rate of receipt of the number of particles at the measuring instrument without knowing the energy they have is not indicative of the harm they might cause. The measurement in Sieverts, however, takes account of the energy of the particle and the effect it might have on the tissue that is exposed to it. It is a direct measurement of the harm likely to be done. The problem is that while the design and operation of a nuclear facility is based on principles such that even in an accident situation the public would be protected from harmful radiation, the releases to the environment by authorized discharges do not necessarily take account of the actual harm likely to be caused by the particular particles included in release. The dangers are two fold; on the one hand a small number of hot particles, those releasing high energy radiation, may be released with permission[175] whereas on the other hand materials releasing larger amounts of low energy particles are being held back for treatment causing high expenditure in resources for very small benefit.

The RWMAC/NuSAC review raised a number of issues relating to the decommissioning process including:

- What is meant by decommissioning being carried out as soon as reasonably practicable?
- Should whole site remediation plans be developed for all sites?
- Confirmation that safe, timely and effective decommissioning is fully consistent with UK obligations under OSPAR; and
- new arrangements associated with the DMA.

Siting Installations for Storage and Disposal of Radioactive Waste

The Nuclear Waste Management Working Group 5 of the International Nuclear Law Association carried out a survey of member countries on the question of

---

[173] Ch.7.12-7.17.

[174] Butler, G. G. (2002), 'UK Radioactive Waste: an overview', *Nuclear Energy*, 41, No. 3 June pp 201-207.

[175] Busby, Chris (2003), *2003 Recommendations of the ECRR*, Green Audit 2003.

institutional control[176] and in response to a set of questions posed the majority of countries indicated that planning permission would be required before a repository could be built and operated and the site would require to be licensed as a nuclear site. The majority of states responding, however, indicated that they did not have a definition of 'Institutional Control' which, according to the OECD-NEA is: 'to guard against inadvertent intrusion or potentially disruptive human actions in the vicinity of the disposal site'.

Planning Permission   Since the failure of NIREX to gain permission to build a rock characterisation laboratory at Sellafield in 1997 with a deep exploratory shaft, the question of the approach to procedures for processing major infrastructure projects was, in 2001-2002, subject to a consultation process.[177] The proposal was abandoned and in July 2003 the *Planning and Compulsory Purchase Bill* was put before Parliament that proposes to give the Secretary of State powers to decide to appoint an Inspector instead of the local authority to report to him on major infrastructure projects. The *Bill* goes some way to reducing delay but does not include the original intention to give Parliament the opportunity to approve projects in principle, nor does it include the right for the public to object prior to Parliamentary debate of the issues and prior to consideration of detailed issues at inquiry. But as pointed out in discussion of *Alconbury*[178] the final decision must always be a matter for the Government or Parliament. A policy that excludes argument at the public inquiry as to where the project should be built, even if endorsed by Parliament, will make the inquiry process seem meaningless. The European Directive on strategic environmental assessment has to be implemented in UK law by 2004 and as described above[179] this will involve public participation at the planning stages of projects and the reporting of progress. Nirex are currently investigating how the framework set out in the directive could be used to enable stakeholders issues and concerns to be addressed.[180] In its proposed programme for action in the proposals for managing solid radioactive waste in the UK[181] the Government indicated that following their decision on the preferred waste management strategy and further consultation on how to implement it, legislation might be necessary in about 2007.

---

[176] Nuclear Inter Jura (2003), Working Group 5, Cape Town, April 2003.

[177] Included in the definition of a major infrastructure was: 3(b) installations designed – (iii) for the final disposal of irradiated fuel; (iv) solely for the final disposal of radioactive waste; (v) solely for the storage (planned for more than 10 years) of irradiated nuclear fuels or radioactive waste in a different site from the production site.

[178] Popham, John and Purdue, Michael (2002), The Future of the Major Inquiry, *[2002] J.P.L* February, pp 137-150.

[179] See European Law chapter five note 75.

[180] Atherton, A. et al (2003), *Strategic Environmental Assessment and Environmental Impact Assessment as Part of a Stepwise Decision Making Process*, ICEM03, Oxford.

[181] *Managing Radioactive Waste Safely*, Chapter 7, Table 1 p 56.

Participation

By entering the consultation process the UK Government has recognised that the attitudes of local committees to proposals for new developments are a material consideration. The example of Finland in determining the way ahead for nuclear energy and the disposal of nuclear waste is a lesson in how to proceed; waste and future energy proposals are intermingled. In its report[182] the INLA Working Group 5 concluded that

> Public participation under well-defined procedures is an adequate means to gain acceptance of the chosen options and the designated sites as well. Experience shows that approaching public concerns at the very early stages of waste management promotes better understanding and wider agree(ment) between populations and those responsible (for) radioactive waste management. Legislation should include appropriate provisions for public involvement to be encouraged and expanded. Societal co-responsibility should be a goal avoiding simple releases of information to be the only way to public participation.

This view was pre-empted in the earlier OECD workshop[183] which noted that the technical aspects of waste management are not of unique importance, the organisational ability to communicate and to adapt, take priority.

> Development projects in general are rejected when stakeholders have not been actively involved in creating them and developed a sense of responsibility for them. Radioactive Waste is not perceived to be a shared societal problem, and the priority assigned to resolving energy-related issues may be low today when economic and energy shortages are just a memory.

An encouraging recognition of the necessity of stakeholder involvement at the early stage of decision-making on practices with rationalisation of radiation risk is the dialogue between the ICRP and the OECD-NEA expert group. The 'road test' of the EGRP proposal referred to in chapter three,[184] to base the authorisation of practices on a system that fits within a common policy framework of other carcinogenic risks was shown to be a useful tool for triggering the involvement of stakeholders.

Pierre Strohl notes[185] that the transparency of information policy and constructive participation procedures imply mutual trust and honest dialogue between qualified authorities and experts and the public. He cautions that decisions relating to the final disposal of radioactive waste raise ethical questions concerning the responsibility for future generations and that this responsibility can only be translated as a legal obligation.

---

[182] Nuclear Inter Jura (2003), *The legal and institutional frame work.* p 16, Cape Town.

[183] OECD-NEA (2000), *Stakeholder Confidence and Radioactive Waste Disposal*, August, OECD Paris.

[184] See ICRP chapter three, note 21.

[185] Strohl, Pierre, 'Disposal of Radioactive Waste: The Question of the Involvement of the Public under International Law', *Nuclear Law Bulletin* 64, December 1999, OECD.

A Personal View

When it comes to pragmatism, 'a stink causes action': the aroma from the Thames on 30 June 1858 caused Parliament to be suspended. Within the following two weeks a Bill to sort out London's water and sewage was introduced. London's smog of the mid 1950s had a similar, but not so immediate effect. The event of 9/11 coupled with the perception of freely available radioactive materials may well have its effect. But there is a need to beware of the backfire; the stink made about nuclear testing and the possibly exaggerated accounts of the effects of fallout still abound and influence the peaceful use of nuclear energy. The methods used to instil caution in handling radioactive materials are based on a series of assumptions that lead to potential exposure to radiation that would give an estimated risk to the life of the most exposed member of the public of one in a million. Is it reasonable to use that same argument to extend that risk to whole populations to give statistically estimated deaths of alarming proportions?

We should not take lightly the possible failure of our energy systems to provide adequate and secure supplies. The problems with brownouts in California led to a lot of perspiration due to loss of air-conditioning; here in the colder north loss of power supplies, even for short periods on a cold winter's day, would lead to hypothermia and deaths of the old and very young. Domestic coal fires were abandoned for environmental improvement and because a secure supply of gas and electricity could be expected. The vision of a low energy, renewable fuel scene must be a common desire, however, the whole scene must be examined and it must be recognised that some countries do not have, yet, the alternative to the use of nuclear power. The Republic of Korea built their first power reactor in the early seventies because they had no alternative to importing oil from Iran and coal from Europe and Australia on credit. Nuclear energy has enormous value as a medical tool; radioisotopes are used as tracers for diagnostic purposes and as lances in surgery all produced using nuclear reactors. Further, until the ideal situation is reached in the UK the gap between reality and the ideal of renewable power sources[186] must be filled and the possibility of brownouts, high fuel costs and air pollution from fossil fuels avoided. To ensure diversity the nuclear option should be available. Abandoning the nuclear option will not solve the problem of disposing of existing waste; that problem is now being tackled and by 2006, if DEFRA keep their programme, there will be an acceptable solution; by (say) 2016 we will have in place a specification for a safe disposal facility and (say) by 2020 existing waste will be safety tucked away in a facility. The reprocessing, recycling and disposal of radioactive material from used fuel from intrinsically safe reactors operating from 2020 to (say) 2060 will be an ongoing process until we have a secure, diverse and interconnected system of renewable energy systems with adequate power storage to provide base load.

Having painted that realistic but possibly optimistic picture let us come back to the present and allow a little to be said about the current situation. Existing

---

[186] An ideal that denies the second law of thermodynamics; there is no such thing as a perpetual motion machine.

reactors, reprocessing and storage facilities are at risk from military style action. They must continue to be defended and the tragedy of 11 September dictates the degree necessary. To some extent technology has recognised the risks and in some cases the effect of a missile, such as a direct crash of a Tornado jet, would be withstood without the release of radiation from the reactor to the environment. All future reactor systems will be designed to withstand credible external forces. The current PWR Sizewell 'B' has a reactor core housed in an 8 inch steel vessel that was designed and manufactured with a probability of failure of 1 in 10 million. The reactor and its cooling system are shielded by one meter of concrete. All of this is housed in a double walled steel and concrete leak tight containment. These are not the flimsy structures of a multistorey office building! Future designs of reactor systems will use the same containment style but with the coolant system disposed to ensure natural cooling in the event of loss of external supplies. In the current style of PWR and future designs an accident such as Chernobyl is impossible. The Three Mile Island (TMI) accident demonstrated the safety of containment; the coolant was lost, the reactor core melted but radioactive releases were contained within the containment vessel. There was no release to the environment that exceeded the regulatory limits.

The problem with nuclear is primarily a social one where a lack of understanding of the risks is exacerbated by obscure scientific explanation and fear is fanned by the media and opponents of anything that might suggest a possibility of nuclear weapons. TMI is a good example. The power company lost an investment but the damage to the environment and the public by radiation was zero, nevertheless, the local population suffered psychological harm and nervous shock from fear of the unknown. The courts allowed damages for that harm. To a large extent the fear of radiation has been caused by the way in which the science of radiological protection has been handled. The situation as a result of the Chernobyl accident serves as an example: radiation levels were accurately measured; estimates were made of the deterministic effects of that radiation and people were evacuated; further estimates were made of the effects of the collective dose (i.e. the probable effects on whole populations of being exposed to varying levels of low level radiation in the form of fallout) and very large numbers of future deaths due to cancer were predicted. The real situation is that 31 people died, about 100 suffered radiation levels that will probably lead to death and 600 children who were infants and babies at the time of the accident and lived in the evacuation area have thyroid cancer that is treatable. A tragic situation but the large number of predicted future deaths from cancer is speculation since cancers would happen in any case due to natural sources of radiation, other cancerous materials in the environment and old age. This use of collective dose while being a useful tool for the comparison of alternative shielding scenarios should not be seen as predicting real outcomes.

Even the estimates of deterministic radiological harm are based on precautionary estimates and then further precautionary limits of dose. The precautionary estimates of harm are based on the evidence of atom bomb casualties, bomb test experiments using military personnel and medical experiments on terminally ill cancer patients. The estimates were made by scientists who were themselves involved in the uses of nuclear weapons. The increase in the measured radiation in the atmosphere caused by bomb testing was detected around the world. So it is unlikely that the estimated values were understated and what an opportunity to put fear into the politicians and (literally) drive testing underground and contain the fallout!

The harm caused by radiation is termed deterministic where the damage is inevitable[187] and is termed stochastic where damage caused by low levels of radiation is not certain and is random,[188] based on projections from damage caused by high doses. A linear no threshold rule is used meaning that even the low levels of radiation below 1 Sv will cause deterministic harm and at a level of 10Sv death is most likely, caused by damage to the cells of the organ tissue. Some people are more susceptible to harm depending on the ability of their body systems to repair the damaged cells. The degree of harm is related to age, the foetus being the most susceptible. Below 1Sv harm is uncertain and random (stochastic) but it is assumed that harm to the cell may occur in some people. The degree of harm is based on statistical studies of people who have been exposed to radiation and have not suffered deterministic harm but who have suffered cancer later and compared with control groups who have not been exposed. These studies used the information from the atom bomb survivors and varying estimates of radiation levels to which they were exposed. Throughout these studies a precautionary approach was adopted. Based on these derived levels safe levels of working were decided for the protection of radiation workers and for the design of shielding. In deciding these levels the effects of the different penetrating power of the different energies of the radioactive particles causing ionising in tissue were taken into account. For example Alpha particles are stopped by a millimetre of polythene but cause high ionisation; Beta particles are stopped by one centimetre of steel and Gamma particles are stopped by one meter of concrete. Appropriate scaling factors were used to reduce the effects of the different types of radiation to a common product, the effective dose, measured in Sieverts (Sv). So below 1 Sv no deterministic effects are likely. Regulatory limits of dose were then decided taking a precautionary approach so that the limit of exposure of the nuclear worker is 20 millisieverts (mSv) per year and the design of nuclear facilities, taking into account design base accidents, is such that a member of the public at the site perimeter will not receive more than 1 mSv per year. This latter limit is also applied for situations outside the nuclear site such as the lamb in North Wales that ingests lichen that shows signs of radiation from the Chernobyl accident of 1986: assuming that a critical group of lamb eaters eat a quantity of meat each day for a year they should not be exposed to radiation from the Chernobyl fallout of more than 1mSv. So the lambs must not be allowed to eat more of that lichen than would cause an aggregation exceeding 1mSv in the meat eater by consumption of their choicest parts. The farmers are therefore paid to move the lambs away from

---

[187] Documents of the NRPB (1996), *Risk from Deterministic Effects of Ionising Radiation*, Vol. 7 No. 3, NRPB Chilton, Oxon.
[188] Documents of the NRPB (1995), *Risk of Radiation-induced Cancer at Low Dose Rates for Radiation Protection Purposes*, Vol. 6, No. 1, NRPB Chilton, Oxon.

certain areas on a rotational basis. A further precautionary approach is evident. The designer also adds his own safety factors and the regulator makes his measurements allowing margins resulting in Precaution to the power five.

This precautionary approach should be contrasted with, as an example, the approach to limiting the release of cancer-causing particles from diesel engines that we are prepared to live with without fear. It is no wonder that the public is scared of radiation. Perhaps the perceived harm from low level radiation should be weighed against the harm of public angst and readjust the safe levels of working accordingly. We might then have a level playing field with the public comparing and making choices on the basis of rationality.

The management of radioactive waste is pivotal for the UK and probably for the rest of the world. The obstacles to a sensible strategy for the management of radioactive waste are not technical but political and unless resolved may threaten civilisation, not by the exposure to radiation but by the effect on energy policy and consequent climate change caused by greenhouse gases from fossil fuels. There appears to be good reason to believe that unless the emission of greenhouse gases is significantly reduced global warming will increase. Policy in the UK is following a precautionary route: reduce greenhouse gases by reducing demand for energy, by making energy generation more efficient and from renewable sources. To avoid energy deficiency in the event that these methods fail to meet the requirements in time and to avoid dependence on gas and oil from unreliable sources, nuclear energy that currently provides 20 percent of electrical power may have to be replaced by new nuclear plant. To ensure that new nuclear plant can be installed without valid opposition and to meet justification requirements two problems remain to be resolved: the first is the question of economics and the second is the management of radioactive waste. The economics of nuclear power will be clarified when the legacy of research, military and development reactors together with the used nuclear fuel and waste associated with that legacy are treated separately along the lines of the current proposals for the Nuclear Decommissioning Authority, leaving the commercial production of nuclear energy un-encumbered by historical burdens. The management of radioactive waste should be resolved by 2007 after the current consultative process. The way should then be clear for the commencement of construction of a series of intrinsically safe, economic reactors and a fuel cycle with zero emissions of both greenhouse gases and radioactive waste and financed entirely by private capital.

Further Reading

Barry, S.F. 'Person years at risk in radiation epidemiology', *Radiation Protection Bulletin* No 81. NRPB.

Beck, Ulrich (1992), *Risk Society: towards a new modernity*, London, Sage Publications.

Beral, V. et al (1985), 'Mortality of Employees of the United Kingdom Atomic Energy Authority 1946-1979' *Brit. Med. J.* 291 (6493), pp 440-447.

Bertell Rosalie (1985), *No Immediate Danger*. The Woman's Press, London.

Busby, Chris (2003), *2003 Recommendations of the ECRR*, Green Audit, Cambrian Printers, Wales.

Butler, G. and Curtis, C. (2003), 'Passive storage of radioactive waste', *Nuclear Energy*, 42, O. 3, June 157-162.

Clarke, Roger (1996), 'Implications of new data on cancer risk', *NRPB Bulletin* No 179 July 1996.

Clarke, Roger (1999), 'Control of low level radiation exposure: time for a change?' *J Radiol Prot* vol. 19 No.2 pp 107-115.

Documents of the NRPB (1995), *Risk of Radiation-induced Cancer at Low Dose Rates for Radiation Protection Purposes*, Vol. 6, No. 1, NRPB Chilton, Oxon.

Duncan, I. J. 'What to do with nuclear waste', *Nuclear Energy*, 2003, 42 No.3. June pp 145-148.

Howe, G. (2002), *Epidemiology: strengths, limitations and interpretation application to studies of low-dose radiation.* 4th International Conference on Health Effects of Low level Radiation, September, Oxford.

Leigh, Dr. W. J. (1997), 'Liability and Regulation - Some Legal Challenges Faced by the Operators of United Kingdom Nuclear Installations'. *[1997] Env. Liability 44.*

Leigh, Dr W. J. and Wakeford, Richard (2001), 'Radiation Litigation and the Nuclear Industry – the Experience in the United Kingdom', Health Physics 81 (6), pp 645-646.

McHugh, J, O and Marshall (1997), 'B, P, Radioactive Waste and "Small Users": The 3Rs-Responsibilities, Rights and Regulation', *[1997] Env.Liability 38.*

Pentreath R. J. (2003), 'A system for radiological protection of the environment: some initial thoughts and ideas', *J Radiol Prot* vol. 12 No.2 pp 117-128.

Pochin, Sir Edward E. (1986), 'The Evolution of Radiation Protection Criteria', *Nucl.Energy* 25 NO. 1, Feb., pp 19-27.

Popham, John and Purdue, Michael (2002), 'The Future of the Major Inquiry', [2002] *J.P.L* February.

Riley, Peter (1997), *The regulation of the user of ionising radiation and the relevance of nuclear facility operators in litigation*, Nuclear Inter Jura '97, Tours, France.

Riley, Peter (2000), 'The precautionary principle and its practice', *Engineering Management Journal*, December Vol.10, No.6.

Riley, Peter (2003), 'Radiation risk in the context of liability for injury', *Journal of Radiological Protection*, Vol.23, Issue 3, September, pp 305-315.

Strand, P and Larsson, C.M. (2001), *Delivering a framework for the protection of the environment from ionising radiation, Radioactive Pollutants, Impact on the Environment*, (Brechignac and Howard eds.), EDP Sciences, Les Ulis, France.

Strohl, Pierre (1999), 'Disposal of Radioactive Waste: The Question of the Involvement of the Public under International Law', *Nuclear Law Bulleting* 64, December, OECD Paris.

Taylor, P. *Consequence Analysis of a Catastrophic Failure of Highly Active Waste Tanks Serving the Thorpe and Magnox Nuclear Fuel Reprocessing Plants at Sellafield*, Nuclear Policy and Information Unit, Town Hall, Manchester, M60 2LA.

The Royal Society (1988), *Management of Separated Plutonium*, Feb.

Wakeford, Antell, Leigh (1998), 'Review of Probability of Causation and its use in a Compensation Scheme for Nuclear Industry Workers in the United Kingdom', *Health Physics* 74 (1), pp 1-9.

Williamson Richard L, Burton Dennis T, Clarke James H and Fleming Lora E (1993); 'Gathering Danger: The Urgent Need to Regulate Toxic Substances That Can Bioaccumulate'. *Ecology Law Quarterly*, Vol 20 (1993) p 604.

International and Government Papers

A Report to the Secretary of State for Trade and Industry by the Director of Civil Nuclear Security (2003), *The State of Security in the Civil Nuclear Industry and Effectiveness of Security Regulation. April 2002 – March 2003,* Office for Civil Nuclear Security, DTI.

DEFRA (2002), *Managing Radioactive Waste Safely, Summary of Responses to the Consultation, September 2001 – March 2002,* July, DEFRA Publications.

IAEA (2002), *Ethical considerations in protecting the environment from the effects of ionising radiation,* IAEA TECHDOC-1270, IAEA, Vienna.

Nuclear Safety Advisory Committee (NuSAC)/Radioactive Waste Management Advisory Committee (RWMAC) (2003), *Joint regulatory review, Structures and principles of the regulation of the nuclear licensed sites,* March, HSE.

OECD-NEA (1995), *The Environmental and Ethical Basis of Geological Disposal. A Collective Opinion of the NEA Radioactive Waste Management Committee,* OECD Paris.

OECD-NEA (2001), *Reversibility and Retrievability in Geologic Disposal of Radioactive Waste. Reflections at an International level,* OECD Paris.

OECD-NEA (2001), *The role of underground laboratories in nuclear waste disposal programmes,* OECD Paris.

OECD-NEA (2002), A *Critical Review of the System of Radiation Protection, The Way Forward in Radiological Protection,* An Expert Group Report, OECD, Paris.

OECD-NEA (2002), *Society and Nuclear Energy: Towards a better understanding,* OECD Paris OECD-NEA (2003), *Radiological protection of the environment. Summary Report of the Issues,* OECD Paris.

RWMAC (2001), *Advice to Ministers on the Process for Formulation of Future Policy for the Term Management of UK Solid Radioactive Waste,* September, DEFRA Publications.

RWMAC (2003), *Advice to Ministers on Management of Low Activity Solid Radioactive Waste Within the UK,* March, DEFRA Publications.

Appendix 1

Nuclear Energy

This brief outline of nuclear energy is intended to provide a background only and is therefore much simplified. The smallest part of an element is the atom. For example, the wooden article can, by burning, be divided into gases and ash. The gas, by chemical separation, can become the elements of carbon, nitrogen, oxygen, sulphur, hydrogen and so on. Similarly the ash by chemical treatment can become the elements of iron, magnesium, copper, aluminium and so on. In turn these elements can be divided into atoms and the atoms into elementary particles. At the centre of an atom, is a nucleus and around the nucleus is a cloud of electrons. The nucleus is made up of protons and neutrons. These particles making the atom have the form of a planetary system and are held together by nuclear and electromagnetic forces. In the earlier part of the last century it was discovered that the system of particles forming the nucleus could be disturbed to release the particles and in so doing also release the energy binding them. A neutron may collide with a nucleus, cause it to disintegrate and to release its constituent particles, leaving an unstable nucleus. The unstable nucleus will release further particles as it successively disintegrates, the process is repeated until a stable nucleus is created. When these unstable nuclei release particles they are said to be radioactive.

Prior to the discovery of nuclear energy the only forms of energy known to man that he could manipulate were his and his animals' muscles, wind, water, heat from chemical reactions, the sun and fire. Only the digestion of food to provide muscle power and fire involved changing matter. By the digestive process and by burning wood or coal the binding energy of the molecules, chemical energy, was released. From the 1930s the binding energy of the nuclei, nuclear energy, could be released.

Alongside the discovery that the nucleus was divisible by artificial means, the process of nuclear disintegration has been found in nature. Certain unstable materials are found naturally, for example, radium. These elements were formed when the earth condensed from the cloud of elementary particles released from the sun or possibly its exploded sister. They have been disintegrating according to the laws of nature ever since. In so doing they release energy; some particles escape and often another element is formed. This new element may have a short life itself, e.g. radon that disintegrates in a few hours or it may be an element that will last forever, i.e. a stable element. This process of disintegration releases particles and radiation. The sun itself is mostly made up of basic particles combining to form elements and disintegrating again from unstable to stable elements; the stable element by collision with a neutron disintegrates and the process starts again. The heat released from this reaction reaches us directly. Some of the particles reach us in the form of cosmic rays, others as light and electro-magnetic radiation, ultra violet and infra red radiation. Much of this radiation is deflected by the earth's atmosphere, hence the higher the altitude the greater the level of background radiation.

We live in an environment that has as a constituent part, radiation from the earth itself, from the solar system and from beyond. The earth, living things and man have developed and live in harmony with a changing scene of radiation. Some scientists believe that it is possible that without radiation man would not have evolved.[1]

Quantification of Radiation

Units of measurement of radiation are given in two main forms. The first measure is in terms of the number of disintegrations undergone by an element, the Becquerel (Bq); 1 Bq is one disintegration per second. This however is not a measure of the harmfulness of the radiation and does not distinguish the type of particle released after disintegration nor the energy of that particle. The Becquerel is used to quantify the gross activity of a source of radiation, the amount of radioactivity present in a material, for example, the radioactivity naturally occurring in a sample of earth, or the radioactive levels in grass in North Wales. The second unit of measurement is the Gray (Gy); a measure of the energy that is absorbed when an emitted particle is brought to rest in a mass of material exposed to the radiation. The effect of different types of particles on tissue is taken into account by applying a quality factor (Q). The value of Q reflects the different capacities for biological damage by each type of particle. The absorbed energy multiplied by the quality factor gives an 'absorbed dose equivalent' the unit being the Sievert (Sv). For gamma radiation the quality factor is 1. The dose equivalent of X Gray of Gamma radiation is therefore X Sv. The quality factor for alpha radiation is 20 and for fast neutrons is 10. The dose equivalent of X Gray of alpha radiation is therefore 20X Sv. Since radiation is absorbed by matter (i.e. its energy is dissipated so that the particle is stopped) materials such as polythene, lead, steel and concrete can be placed between the source of radiation and the person to prevent the particle reaching the person. Gamma particles pass through tissue, imparting only part of their energy; alpha particles are stopped by tissue thus causing more damage because all of the energy is dissipated in the tissue. Conversely it is easy to shield from alpha particles by using, for instance, a polythene sheet. Gamma radiation and neutrons are stopped by inches of lead, or feet of concrete.

---

[1] Fremlin, (1985), *Power Production - What Are the Risks?* Adam Hilger Ltd. pp 53-57.

Sources of Processes of Artificial Radiation

Nuclear Weapons

Nuclear energy and radiation are released in all their forms in a nuclear weapon. The nuclear energy is dissipated promptly in an explosion. Radiation is released via three mechanisms; firstly by direct radiation and by the primary particles released, secondly, by secondary radiation from fission products, i.e. the unstable elements formed on disintegration of the bomb material in the case of a fission (atom) bomb, and thirdly, secondary radiation from materials made unstable by neutron irradiation. The disintegration of the atoms of uranium and other fissile materials causes the release of all types of primary particles. These particles are brought to rest in the immediate vicinity of the explosion, about 1500 metres in air.[2] Depending on where the explosion takes place, material near to the centre will be irradiated by collisions with the released particles. The bomb container, the earth and the supporting structure will be irradiated by these particles and will become radioactive. The fissile materials and the products of fission will be radioactive. The bomb blast will spread some of these radioactive materials (contamination) into the atmosphere, primarily the troposphere and the stratosphere. The larger material will fall out in the vicinity of the bomb site and the finer material will be distributed over a large part of the earth's surface. Calculation of the effect of global fallout from all the weapons exploded, a total of 1493[3] is a lifetime collective dose equivalent of about 0.004 Sv per head of world population, i.e. the equivalent of about two years of exposure to the natural background radiation in the UK. Nuclear energy released during underground testing is contained below ground and the surface is shielded from primary particles, fission products and irradiated materials.

Nuclear Reactors

Nuclear energy and radiation is released from the fission of nuclear fuel in reactors. Reactors are built behind shielded containments made primarily of steel and concrete. The nuclear energy is released slowly, raising the temperature of the reactor core. This temperature rise is used to convert water to steam and the steam is used to turn a turbine to rotate an electrical generator and make electricity. The radioactive particles are brought to rest by the shielding within a few metres of the centre of the reactor. Radioactive material is confined within the reactor primary containment. Material taken from the reactor, used fuel and mechanical components, the coolant and materials added to the coolant, and the shielding materials surrounding the reactor are irradiated by neutrons and become radioactive and emit radiation. Such material is confined to the area immediately around the reactor by a secondary containment or taken out of the secondary containment and stored in shielded vaults or under water. About one metre of water provides good shielding and also allows observation of the material stored

---

[2] Arnold, Lorna, *British Atomic Weapons Trials in Australia.* (HMSO) p 304.
[3] ibid p 289.

beneath the surface. In the event of accidental damage to the reactor the radioactive materials may be released into the containment; this happened in the Three Mile Island accident. In the Chernobyl accident the containment was damaged by an explosion and radioactive materials were released from the containment into the atmosphere. The Windscale reactor fire in 1957[4] occurred in an uncontained reactor and released radioactive material into the atmosphere.

Mining and Refining

In the mining of uranium ore, as in the mining of coal and many other ores, naturally occurring radioactive material such as radon gas is released. In refining natural uranium, traces of naturally occurring radioactive materials are concentrated in the waste products. Used fuel from reactors is reprocessed to recover unused uranium and other elements such as plutonium for recycling as fuel in reactors and for the manufacture of weapons. The materials extracted are radioactive and are stored in vaults. The by-products of reprocessing are concentrated and stored for future disposal. In the process of refining and concentration, solutions of weak radioactive materials are formed and lightly contaminated materials accumulate. Some of the solutions are so dilute as to be considered safe enough to release to the environment and are piped into the sea. Similarly in research and other facilities such as hospitals, weak solutions containing traces of radioactive materials are released to inland waterways, sewers and drains. Lightly contaminated materials, workmen's overalls and gloves, which may have traces of radioactive materials handled in the operation and maintenance of the plant, are collected and disposed of into low-level waste depositories.

Isotopes in Industry and Medicine

Radioactive materials are produced for special purposes; isotopes produced by irradiation in reactors, are used as tracers in medicine and in geological investigations; for use as x-ray sources for industry and medicine; as sources of radiation for food preservation; for use in fire detectors, thickness gauges and many other applications. In such production radioactive materials are accumulated as waste, as leftover materials and equipment and as protective clothing that is contaminated with traces of radioactive material. Such material is collected and graded for disposal to vaults on the factory site or sent to low level waste depositories on licensed nuclear sites. Liquids and gases with radioactive contamination below allowed levels are dispersed into the environment after they have been checked for the amount and type of radiation.

Radioactive materials are used in factories and hospitals. These materials release particles and are therefore shielded to reduce the release outside the containers to a level which complies with regulations and are handled by authorised operators. Machines that generate radiation, such as x-ray machines, are used in factories, research establishments, universities and hospitals; these are installed in shielded facilities. Waste is accumulated in such facilities; traces of the

---

[4] Accident at Windscale No 1 Pile. Oct 1957. Cmnd 302.

radioactive materials are attached to protective clothing and washing liquids contain traces of radioactive materials. Solid material is collected and sent to a low level waste depository. The liquid is held in delay tanks, checked and if below the authorised level is then despatched to the drains.

The Hazards of Radiation

The study of the effect of radioactivity on man and animals under varying conditions has led to an understanding of the effects at high radiation dose levels and allows predictions of the effect of low radiation dose levels. Studies have been made of the consequences of the atom bombs at Hiroshima and Nagasaki; observations of the use of radiation therapy in medicine and medical treatment; the effects on early research workers;[5] [6] studies of workers in nuclear facilities[7] [8] and more recently the effects on workers and firemen after the Chernobyl accident.[9] [10]

The effects of radiation on the person, (somatic effects), fall into two categories; early effects which are related to the amount of radiation received (deterministic) and late effects the severity of which are not related to the dose level received (stochastic). The probability of a late effect is, however, related to the dose level received. The early effects (from which recovery is unlikely) are skin loss, loss of hair, reduction in fertility, damage to gut, blood cells and bone tissue and death within a few weeks from the exposure. The amount of radiation that would cause these effects is an absorbed dose in excess of 10 Sv to the whole body over a short period of time.[11] Below an absorbed dose of 1 Sv over a short period no early death would occur. While local absorbed doses of the order of 10 Sv and higher are used in medical therapy to kill cancer in the body such a dose to the whole body, with every cell in the body exposed to absorb the radiation, would be fatal. Such lethal levels of radiation are produced in the area immediately around a nuclear explosion or within a few metres of a reactor core.

The present assumption regarding delayed effects of radiation and the development of cancer is that there is no lower threshold below which no harm will occur.[12] [13] There may always be a risk from radiation in the environment but this

[5] Bertell, Rosalie (1985), *No Immediate Danger*, (The Womans Press) p 50.

[6] Beral V. et al (1985), 'Mortality of Employee's of the United Kingdom Atomic Energy Authority 1946-1979', *Brit Med J*, 291, (6493), pp 440-447.

[7] Fremlin (1985), *Power Production - What are the Risks?* Adam Hilger Ltd p 263.

[8] Kendall G.M. and Muirhead C.R. (1992), 'First Analysis of the National Registry for Radiation Workers' *NRPB Radiological Protection Bulletin* No 128 Jan 1992, NRPB Chilton, Didcot, Oxon.

[9] OECD-NEA (1995), *Chernobyl Ten Years On. Radiological and Health Impact.* An appraisal by the NEA Committee on Radiation Protection and Public Health, OECD Paris.

[10] Directorate - General Science, Research and Development (1993), *Thyroid cancer in children living near Chernobyl. Expert panel report.* EUR 15248 EN. Luxembourg.

[11] Saunders P.A.H. (1986), *The Effects and Control of Radiation* UKAEA.

[12] Pochin, Sir Edward E. (1986), 'The Evolution of Radiation Protection Criteria' *Nuclear Energy*, 25 No 1, Feb pp 19-27.

risk is very difficult to quantify and would involve a study incurring several million-person years to expect any hope of a significant result.[14] The risk is of damage that causes the cells to multiply out of control and is not overcome by the defence mechanisms within the body; this is cancer. Radiation may kill the cell; this will not cause harm to the body unless so many cells are killed as to impair the function of the organs and so cause early death as mentioned above. Radiation is only one of many causes of cancer; others are asbestos fibre, smoke tars and many chemicals. Intense study has been carried out on people and animals who have been exposed to radiation and at this time the link between radiation and cancer death shows that assuming a linear relationship and interpolating from high doses, a dose rate of 2mSv per year is associated with a fatal accident rate of one in twenty five million per year or of three and three-quarter years lost in one thousand man years.[15] The Natural background in the UK gives an average absorbed dose equivalent of about 2.2mSv per year and the artificial sources of radiation contribute an average absorbed dose equivalent of about 0.4mSv per year of which ninety-four percent is due to medical uses.

So on these assumptions, doubling the background will, on average, shorten a one hundred year life span by about five months. A dose rate of 30mSv per year would give a fatal accident rate of one in four hundred million per year and loss of fifty years in one thousand man years, which means that if the environmental background were raised by thirty times, the average shortening of a one hundred year life would be five years. The validity of such estimation by extrapolation from the death rate caused by high radiation levels is a source of some debate. On the one hand it is argued that any increase above the natural background must be avoided because of unknown factors; the occurrence of leukaemia clusters is seen by some to be an indicator of these unknown factors.[16] On the other hand it is thought that the rate at which the dose is administered may affect the carcinogenic risk[17] and that these linear extrapolations of the effect of high doses may lead to undue pessimism about the effects of low doses.

The policy of dose limitation practised internationally is to assume a linear relationship until this alternative theory is proved or rejected by continued observation of the effects of low doses. Concern about radiation and cancer must be considered against a background of cancer as the cause of one in five of all deaths. To place the problem in perspective, radiation levels of ten times the natural background level will increase cancer deaths from two hundred thousand in one million to two hundred thousand one hundred and twenty five in one million.

---

[13] Pochin, E.E. (1984), 'The 1984 Sievert Lecture. Sieverts and Safety' *Health Physics* Vol 46 No 6, pp 1173-4.

[14] United Nations (1985), *Radiation. Doses, Effects, Risks.* United Nations Environment Programme, p 57.

[15] ICRP Publication 45 (1985), *Qualitative basis for developing a unified index of harm.* Annals of the ICRP, Pergamon Press. 15, (3).

[16] Stewart A (1986), Evidence to the EDRP Inquiry at Thurso.

[17] Barry S.F., 'Person years at risk in radiation epidemiology', *Radiation Protection Bulletin* No 81. NRPB.

From the study of animal populations, radiation as well as having late effects, is known to have hereditary effects on animal populations. The estimates of possible hereditary effects on man are based on extrapolation from results in other species, in particular mice.[18] even though no unequivocal evidence of similar effects in humans is evident at any dose level. However, radiation of the foetus in pregnant women is known to cause leukaemia in the child.[19] The practice of x-ray examination of pregnant women has ceased.[20]

Avoidance of the Hazards of Radiation

The hazards of radiation will be realised by the explosion of a nuclear weapon, by an accident at a nuclear facility that is not contained or by contact with radioactive material.

Nuclear weapons are exploded by deliberate action of a sovereign State. It is possible, however, that a nuclear weapon could be exploded by a terrorist organisation if suitable radioactive material could be obtained and the organisation had access to suitable manufacturing facilities. Such facilities would have a capital value of many tens of millions of pounds sterling. The explosion of a nuclear weapon by a State can only be avoided by agreement between all States able to manufacture such a weapon. Similarly, the diversion of materials to terrorists can only be avoided by co-operation between States.

Effective licensing and regulation avoid the potential hazards of operating nuclear facilities and dangerous contact with radioactive material. In formulating rules to avoid the hazards of radiation it has been assumed, by the regulating authorities, that the degree of harm is in linear proportion to the amount of radiation exposure and that there is no lower limit below which radiation is harmless. International consensus is obtained by following the International Commission on Radiological Protection (ICRP) recommendations.

Activities that add radiation exposures or risks are called 'practices'. Other human activities can decrease the overall exposure by removing the source, modifying the pathways or reducing the number of exposed individuals. These activities that subtract radiation exposures are called 'intervention'. For 'practices' the system of protection recommended by the Commission is based on the following general principles:

The dose limits recommended by the ICRP are an average of 0.02 Sv per year over 5 years (0.1 Sv in 5 years) with no more than 0.05 in a single year for radiation workers and 0.001 Sv per year for the general public. However, the National Radiological Protection Board (NRPB) has recommended that individual workers should be controlled so as not to exceed an average effective dose equivalent of 0.015 Sv per year. For individual members of the public, it is recommended that the effective dose equivalent should not exceed 0.0005 Sv per year from effluent discharges from a single site. This recommendation comes after

---

[18] Layfield, Sir Frank, *Sizewell B Inquiry*. Ch 11, para 67-69.
[19] ibid Ch 11 para 73-76.
[20] Stewart A. et al (1956), 'Malignant Diseases in Childhood and Diagnostic Irradiation in Utero' *Lancet* (ii) 447.

a preliminary re-assessment by the ICRP of the data from Hiroshima and Nagasaki that has raised the fatal cancer risk estimate by the order of two.[21] [22] [23] In 1984 the average dose equivalent of occupational exposure to radiation in the UK was 1.4mSv per worker year; the major deviations from this were non-coal miners 2.6mSv, fuel reprocessors 7mSv, radiotherapy staff 2.6mSv. As will be seen later, international and domestic regulations are based on those ICRP recommendations. However, it is recognised that a significant part of the wastes from the application of radioactive materials in industry, research, medicine and the nuclear fuel cycle is contaminated to such low activity levels, and the consequent risks to health are so minimal, that the application of regulating processes seems unwarranted. The International Atomic Energy Agency (IAEA)[24] has considered a *de minimis* policy whereby exception from notification, registration and licensing of artificial radioactive sources of practices would be allowed where:

> the amount of effective dose equivalent to individuals of the critical group at no time exceeds 0.01mSv, and the annual dose equivalent to skin does not exceed 0.5mSv, and

> the collective effective dose equivalent commitment from the excepted sources or practice is of the order of 1 man Sv or less.

The critical group referred to above is a well-defined group of people who would receive more radiation than any other defined group.[25] The collective dose equivalent commitment means the total dose received by the whole of the critical group. Such arrangements would limit the relentless pursuit of unnecessarily low levels of dose equivalent by the application of a policy of releases being as low as technically achievable (ALATA). At the same time such arrangements would prevent release (by dilution) of an unlimited amount of radioactive materials to the environment. A critical view of the ICRP recommendations may be seen in *Russell Jones and R Southwood*.[26]

The OECD-NEA Committee on Radiation and Public Health (CRPPH) is reviewing the system of radiation protection and has issued an interim paper 'A critical review of the system of radiation protection'.[27] As part of this review process Professor Roger Clarke, the chairman of the ICRP, proposed a series of

---

[21] ICRP (1990), *International Commission on Radiological Protection Publication 60, Recommendations of the International Commission on Radiological Protection*. Annals of the ICRP. 21, 1 - 3, 1991.

[22] NRPB (1987), *Interim Guidance on the Implications of Recent Revisions of Risk Estimates and the ICRP 1987 COMO Statement*. NRPB - GS9. ICRP to Review Recommendations. Atom 374 Dec pp 12-13.

[23] Preston D.L. and Pierce D.A. (1987), *The effect of changes in dosimetry on the cancer mortality risk estimates in the atom bomb survivors*. Technical Report of the Radiation Effects Research Foundation.

[24] Linsley G.S. (1986), 'Exemption from Regulatory Control - International Developments' *Radiation Protection Bulletin* No 81. NPPB.

[25] Glossary of Atomic Terms (UKAEA, 1982).

[26] Jones, Russell and Southwood R. (1987), *Radiation and Health*, John Wiley, London.

[27] [www.rea.fr/html/op/reports/2000].

ideas for simplifying the system or radiation protection.[28] For a balanced view see the views from the Nordic countries.[29] The philosophy of protection of the environment is also being reconsidered.[30]

Summary of the Potential for Damage Caused by Radiation

Primarily the damage caused by the explosion of a nuclear weapon is that caused by the blast. Radiation from the nuclear reaction in the exploding weapon will cause death within about a mile of the centre of the explosion. Radiation from the debris will cause damage depending on the amount of radiation and may lead to an increased incidence of death from cancer many years later. Future generations will be affected by the remaining radioactive debris and by genetic changes from exposure of parents. An accident to a nuclear reactor may have similar effects. In the Chernobyl accident 31 people died from the non-stochastic effects and it is estimated that an additional 1000 people in Europe face death from cancer in the next 50 years.[31] In an analysis made for the Sizewell B public inquiry[32] of the worst credible predicted accident, (a degraded core accident in which the reactor core melts and the containment fails, thus releasing radioactive material to the environment), it was calculated that about seven people would die from non-stochastic effects and 1300 people would die of cancer in the following 40 years.

The mishandling of industrial or medical equipment that uses radioactive materials may cause radiation damage. In September 1987 a shielded radioactive source was removed by scavengers from an abandoned clinic in Goiânia, Brazil and was later broken open. Many people handled the source: approximately 250 were exposed to large doses of radiation; of these, 50 showed signs of whole body irradiation and local acute irradiation and internal or external contamination; 14 developed bone marrow injury; ultimately 4 of these died of bleeding and sepsis and radiation skin injuries were observed in 28.[33]

Property irradiated by a nuclear reaction or contaminated by radioactive dust is potentially dangerous. The long-lived nature of some of the components of the radioactive contamination causes the need to control them at lower levels than are dangerous so as to limit their concentration, via the food chain, to safe levels. This is possible since all radioactive materials decay in strength over time. Economic

---

[28] Clarke, R. (1999), 'Control of low-level radiation exposure: time for a change?' *J Radiol Prot* vol 19 No 2, 107-115.

[29] Views expressed in the Nordic countries on the suggested modifications to the ICRP approach [www.nsfs.org/irpa_nsfs.html].

[30] Pentreath, R.J. (1999), 'A system for radiological protection of the environment: some initial thoughts and ideas'. *J Radiol Prot* vol 19 No 2, 117-128.

[31] Linsley G.S. (1986), 'Exemption from Regulatory Control - International Developments' *Radiation Protection Bulletin* No 81, NPPB.

[32] UKAEA (1987), 'Degraded Core Analysis for the PWR' *Atom* 362 Oct 1987 pp 7-13.

[33] Brandao-Mello, Carlos Eduardo, MD; de Oliveira, Alexandre Rodrigues, MD and Farina, Rosana MD (1993), *A Medical Follow-Up of the 137Cs Goiania Radiation Accident,* International Nuclear Law Association, Sept, Rio de Janeiro, Brazil.

loss may therefore be caused by the restriction of use or movement of property; for example the delay of the slaughter of sheep following the Chernobyl accident.

Radiation is released by many processes and can cause harm to man directly and possibly to future generations. The contamination of property by radioactive materials may render it unusable. Persons may suffer anxiety either because of knowledge of contact with radiation or fear of the unknown. The deployment of resources to reduce the levels of radiation release to the environment to lower and lower levels may starve investment from other socially needed measures.

One of the major sources of natural radiation is the decay of radon gas which is issued from the earth and which accumulates in houses. Professor Roberts of the University of East Anglia has observed:

> The standards applied to excess radiation levels arising in industry are those appropriate to a safe working industry, while those applied to radon in homes are, perhaps, appropriate to the usual standards of domestic safety. Home is known to be a much more dangerous place than the workplace.

Appendix 2.1

International Commission on Radiological Protection: History, Policies and Procedures[1]

Compiled for the ICRP by Bo Lindell,[2] H John Dunster,[3] and Jack Valentin[4]

Abstract

This report briefly reviews the history, mode of operation, concepts, and current policies of the International Commission on Radiological Protection (ICRP). It touches upon the objectives of the Commission's recommendations, the quantities used, the biological basis of the Commission's policy, the quantitative basis for its risk estimates, the structure of the system of protection, some problems of interpretation and application in that system, and the need for stability, consistency, and clarity in the Commission's recommendations.

1 Introduction

The International Commission on Radiological Protection (ICRP) recently issued a review of its history, mode of operation, concepts, and current policies. [1] The present paper summarises that report. It is assumed that the reader is broadly familiar with the current Recommendations and Publications of the Commission.

2 History and Affiliation

ICRP was established in 1928 as a Commission linked to the International Congresses of Radiology. Formally, its parent organisation is still the International Society of Radiology, but its field of work has widened from protection in medical radiology to all aspects of protection against ionising radiation. The Commission is supported by a number of international organisations and by many governments. It issues recommendations on the principles of radiation protection. Its

---

[1] Taken from the ICRP website with kind permission of the ICRP and formatted to suit the style of the book.

[2] Swedish Radiation Protection Institute (SSI), SE-171 16 Stockholm, Sweden.

[3] National Radiological Protection Board, Chilton, Didcot, Oxon OX11 0RQ, UK.

[4] International Commission on Radiological Protection (ICRP), SE-171 16 Stockholm, Sweden.

recommendations form the basis for more detailed codes and regulations issued by other international organisations and by regional and national authorities. The Commission is registered as an independent charity in the United Kingdom and is financed mainly by voluntary contributions from international and national bodies with an interest in radiological protection. Some additional funds accrue from royalties on the Commission's publications. Members' institutions also provide financial support to the Commission by making the members' time available without charge and, in some cases, contributing to their costs of attending meetings. Many of these institutions also provide substantial resources without charge to the Commission. The Commission issued its first report in 1928. The first report in the current series, subsequently numbered Publication 1[2], contained recommendations   adopted   in   September   1958.   Subsequent   general recommendations have appeared in 1964 as Publication 6[3], in 1966 as Publication 9[4], and in 1977 as Publication 26[5]. Publication 26 was amended and extended by a Statement in 1978[6] and further clarified and extended by a succession of Statements between 1980 and 1987[7, 8, 9, 10, 11]. The recommendations were completely revised and issued in 1991 as Publication 60[12]. Reports on more specialised topics have appeared as intermediate and subsequent Publication numbers. The more recent reports are listed in Table 1. (below)

The Commission has always been an advisory body. It offers its recommendations to regulatory and advisory agencies at international, regional, and national levels, mainly by providing guidance on the fundamental principles on which appropriate radiological protection can be based. The Commission does not aim to provide regulatory texts. Authorities need to develop their own texts in the context of their own regulatory structures. Nevertheless, the Commission believes that these regulatory texts should be developed from, and have aims that are broadly consistent with, its guidance. In addition, the Commission hopes that its advice is of help to management bodies with responsibilities for radiological protection in their own operations, to the professional staff whom they use as their advisers, and to individuals, such as radiologists, who have to make decisions about protection in the use of ionising radiation.

3 The Structure and Mode of Operation

The Commission ICRP is composed of a Main Commission and four standing Committees. The Commission consists of twelve members and a Chairman. They are elected by the Commission itself, under its rules, which are subject to the approval of the International Society of Radiology. The Committee members are appointed by the Commission, and each Committee is chaired by a Commission member. From 1962 to the present, 1998, there have been four Committees:

- Committee 1 on Radiation Effects,
- Committee 2 on Derived Limits,
- Committee 3 on Protection in Medicine, and
- Committee 4 on the Application of the Commission's Recommendations.

The Commission uses Task Groups and Working Parties to prepare reports to be discussed by the Committees and finally approved by the Commission. Task Groups are appointed by the Commission to perform a defined task, usually the preparation of a draft report. A Task Group usually contains a majority of specialists from outside the Commission's structure. Working Parties are set up by Committees, with the approval of the Commission, to develop ideas for the Committee, sometimes leading to a Task Group. The membership is usually limited to Committee members. The Commission's secretariat is managed by a Scientific Secretary with a minimum of bureaucracy.

4 The Objectives of the Commission's Recommendations

The main objective of the Commission's recommendations is to provide an appropriate standard of protection for man without unduly limiting the beneficial practices giving rise to radiation exposure. This aim of providing an appropriate standard of protection, rather than the best possible standard regardless of costs and benefits, cannot be achieved on the basis of scientific concepts alone. Members of the Commission and its Committees have the responsibility for supplementing their scientific knowledge by value judgements about the relative importance of different kinds of risk and about the balancing of risks and benefits. The Commission believes that the basis for such judgements should be made clear, so that readers can understand how the decisions have been reached.

5 Quantities

The *absorbed dose* is the radiation energy imparted per unit mass of an irradiated body. It is measured in joule per kilogram, a unit which is also called the *gray (Gy)*. Multiplying the absorbed dose by appropriate weighting factors depending on the type of radiation, creates the *equivalent dose* in the relevant organ or tissue. By weighting the equivalent dose in each organ in proportion to the probability and severity of the harm done by radiation, and adding the weighted contributions from each organ to a total body dose, a third dose, the *effective dose* is obtained. The *effective dose* is defined by the Commission as the sum of the equivalent doses in the principal tissues and organs in the body, each weighted by a *tissue weighting factor*, w_T. This weighting factor takes account of the probability of fatal cancer, the probability of nonfatal cancer, weighted for severity, and the average length of life lost due to an induced cancer. A contribution for severe hereditary disorders is also included. Detriment, as used by the Commission, can be thought of as the probability of causing a level of total harm judged to be equivalent to one death that causes, on average, a loss of lifetime of 15 years. The *committed effective dose* is the sum of the committed equivalent doses each weighted by the appropriate tissue weighting factor. In radiation protection it is usually the effective dose that is determined for comparison with dose limits or for assessments of risks. Both the equivalent dose and the effective dose are also measured in joule per kilogram, but in these cases the unit is called the *sievert (Sv)*. For x rays and gamma rays the absorbed and equivalent doses in gray and sievert are numerically equal.

In publications before *Publication 60*, the Commission defined a *mean quality factor*, Q, for spectra of mixed values of linear energy transfer. In addition, the Commission stated that it was permissible to use approximate values for Q and provided tables of values[5]. In *Publication 60*[12], the Commission replaced the dose equivalent defined at a point by the *equivalent dose*, derived by weighting the mean absorbed dose in an organ or tissue by the *radiation weighting factor*, wR. This factor was an updated value of the previous permissible approximation for Q, but now became the definitive weighting factor. Doses in organs within the body cannot be measured directly, so practical quantities, measurable outside the body, are needed. For radiation fields outside the body, measurable quantities, called *operational quantities*, have been recommended by the International Commission on Radiation Units and Measurements. These quantities were specified before the introduction of the radiation weighting factor, and use quality factors (related to linear energy transfer) rather than radiation weighting factors. Nevertheless, they still provide a set of field quantities that, in most practical situations, adequately reflect the protection quantities used by ICRP[13]. For sources inside the body, the relevant measurable quantity is the activity of radioactive material taken into the body, the *intake*. This material causes a continuing distribution of equivalent doses within the body. The time integral of the resulting equivalent dose rate is called the *committed equivalent dose*. The integration time is 50 years for an adult and from the time of intake to age 70 years for children. In source-related assessments, the individual doses have to be supplemented by information on the number of people exposed. The simplest quantity to reflect both the dose and the number of people is the *collective dose*. The collective effective dose may sometimes be used as a measure of the expected collective harm, the radiation health *detriment*. The collective dose is most useful when the individual doses are all of much the same magnitude and are all delivered in times not greatly exceeding a few years. If the distribution of individual doses covers many orders of magnitude and the time distribution covers centuries, the simple collective dose is less useful because it aggregates too much diverse information. It is then better to present partially disaggregated data in the form of blocks of collective dose each covering a narrower range of individual dose and a narrower range of time.

6 The Biological Basis of the Commission's Policy

There are two types of harmful radiation effects to be protected against. High doses will cause inevitable harm, the *deterministic effects*, which do not appear if the dose does not exceed a *threshold value*. The primary protection policy is then to prevent high doses. Both low and high doses may cause *stochastic*, i.e. randomly occurring, effects (cancer and hereditary disorders). At low doses, of the order of those caused by natural sources of radiation, these effects will occur only with a small probability, which is judged by the Commission to be in proportion to the dose. This proportionality (the linear, non-threshold dose-response relationship) has characteristics that facilitate the administration of radiation protection. For example, it makes it possible to consider each source and exposure separately from other sources and exposures – the probability of harm per unit dose will always be the same. However, the probabilistic nature of the stochastic effects makes it impossible to make a clear distinction between 'safe' and 'dangerous', a fact that causes problems in explaining the control of radiation risks. The major policy implication of a non-threshold relationship for stochastic effects is that some finite risk must be accepted at any level of protection. Zero risk is not an option. This leads to the basic system of protection which has three components –

(1) the justification of a practice, which implies doing more good than harm,

(2) the optimisation of protection, which implies maximising the margin of good over harm, and

(3) the use of dose limits, which implies an adequate standard of protection even for the most highly exposed individuals.

A simple proportional relationship also has some important practical implications. It allows –

(a) doses within an organ or tissue of the body to be averaged over that organ or tissue,

(b) doses received at different times to be added, and

(c) doses received from one source to be considered independently of the doses received from other sources.

These practical aspects are of overwhelming importance in radiological protection because of the complexity of the dose distributions in both time and space and because of the ubiquitous presence of natural sources of radiation.

7 Concepts

The Commission makes a distinction between what it calls *practices* and *intervention*. A practice is a human activity that is undertaken by choice but which increases the overall exposure. For that reason, practices have to be controlled so that additional doses are appropriately restricted. Intervention is an action against radiation exposures that already exist, for the purpose of reducing the exposures. Both practices and intervention are justified when they cause more good than harm. The main protection principle in both cases is that protection should be *optimised*, *i.e.* all doses should be kept as low as reasonably achievable, economic and social factors being taken into account. For equity reasons (because those who are exposed are not necessarily those who gain by a practice) some dose or risk limitation is necessary to prevent the optimised situation from being one where a few individuals receive inappropriately high doses. In addition to source-related constraints for this purpose, various levels for actions are recommended (levels for intervention, for recording, for investigation, etc.).

The Commission also differentiates between three types of exposure: occupational exposure, which is the exposure incurred at work, and principally as a result of work; medical exposure, which is principally the exposure of persons as part of their diagnosis or treatment; and public exposure, which comprises all other exposures. A distinction is also drawn between source-related assessments, which are concerned with the exposures resulting from a single source and individual-related assessments, which deal with the exposure of a single individual from many sources.

The process of the optimisation of protection involves some degree of balancing of detriments and benefits. Unless the individual detriments are small, this process raises ethical problems of inequity when the detriments and benefits accrue to different people, as is usually the case. It is in order to limit this inequity that the Commission recommends the use of *source-related constraints,* aimed at excluding from the process of optimisation any protection options that would involve individual doses above the selected constraint. Over the years there has been confusion over the meaning of the Commission's *dose limits.* The Commission now regards these as being close to the point where the doses from the sources to which the dose limits apply result in a level of risk that, if continued, could legitimately be described as unacceptable for those sources in normal circumstances. Compliance with dose limits is then a necessary, but not a sufficient, condition for complying with the Commission's recommendations. A dose limit is not a measure of the degree of rigour implied by the recommendations. That should be judged by the overall impact of the system of protection, of which the optimisation of protection is the most onerous and effective component. It must be remembered that dose limits do not apply to medical exposure. Particular confusion has been caused by the dose limit for public exposure. This limit applies to the doses from (*i.e.* attributable to) deliberate practices and, within these practices, from those radiation sources that can reasonably be controlled by human actions. The value selected is less than the total dose from all sources, many of which are natural sources that cannot be controlled, e.g. the dose from natural potassium in the body or from cosmic rays at ground level. This position, while logical, is not easily explained. The presence of doses from natural sources of radiation does not justify the doses from controllable sources. It is proper to control these sources, even if the doses are less than the background doses from uncontrolled natural sources. However, this background does provide a useful basis for comparisons.

As with practices, the *justification of intervention* requires that the intervention should do more good than harm. Intervention is justified if the reduction of exposures and thus of radiation induced detriment is sufficient to offset the costs, risks, and social disadvantages of the actions (countermeasures) that comprise the intervention. The decision to intervene is made easier by the selection of intervention levels of averted dose linked to specified actions. The Commission has recommended ranges of such intervention levels[14,15]. All these concepts relate to situations in which the dose has already occurred or will occur in the future. However, there are many situations in which an exposure (and thus a dose) is not certain to occur and may have only a small probability of occurring. Such exposures are called *potential exposures.* The detriment associated with a potential exposure of an individual can be expressed as the product of the conditional detriment, given that the dose has occurred, and the probability of the dose being delivered. Even for an individual potential exposure, the aggregation implied by this product may be excessive. For example, an event with a high probability of causing a dose that, if incurred, would carry a low probability of death and an event with a low probability of causing a high dose carrying a certainty of death may have the same potential detriment as given by this product. But the two events may not be judged to be of equal importance.

Reference levels are values of measured quantities above which some specified action or decision should be taken. They include recording levels, above which a result should be recorded, lower values being ignored; investigation levels, above which the cause or the implications of the result should be examined; intervention levels (of dose averted by a defined remedial action), above which the remedial action should be considered; and, more generally, action levels above which some specified action should be taken. The use of these levels can avoid unnecessary or unproductive work and can help in the effective deployment of resources.

8 The Quantitative Basis for Risk Estimates

The Commission bases its recommendations on risk estimates derived from several sources. Direct evidence on deterministic effects on humans is obtained from observations on individuals who have been exposed to high doses by accident or intentionally in radiotherapy. For stochastic effects no direct cause-effect relation can be observed and assessments on risks to humans must be based on epidemiological studies with statistical methods. Because these effects are no different from cancers and hereditary disorders from other causes, statistical limitations prevent significant observations at low doses. The epidemiological information therefore has to be supplemented by inference from radiobiological research on mechanisms for stochastic effects. The information on which the Commission bases its quantitative estimates of the probability of stochastic effects comes primarily from epidemiological studies of human populations. However, cancer and hereditary disorders are common in man and the detection and quantification of small increases depends on two features of the study. One is the statistical power of the study, which relates to the size of the population studied and the level of risk to detect. As information is sought at lower and lower doses, the statistical power ceases to be adequate and no conclusions can be drawn about the presence or absence of effects. The other limitation of low-dose epidemiological studies is the inability to control for confounding factors, such as tobacco use, where slight differences between exposed and comparison groups can be much more significant than the anticipated radiation risk.

9 The Structure of the System of Protection

Because of the complexity of radiological protection and of the need to achieve a consistency across a wide range of applications, the Commission has established a formal System of Protection. The main aim of this system is to encourage a structured approach to protection. The principal subdivisions in the system are summarised as follows:

- Practices that increase the exposure of people or the number of people exposed;
- Intervention that decreases the exposures from existing sources;
- Source related and individual related assessments;
- Classification of types of exposure into occupational exposure, medical exposure and public exposure;
- Justification of a practice, optimisation of protection, and dose limits;
- Justification of intervention and optimisation of the type and scale of intervention;
- Potential exposure and accident prevention;
- Emergency planning;
- Implementation of the recommendations by operating managements and regulators.

10 Problems of Interpretation and Application in Protection

The Commission's *risk estimates* are called 'nominal' because they relate to the continuous exposure of a nominal population of males and females with a typical age distribution. For populations with an age distribution very different from the nominal populations it may be desirable to use adjusted risk coefficients, but not to seek for different sets of radiation and tissue weighting factors because these would confuse the use of effective dose. The borderline between practices and intervention is usually clear, but there are some difficult cases. The clearest differentiation is provided by the ability to choose whether to accept the sources and the consequent exposures. If that choice is still available, the exposure can usually be said to be due to a practice and steps to reduce doses are improvements to the practice, not intervention. If the choice does not exist because the sources and the exposures already exist, any action taken to reduce exposures is intervention. The decision to intervene is then made on the basis of the dose that can be averted. In the early years of radiological protection, the limited control of exposures made it desirable to check for the occurrence of detectable effects in workers. Pre-employment and routine medical surveillance were integral parts of protection. In recent years, the medical needs have changed. As in any occupation, there is still a need for confirmation that workers are fit for their duties, but the normal level of radiation exposure is not now a factor that should influence the extent of the conventional occupational health surveillance. Exceeding a dose limit is an indication of a failure of managerial control but, unless the dose is much higher than the dose limit, does not call for medical action. Some confusion has been caused by attempts to limit the definition of *occupational exposure* to annual doses above some value, often 1 mSv. This is not the Commission's intention. All exposures incurred at work are occupational, although the Commission intends that its recommendations on occupational exposure should apply only to those occupational exposures that can reasonably be regarded as the responsibility of the operating management. The decision to use individual monitoring or to require special training should be based on an assessment of the need, rather than on any estimates of current or future exposure. Occupational exposures directly due to an accident can be limited only by the design of the plant and its protective features and by the provision of emergency procedures. Ideally, the aim should be to keep the doses within those permitted in normal conditions, but this may not always be possible in serious accidents. In addition to the exposures resulting directly from the accident, there will be exposures of emergency teams during emergency and remedial action. The doses incurred are likely to be higher than in normal situations and should be treated separately from any normal doses. Emergencies involving significant exposures of emergency teams are rare, so some relaxation of the controls for normal situations can be permitted in serious accidents without lowering the long-term level of protection. This relaxation should not permit the exposures during the control of the accident and the immediate and urgent remedial work to give doses approaching thresholds of deterministic effects. Furthermore, life-saving actions can rarely be limited by dosimetric assessments. Once the emergency is under control, remedial work should be treated as part of the occupational exposure incurred in a practice.

11 The Need for Stability, Consistency, and Clarity

The Commission's recommendations are widely used by international and regional agencies, by national regulatory agencies, and by operating managements and their protection advisers. The time-scale on which these bodies can respond to a change in recommendations varies widely, but none of them welcomes frequent changes. The Commission recognises this and avoids making frequent changes in its principal recommendations. Intervals of not less than ten to fifteen years seem to be appropriate. There is also an expectation that the recommendations will be internally consistent. This is fairly straightforward in the principal recommendations but more difficult in the separate detailed guidance issued on specialised topics.

Table 1 Summary of ICRP Publications from Publication 60 Onwards

Pub.60 1990 Recommendations of the International Commission on Radiological Protection Vol. Vol.21 (1-3) - Risks Associated with Ionising Radiations Vol.22 (1)

Pub.61 Annual Limits on Intake of Radionuclides by Workers Based on the 1990 Recommendations Vol.21 (4)

Pub.62 Radiological Protection in Biomedical Research Vol.22 (3)

Pub.63 Principles for Intervention for Protection of the Public in a Radiological Emergency Vol.22 (4)

Pub.64 Protection from Potential Exposure Vol.23 (1)

Pub.65 Protection Against Radon-222 at Home and at Work Vol.23 (2)

Pub.66 Human Respiratory Tract Model for Radiological Protection Vol.24 (1-3)

Pub.67 Age-dependent Doses to Members of the Public from Intake of Radionuclides: Part 2. Ingestion Dose Coefficients Vol.23 (3-4)

Pub.68 Dose Coefficients for Intakes of Radionuclides by Workers Vol.**24** (4)

Pub.69 Age-dependent Doses to Members of the Public from Intake of Radionuclides: Part 3. Ingestion Dose Coefficients Vol.**25** (1)

Pub.70 Basic Anatomical and Physiological Data for use in Radiological Protection: The Skeleton Vol.**25** (2)

Pub.71 Age-dependent Doses to Members of the Public from Intake of Radionuclides: Part 4. Inhalation Dose Coefficients Vol.**25** (3-4)

Pub.72 Age-dependent Doses to Members of the Public from Intake of Radionuclides: Part 5 Compilation of Ingestion and Inhalation Dose Coefficients Vol.**26** (1)

Pub.73 Radiological Protection and Safety in Medicine Vol.**26** (2)

Pub.74 Conversion Coefficients for use in Radiological Protection against External Radiation Vol.**26** (3-4)

Pub.75 General Principles for the Radiation Protection of Workers Vol.**27** (1)

Pub.76 Protection from Potential Exposures: Application to Selected Radiation Sources Vol.**27** (2)

Pub.77 Radiological Protection Policy for the Disposal of Radioactive Waste Vol.**27** (Supplement)

Pub.78 Individual Monitoring for Intakes of Radionuclides by Workers: Replacement of ICRP Publication 54 Vol.**27** (3-4)

Pub.79 Genetic Susceptibility to Cancer Vol.**28** (in press)

Pub.80 Radiation Dose to Patients from Radiopharmaceuticals: Addendum 2 to ICRP Publication 53 Vol.**28** (in press)

References

1 ICRP (1998). International Commission on Radiological Protection: History, Policies, Procedures. Elsevier Science Ltd, Oxford.

2 ICRP (1959). Recommendations of the International Commission on Radiological Protection. ICRP Publication 1, Pergamon Press, Oxford.

3 ICRP (1964). Recommendations of the International Commission on Radiological Protection. ICRP Publication 6, Pergamon Press, Oxford.

4 ICRP (1966). Recommendations of the International Commission on Radiological Protection. ICRP Publication 9, Pergamon Press, Oxford.

5 ICRP (1977). Recommendations of the International Commission on Radiological Protection. ICRP Publication 26, Annals of the ICRP 1(3), Pergamon Press, Oxford.

6 ICRP (1978). Statement from the 1978 Stockholm meeting. In: Annals of the ICRP 1(3), Pergamon Press, Oxford.

7 ICRP (1980). Statement from the 1980 Brighton meeting. In: Annals of the ICRP 4(3/4), Pergamon Press, Oxford.

8 ICRP (1984). Statement from the 1983 Washington meeting. In: Annals of the ICRP 4(3/4), Pergamon Press, Oxford.

9 ICRP (1985). Statement from the 1985 Paris meeting. In: Annals of the ICRP 15(3), Pergamon Press, Oxford.

10 ICRP (1987a). Statement from the 1987 Washington meeting. In: Annals of the ICRP 17(2/3), Pergamon Press, Oxford.

11 ICRP (1987b). Statement from the 1987 Como meeting. In: Annals of the ICRP 17(4), Pergamon Press, Oxford.

12 ICRP (1991a). 1990 Recommendations of the International Commission on Radiological Protection. ICRP Publication 60, Annals of the ICRP 21(1-3), Pergamon Press, Oxford.

13 ICRP (1995). Conversion Coefficients for use in Radiological Protection against External Radiation. ICRP Publication 74, Annals of the ICRP 26(3/4), Pergamon Press, Oxford.

14 ICRP (1991b). Principles for Intervention for Protection of the Public in a Radiological Emergency. ICRP Publication 63, Annals of the ICRP 22(4), Pergamon Press, Oxford.

15 ICRP (1993). Protection Against Radon-222 at Home and at Work. ICRP Publication 65, Annals of the ICRP 23(2), Pergamon Press, Oxford.

Appendix 2.2

Constitution of the International Commission on Radiological Protection[5]

Approved at a meeting of the Commission at Como, Italy in September 1987

1. Name

The name of the organisation is The international Commission on Radiological Protection (hereinafter called 'the Commission' or 'ICRP').

2. Objects and Powers

2.1. The Commission is established to advance for the public benefit the science of Radiological Protection, in particular by providing recommendations and guidance on all aspects of radiation protection. In preparing its recommendations, the Commission considers the fundamental principles and quantitative bases upon which appropriate radiation protection measures can be established, while leaving to the various national protection bodies the responsibility of formulating the specific advice, codes of practice, or regulations that are best suited to the needs of their individual countries.

2.2. In furtherance of the said objects, but not otherwise, the Commission may:

2.2.1. Employ and pay any person or persons not being a member of the Management Committee to supervise, organise and carry on the work of the Commission and make all reasonable and necessary provision for the payment of pensions and superannuation to or on behalf of employees and their widows and other dependants;

2.2.2. Bring together in conference representatives of voluntary organisations, Government departments, statutory authorities and individuals;

2.2.3. Set up specialist advisory committees and task groups;

2.2.4. Promote and carry out or assist in promoting and carrying out research, surveys and investigations and publish the useful results thereof;

2.2.5. Arrange and provide for or join in arranging and providing for the holding of exhibitions, meetings, lectures, classes, seminars and training courses;

2.2.6. Collect and disseminate information on all matters affecting the said objects and exchange such information with other bodies having similar objects;

2.2.7. Undertake, execute, manage or assist any charitable trusts which may lawfully be undertaken, executed, managed or assisted by the Commission;

---

[5] Taken from the ICRP website with kind permission of the ICRP.

2.2.8. Cause to be written and printed or otherwise reproduced and circulated, gratuitously or otherwise, such papers, books, periodicals, pamphlets or other documents or films or recorded tapes (whether audio, visual, computer readable or any combination) as shall further the said objects;

2.2.9. Purchase, take on lease or in exchange, hire or otherwise acquire any property and any rights and privileges necessary for the promotion of the said objects and construct, maintain and alter any buildings or erections necessary for the work of the Commission;

2.2.10. Make regulations for any property which may be so acquired;

2.2.11. Subject to such consents as may be required by law, sell, let, mortgage, dispose of or turn to account all or any of the property or assets of the Commission;

2.2.12. Subject to such consents as may be required by law, borrow or raise money for the said objects and accept gifts on such terms and on such security as shall be deemed to be necessary;

2.2.13. Raise funds and invite and receive contributions from any person or persons whatsoever by way of subscriptions and otherwise provided that the Commission shall not undertake permanent trading activities in raising funds for the said objects;

2.2.14. Invest the monies of the Commission not immediately required for the said objects in or upon such investments, securities or property as may be thought fit, subject nevertheless to such conditions (if any) as may for the time being be imposed or required by law;

2.2.15. Do all such other lawful things as are necessary for the attainment of the said objects.

3. Structure and Membership

3.1. The Commission shall be composed of a Chairman and not less than six and not more than twelve other members. At least one Member of the Commission shall be resident in England or Wales. The selection of the Chairman and members shall be made by the Commission. When changes occur in the membership, the Chairman shall inform the Executive Committee of the International Society of Radiology. Members of the Commission shall be chosen on the basis of their recognised activity in the fields of medical radiology, radiation protection, physics, health physics, biology, genetics, biochemistry, biophysics and other disciplines relevant to the objects of the Commission, with regard to an appropriate balance of expertise rather than to nationality.

3.2. The membership of the Commission shall be selected for services until the end of the succeeding International Congress of Radiology, or until new members are appointed. Not less than three but not more than five members shall be changed at any one such Congress. In the intervening period vacancies may be filled by the Commission.

3.3. In event of a member of the Commission being unable to attend a meeting of the Commission, a substitute may be selected by the Commission as a temporary replacement. Such a substitute shall not have voting privileges unless specifically authorised by the Commission.

3.4. The Commission shall be permitted to invite individuals to attend its meetings to give special technical advice. Such persons shall not have voting privileges, but their opinions may be recorded in the minutes.

3.5. The Chairman shall be elected by the Commission from among its members, to serve until the end of the succeeding International Congress of Radiology, or until his successor is elected. The choice shall not be limited to a national of the country in which it is proposed to hold the succeeding Congress. The Chairman shall be responsible for reporting the proceedings and recommendations of the Commission at the next Congress.

3.6. The Commission shall elect from among its members a Vice-Chairman who will serve in the capacity of Chairman in the event that the Chairman is unable to perform his duties. The Chairman and Vice-Chairman shall constitute the Honorary Officers of the Commission.

3.7. Minutes of meetings and records of the Commission shall be made and maintained by a Scientific Secretary selected by the Chairman of the Commission, subject to the approval of its members. The Scientific Secretary shall not be a member of the Commission. The records of the Commission shall be passed on to the succeeding Scientific Secretary.

3.8. The Chairman, in consultation with the Vice-Chairman and Scientific Secretary, shall prepare a programme to be submitted to the Commission for discussion at its meetings. Proposals to be considered shall be submitted to the Chairman for circulation to all members of the Commission and other specially qualified individuals at least 56 days before any meeting of the Commission.

3.9. Decisions of the Commission shall be made by a majority vote of the members. (Voting may be at meetings or by postal ballot. Organisation of voting and the recording of results is the responsibility of the Scientific Secretary.) A minority opinion may be appended to the minutes of a meeting if so desired by any member upon his submission of the same in writing to the Scientific Secretary.

3.10. The Commission may establish such committees as it deems necessary to perform its functions. No such committee shall incur expenditure on behalf of the Commission except in accordance with a budget which has been agreed by the Commission or the Management Committee hereinafter described.

4. Management Committee

4.1. The Commission shall from time to time, but not less often than once in each year, constitute itself as the Management Committee, with the same officers as the Honorary Officers of the Commission. The Management Committee shall direct the policy and general management of the Commission.

4.2. The Management Committee shall appoint one or more qualified auditors.

4.3. The Chairman, after consultation with the Management Committee, shall appoint and fix the remuneration of the Scientific Secretary.

4.4. All questions arising at a meeting of the Management Committee shall be decided by a simple majority of those present and voting. In the event of an equality of votes, the Chairman of the meeting shall have a second or casting vote.

4.5. The proceedings of the Management Committee shall not be invalidated by any failure to elect or any defect in the election, appointment, co-option or qualification of any member.

5. Meetings of the Commission

5.1. The first General Meeting of the Commission shall be held not later than September 1988 and once in each year thereafter an Annual General Meeting of the Commission shall be held at such time (not being more than 18 months after the holding of the preceding Annual Meeting) and place as the Committee shall determine. At least 56 clear days' notice shall be given in writing by the Scientific Secretary to each member. At such an Annual General Meeting the business shall include the consideration of an annual report of the work done by or under the auspices of the Management Committee and of the audited accounts; and the transaction of such other matters as may from time to time be necessary.
5.2. The Chairman of the Commission may at any time at his or her discretion and the Scientific Secretary shall within 21 days of receiving a written request to do so, signed by not less than four members of the Commission, and giving reasons for the request, call a Special General Meeting of the Commission.

6. Nominations of Honorary Officers

Only members of the Commission shall be eligible to serve as Honorary Officers of the Management Committee. Nominations for Honorary Officers must be made by members of the Commission in writing and must be in the hands of the Scientific Secretary at least seven days before an Annual General Meeting. Should nominations exceed vacancies, election shall be by ballot.

7. Rules of Procedure at All Meetings

7.1. The quorum at a meeting of the Commission or Management Committee shall be seven members.
7.2. All questions arising at any meeting shall be decided by a simple majority of those present and entitled to vote thereat, so however that any matter that is to be recorded as a Decision for the Commission shall be determined in accordance with Item 3.9. No person shall exercise more than one vote, but in the case of an equality of votes the Chairman of the meeting shall have a second or casting vote.
7.3. Minutes shall be kept of all meetings of the Commission, the Management Committee and all other committees, and the appropriate secretary shall enter therein a record of all proceedings and resolutions.
7.4. The Management Committee shall have the power to adopt and issue Standing Orders and/or Rules for the Commission and its committees. Such Standing Orders and/or Rules shall come into operation immediately provided always that they shall be subject to review by the Commission in General Meeting and shall not be inconsistent with the provisions of this Constitution.

8. Finance

8.1. All monies raised by and on behalf of the Commission shall be applied to further the objects of the Commission and for no other purpose provided that nothing herein contained shall prevent the payment in good faith of reasonable and proper remuneration to any employee of the Commission (not being a member of the Management Committee) or the repayment to members of the Commission, the Management Committee, or other persons associated with the work of the Commission of reasonable out-of-pocket expenses.

8.2. The Scientific Secretary shall keep proper accounts of the finances of the Commission.

8.3. The accounts shall be audited at least once a year by the auditor or auditors appointed by the Management Committee.

8.4. An audited statement of the accounts for the last financial year shall be submitted by the Management Committee to the Annual General Meeting as aforesaid.

8.5. A bank account shall be opened in the name of the Commission with such bank or banks as the Management Committee shall from time to time decide. The Management Committee shall authorise in writing the Chairman, the Vice-Chairman, the Scientific Secretary to the Commission and one other member of the Management Committee to sign cheques on behalf of the Commission. All cheques for amounts above £5,000, or such other sum specified by the Management Committee, must be signed by not less than two of the four authorised signatories.

8.6. Except for temporary deposits of monies in other countries for funding activities in those countries, the monies and assets of the Commission shall be held in England or Wales.

9. Trust Property

The title to all real or personal property which may be acquired by or on behalf of the Commission shall be vested in a corporation lawfully entitled to act as Custodian Trustee, or shall be vested in Trustees who shall be appointed by the Management Committee and who shall enter into a deed of trust setting forth the purposes and conditions under which they hold the said property in trust for the Commission. The number of Trustees shall not be less than seven nor more than thirteen.

10. Alterations to the Constitution

Any alteration to this Constitution shall receive the assent of not less than two-thirds of the membership of the Commission for the time being present and voting at a meeting specially called for that purpose provided that notice of any such alteration shall have been received by the Scientific Secretary in writing not less than 70 clear days before the meeting at which the alteration is proposed. At least 56 clear days' notice in writing of such a meeting, setting forth the terms of the alteration, shall be sent by the Scientific Secretary to each member of the Commission provided that no alteration shall be made to clause 2 (objects), clause 11 (dissolution), or this clause until the approval in writing of the Charity Commissioners or other authority having charitable jurisdiction shall have been obtained, and no alteration shall be made which would have the effect of causing the Commission to cease to be a Charity at law.

11. Dissolution

If the Management Committee decide at any time that on the ground of expense or otherwise it is necessary or advisable to dissolve the Commission, it shall call a meeting of all members of the Commission who have the power to vote, of which meeting not less than 56 days' notice (stating the terms of the Resolution to be proposed thereat) shall be given. If such a decision shall be confirmed by a two-thirds majority of those present and voting at such a meeting the Committee shall have power to dispose of any assets held by or on behalf of the Commission. Any assets remaining after the satisfaction of any proper debts and liabilities shall be given or transferred to such other charitable institution or institutions having objects similar to the objects of the Commission as the Committee may determine.

12. Notices

Any notice may be served by the Scientific Secretary on any member personally or by sending it through the post in a prepaid letter addressed to such member at his/her last known address. Any letter so sent shall be deemed to be received within 28 days of posting.

13. Interpretation

For the interpretation of this Constitution, the Interpretation Act 1978 shall apply as it applies to the interpretation of an Act of Parliament.

Bibliography

Barnes, M. QC (1990), *The Hinckley Point C Public Inquiries*. A Report, HMSO, London.

Beral V. (1985), 'Mortality of Employee's of the United Kingdom Atomic Energy Authority 1946-1979', *Brit Med J*, 291, (6493), pp 440-447.

Bertell, R. (1985), *No Immediate Danger*, The Woman's Press, London.

Boon, A. (1988), 'Causation and the Increase of Risk', 51 MLR 508.

Boyle, A.E. (1989), 'Nuclear Energy and International Law: An environmental perspective', *British Yearbook of International Law*, Vol LX.

Boyle, A.E. (1991), 'Making the Polluter Pay? Alternatives to State Responsibility in the Allocation of Transboundary Costs' in F. Francioni and T. Scovazzi (eds), *International Responsibility for Environmental Harm*, Graham & Trotman, London.

Busby, C. (2003), *2003 Recommendations of the ECRR*, Green Audit. Cambrian Printers, Wales.

Butler, G. and Curtis, C. (2003), 'Passive storage of radioactive waste', *Nuclear Energy*, 42, No.3, June, pp 157-162.

Cameron, P. (1999), *The Safety of Radioactive Waste Management: new steps forward in the law*, Nuclear Inter Jura 1999, Washington DC.

Clarke, R.H. (1996), 'Implications of new data on cancer risk', NRPB *Bulletin* No 179 July.

Clarke, R.H. (1999), 'Control of low-level radiation exposure: time for a change', *Journal of Radiological Protection*, Vol 19 No.2, 107-115.

de Kageneck, A. and Pinel, C. (1998), 'The Joint Convention on the Safety of Spent Fuel Management and on the Safety of Radioactive Waste', *International and Comparative Law Quaterly*, Vol 47 April.

Decleris, M. (2000), *The Law of Sustainable Development-General Principles*. A report produced for the European Commission, Office for Official Publications of the European Communities, Luxembourg.

Department for Environment, Food and Rural Affairs (2002), *UK Strategy for radioactive discharges 2001-2020*, DEFRA Publications, London.

Department for Environment, Food and Rural Affairs, the Scottish Executive and the Welsh Assembly (2001), *Managing Radioactive Waste Safely, proposals for developing a policy for managing solid radioactive waste in the UK*, DEFRA Publications, London.

Department for Environment, Food and Rural Affairs, the Scottish Executive and the Welsh Assembly (2002), *Managing Radioactive Wastes Safely, summary of responses to the consultation, September 2001 – March 2002*, DEFRA Publications, London.

Department of the Environment (1995), *Review of Radioactive Waste Management Policy, Final Conclusions*, Cm 2919, HMSO, London.

Department of Trade and Industry (2002), *Managing the Nuclear Legacy – A Strategy for Action*, White Paper, (Cm5552), HMSO, London.

Department of Trade and Industry (Office of Civil Nuclear Security) (2003), *The State of Security in the Civil Nuclear Industry and Effectiveness of Security Regulation April 2002 – March 2003*, A Report to the Secretary of State for Trade and Industry by the Director of Civil Nuclear Security, Office for Civil Nuclear Security, HMSO, London.

Department of Trade and Industry and DEFRA (2003), *The Energy White Paper. Our Energy Future – creating a low carbon economy*, (Cm 5761), HMSO, London.

Doll, Sir R. (1988), *Healthy Worker Effect*, Imperial Cancer Research Fund Cancer and Epidemiology and Clinical Trials Unit, Radcliffe Infirmary, Oxford.

Duncan, I.J. (2003), 'What to do with nuclear waste', *Nuclear Energy*, 42 No.3, June pp 145-148.

European Commission (2000), *Innovation in a knowledge-driven economy*, COM (2000) 567, Brussels.

Evans, A. (2003), *The Generation Gap: scenarios for UK electricity in 2020*, Institute of Public Policy Research, London.

Farquhar, J.T. (1986), 'Best Practicable Means (and the thought that Nanny may have known best after all)' *Chemistry and Industry*, Aug., pp 541-543.

Fremlin, J. (1989), *Power Production – What are the Risks?* Adam Hilger, London.

Galizzi, P. (1966), 'Questions of Jurisdiction in the event of a nuclear accident in a member state of the European Union', *Journal of Environmental Law*, Vol 8 No 1 p 71.

González, A.J. (2000), 'The Safety of Radioactive Waste Management. Achieving internationally acceptable solutions', *IAEA Bulletin*, Vol 42, No. 3, pp 5-18. Vienna, Austria.

Gorka, G. (2001), 'Waste Legislation in the European Union', *European Environmental Law Review*, Dec.

Grecos, M. (2002), 'Human Rights and the Environment', *[2002] 2 Env. Liability* 95.

Guruswamy L.D. and Tromans S.R. (1986), 'Towards an Integrated Approach to Pollution Control. The Best Practicable Environmental Option and its Antecedents', *Journal of Planning and Environment Law*, August pp 643-655.

Health and Safety Executive (1992), *Safety Assessment Principles for Nuclear Plants*, HMSO, London.

Health and Safety Executive (1992), *Tolerability of risk from nuclear power Stations*, HSE Books, London.

Health and Safety Executive (1999), *Reducing Risks, Protecting People*, HSE Discussion Document, HMSO, London.

Health and Safety Executive on behalf of DEFRA (2003), *National Report on conformance with the obligations of the Joint Convention on the Safety of Spent Fuel Management and on the Safety of Radioactive Waste Management*, HMSO, London.

House of Lords (1999), Session 1998-9, *Third Report of the Select Committee on Science and Technology, Management of Nuclear Waste*, HL Paper 41, HMSO, London.

Howe, G. (2002), *Epidemiology: strengths, limitations and interpretation application to studies of low-dose radiation*. 4th International Conference on Health Effects of Low-level Radiation, September, Oxford.

Hughes, D.J (1995), 'The Status of the "Precautionary Principle" in Law,' *Journal of Environmental Law* Vol 7 p 224.

Hunt, C.A. (2002), 'Example of a BPEO study at AWE Aldermaston', *Nuclear Energy*, 41, No. 6, Dec, pp 369-373.

International Atomic Energy Agency (2002), *Ethical considerations in protecting the environment from the effects of ionising radiation*, IAEA TECHDOC-1270, IAEA, Vienna.

International Atomic Energy Agency (2002), *Scientific and Technical Basis for the Near Surface Disposal of Low and Intermediate Level Radioactive Waste (LILW)*, Technical Report Series No 412, IAEA, Vienna.

International Atomic Energy Agency (2003), *Scientific and Technical Basis for Geological Disposal of Radioactive Waste*, Technical Report Series No. 413, IAEA, Vienna.

Isted, J. (2003), *Novel developments in the use of international law to oppose nuclear activities*, International Nuclear Law Association Congress, Cape Town.

Janssens, A. (2002), 'Environmental radioactivity surveillance under the Euratom Treaty', *Nuclear Energy*, 41, No. 5, Oct., 339-346.

John, Edward (1995), 'Access to Environmental Information: Limitations of the UK Radioactive Substances Register', *Journal of Environmental Law*, Vol 7 No 1.

Lee, M. (2000), 'Civil Liability of the Nuclear Industry', *Journal of Environmental Law*, Vol 12, No.3.

Leigh, W.J. (1997), 'Liability and Regulation - Some Legal Challenges Faced by the Operators of United Kingdom Nuclear Installations', [1997] *Env. Liability* 44.

Leigh, W. J. (2003), 'The Principle of Justification: the Application of the Principle to the Manufacture of MOX Fuel in the UK.' *Nuclear Law Bulletin* 71 Vol 2003/1. OECD Paris.

Leigh, W.J. and Wakeford, Dr Richard (2001), 'Radiation Litigation and the Nuclear Industry – the Experience in the United Kingdom', Health Physics 81 (6), pp 645-646.

Lochard, J. and Boehler, M-C. (1993), 'Optimising Radiation Protection-the ethical and legal bases', *Nuclear Law Bulletin* 42.

Lofstedt, Ragnor, E et al (2000), 'Risk Management across the Globe: Insights from a Comparative Look at Sweden, Japan and the United States'. *Risk Analysis*, Vol 20, No 2.

McHugh, J. (2002), *The Way Forward in Radiological Protection*. An Expert Group Report, OECD, Paris.

McHugh, J.O. and Marshall, B.P (1997), 'Radioactive Waste and "Small Users": The 3Rs-Responsibilities, Rights and Regulation', [1997] *Env.Liability* 38.

National Radiological Protection Board (1995), *Risk of Radiation-induced Cancer at Low Dose Rates for Radiation Protection Purposes*, Documents of the NRPB,Vol 6, No. 1, NRPB Chilton, Oxon.

Nuclear Safety Advisory Committee/Radioactive Waste Management Advisory Committee (2003), *Joint regulatory review, Structures and principles of the regulation of the nuclear licensed sites*, March, HSE, London.

Organisation for Economic Cooperation and Development-Nuclear Energy Agency (1995), *The Environmental and Ethical Basis of Geological Disposal*, A Collective Opinion of the NEA Radioactive Waste Management Committee, OECD, Paris.

Organisation for Economic Cooperation and Development-Nuclear Energy Agency (1997), *Radiation in Perspective: Applications, Risks and Protection*, OECD, Paris.

Organisation for Economic Cooperation and Development-Nuclear Energy Agency (1999), *Reform of Civil Nuclear Liability*, OECD, Paris.

Organisation for Economic Cooperation and Development-Nuclear Energy Agency (2000), *Nuclear Energy in a Sustainable Development Perspective*, OECD, Paris.

Organisation for Economic Cooperation and Development-Nuclear Energy Agency (2000), *Society and Nuclear Energy: Towards a Better Understanding*, NEA Secretariat, OECD, Paris.

Organisation for Economic Cooperation and Development-Nuclear Energy Agency (2000), *Nuclear Legislation: Analytical Study*, OECD, Paris.

Organisation for Economic Cooperation and Development-Nuclear Energy Agency (2000), *Radiological Impacts of Spent Nuclear Fuel Management Options: A Comparative Study*, OECD, Paris.

Organisation for Economic Cooperation and Development-Nuclear Energy Agency (2001), *Chernobyl 15 years on*, OECD, Paris.

Organisation for Economic Cooperation and Development-Nuclear Energy Agency (2001), *Reversibility and Retrievability in Geologic Disposal of Radioactive Waste. Reflections at an International level*, OECD, Paris.

Organisation for Economic Cooperation and Development-Nuclear Energy Agency (2001), *The role of underground laboratories in nuclear waste disposal programmes*, OECD, Paris.

Organisation for Economic Cooperation and Development-Nuclear Energy Agency (2002), A *Critical Review of the System of Radiation Protection, The Way Forward in Radiological Protection*, An Expert Group Report, OECD, Paris.

Organisation for Economic Cooperation and Development-Nuclear Energy Agency (2002), *Society and Nuclear Energy: Towards a better understanding*, OECD, Paris.

Organisation for Economic Cooperation and Development-Nuclear Energy Agency (2003), *Radiological protection of the environment*, Summary Report of the Issues, OECD, Paris.

Pentreath, R.J. (2003), 'A system for radiological protection of the environment: some initial thoughts and ideas', *Journal of Radiological Protection*, Vol 12 No.2 pp 117-128.

Pochin, E.E. (1978), 'Estimates of Industrial and Other Risks', *Journal of the Royal College of Physicians*, Vol 12 No 3 pp 210-2.

Pochin, E.E. (1984), 'The 1984 Sievert Lecture – Sieverts and Safety' *Health Physics*, Vol 46, No. 6, pp 1173-9.

Pochin, E.E. (1986), 'The Evolution of Radiation Protection Criteria', *Nucl.Energy* 25 No. 1, Feb., pp 19-27.

Popham, John and Purdue, Michael (2002), 'The Future of the Major Inquiry', *Journal of Planning and Environment Law*, February, pp 137-150.

Radioactive Waste Management Advisory Committee (2001), *Advice to Ministers on the Process for Formulation of Future Policy for the Term Management of UK Solid Radioactive Waste*, DEFRA Publications.

Radioactive Waste Management Advisory Committee (2003), *Advice to Ministers on Management of low activity solid radioactive waste within the UK*, DEFRA Publications.

Renn, O. (1988), 'The Role of Risk Communication and Public Dialogue for Improving Risk Management', *Risk, Decision and Policy*, Vol 3, No.1, Routledge, London pp 5-30.

Riley, Peter (1991), 'The Legal Control of Nuclear Energy between States', *California Western International Law Journal*, Vol 21, No 2 pp 303-328.

Riley, Peter (2000), 'The precautionary principle and its practice', *Engineering Management Journal*, Vol 10, No.6, December, pp 281-287.

Riley, Peter (2002), 'Nuclear Energy; a sustainable future?', *Engineering Management Journal*, Vol 12, No.2, April, pp 97-104.

Riley, Peter (2003), 'Radiation risk in the context of liability for injury', *Journal of Radiological Protection*,Vol 23, Issue 3, September, pp 305-315.

Rockwood, L. (1995), 'The Nuclear Non-Proliferation Treaty: A permanent commitment to disarmament', *Nuclear Law Bulletin 56*, OECD, Paris.

Rockwood, L. (1997), 'Strengthening the effectiveness and improving the efficiency of the IAEA Safeguards System', *Nuclear Law Bulletin 60*, OECD, Paris.

Royal Society (1983), *Risk Assessment: Report of a Royal Society Study Group*, Royal Society, London.

Royal Society (1988), *Management of Separated Plutonium*, Royal Society, London.

Sands, P. (1996), 'Special Issue on International Nuclear Law', *Review of European Community and International Environmental Law*, Vol 5, issue 3, Bladeswell.

Scheinman, L. (2001), 'Transboundary Sovereignty in the management of nuclear material', *IAEA Bulletin*, Vol 43, No. 4, Vienna, Austria.

Smith, R.E. (2002), 'Some observations on the concept of best practicable option (BPEO) in the context of radioactive waste management', *Nuclear Energy*, 41, No. 4, Aug., pp 271-181.

Steele, J. (2001), 'Participation and Deliberation in Environmental Law: Exploring a Problem-solving approach', *Oxford Journal of Legal Studies*, Vol 21, No. 3, pp 415-442.

Stokes, E.R. (2003), 'Precautionary Steps: the development of the precautionary principle in EU jurisprudence', *Environmental Law and Management* 15.

Strand, P. and Larsson, C.M. (2001), *Delivering a framework for the protection of the environment from ionising radiation*, Radioactive Pollutants, Impact on the Environment, (Brechignac and Howard eds), EDP Sciences, Les Ulis, France.

Strohl, Pierre (1999), 'Disposal of Radioactive Waste: The Question of the Involvement of the Public under International Law', *Nuclear Law Bulletin* 64, December, OECD, Paris.

The Environment Agency (2002), *Proposed decision for the future regulation of disposals of radioactive waste from British Nuclear Fuels plc, Sellafield*, EA Publications.

The Royal Commission on Environmental Pollution (2000), *Energy - The Changing Climate*, 22nd Report Cm 4749, The Stationery Office, London.

Tromans, S. (1997), *The Law of Nuclear Installations and Radioactive Substances*, Sweet and Maxwell, London.

US Department of the Environment (2002), *The National Waste Management Plan, Rev 3*, Field Office (CBFO), Carlsbad, USA.

Wakeford, Antell, Leigh (1998), 'Review of Probability of Causation and its use in a Compensation Scheme for Nuclear Industry Workers in the United Kingdom', *Health Physics* 74 (1), pp 1-9.

Warner, Sir F. (1983), 'Risk Management', *Study Group Royal Society*, London.

Williamson R.L. (1993), 'Gathering Danger: The Urgent Need to Regulate Toxic Substances That Can Bioaccumulate', *Ecology Law Quarterly*, Vol 20, p 604.

Woolf, Lord (2001), 'Environmental Risk: The Responsibilities of the Law and Science', *Environmental Law and Management* 13[2001] 3, pp 131-7.

Wynne, B, (2000), *Public Participation in Scientific Issues: What is the recent fuss about and how should we address it?* Public Consultation in Science, British Council Lecture, Amsterdam, Netherlands.

Index